CW01507852

Contents

PEACH
STREET
TO
Lobster
LANE

FELICITY CLOAKE

PEACH STREET TO Lobster LANE

COAST TO COAST IN SEARCH OF AMERICAN CUISINE

MUDLARK

Mudlark
HarperCollins*Publishers*
1 London Bridge Street
London SE1 9GF

www.harpercollins.co.uk

HarperCollins*Publishers*
Macken House, 39/40 Mayor Street Upper
Dublin 1, D01 C9W8, Ireland

First published by Mudlark 2025

10 9 8 7 6 5 4 3 2 1

Text © Felicity Cloake 2025
Illustrations © Dina Ruzha

Felicity Cloake asserts the moral right to be identified as the author of this work

A catalogue record of this book is available from the British Library

ISBN 978-0-00-868765-6

Printed and bound in the UK using 100% renewable electricity at CPI Group (UK) Ltd

This book contains FSC™ certified paper and other controlled sources to ensure responsible forest management.

For more information visit: www.harpercollins.co.uk/green

For Daphne and Freddie,
the best excuses ever

INTRODUCTION: IN WHICH EVERYONE TRIES TO PUT ME OFF

*'He was fairly happy, except that, like many people living in Europe,
he would rather have been in America'*
Ernest Hemingway, *The Sun Also Rises*

'Don't be ridiculous, you won't *die.*'

As parting words before a bike ride go, these aren't exactly reassuring – but then I have just spent my farewell meal warning everyone I might be coming home in a box. Not that death is on the official itinerary; in fact, in the excitement of preparation, the possibility of expiring en route hadn't really occurred to me. It was only when I began telling people that, having pedalled round France and the UK for previous books, my next cycle tour would take place across the Atlantic that this sunny optimism took a knock. While I waffled about the joy of the open road, a surprising number of them merely frowned and said, 'Yes, but is it *safe?*'

The Olympic gold-medal-winning rower who now describes himself as 'the man who used to be James Cracknell' following a near-fatal collision with a petrol tanker and a serious brain injury while cycling in Arizona in 2010 comes up more than once in these conversations.* Despite not having heard his story, the American friends of friends who've kindly offered to host me in Beverly Hills are so independently anxious about my plans that, after trying and failing to dissuade me with links to newspaper articles on cyclist fatalities, they send our mutual acquaintances a touching email with the subject line 'PLEASE TRY TO CONVINCE FELICITY THAT CYCLING FROM SF TO LA IS A BAD IDEA'.

The question often goes beyond a dearth of bicycle lanes, however: America itself is apparently one step away from the Foreign Office red list in the minds of many Brits. Even my mother, whose attitude to her offspring is best described as 'no-nonsense', makes me promise her – fingers crossed behind my back – that, having success-fully navigated most of the way around both France and the UK solo, I'll never be alone on this trip, revealing a hitherto unguessed-of (and quite irrational) conviction that the US is full of serial killers with nothing better to do with their time than lie in wait for idiots like me to ride past.

A few people more reasonably bring up the 'cicadapocalypse', the Biblical plague of insects due to erupt in the Midwest in spring 2024, which I have to concede does sound like a pretty bad omen, as is the unnerving news that the road I'm planning to take out of San Francisco has just fallen into the Pacific Ocean. Others fret that I'm going to die either of starvation in a lonely desert, or of a surfeit of saturated fat in a drive-thru car park. (Seemingly Ameri-cans exist solely on fast food in the European mind.) 'Well, I hope you like hamburgers,' my dad says with a wry laugh, as if the pros-pect of eating nothing else for three months straight is going to put me off. As it happens, I love hamburgers . . . but I'm also pretty

---

* Pointing out that he'd made a full recovery and was now the Conservative Party candidate for Colchester didn't seem to help much, oddly enough.

confident that this unimaginably large and incredibly diverse country has a little more to offer.

Plus I've already booked my outbound ticket, and it's non-refundable.

In truth, this is a long-cherished dream of mine, not easily punctured by even the most well-meaning worry warts. Even before I discovered the profound joy of cycle touring, I was in love with the time-honoured trope of the American road trip: just catching sight of the old Rand McNally atlas on the bookshelf, souvenir from a long-ago holiday, has always been enough to make my feet itch with the urge to disappear into that vast, seductive emptiness across the ocean. Perhaps it's living in a tiny one-bedroom flat in the middle of the biggest city on the small dark island of Great Britain that makes me yearn for space . . . but I don't think I'm alone in feeling drawn to the notion of the lonely road, the fantasy of following it into an endless horizon.

Who, Brit or not, hasn't watched *Thelma & Louise* or *Into the Wild* and dreamt of a similar, if ideally less definitive, escape? As travel writer Jamie Jensen, who grew up along Route 66, puts it, 'Poets and artists from Walt Whitman to Muddy Waters have long sung the praises of rolling down the highway, and no matter how times have changed we still believe there's nothing more essentially American than hitting the road and seeing the country.'

Because, established by those escaping cramped, claustrophobic societies, the United States has always been a country on the move: new arrivals pushing ever further west in their quest for life, liberty and the pursuit of happiness. This national restlessness was encouraged by the rapid spread of the car,* and the expansion of the road

---

* Astonishing fact: in 1927, 80 per cent of all motor vehicles worldwide were in America.

network, which turned travel from a chore into a pleasure. Or a potential pleasure anyway; when I first crossed the Atlantic at the age of eleven, it was to be a queasy backseat passenger on a road trip from Boston to Quebec, a nausea only exacerbated by my first encounter with a plastic-wrapped blueberry muffin the size of my fist. As well as making my dad pull over a couple of hours later so I could be sick, I remember the thrill of pancakes for breakfast, of revolving pie cases in steamy-windowed diners and the jaw-dropping novelty of the Ben & Jerry's factory. (The rumours are true: before Chunky Monkey even launched in the UK, I had the t-shirt. What can I say? I was a very cool child.*)

Since then, American food – by which I mean food in America, not the bland stuff served up from Bognor to Bogota by the country's many wildly successful global chains – has always felt exotic, glamorous even. And though I'm in the minority if opinions online are anything to go by – 'Are you mad?' is just one of the responses I get when I share my plans on social media – exploring it in all its infinite variety is one of the things I love most about travelling to the USA. There's a free-wheeling, anything-goes attitude to sustenance on display that strikes the traveller from the moment they make it through the stress of Homeland Security and attempt to revive their battered spirits with a coffee, only to be asked if they want it cinnamon-roll, blueberry, hazelnut or vanilla flavoured, with skim, regular, almond or soya milk, or the perennially mysterious half and half. It's like walking into a culinary theme park where none of the usual rules (coffee-flavoured coffee, for example) apply. In America, it appears, you can be anyone you want to be – even someone who drinks blue raspberry lattes.

---

* Recollections may vary.

Yet it's just this cavalier attitude towards rules that seems to have given much of the world the impression that there is no such thing as 'American cuisine', on the basis that if anything goes then nothing is sacred. To wit, I'm surprised to discover how many otherwise open-minded people are happy to dismiss the idea of America having any food worth travelling for.* Online, complete strangers describe my plan to eat my way across the US as 'unworthy' of my 'talents' – which is weird because if my talents lie anywhere, it's in eating.

I'd put all this negativity down to simple, if silly, anti-Americanism of the kind sadly common when people assume an entire nation to be represented by its loudest voices, but the question of whether America has a food culture is one that's been simmering away both at home and abroad for decades. As far back as the 1870s, the Russian Grand Duke Alexis, fresh from a two-year tour of the US, declared that there was no such thing as American cuisine. A few decades later the *New York Times* noted the common European belief that 'America is a land without leisure for gastronomic appreciation'. Even the current francophone Wikipedia entry on the subject kicks off with the note that US cuisine is 'very diverse and difficult to define'; not a problem I imagine the French have when it comes to their own culinary heritage.

The sneering isn't confined, if I may quote Groundskeeper Willie, to cheese-eating surrender monkeys: from influential Southern food writer James Villas to Ronald Reagan's director of speechwriting, many proud Americans have claimed, in the words of the latter, that 'there is virtually no such thing as American cuisine'. Yet New Jersey-born anthropologist Sidney Mintz found himself in hot water when he made a throwaway reference to this idea while delivering a lecture to a class of students in the mid-1990s.

---

* In much the same way, I quickly discover that Americans don't believe Britain has much to offer the world culinarily beyond fish and chips.

It quickly became apparent, he wrote later in his essay 'Eating American', that many in his audience believed that to have no cuisine was to have no culture.

Mintz claimed he had not intended the observation as a criticism, noting that the United States is a large and highly mobile country made up of people of many different backgrounds and traditions. So far, so uncontroversial. One can, he says, describe what is actually commonly eaten: 'certainly hamburgers, and probably Southern fried chicken and clam chowders and baked beans, steak, ribs, and perhaps chilli, and hot dogs, and now pizza, and baked potatoes with "the works" . . . A dessert list beginning with apple pie . . . and many dishes based on maize.' Yet despite this, he goes on, a list of ten favourite 'entrees'* for 1994 collected by the NPD market research group starts off with pizza and ham sandwiches and hot dogs and ends with cheese sandwiches, hamburger sandwiches and spaghetti, concluding triumphantly: 'I don't think anyone wants to call that array a cuisine.'

It's at this point he loses me. Though such things are clearly not all America has to offer, it seems to me churlish to deny that they are unworthy of being labelled a cuisine. After all, Italians also enjoy pizza, the French croque monsieur, the Koreans fried chicken, and no one seriously claims that any of these demean their wider culinary cultures, let alone disprove their very existence.

The contemporary American food writer Alicia Kennedy, who produces a thoughtful argument against the usefulness of national cuisines as a concept, notes that 'our commonalities across all differences in the U.S. emerge through interaction with fast and widely available processed foods'. Though growing up in Long Island she ate a lot of Puerto Rican food, sushi and bagels, she

---

* Entree, as any visitor to the States will quickly learn, refers to the main course, rather than a starter (which is known as an appetiser). This is actually closer to its historical meaning in French, though not its modern one.

would, she suggests, still be able to 'compare notes on breakfast cereals [and] go-to childhood McDonald's orders' with someone raised in the South or Midwest . . . Just as, I suspect, someone born in Bangalore might be able to bond over Limca sodas, or Amul ice cream, with a Bengali, in spite of their very different food cultures.

In short, I'm convinced that there is a cuisine, which is to say a style of cooking, a manner of eating, that's unmistakably, distinctively, primarily American – and on this trip I'm determined to find this unicorn, cover it with ketchup and pickles and have it for lunch.

While I concede experts like Sidney and Alicia may have a head start on a tourist like me, nevertheless I realise to my surprise as I embark upon the aggressively time-consuming American visa application process that I've been to the States twelve times since the incident with the muffin. I've danced at a Jewish wedding in Brooklyn, met with a National Rifle Association lobbyist in the Capitol, and eaten deep-fried butter at the South Carolina State Fair . . . but mostly my visits have taken the form of road trips, down the Pacific Coast Highway, around the Deep South, through the Nevada desert. And despite occasional dramas like nearly losing a finger trying to rescue* a snapping turtle from the middle of a Georgia road or being pulled over for (barely) speeding in the Olympia National Forest (where the cop appeared perplexed and then mildly amused by the panic on my friend's face as she unthinkingly scrabbled for her passport in the glovebox and then shouted, 'OFFICER, I'VE NOT GOT A GUN!'), the road element of these trips consistently failed to live up to my romantic expectations.

---

* Though you should of course avoid running them over, it's advisable to use a car mat to slide a snapping turtle safely across the road if you're concerned for their safety – they have long necks and a nasty bite.

For a start, unlike in the movies, with their scenic spools of blacktop, the most sensible route to anywhere always appeared to involve a featureless freeway. Such systems are designed to be perfectly efficient – and like many perfectly efficient things, from meal-replacement shakes to internet grocery shopping, they're dull. That's actually their raison d'être – minimum distraction, maximum speed, which means no diners, no Amish buggies, and definitely no roadside attractions like the world's largest ball of sisal twine,* or California's International Banana Museum. The most you get on a freeway is a billboard advertising what you're missing at the next exit (mostly the same generic fast food that you missed twenty minutes ago). In vain I would plead with my holiday companions for a ninety-minute detour for barbecue ribs, or to sample the delights of a grasshopper pie: the ease of the freeway always won out. And for all the damage they inflicted on small towns and marginalised communities,† these huge roads have undoubtedly saved Americans, who seem to be in a tearing hurry, an awful lot of time. But I won't be in a rush – quite the opposite in fact, because I'll be on a bike.

My previous bike-based adventures‡ have convinced me that there's no better way to really connect with a place than on two wheels, and I have a feeling this will prove especially true in a US context where the greater distances involved will presumably force

---

*   719 Wisconsin Street, Cawker City, Kansas.
†   In cities, the new roads were disproportionately routed through historically Black neighbourhoods, displacing or further segregating established communities and creating repercussions that continue to be felt to this day. Commenting on marchers blocking Interstate 94 as they marched from the Minnesota State Capitol to Minneapolis in May 2020 to protest against the murder of George Floyd and the treatment of Black Americans by law enforcement, state governor and future Vice Presidential candidate Tim Walz acknowledged that highway expansion in St Paul 'wasn't just physical – it ripped a culture, it ripped who we were'.
‡   Quests for perfect patisserie and fabulous fry-ups respectively.

me into small towns for sustenance, and on to small roads for safety. Not only does this type of travel allow a privileged glimpse into everyday life – slow enough to read yard signs and bumper stickers, take note of what people grow on their farms and want in their strip malls – like it or not, you get a sense of the landscape too. The cyclist doesn't need to see the sea to taste the salt and feel the crunch of sand under their tyres; doesn't need a map to know they're in the foothills of the Rockies. And, homogenous as modern America is often claimed to be, I have faith that, just like anywhere else, it'll look quite different at 15mph.

Perhaps even more of a draw than the opportunity for some serious nosiness, however, is the prospect of working up a real appetite: one of my chief disappointments on petrol-powered road trips has been the difficulty of doing justice to breakfast, lunch and dinner on a daily diet of sitting on one's ever-expanding bottom. Cycling, I fondly hope, will leave me hungry enough for all of the above, and an ice cream on top – hopefully at the hidden gems I'm praying I find off the interstate.

That said, unlike anywhere else I've been previously, travelling by bike in America comes with connotations of daring – even the name of the Missouri-based Adventure Cycling Association suggests this is not a land where it's considered an everyday mode of transport. Instead of relying on my own somewhat questionable navigational skills, I find myself on their website downloading dedicated cycle routes but, desperate as I am to pedal to the lip of the Grand Canyon, or through Utah's Monument Valley, America in general feels exotic enough that I'm almost equally thrilled at the idea of riding down the average Main Street and getting a free refill from a waitress who calls me honey.

Indeed, though I have every faith that humans are fundamentally similar wherever you are in the world, America's unusual openness towards strangers is one of the things I love most about travelling there, and I'm looking forward to chatting to some of the people whose opinions never show up on my newsfeeds. Despite the warnings, it seems to me that a bike is the perfect vehicle to make the familiar strange; to see America, still the capital of global popular culture, with fresh eyes and an empty stomach. And, given how unusual cycling seems to be, parts of my journey might perhaps be new to US readers as well; after all, as my former MP Diane Abbott once said, 'Outsiders often have an insight that an insider doesn't quite have.' While insight might well be a little aspirational for a person with no grander plan than cycling round eating stuff, it's always interesting to glimpse your own country through a new lens – and I hope, given the sheer scale of this one, fully paid-up, allegiance-pledging Americans might even discover a novel nugget or two en route, too.

To recap, it appears I'm setting off on my bike across a country where no one cycles, to explore a cuisine that doesn't exist. Happily I've always enjoyed a challenge, even one involving extracting a media visa from the US Embassy in London – of which the less said the better – and booking a bike on to a transatlantic flight with the dubious help of a British Airways chatbot.

Naturally Eddy,* the handsome green touring bike who has taken me from Marseilles to Muckle Flugga, was always going to be part of the plan. So much about this trip is going to be different from my previous expeditions – I've never had to negotiate time zones and visas before, for a start – that the idea of navigating a strange continent without his reassuring presence would be too much to bear. Thus, in a sign I may not have my priorities quite right, he's safely packed up in a cardboard box in my hall weeks

---

* For new readers, Eddy is named after the great Belgian cyclist Eddy Merckx, who once said, 'They always say cakes are bad for cyclists . . . But it's not the cakes, it's the climbs.'

before my actual visa arrives, tenderly dismantled by Condor Bikes on Grays Inn Road, the London shop that built him for my French adventure back in 2018.

In theory I, a person who still has to watch a YouTube video to fix a puncture, will be reassembling him alone in San Francisco, so I stand over Adrian, the mechanic, like an inept hawk, making notes like 'take the wheels off'. As he carefully wraps the chain in layers of cloth, Adrian casually mentions that he was fitted with a pacemaker at the age of forty, after being diagnosed with a complete heart block, and, during his recovery, promised the doctors he would pass his new energy on in whatever way he could: 'send a little spark travelling around the world' as he rather charmingly puts it while reinforcing the corners of the box with tape.

Having embarked on a frankly deranged campaign to loop Swains Lane, 'the toughest climb in London' according to *Cyclist* magazine (and me, the only time I attempted it), a thousand times to raise money for the British Heart Foundation, he then gives me a piece of advice that pops into my head on every slope from San Francisco to the Brooklyn Bridge: 'It's not about getting to the top, forget the top – all you need to concentrate on is turning those pedals once. Just once.'

This is not the only professional help I've sought in my preparation for a trip that feels like a much bigger deal than my previous expeditions. The USA is many times larger than the UK or France* and far more sparsely populated – which means the chances of running into the kind of handy older gentleman who usually miraculously pops up by the side of the road to fix my mechanical issues are slim. Instead, I book myself into an emergency roadside repairs course at the London Bike Kitchen.

---

* In fact, the state of Texas alone is bigger than either.

Jeni, the owner, kicks off by asking our greatest fear, 'in this context'. My fellow pupil, who is planning to cycle the Continental Divide trail from the Canadian to the Mexican borders, says he doesn't really have any fears as such, he just wants to know he can get back on the road as fast as possible. I say I'm worried about getting eaten by coyotes and dying alone with a tyre lever in my hand. She says she can't help with wildlife.

Truthfully, my route is not going to take me anywhere very remote, primarily because I've designed it around food, which tends to require the presence of people. I've decided to start in San Francisco in late April on the basis that the Pacific Coast Highway (the route Dan, my host in Beverly Hills, is so concerned about me taking) will only get busier as the weather improves, and also because, as a person who got sunburnt in the north of Shetland, I want to hit the South as early as possible. But before I do, I have a few things to tick off on the West Coast, the birthplace of Chinese-American and California cuisines, McDonald's and Mission burritos – all surely indisputably US creations.

From Los Angeles I'll head east through the deserts of the Southwest in search of Tex-Mex, ending up in Louisana, home of Cajun and (American) Creole cooking. Tennessee and Kentucky seem good places to explore the wonderful worlds of fried chicken and real barbecue en route to the Midwest, epicentre of both good plain cooking and the modern fast-food industry. Chicago is a must for deep-pan pizza, Italian beef and chocolate brownies before I hop east to Washington DC, where I'm hoping to find out more about Native American foodways in the capital's many museums, and pay a visit to Thomas Jefferson's Monticello, where the third president penned the first American recipe for ice cream. Leafy Virginia yields to fir-trimmed Maine, the most north-easterly state in the union, famous for its lobster rolls, and the beginning of the wild Atlantic-coast bike route I'll take through New England, with its clam chowders and Boston baked beans, as far as New York, from where I plan to fly home in an explosion of Fourth of July fireworks – after eating my baggage allowance in bagels and hot dogs, naturally.

On my travels round France, I made it my mission to eat, and rate, as many croissants as possible. In the UK, it was fry-ups. The US is trickier: after much debate and furrowed brow over what food unites this vast nation (can I really face eating every burger I come across? Will too many donuts give me diabetes?), I decide on the sweet pie – distinctly American, in that they're found in every diner in the country, yet relatively rarely elsewhere in the world (British pies are, of course, almost always savoury) and with enough regional variation to keep things interesting. As a bonus, they often contain fruit, and if I'm honest, the availability of fruit and veg is one of the things I'm most worried about.

The only thing that grieves me about this itinerary – apart from all the bits I'm having to leave out, due to the sheer size of the country, and the limited time I can afford to stay, both financially and without greatly vexing the dog – is that it includes several trains. I'll be away from late April to early July; almost three months, longer than any of my previous trips, and yet will still barely skim the surface of a country with nine time zones plus, at the time of my visit, rampant inflation. I know how to travel on a budget in Europe, but the US, with its many cities and serious lack of affordable campsites, is a pricier proposition even before factoring in the flights.

The same things also make it harder for friends to join me – hopping across the Channel or up to Scotland is one thing; booking a plane ticket is quite another. Even Gemma, my faithful domestique from past expeditions, has gone to the quite extraordinary lengths of having a baby to avoid coming along for the ride, while Matt, who purchased an electric bike to tackle East Anglia after I nearly killed him in Normandy, has ensured cycling will not be on the agenda this time by arranging to meet me in Los Angeles.

As it seems I'll largely be on my own this time, and possibly many miles from the nearest shop, I've been convinced by my friend Emily, after one too many martinis, to buy a portable solar panel, as if I'm going full Pole to Pole as opposed to pedalling from one diner to the next. Hoping to really embrace the pioneer spirit, I've also invested in a new, much smaller sleeping mat and bag, and borrowed Gemma's absurdly tiny tent. As it's pouring with rain when I go to collect it, she supervises me struggling to pitch it in her parents' kitchen, while the baby wails ominously and Wilf sits unhelpfully in the middle of the flimsy nylon, looking nervous. (It's almost as if my furry sidekick knows that, after reading Steinbeck's account of his road trip with a French poodle, *Travels with Charley*, I briefly looked into bringing him along for the ride before concluding that the hold of an A380 is no place for an eleven-year-old terrier under the impression he's a celebrity. First Class, maybe.)

My friend Sam, who is going to be helping to dance attendance on said terrier for the next few months, also kindly takes the morning off work to escort me to the airport on a drizzly day towards the end of April, shouldering my two usual panniers, plus a large kitbag that in theory clips over the top of them. As the last arrived too late for a test run, I'm winging it,* but despite this extra room, I've attempted to keep my packing down to a minimum: Adrian at Condor might think I need more than two pairs of socks; I know better (spoiler, I end up buying more socks).

---

* Don't do this – it's too wide for my narrow rack and, tired of scooping it off the back tyre, I end up sending it home from Texas.

Here, in case it's useful to anyone planning a similar expedition, is my packing list:

Pannier 1:
Tiny tent
Sleeping mat
Sleeping bag
Solar charging panel (could have done without this)
Phone charger and plug adaptor
Battery pack
Towel (Swahili kikoi: quick-drying and large enough to be used
   as a sarong or knotted as a scarf as temperatures demand)
Eye mask and earplugs (best not to know you're going to be
   murdered until it happens)
Inner tubes
Tyre patch kit
Tyre levers
Tyre tool (cannot recommend this highly enough if you have
   tight tyres)
Mini pump
Chain tool and 2 × quick links
FiberFix spoke replacement
Front and back light and charging cables
Allen keys (I only took the ones I needed for my bike)
2 × 900ml water bottles
Serious lock (1.7kg of peace of mind)

Duct tape and scissors
Cable ties (for quick fixes, not abductions)
Voile adjustable strap (never worked out how this worked)
Pocket knife, spoon, fork

Pannier 2 (in packing cubes):
Half cycling gloves (useful for absorbing some of the vibrations
  from the road)
Cycling cap (invaluable for keeping the sun off your head)
Reflective waterproof jacket
Reflective gilet
Arm warmers
Fleece jumper
Cycling jerseys × 2
Cycling bib shorts × 2
Socks × 2
Cycling shoes
Sunglasses
Cotton trousers
Shorts
2 × t-shirts
1 × seersucker cotton dress (handily pre-crumpled)
Woolly cardigan
T-shirt and leggings to sleep in
Underwear × 3
Flip-flops
Swimming costume
Vaguely waterproof, light and grippy trainers (I went for Adidas
  Sambas, shortly before the prime minister was pictured in
  the very same pair. Thanks, Rishi)
Basic toiletries and first aid (NB always pack rehydration tablets for
  hot weather. Preferably more than the one sachet in my
  luggage)

Insect repellent

Tick removal tool, borrowed from the dog

Wet wipes and anti-bac gel (spilled on the plane, never replaced)

Face flannel/cloth (OK, I bought this in Ohio, but I wish I'd
    brought one; necessary for when you're the kind of dirty
    that requires active scrubbing)

Hairbrush and hairbands

Book*

Handlebar bag:

Wallet

Passport

Keys

Lip balm

Suncream

Battery pack

Notebook

Propelling pencil

Sweets: boiled are best, as they offer the longest sugary
    distraction on hills – the ubiquitous jelly sweet is gone too
    quickly, chocolate melts in the sun

Plus, of course, a bike helmet

---

* Negligible weight and it's always useful to have a book with you when travelling. The same goes for a pack of cards if you're in company or enjoy playing patience. In the course of my travels I got through *America Day by Day* by Simone de Beauvoir, *Housekeeping* by Marilynne Robinson, *The Death and Life of the Great Lakes* by Dan Egan, *The Jungle* by Upton Sinclair, *Pineapple Street* by Jenny Jackson and *How to Say Nothing* by Jenny Odell, donating them to free libraries as I went and then replacing them in the next independent bookshop (of which America seems to have a gratifying number).

In fact, given I'm doing the first bit of the trip on my own, Sam is potentially the last friend to see me alive – as I point out after he's helped me manhandle poor Eddy onto the oversized luggage belt at Heathrow.

He looks genuinely worried.

'If you die . . . what happens to Wilf?'

1
CHINATOWN USA

In search of the truth inside the fortune cookie

'An Exciting Opportunity Lies Ahead of You'

From the moment I board my flight to San Francisco, lugging my orange kitbag of Marmite cashews and books past a wannabe tech-bro in Business Class reading (and I swear I'm not making this up) *Software Licensing for Dummies*, everything feels exciting, even my vegetable biryani, a last taste of home. Hours of ice and emptiness pass below my window before the Canadian wilderness finally shows signs of human activity . . . and then I realise with a sudden thrill that the bright line on the horizon must be the Pacific Ocean. By the time we're close enough to see the Bay Bridges my heart is fluttery with anticipation despite the many warnings I've had about 'staying safe' in San Francisco in recent weeks.

In the end, by the time I make it through Homeland Security, find Eddy's box abandoned by a conveyor belt, manhandle it onto a trolley, discover it's too wide to fit through the bollards, manhandle it off the trolley attracting the attention of the customs staff, am eventually released, learn no one offering assistance knows anything about the designated bicycle assembly stations mentioned on the airport website, realise the box is also too wide to fit in the lifts on the trolley, abandon the trolley and somehow push the enormous box and my panniers down to ground level, spend a sweary forty-five minutes in a bus stop reassembling him while security eyes me suspiciously, make it on to the train, which smells strongly of skunk, and then notice I've put his back wheel on wrong . . . well, by that point, I'm basically beyond caring.

That fixed, but still anxious about actually getting on the bike, on the wrong side of the road, after a ten-and-a-half-hour flight, I wheel Eddy from the subway station to the hostel where I'll be staying, my mouth hanging open like a medieval yokel at the sheer scale of everything around me. The grey stone buildings occupy entire city blocks, the doorways are large enough to accommodate an elephant in a top hat, and the streets wide enough for a whole parade of the things. It's just all so extraordinarily American; so familiar from screens, so discombobulating to see in three dimensions.

As she checks me in, the friendly girl behind the reception desk, perhaps sensing I feel a little unmoored, tells me she has friends on a work placement 'somewhere in the North of England, I don't know where but the trains are really bad?' and, she continues dreamily, 'all they see are sheep. I'd love to see a sheep and . . . and one of those hairy orange cows?' These musings remind her of a local attraction I really shouldn't miss: 'There's a place not too far from here where you can pay $20 to go and cuddle a cow and they put their heads on your shoulder and you can just, like, go to sleep, and then they come back in two hours and wake you up?' Gosh, I say. That's quite something. I'll certainly look out for it.

I don't need any bovine assistance to help me sleep tonight though. I'm out like a light, and emerge fizzing with energy at 7am into an empty breakfast room; even the friendly rat mentioned as 'looking a bit lost' in a recent TripAdvisor review of the hostel seems to still be in bed. I sip weak black coffee out of a mug advertising Geere Family Mortuary and Cremation Services and watch two shiny pink-cheeked girls doing sprints and press-ups outside next to someone huddled under a filthy duvet. As tableaux on inequality go, it feels distinctly heavy-handed.

I pass on the complimentary bagels and peanut butter – less because the bagels look rubbish and the Skippy sugary than what lies ahead. There's a lot on the menu in San Francisco, including America's oldest Chinatown, the birthplace of California Cuisine and the famous local sourdough, and with only two days here before I hit the road, I have to be strategic.

While no one's claiming that a city younger than Edinburgh's New Town came up with the concept of naturally leavened bread, it's become so synonymous with the stuff that when the strain of bacteria that gives sourdough its characteristic tang was isolated in the 1970s, it was named *Fructilactobacillus sanfranciscensis*. This association stems from the notion that sourdough starters were easier for the prospectors who rushed to the area after gold was discovered in the Sierra Nevada foothills in 1848 to maintain in remote camps than yeast – and, so the story goes, the taste for it just stuck. (A cynical person might observe that before the introduction of commercial baker's yeast in the 1870s, sourdough was pretty standard fare wherever you were, but I am not that person.) Unsurprisingly, perhaps, given they didn't have breadfluencers to teach them, the miners' sourdough is believed to have been a bit rubbish, but happily San Francisco also saw an influx of French and Italian immigrants who made loaves good enough to survive the Industrial Revolution, and still be sold today.

Boudin, which opened in 1849, the year of the Gold Rush, is the city's oldest bakery (and continuously operating business), but the best known to bread nerds like me is Tartine, which has only been going since 2002, but, according to the *San Francisco Chronicle*, 'redefined sourdough bread in San Francisco'. It's even received the seal of approval from the city's most celebrated chef, Alice Waters, who's been known to order her birthday cakes there.

Launched just as the dot-com bubble burst, like the tech industry Tartine has weathered some choppy waters, but though not all of its offshoots have prospered, there are still three sites in the Bay Area, six in Los Angeles, and, I'm surprised to learn, the same number in South Korea* – making them, I suppose, a small chain. Yet the original location, on the corner of Guerrero and 18th Streets in the Mission District, its colourful Victorian bay-windowed houses standing out against the grey sky, doesn't feel like it on a Tuesday morning in late April; charmingly cramped and busy with hanging plants and hippyish art.

I'm here to try their sourdough, but I can't go toting a $14.75† loaf around the city, so I go for the most Californian thing on the menu: an avocado tartine with 'salsa seca, nutritional yeast, cilantro' ($16.75) on a slice of their celebrated country loaf and a filter coffee ($4.75!). At the till I have my first experience with the infamous American tipping system when the cashier unexpectedly flips the screen over to reveal options beginning at 15 per cent, which is at least an improvement on the old days, when you were expected to calculate your gratitude on the hoof. Taken aback, I concede they do have to toast the bread and peel the avocado – not wanting to look like a cheapskate, I poke begrudgingly at 18 per cent even though I have to wait around for, and collect, the coffee myself.

While I'm standing around, I message Cecilia, a friend recently returned to the city after several years in London, to ask her advice

---

* Baker Chad Robertson has spoken of his long interest in Korean culture, and in truth they weren't even the first SF bakery to open in Seoul, which is an appreciative and lucrative market for artisan pastries.
† The exchange rate is $1 = 80p, making this loaf £11.85.

on tipping etiquette, worried about coming across as a stereotypical mean Brit . . . but more worried about my budget if I'm expected to maintain this level of generosity. A voice note comes back: 'To be honest, I'm still super confused after living abroad for so long, but just so you know, you don't have to tip anywhere where you're not sitting down and being served. So for example if you're at Tartine and you're just getting a coffee and a pastry . . . you still don't have to tip, it's only in a restaurant where there's a server coming over, taking your order, bringing it to you: at the end of *that* meal you'd tip between 15 and 18 per cent, you don't need to do any more than that.' ANY MORE THAN 18 per cent? I think wildly.

'Now with the technology with paying,' she continues, 'they make it really easy when you're buying a coffee for it to say how much do you want to tip, when actually you don't have to tip if you're just getting a coffee and sitting down or taking it away, SO' – she pauses for emphasis, speaking slowly as if to a child, or someone newly arrived from outer space – 'I just want you to know that.' I'm so shocked* I forget how hot my coffee is likely to be, and almost scald my mouth.

Happily, however, when it arrives the avocado toast feels . . . if not, perhaps, worth the almost $20 I've voluntarily paid for it, at least extremely satisfying: generous with the avocado (as it ought to be for that price, my inner dad grumbles), the toast crisp and garlicky, almost fruity rather than overtly sour. Online, people mutter darkly that, as the baker Chad Robertson's technique delivers at most a mild tanginess, it's not real San Francisco sourdough, he's just 'cashing in' on the association, but as a bread fan, rather

---

* Naturally for the rest of the trip I tip for everything, because it's very hard to look someone in the eye and press 'no tip', so I estimate I probably spend about 20 per cent more than is strictly necessary, in a country where food prices are already noticeably higher than at home.

than obsessive, who's lucky enough to live near a few of London's finest bakeries,* I think it's up there with the best.

I walk back to the station fortified, if a little concerned about how expensive this trip is going to prove. Though I haven't drawn up a formal budget, because, well, to be honest it never really occurred to me, being more of a spend-and-repent-at-leisure type person, I'd always thought of America as a fairly cheap place to travel once you got there, so the cost of breakfast has been a revelation. I comfort myself with the fact I'll soon be on the bike in camping country, which should surely save a few dollars. Cities, I reason, are always expensive.

Sourdough may not be a San Francisco invention, but American-Chinese food can be said with some degree of certainty to have originated here: the city's Chinatown, which it claims is the largest outside Asia, is the oldest in North America. 'Unequivocally a food town from its beginning' according to Professor Yong Chen, author of Chop Suey USA, it was first settled in the late 1840s, when the severe weather and high taxes that had been driving many Chinese to seek work abroad brought them to the California gold mines. The rush swelled the city's population by thirty-five times in two years, and by 1850, the *New York Tribune* noted that it boasted three Chinese restaurants 'much frequented by Americans', which an English traveller, William Shaw, called the 'best eating houses in San Francisco . . . The dishes are mostly curries, hashes and fricassee served up in small dishes and . . . exceedingly palatable.' By 1856, food (thirty-three grocers, five restaurants and five meat markets) drove nearly half the businesses in this new Chinese community.

---

* Dusty Knuckle and Quince Bakery since you didn't ask.

COFFEE BREAK
The "Forgotten War"*

Though Chinese restaurants may have quickly become part of the American culinary landscape, this didn't necessarily indicate wider racial tolerance – contemporary reports suggest the quantity of food on offer was initially the biggest draw for a population that was at that time largely single, male and itinerant.

As the Chinese community in America grew, it faced increasing prejudice, culminating in the Chinese Exclusion Act of 1882, the first immigration ban in US history (which was only finally repealed out of military necessity in 1944). In a pattern that may feel bitterly familiar to the proprietors of Indian and Bangladeshi restaurants in the UK, Chinese people themselves may not have been welcome, but their cooking very much was. Decades before the advent of fast food, Professor Chen makes a strong argument that Chinese restaurants played a pivotal role in turning America into the dining-out culture it is to this day.

The food in these restaurants was not, strictly, Chinese, reflecting instead the ingredients available, and the tastes of the clientele – as well as the fact that many of those in the kitchen had only turned to cooking in America to make a living. Not only did they commonly offer Western dishes like ham and eggs but their 'Chinese menu' tended to include chow mein and the hugely popular chop suey – a dish often decried, even in its heyday, as 'about as much Chinese as a concoction mixed in an American bar in Paris is an American cocktail' as the *New York Times* put it.

* A phrase coined by academic and author Jean Pfaelzer.

More recently, experts including Chen have observed that chop suey, a meat and vegetable stir-fry in a starch-thickened gravy, is just a more saucy version of a dish common in Chinese home cooking. What is distinctly American, he points out, is the way that this dish emerged 'as the first big brand name of the burgeoning mass-consumer food market . . . It was, simply put, the Big Mac in the pre-McDonald's era.'

Though chop suey has fallen out of favour, it's been replaced on Chinese menus by other American dishes like:

- **Moo shu pork** – stir-fried pork and vegetables served with pancakes and hoisin sauce
- **Crab Rangoon** – fried wonton stuffed with surimi (mock crab) and cream cheese
- **General Tso's chicken** – deep-fried battered chicken in a ginger, garlic, spring onion and chilli sauce
- **Orange chicken or beef** – deep-fried battered meat in a sweet, mildly hot orange sauce
- **Mongolian beef** – fried beef with onions or spring onions in a sweet, spicy brown sauce

---

If the Mission District, where Tartine is located, is a mixture of arty hipsters and Mexican-American families (the Spanish-Colonial Mission High School stops me in my tracks: it's so like something out of a Brat Pack movie that I half expect to see Emilio Estevez and Molly Ringwald slouch down the steps) and arty hipsters, Chinatown is very much still Chinese. Looking down Stockton Street to the water feels like being in a low-rise Asian city, bristling with wires and signs for dim sum and massage spas, benevolent associations and traditional medicine, and endless fluttering Taiwanese flags. My friend Nina tells me later that the local Taiwanese population is so large that her mum, who came to

America as a young woman, now attends elementary school reunions in the Bay Area.

Dodging tables of dried mussels and reflexology sandals, I turn into a narrow alleyway strung with red lanterns, deserted save for a woman sitting on a plastic chair outside a bubble tea shop, and catch the buttery smell of my destination, the Golden Gate Fortune Cookie Factory. Chop suey may be up for debate, but these sweet half-moon-shaped wafers are definitely American . . . or so I assume, given I've rarely seen them anywhere else.

Indeed, the fortune cookie as we know it today first popped up in Californian Chinese restaurants in the 1940s, and was so rapidly assimilated into American popular culture that by the 1960s it was a common political campaign tool. (Sample fortune from the 1968 presidential election: 'A tall, dark, handsome man will come into your life. He supports KENNEDY'.) Research by Yasuko Naka-machi, however, suggests that the idea came to the States with Japanese rather than Chinese immigrants in the form of *tsujiura senbei*, crisp, sweet little crackers once served at the Japanese Tea Garden in Golden Gate Park. With the Japanese population interned in camps in the wake of Pearl Harbor, the Chinese-American community appears to have taken over production, at some point replacing the sesame and miso in the original recipe with more American-friendly butter and vanilla.

Today they're considered as Chinese as egg rolls* – author Jennifer 8. Lee grew up in New York believing them to be Chinese . . . as did her Taiwanese-born mother, who had never visited mainland China: the shock 'was like learning I was adopted while being told there was no Santa Claus', she writes in her book *The Fortune Cookie Chronicles*. Yet their origins are still sufficiently murky as to have been the subject of a mock trial pitting a Chinese

---

* A sturdier take on a spring roll invented in New York's Chinatown, which uses a wonton wrapper instead of the usual spring roll pastry.

immigrant to LA against Makoto Hagiwara, proprietor of the Golden Gate tea garden back in 1983. The judge decided in favour of San Francisco . . . but as there's little concrete historical evidence, the dispute rumbles on.

I'm hoping that the Golden Gate factory, which opened in 1962 and proudly claims to be the city's oldest handmade fortune cookie producer (and the last operating in Chinatown) will be able to clarify matters. Kevin Chan, the co-owner, and son of one of the founders, is currently in China but assures me someone will be there to 'represent him' – though when I step into the tiny shop I quickly realise it isn't quite the slick visitor attraction I'd assumed from its website. Instead, the space is just about large enough to hold two ancient-looking *Wallace & Gromit*-style machines hard at work filling a rotating conveyor belt of small round hot plates with yellow batter. By the time the batter reaches the two masked, gloved women on the line it's firm enough to be picked up, but they only have a few seconds to deftly bend it into shape over a metal stick, adding a fortune to each from a box in front of them. Apparently they can make up to 10,000 cookies a day like this, though they don't seem in much of a hurry this morning, chatting happily away with a man leaning casually against the counter as they reach, fold, drop and repeat.

He ambles over and, after I explain who I am, mutely signs that the person I need is out back, on the phone, and goes back to his perch. While I wait, I inspect the merchandise; unable to compete with mechanised producers on price, the Golden Gate has diversified, offering, in addition to the traditional variety, giant fortune cookies, green tea, strawberry and chocolate fortune cookies, chocolate-dipped fortune cookies with sprinkles, personalised fortune cookies (popular, I learn, for marriage proposals) and, intriguingly, adult X-rated fortune cookies – though as I'm visiting a young family this evening, I steer clear. Framed photos of Kevin with local dignitaries and celebrity visitors crowd the walls, along with an array of police badges, Chinese calligraphy, watercolours and the odd smiling Buddha. Even police dogs seem to love Golden Gate – I can't help wondering how they stop them eating the fortunes along with the cookies. That's police training for you, I suppose.

Eventually, the one person in the place who will admit to speaking a little English appears, but the word journalist seems to unnerve her, despite my repeated dropping of Kevin's name while doing my best not to look like a health inspector on an unannounced visit – 'You must talk to him,' she repeats, though she does unbend sufficiently to answer my question: are fortune cookies Chinese, Japanese or American. No hesitation there – 'American!' she says firmly.

Matter settled, and with little else to detain me, I pay for a bag of cookies, and she shoves a couple of warm unfolded wafer discs in there too, which I find as unaccountably exciting as the solid chocolate KitKat I was blessed with in a school packed lunch back in 1993. Consumed mindfully, as Californians might say, rather than tossed down carelessly at the end of a meal, the cookies are nicer than I remember; richer and more buttery, with a more distinct vanilla flavour.

After crunching around Chinatown spewing crumbs for a while, I duck into St Mary's Cathedral and Chinese Mission to light a candle for my safe travels. Ten minutes later, while powering down to Fisherman's Wharf, I realise I've left my bag with my passport, wallet and notebook in the loving care of Our Lady. Fortunately it's still where I left it – but as I walk out, sweating slightly, I can't decide whether this is a good sign, or a warning from the heavens.

Having established that fortune cookies are American (if not who exactly is responsible), I have a side mission involving Chez Panisse in Berkeley, the Bay Area's most famous restaurant and birthplace, it's often said, of the once terribly fashionable California Cuisine (aka the reason that goat's cheese salads, sun-dried tomatoes and gourmet pizza dominated the British dining scene at the turn of the century), though I'm eating at the cheaper upstairs cafe, because even I'm not that bad at budgeting.

Berkeley immediately feels different when I step off the train from the touristy bustle of the wharf across the water, with quiet, citrus-lined streets of colourful clapboard houses trailing perfumed climbers. A yard with a beautiful crop of rainbow chard also sports a BERNIE FOR PRESIDENT sign and more than one porch has a poster declaring that the residents within believe some variation on 'Black lives matter; women's rights are human rights; no human is illegal, science is real; love is love; kindness is everything'. It's a lot to share with the world – after a decade I have very little idea of what my own neighbours think about most of these issues, and I chat to some of them almost every day.

Chez Panisse itself is housed in a curious little wood-shingled building with a huge, very Californian-looking tree of some kind towering above it and white wisteria just coming into bloom on the front fence. On the other side of the road a chap towing what appear to be all his possessions in a supermarket trolley shouts racist abuse at no one in particular, while someone with a long beard and even longer hair wobbles past on a folding bike with two flat tyres, their flowery tea dress floating gracefully behind them.

I pass under a wooden arch as if entering some sort of summer camp for wealthy arugula enthusiasts, past the restaurant dining room, panelled in rich, glowing local redwood, and upstairs to the cafe, flattening myself against the wall to make room for a glamorous woman who sweeps past without acknowledgement, exclaiming, 'Can you *believe* I ate all of that pasta?' Waiting for my table, I see a poodle up on a chair, being fed sourdough pizza crusts by a person in a cardigan with CHRISTIAN DIOR written in two-inch-high letters across the back, and feel this alone has been worth the investment.

The menu changes daily – all part of founder Alice Waters' culinary philosophy to use good local ingredients at their best, which sounds pretty old hat now, but, according to those who were there, was pretty revolutionary when they opened up back in 1971. Phil Rosenthal of Somebody Feed Phil fame has described Waters as 'the most charming, lovely lady [who] also happened to create the way we eat in America. She started the farm to table movement, almost single handedly.'

Waters' 'one unbreakable rule' has always been 'to use only the freshest and finest ingredients available' – which is why I order the garden lettuces (sourced, the menu notes, from Star Route Farms, set up in 1974 by a Berkeley PhD student) with Banyuls vinaigrette,* to see what magic her kitchen might work on a green salad, followed by the wood-fired pizza di Michele, topped with goat's cheese, prosciutto and fried rosemary – California loves a gourmet pizza.

As I tuck into bread and butter and some sort of house-made kombucha, I eavesdrop on the couple next to me, whose conversation ranges from interest rates to the absolute necessity of drinking thirteen glasses of water a day. As the meal progresses they move on to their real estate investments and why a particular property might not be selling, at which point I hear the man say quite seriously, as if imparting a little-known fact, 'You know, not everyone makes a quarter of a million dollars a year.' When I tell my dinner hosts about this later, Adele rolls her eyes and says, 'That's *so* Berkeley.'

I don't know what I'm expecting from a plate of lettuce, but impeccably sourced though it no doubt is, I can't help wishing for

---

* Banyuls being a French sweet red wine vinegar that retails for about $22 a bottle.

some salt, though I'm too scared to expose my debased palate to ridicule by asking for it. The pizza, with its crisp, blistered crust, sweet ham and creamy cheese, is unsurprisingly a lot tastier, and feels unmistakably American, rather than Italian – an elevation of a cheap and cheerful staple into something altogether more luxe. As the *New York Times* sniffed back in 1991, 'pizza has not been the same since California discovered goat cheese', or indeed barbecued chicken or smoked salmon or nettles, the last one of Waters' most famous seasonal toppings.

My favourite part of the meal, however, turns out to be the extraordinarily zingy tangerine sherbet with candied kumquats, blood orange and citrus blossom ice cream I order for dessert – like a very elegant rave in an organic orange grove. Discreetly wiping my finger across the plate to pick up every last atom of flavour, I watch a woman across the room clap her hands with pleasure when she receives a gold bowl containing a single Churchill-Brenneis Orchard Pixie tangerine ($9!), proclaiming it 'the perfect dessert'. I wonder how long it will take me to attain this level of consciousness.

TANGERINE SHERBET WITH CANDIED KUMQUATS, INSPIRED BY CHEZ PANISSE

This gloriously refreshing ice sounds more work than it actually is if you have an ice cream maker. You can also strain out the zest if you'd prefer a silkier result. The alcohol is not obligatory, but again, will give a smoother finish.

Serves 4 to 6
1kg/2 pounds 3 ounces tangerines
100g/½ cup white caster/superfine sugar
¼ tsp fine salt

1 tbsp vodka or orange-flavoured liqueur
120ml/½ cup double/heavy cream

For the candied kumquats
100g/about ⅔ cup kumquats
125g/½ cup + 1 tbsp caster/superfine sugar
2 green cardamom pods, roughly crushed

To serve
2 tangerines or 1 large orange

1. Finely grate the zest from a couple of the tangerines into a medium saucepan, then squeeze in the juice of all the fruit, removing any seeds as you go.
2. Add the sugar and salt to the juice and heat gently until they've dissolved. Take off the heat, stir in the vodka and chill.
3. Once cold, stir in the cream, then churn in an ice cream maker until smooth.
4. Chop the kumquats into slices about 3mm (⅛ in) wide, removing any seeds as you go.
5. Put the sugar and cardamom pods into a pan with 125ml/½ cup plus 1 teaspoon of water and bring to the boil, stirring occasionally to dissolve the sugar.
6. Add the sliced kumquats and bring back to a simmer, then cook, stirring occasionally, until the syrup thickens around the fruit – about 10 minutes. Tip into a clean jar and allow to cool.
7. Peel the fresh fruit and remove as much pith as possible. Cut into thin slices and chill. When ready to serve, divide these between small bowls or plates and top with a spoonful of sherbet and some kumquats and syrup.

Floating on a sherbet cloud, I drift down University Avenue, past an anarchist t-shirt collective and a giant hamburger joint, to meet my friend Nina – she of the Taiwanese mother – at the Cultured Organic Pickle Shop, where I find a man chopping untidy piles of beet tops for kimchi in an industrial kitchen lined with rainbow vats of liquid. Keen as I am to try the seasonal pickles,* I confine myself to a fennel and blood orange green tea kombucha, which is so lively that it requires detailed opening instructions – and then, when I fail to heed them, some emergency tissues.

Nina, an author/musician/techie/renaissance woman, takes me on a tour of the UC Berkeley campus, where we have to duck past several graduation photoshoots involving East Asian students wearing sashes, which she says is 'probably a Greek thing'. I ponder this in silence for a minute, and then realise she means the fraternity and sorority system (which I somehow still didn't quite believe existed outside *Legally Blonde*) rather than anything to do with souvlaki and Socrates.

Skirting the Gaza Solidarity Encampment in Sproul Plaza, we hit a Taiwanese bakery, 'the kind of place I used to come a lot with my mom as a kid', and end up in a bubble tea shop – or boba, as it's known here. 'My friends and I didn't really drink a ton as teenagers,' she recalls, 'so we'd meet up in tea shops, but back then it was called pearl milk tea. Apparently only old ladies call it that these days.' She scrutinises the colourful menu sceptically. 'All these options make *me* feel so old! What the hell is a tornado swirl?'

As I slurp salted cream cheese *tie guan yin* between bits of fluffy spring onion bun, she points at a shop across the road. 'What do you think that place is?' It's black and sleek, with well-tended greenery, and a sign that simply reads 'Apothecarium: dispensary'. I guess

---

* Today, beets with fennel, kohlrabi with caraway and leek, mustard greens with turmeric and fennel seed.

either a cocktail bar or some sort of high-end skincare clinic. 'Weed,' she says. 'Want to take a look?'

Though she's not even allowed in the building without ID, the affable man behind the reception desk signs me in, and tells me to take all the time I want, 'photos too, just make sure you don't get any faces in there'. I'm not sure what I was expecting – probably the goth and poppers vibe of the head shops of my youth – but this brightly lit showroom, with its blond wood and curated glass display cases, definitely wasn't it. Smiling my thanks to the helpful man, I slink out and tell Nina it reminds me of an Apple store. 'Weird, huh,' she says. 'Very California.'*

Nina kindly drops me off at the Central Berkeley home of friends Richard and Adele, whose three small boys are playing outside on the sidewalk with neighbouring kids in what seems an almost comically wholesome fashion to me, fresh from the mean streets of London. Adele gathers them in for taco salad ('You've never had a taco salad?' one asks incredulously) and my fortune cookies, which prove a big hit, and tells them I'm writing a book about American food. We discuss favourites. 'Burger and fries,' Felix says firmly. 'Fries . . . and Skittles,' his twin brother, Simon, counters. Hugo, the youngest, is also the loudest: 'PIZZA, PIZZA, PIZZA!' he shouts. 'Come and see our treehouse.'

Adele happens to casually mention, as Richard comes in from work and, finding we've polished off the taco salad, cuts himself some cheese made on her family farm in Maine, that the aunt and

---

* I discover later that, although marijuana remains illegal under federal law, many states have decriminalised it for medical, or, like California, recreational use, which explains why it's the defining smell of my trip. The state is estimated to produce 40 per cent of the nation's weed; according to a CNN report into the unlicensed growers undercutting legal operations, the Golden State's cannabis 'enjoys a global reputation similar to that of Napa Valley wines'.

uncle who produce it happen to be part of the McIlhenny clan of Tabasco fame – perhaps I'd like an introduction?

I almost bite her hand off, so much would I like this, not only has it been a lovely evening, but potentially a useful one too, which, on day one (how have I only been here twenty-four hours?), feels like a good start.

Having seen several people with a full complement of limbs cycling around Berkeley, I decide to take the plunge the next morning by dusting Eddy off to meet the friends of friends who have offered to take me for a swim in the Bay. Almost queasy with nerves thanks to all the warnings about American drivers, as well as a deep sense of my own mechanical incompetence, I wobble onto the inconveniently hilly city streets and find, to my amazement, everything seems to work perfectly . . . until I hit a particularly steep descent and realise the handlebars, and thus the brakes, are rotating alarmingly away from my trembling grasp.

Thankfully I manage to stay on board, sweating slightly with terror, all the way down to the Dolphin Club on the grey, chilly waterfront, a members' sailing and swimming organisation established by German immigrants in 1877. Johan, a Frenchman, and Benedetta, his Italian wife, show me the wooden boats watched over by decades of club photos, from stiff-looking Victorian men in suits and walrus moustaches to the happier and more diverse crowd of recent years.

Once we're in the water the temperature isn't as bad as I'd feared – Johan estimates it's about 64°F (18°C), so visions of embarrassing myself by going into cardiac arrest prove needless – and the joy of being in the slatey ocean, as opaque as mercury from a distance but absolutely clear above my pink limbs, is profound. Thirty-six hours after touching down I realise I finally feel grounded.

Almost everyone I meet here seems to work in tech in some capacity. Johan, who spent fifteen years at Google, recalls that in the early days the food was 'ridiculous . . . lobster, steak, almost anything you could wish for'. More recently, he says, there's been a drive towards helping people to make healthier choices, 'because for a while, your desk was never more than ten yards from a bad decision'. Afterwards, Benedetta and I retreat to the ladies' sauna, where a group of older women, clearly regulars, are discussing the city's public transport – 'You know, I never took a bus until last month,' one says, 'and then my daughter made me, when we went to see Bruce Springsteen. I was so scared – but you know what, it was fine!' Not that she's taken the bus since. (That was very American, Benedetta says fondly when they leave; everyone here drives everywhere. This puzzles me, given the Bay Area seems to have decent public transport – but with a few, mostly East Coast exceptions, driving just seems to be the American way. Perhaps, we ponder, the autonomy of the car assumes particular significance in this proudly individualist country.)

Waving the couple goodbye, I tighten my handlebars at the nearest bike shop* before battling the wind across the Golden Gate Bridge, the waters of the Bay below looking distinctly less inviting from this angle. I spot Alcatraz through the famous red cables, squatting grimly on its lonely rock under looming clouds. Johan has recommended a scenic bike route up to a lighthouse on the other side, but by the time I've made it past the slow-moving queue of heavy rental bikes wobbling across the bridge's narrow cycle lane, I have to turn round and head back for my lunch date with Cecilia in the Mission.

Feeling confident now, I pedal through the cool, dark woods of the Presidio, the site of an old Spanish fort and now home to several alarming warnings about coyotes (I realise after stopping to take a

---

* Thanks to Rapha for the loan of the tool and the very welcome cortado.

picture that I have absolutely no idea if coyotes are dangerous to humans, or even what exactly they might look like outside Looney Tunes), through the old hippy stronghold of Haight Ashbury, now disappointingly respectable, and meet her at La Taqueria, a local favourite since 1973, which, the *Michelin Guide* reports, 'always has a queue because everyone loves it – from tech bros in hoodies to families out for Sunday lunch'. It serves Mission-style burritos, though its version pre-dates the term: 'It's my own style,' owner Miguel Jara told Eater a few years ago. 'A lot of people call it a Mission-style burrito, but I don't know what a Mission-style burrito is.' (If you too are in the dark, it's a larger-than-average style made with a flour tortilla, meat, rice and beans: the *New York Times* suggests that 'the enlargement of the burrito to humongous, Americanized proportions may be the Mission's supreme contribution to Western civilization'.)

Cecilia, a local who – you guessed it – once worked in tech, and now writes about the ethical and philosophical issues around artificial intelligence, deftly orders a vegetarian version in Spanish; I get as far as '*lengua* [tongue] *por favor*' and a smile, which seems to do the trick – the burrito is huge, stuffed tight in its skin with stickily rich meat and earthy pinto beans, plus salsa and not a single grain of rice. This surprises me, given that La Taqueria's version is held up as an iconic Mission burrito, a dish in which rice seems to be a defining ingredient . . . it's a bit like going to somewhere that does a great roast beef and finding out there's no Yorkshire pudding, except less disappointing, because actually, if I were designing the perfect Mission burrito, I'd probably keep the size and drop the rice too. Less rice means more meat and beans; all killer, no filler.

A mariachi band wanders around serenading workers on their lunch break. I spill green salsa down my only clean t-shirt. Time to head back to the hostel and wash everything I own, ready to hit the coast road tomorrow. Los Angeles here I come!

Ridden: 19 miles
Climbed: 804 feet
Pies consumed: 0
All-American foods discovered: fortune cookies, gourmet pizzas, taco salad, Mission burritos

2
HITTING THE HIGHWAY

In search of the artichoke capital of the world

'*The journey is part of the experience – an expression of the seriousness*
of one's intent. One doesn't take the A train to Mecca.'
Anthony Bourdain

I wake at dawn with mixed feelings. On the one hand, I'm raring
to get on the road. On the other, Dan's warnings regarding the
Pacific Coast Highway are still living rent free in my head, prompt-
ing my decision to dodge city traffic by taking the train down to
Colma, a town originally built as a necropolis (there are no cemeteries in San Francisco itself – the land is too valuable) and where
the dead still outnumber the living by a thousand to one. As signs
and portents go, it's not a great place to start, but as a way to put
off getting on the highway, it works fine.

By the time I finally load Eddy up for the first time, wobble my
way nervously to the station, negotiate the trains to Colma and find
the ocean road, it's already 8.30am, and I'm tempted to stop almost
immediately at the promisingly named Porridge King . . . but it's
still closed, so no breakfast congee for me. Finally there's nothing
for it but to actually do a bit of cycling.

Turning on to Skyline Drive I realise, with a sinking heart, that my journey across America begins with a long hill – but, having made it to the top (Adrian's words ringing in my ears at every puffing pedal stroke), I find myself blown away by the sight of the coast spooling away in front of me. The ocean may be choppy and grey but it promises wildness and adventure, and suddenly I'm coasting downhill and there's nowhere I'd rather be. It's hard to explain the profound pleasure I get from a day on the bike with nothing to do but turn my legs around, enjoy the scenery and occasionally stop to refuel – it's the simplicity of it, plus the deep satisfaction of being entirely self-sufficient, like a snail with emergency rations tucked inside its shell.

I stop, already elated, in Pacifica for an egg and cheese bagel and the hottest coffee on earth. Hearing my accent, the man behind the counter says, without preamble, 'So, Prince Harry, huh?' After I recover from the shock of scalding my oesophagus, we spend an enjoyable few minutes trading unfounded royal rumours before I go outside, open the wrapper and discover that cheese here, without further qualification, apparently refers to processed slices. It seems I'm going to have to do some work on myself to accept this stuff into my life and heart if I'm to survive the next few months because right now, hungry as I am, its gloopy texture really turns my stomach.

Though the weather is relentlessly overcast, with a chilly wind that feels like it blew straight in from Great Yarmouth, I'm still taken aback to pass an English Pub and Inn in Half Moon Bay with a Routemaster claiming to be 'the world's only double decker smoking bus as seen nationwide on TV' parked outside next to a red phone box. Mostly, however, it's rolling green countryside to the left and ocean to my right, bordered by a cliff-top carpet of succulents and pink and yellow flowers. Just before 1pm I turn off Highway 1 and head two miles inland to Duarte's Tavern in the little town of Pescadero, a place I'd noted on my phone while chatting to my parents' American friend Dennis over a post-Mass sherry in Broadstairs, Kent – it seems quite extraordinary to actually be here, just weeks later. Duarte's pies, apparently, are out of this world, and it's high time I got going on my mission to try as many as possible.

Pescadero, despite its Spanish name,* has a large Portuguese-heritage community, and signs by the highway advertise the 124th annual Holy Ghost Celebration organised by the IDES, or Sociedade Da Irmandade do Divino Espirito Santo. There's even a free barbecue in honour of the Ghost, but sadly I'm a few weeks early, so I have to content myself with a large fried sole sandwich on fluffy white bread, with good fries, crinkle-cut pickles and a root beer. It's not quite fish and chips as I know it, but it's delicious, and, sitting at the counter, where I suspect I'm placed to avoid putting the other customers off their lunch, I feel like I'm finally living the kind of road trip I've always dreamed of. (I also get my first taste of the American commitment to efficiency when the bill arrives while I'm still eating, a common practice I do not find conducive to relaxed enjoyment of the food. Why everyone is in such a rush on a Thursday lunchtime I can't think.†)

Keen to get back on my way – it's still thirty-five miles to Santa Cruz, where I'm staying the night – I add a large slab of something called oliaberry pie to the check and coast back down to the ocean road (spotting yet another red phone box in someone's front garden en route. It's a wonder there are any left at home to

---

* Meaning 'fishmonger'.
† A recent YouGov poll found over half of Americans surveyed didn't agree with the idea it was acceptable to take 'an extended period of time to decide what to order', which explains why I – a leisurely eater who likes to study the menu – feel so consistently rushed in restaurants, where the server often arrives to take my dessert order shortly after I've started my main course, then brings it to sit on the table in front of me like I'm in a cafeteria, along with the bill. Though I come to realise this is just standard etiquette here, I can't help but feel I've outstayed my welcome.

vandalise). A few miles later, I pass signs exhorting me to SLOW FOR PIE – but I feel I can't in all conscience take on two slices, especially given that my left pannier keeps coming loose, at one point falling off into the road, which is less than ideal for the pastry on top. I can't work out what's wrong, but it's losing me time, and, though I had been happy with my progress, the last few miles of the afternoon are a grind, my mood not helped by the charred trunks of redwoods stacked up next to huge piles of orange woodchips, grim reminders of recent forest fires soon followed by the gaping wound of an even more recent landslide.

Later, curious about this apparently unfortunate series of events, I learn that increasingly heavy rainfall has left the coast road, Highway 1, already on shaky ground, more vulnerable than ever to landslides. This is exacerbated by the also increasingly frequent wildfires which strip away the vegetation holding the soil together. I had originally hoped to cycle Big Sur, widely touted as one of the most beautiful drives in the world ('the California that men dreamed of years ago . . . the face of the earth as the Creator intended it to look' as local resident Henry Miller put it) but it's been closed for the last year, not helped by another rockslide in late March. 'But hey, that's climate change for ya, honey,' the woman in the hostel says when I check in. 'We created it, now we gotta live with it.'

I grimace, both sympathetically and because I've still got approx-imately 100 oliaberry seeds stuck in my molars from the pie, eaten by the side of the road after a wayward pannier cast it into a particularly thorny bush. Once a few ants have been flicked off, it turns out to have a very thin, delicate base, in contrast with its crisp, biscuity sides and top, and boasts a solid 5cm of tart-sweet purplish filling; from the colour and seeds I guess an oliaberry is a type of blackberry. An excellent first example to kick off with, setting the bar high with an 8.5/10; though the fruit to pastry ratio is a little high for my taste.

Pie, according to the Farm Journal's *Complete Pie Cookbook* of 1965, 'is America's top dessert. It appeared on New World tables almost from the start – long before the Stars and Stripes flew from a flagpole or the Fourth of July was an extraordinary day.' More recently, it was pie that the Singaporean-born amateur baker and wannabe-American Stacey Mei Yan Fong decided to focus on to destress while waiting for her permanent visa to be approved back in 2016, which led to a book: *50 Pies, 50 States: An Immigrant's Love Letter to the United States Through Pie*. From pioneer pumpkin to Fong's South Dakota wild rice pudding pie, nothing, it seems, unites the States like pie.

American sweet pies fall into three principal categories: fruit pies, like cherry, apple or blueberry; cream or icebox pies, like chocolate, pumpkin and key lime; and sugar pies, a category that, as well as pecan, includes such idiosyncratic examples as chess (with a starchy sweet custard filling) and shoo-fly (an Amish speciality involving molasses). There are hundreds, if not thousands, of variations on these themes, from lurid-green grasshopper to mock mincemeat made with green tomatoes.

For me, the delight of the pie is as much in the shell as the filling – we're past the days of Mark Twain's bullet-proof crusts – and both elements will be awarded equal weight in my very scientific judging process, similar to my ongoing quest to rate every croissant I think looks worth eating, and every mince pie I can lay my hands on in the month of

December. Some people may say this takes the joy out of such treats; for me, eating critically only increases my pleasure in good examples.

Though the type of pastry will vary with the pie, I generally prefer them to be fairly savoury, even a little salty, to counteract the sweetness inside; crisp and buttery for a fruit filling, snappy and plain for something richer. To my mind the two should complement rather than echo each other, and neither should dominate – sometimes you can have too much of a good thing.

Though sugar-based pies in particular are, by their very nature, extremely sweet, I like fruit pies to retain some of the natural tartness and texture of the fruit itself, and ideally, not to be too starchy or jellied. A soggy crust is, to my mind, preferable to a stodgy, over-thickened filling. In the icebox category, whipped cream should not be so copious, or so sweet, that it has to be scooped off the top.

1/10: probably not even a pie to be honest.

2–4/10: a pie all right, but not one worth finishing.

5–6/10: suggests either the pastry or the filling has serious deficiencies, but you'd probably finish the other bit.

7/10: decent workaday pie, but not one you'd recommend to others when they message you in six months' time to ask what they should eat in Toad Suck, Arkansas.

8/10: a good pie, the kind you'd recommend someone travelled to Toad Suck for from as far afield as, say, Lost Corner or Sulphur Springs.

9/10: a really great pie, the kind of pie worth a detour via Toad Suck when driving from Seattle to Portland.

10/10: perfection does not exist in this life, even in Toad Suck: you're either drunk or dead.

After the open, wind-blasted coast road I've been pedalling all day, Santa Cruz, with its tall palms and wide, sandy beaches, feels truly Californian at last. The ocean-front fairground, with its retro neon signage and concessions offering monster corn dogs and French-fried artichoke hearts, may be closed, but walking the pier I spot a sea otter floating nonchalantly on its back, casually eating something held between its front flippers, which as amusements go is surely better than any pirate ship ride.

After two cold pints and a wedge salad (like the French, the Americans understand that salad doesn't have to be self-flagellation in a bowl) at a brewpub, I wander back to find I have two room-mates in tonight's dorm. Melinda, a middle-aged single mother of two, is travelling on her own and seems cock-a-hoop about this sudden freedom. Cindy, a twenty-two-year-old East Coaster study-ing engineering in Austin, is taking time out to work out what she wants to do with her life, telling us she feels caught between the obligation to get a job and pay off her college debts – which will take the pressure off her Chinese immigrant parents – and her secret desire to work a ski season in Tahoe. Both Melinda and I urge her to take a little time out before getting a serious job – though I'm conscious as we say our goodnights, Walton-style, that I might have taken this whole not-getting-a-serious-job thing a bit too far.

So keen is Melinda on the idea of getting back into travelling that she appears at my side at 7.15 the next morning, wanting to look at my bike as I'm inserting a spare widget* I hope should stop my disobedient pannier falling off every quarter of an hour (which it eventually does, once I've finally located the correctly sized widget

---

* More thanks due to Adrian at Condor for insisting a spare packet of these widgets might come in handy; if only I'd taken a look before leaving London.

later that afternoon, and replaced it a second time). 'I'd love to do something like this,' she says dreamily. 'I haven't spent any time on my own in twenty years.' It's nice to be reminded how lucky I am, and I set off along the coast with spirits high, waving to the dog walkers and treasure hunters already out on the beach, and narrowly avoiding ending up under the wheels of a speeding Jeep convertible bearing the bumper sticker: TRUMP DON'T SURF – quite the mental image before 8am.

The sun even comes out, which is great, until the road heads inland through forest, and things become stickily unpleasant. I stop in Seacliff for breakfast, lured by the gloriously late 50s styling of the Sno-White Drive-In (opened in 1957, now owned by Cambodians, which explains the slightly random spring roll on the menu between fried chicken and corn dogs), and the prices: $5.49 for an English muffin with cheese and egg, and, a special order, hash browns instead of bacon or sausage ('You don't want meat in there?' – the woman behind the counter confirms, apparently astonished).

Clutching a cardboard cup of watery coffee, I sit under the angular concrete canopy listening to the people next to me, who seem to be neighbours who have bumped into each other unexpectedly. The woman, tucking enthusiastically into a muffin, explains she doesn't eat breakfast as a rule, no, nor lunch either, dinner is her thing, and she likes to have meat: 'a big ol' baked potato and STEAK'. It dawns on me that this is not the California of Gwyneth Paltrow.

Spotting a branch of Ferrells, the doughnut . . . sorry, donut* shop Cindy waxed lyrical about last night, I stop again to pick one up for the road – though they have European roots, the modern

---

* In keeping with their general efficiency, Americans tend to go with the phonetic 'donut', in use there since at least 1870, while in the UK, 'doughnut' is the preferred spelling.

American donut, in all its over-the-topness, is very much a New World creation. Despite the forty-one varieties advertised in this out-of-the-way little shop (who could possibly need, or even want, so much choice?), nothing on display is labelled, and when I ask the woman behind the counter what she has, she sighs heavily, though I'm the only customer, and then coughs into her hand. 'What, you want me to tell you *all* of 'em?' This is clearly a rhetorical question. Perhaps, I think, donut identification is something you learn in school here. I meekly pick the plainest thing I can find, which she grumpily puts in a bag, and pay by cash, in case she expects a tip.

Looking at my watch, I quicken my pace; as there's currently no way through the Big Sur landslide, and accounts of the inland detour are uninspiring, I'm planning to catch a train from Salinas south to Santa Barbara, where I can rejoin the coast road. It's 9am, the train is at 12.06pm, and Salinas lies forty miles to the south, in prime agricultural country arguably more representative of the Golden State – which produces three-quarters of the country's fruit and nuts and a third of its vegetables – than these wealthy enclaves along the coast. In short, I'm in a hurry.

It's not long before beachfront condos are replaced by crops; mainly spiky artichokes (every roadside cafe seems to offer them deep-fried, which I sorely wish I had time to sample) and low rows of what I assume, from the number of signs advertising them for sale, to be strawberries. The surface becomes increasingly cracked and rutted with mud and I battle a stiff headwind, though I suspect my travails are nothing compared to those bent double in the fields – as the morning wears on I'm passed at speed by several rickety Mexican food trucks, all presumably headed for the lunchtime rush: 96 per cent of farmworkers in California identify as Hispanic, according to La Cooperativa Campesina de California 75 per cent are undocumented.

There's not even time to tarry in Castroville, the Artichoke Capital of the World (a fact underlined by the many enormous model artichokes on display by the side of the road); instead I push on across the plain, dead flat now, and neatly striped on both sides with crops as far as the eye can see. I get to Salinas station with about half an hour to spare, only to discover, standing in the beautiful, wood-beamed 1940s ticket hall with its tiled mural of workers loading crops onto wagons, that I could have stopped for an artichoke after all. The man behind the desk is telling the couple in front of me that there's some delay up in the mountains, and though the board is suggesting the 12.06pm should arrive at 6.25pm, he personally wouldn't bet on seeing it before 10pm 'at the earliest'.

Fortunately, once it's my turn to explain my plight, he's more helpful than I anticipate, booking me, bike and all, onto a coach as far as San Luis Obispo and another train south from there, and offering to store Eddy 'free of charge' (I understand this to be a great concession from his tone) while I go and get something to eat: 'El Charrito just down the street, you can't go wrong.'

He's not the only person to think so; the queue for the parking lot of this Mexican canteen blocks the pavement, and the line inside fills the building. Burritos seem to be the move here judging by what people are picking out from the steam trays at the front, and caught between so many tempting options I plump for the least familiar, a chile relleno, a large chilli pepper stuffed with cotija and fresh cheeses and topped with salsa verde, refried beans and rice.

It's smaller than the Mission burrito, more Mexican in that way perhaps (debate rages online about how Mexican the burrito as a concept is: the Texan food expert José Ralat reckons they're simply a type of taco found in the borderlands, though it can't be denied that the panoply of fillings probably originated towards the north of that line), but the tortilla is out of this world, freshly made, flaky and rich and a very satisfying thing to eat sitting on the kerb outside the station, washed down by an extremely sweet cup of horchata, a kind of rice and cinnamon milkshake. If I didn't have places to be, I'd seriously consider going back to try their carnitas.

The bus, once it finally pulls in, proves so cold I have to get out my towel to cover my legs, and stops only once,* at McDonald's in King City, where I treat myself to a tip-free coffee. Two and a half hours later we reach San Luis Obispo, a sunny university town where the streets are called things like Peach, Pepper and Walnut, and I haul Eddy on board the Surfliner train to Santa Barbara, a lovely line hugging the palm-fringed ocean. Wooden lifeguard chairs on sand glowing golden in the evening sun give me a little thrill of recognition – it feels like I've arrived in a Beach Boys song.

Cycling to my hostel from the station (having reluctantly decided the delay means it's now too late to cycle to the nearest campsite, thirteen dark miles down the coast), I pass restaurants already full of Friday-night revellers in body-con dresses and artfully gaping shirts. Hoping to find somewhere a little cheaper, I check in ('smile more, laugh more, LOVE MORE' a stone on reception advises me) and ask about grocery stores in walking distance. The receptionist shrugs, says he's not sure there is one, I'd be better off taking a cab – but I finally find a Mexican place bursting at the seams with fresh produce, much, presumably, grown nearby. This yields a family-sized bag of carrots and a box of the biggest strawberries I've ever seen – freakishly big, in fact – which, paired with some tortilla chips, guacamole and salsa from the adjoining restaurant, make a fine dinner back at the hostel (where two men are watching *Men in Black* at an ear-splitting volume) chased down by the unexpectedly salty squashed Ferrells donut I discover while looking for ear plugs.

---

* It does, however, give me a glimpse of the city's once-thriving Chinatown, via a battered sign advertising Chop Suey on a derelict Mission-style building – formerly the largest between San Francisco and Los Angeles, it went into a decline in the 1950s when Asian-Americans were finally allowed to own land elsewhere.

With its palm trees and manicured mansions, Santa Barbara feels even more like Instagram California than Santa Cruz, with a photogenic farmers' market to match. Longingly ogling the colourful riot of fruit and vegetables, from Meyer lemons to cherimoya, I buy a strawberry pie, an avocado from an elderly woman who goes through a great pile to find the ripest for me and a bag of dried Mission figs from one of the many people to assume I'm Australian ('I've never been to Europe,' the stallholder shrugs when I correct her, 'we only travel to hot places') but for me, the people-watching is even better than the produce.

A long-haired John Lennon type in cheesecloth, beads and soft, expensive-looking moccasins complains down the phone about his therapist as he idly fondles some wheatgrass – 'they shouldn't be like, this is how *I* feel, they're here to ask how do *you* feel?' – a woman protests loudly that she '*loves* homeless people', and I witness a quite heated argument over the carb content of strawberry juice. There is, however, nowhere selling anything resembling breakfast, so I relocate to a Mexican bakery down the road, where I buy a bread roll and beg a little salt in a twist of paper to season my perfect, buttery yellow avocado. Consumed sitting on a sunny park bench, it's the best breakfast I've had so far. Sorry, Tartine, but context is everything.

On the way out of Santa Barbara – after taking a photo of myself next to the No Wankers sign on the door of the Old Kings Road pub and wondering whether local resident the Duke of Sussex ever pops in for a pint – I'm accosted by a deeply tanned topless man on a tricycle, who wants to know 'my deal'. As he seems to consider himself a sort of expert on the Pacific Coast Highway, I ask if what I've read online about the suspension of the 'hiker biker' policy* in southern California due to a problem with

---

* A few states have policies, official or otherwise, of not turning anyone away who arrives at their campgrounds on foot or bicycle.

'long-term campers' is true. The man frowns and tells me quite aggressively I should stop listening to the mainstream media and other people's opinions and start thinking for myself. I thank him and resolve to try to contact the sites by phone instead – though so far mine seems to be having issues connecting to outgoing calls, which isn't ideal frankly, from a practical or indeed an emergency point of view. My current game plan is just to wait it out and hope it magically resolves itself.

Passing through Montecito, home to Harry and Meghan, I sail through my first roundabout of the trip – no wonder he feels at home – and, capitalising on a brief glimpse of a man on a polo pony at the Santa Barbara Polo and Racquet Club, immediately message friends to say I've spotted the erstwhile prince. Disappointingly though, like many places favoured by the mega rich, Montecito doesn't encourage the casual visitor to linger – there's not even anywhere I can stop in to say I've had a latte at the Duchess's local caff.

After getting lost crossing the freeway and being told off by a gang of Lycra-clad roadies for blocking their path while I snap a photo at Mussel Shoals after confusing it with an album by 90s Brummie rockers Ocean Colour Scene,* I find myself back by the ocean. The sun is out and the views would be fabulous if it weren't for a wall of white plastic between me and the water. From here to Los Angeles stretches an almost solid line of RV parking where families set up camp in their huge homes on wheels, often with a sizeable truck parked alongside for good measure. It's fascinating to see how much they bring with them: satellite dishes sit propped on the tarmac, sports team flags fly from windows, men char meat on enormous outdoor grills, and

---

* In my defence, I wasn't expecting to see any other cyclists given tricycle man is the only other one I've encountered in three days, but it's Saturday morning and weekend warriors are apparently a global phenomenon.

I even spot a solid metal American flag propped up reverently on a folding chair – patriotism never takes a vacation, it seems. The whole scene reminds me a little of beach huts at home, in spirit if not detail given that the vibe there is more Thermos flasks and flapping newspapers.

The surfers are out in force in Ventura where I stop for tacos on the pier – grilled fish with crunchy colourful slaw and spicy corn relish. Though fish tacos are a speciality of Baja California, which lies south of the border, there they tend to be a simpler affair; battered white fish, shredded white cabbage and a creamy sauce; up here you might get avocado, cilantro lime slaw and chipotle cream on top, too. As both are on the menu, I eat both . . . and honestly I'd be hard pressed to say which version I prefer.

EARLY CALIFORNIA TACOS, INSPIRED BY VENTURA PIER

Much as I love the battered fish tacos of Baja California, these grilled versions, colourful with the fresh produce of the Sunshine State, are equally delicious, but without the need for firing up your nerves for deep frying. Note that UK sour cream tends to be thinner than the US version; full-fat crème fraîche works better as a substitute.

Serves 4
½ a small red onion, very thinly sliced
Salt and black pepper
2 limes
2 tbsp olive oil
225g/1¾ cups sweetcorn kernels, cut from a fresh cob, drained from
    a tin, or defrosted
1 jalapeño pepper or other fairly mild chilli, seeded and sliced
8 cherry tomatoes, quartered

*100ml/½ cup sour cream or (better in the UK) full-fat crème fraîche
(French brands tend to be thickest)*
1 chipotle in adobo sauce, plus 2 tsp of the sauce
1 ripe avocado
10g/½ cup roughly chopped fresh coriander/cilantro
12 corn tortillas
400g/1 pound firm white fish fillets
*¼ of a small red cabbage, woody core trimmed, leaves finely
shredded*

1. Put the red onion into a bowl, lightly salt, and squeeze over the
   juice of 1 lime. Leave to soak while you make the rest of the
   dish, turning occasionally to ensure it soaks evenly.
2. Put 1 teaspoon of oil into a large frying pan over a high heat.
   Once it's hot, toast the corn and jalapeño, stirring regularly,
   until slightly charred. Tip into a bowl and add the tomatoes and
   the juice of the second lime. Toss well.
3. To make the cream, whizz together the sour cream or crème
   fraîche, chipotle and 2 teaspoons of its sauce (or more if you
   like things hot). Season to taste.
4. Peel and stone the avocado and slice. Stir the chopped
   coriander into the corn salsa and check the seasoning. Put
   a griddle pan on a medium-high heat (or do this on an
   outside grill). Heat your corn tortillas in a dry frying pan,
   or over an open flame, and wrap tightly in a tea towel to
   keep warm.
5. Rub the fish with olive oil and season well. Put on the hot
   griddle and cook for 2 to 4 minutes if the pieces are very thick,
   undisturbed, then turn over and repeat; the fish should be
   cooked through but not falling apart.
6. Lift onto a plate and begin assembling the tacos (or allow
   people to do their own), starting with a handful of cabbage,
   then a few chunks of the fish, topped with the corn salsa,

avocado, chipotle cream and drained onions. Eat immediately, with a napkin on hand.

As I wait for my tacos, I confirm my suspicion that there's not much accommodation between here and Malibu given that most of the intervening forty-five miles is occupied by the Point Magu State Park (where, hiker biker or not, the campgrounds all seem to start at $45 a night, which seems steep given that my tent is barely bigger than my body), so I decide to book a motel for the night in the last settlement before the wilderness, Port Huemene.

This is to prove one of the worst decisions of the entire trip; when I mention Port Huemene to Californians later, they either say 'Where?' or sigh 'I wish you'd asked me first.' Though I'm sure the town, which hosts a large naval base, is lovely in parts, my first impression is less than charming as the beach view is replaced by a stagnant-smelling marsh and a large power station, and the road widens into a fast dual carriageway. As it's still only 3pm, I head to its one and only tourist attraction: the Seabee Museum. I'll be honest, going in I have absolutely no idea what a Seabee is beyond a faint hope they're flying comrades of the US military dolphins. Disappointingly they turn out to be the (human) service corps for the US Navy, but nevertheless their museum is not without interest for the desperate; I particularly enjoy the Gulf War ration packs with extras of Tabasco, peanut butter and iced tea mix. Having wrung the place dry of all possible excitement, I head to my motel. It's never the best sign when the receptionist is barricaded behind a glass screen, or when she won't meet your eye as she reveals that the web price did not include various taxes and charges, which means she will be charging you $177 for a night at a one-star motel opposite a 'wastewater' processing facility. I'm startled into silence – there are no other options round here, and we both know it. 'Oh . . . OK,' I squeak conciliatorily as she turns away with my passport. 'Thanks so much!'

I stamp crossly over to my room, in which the otherwise mismatched furniture is united in being far too big for the space, a mystery solved when I open a drawer later in a futile hunt for a hairdryer and find it the property of 'Hilton Hotels'. Perhaps the price is explained by the number of amenities that are crammed in, viz. two large desks, an office chair, three chests of drawers and a 'kitchenette' consisting of a mini fridge and a microwave with pizza or popcorn settings, which is occupying the only visible plug point right by the door. There is no Wi-Fi, and the shower is a warm trickle.

As the parking lot outside quickly fills with trucks, I keep the curtains closed and make use of the room's only virtue, an enormous flat-screen TV, quickly becoming quite engrossed in a drama on the Tri State Christian network (the number of specialist television channels in the States never fails to thrill me, even if at least 80 per cent of them are showing pharmaceutical commercials at any one time), in which an evangelical student finds herself the sole voice of reason at her liberal college. Once she bumps into Jesus in the cafeteria, everyone lives happily ever after, except me because the pie I bought this morning in Santa Barbara has floppy, underbaked pastry and a filling jellied by tapioca starch. To be honest, I never see the point of cooking strawberries – they lose all their perfume and acidity; a mere 6/10 I'm afraid, a score perhaps not helped by my surroundings.

Dinner options locally are similarly uninspiring, so I plump for one of the strip-mall Chinese buffets that dominate the provincial American dining scene – there are, it is said, more Chinese restaurants in the USA than McDonald's, Burger King, KFC and Wendy's combined, and, as in the UK, they're often the only option in rural areas (to take one particularly remote example, North Pole Alaska, pop. 2,373, has two Chinese restaurants, one of them located on Santa Claus Lane). Here in Port Huemene, the Fuji Buffet is heaving.

Having paid my $17.99 to an elderly lady in an embroidered silk blouse, I join a queue of about forty people, mostly Hispanic, like the boy behind me talking urgently in English about his plan to apply to CalPoly, before switching into Spanish to scold his younger siblings. Once I'm finally seated – feeling, it's fair to say, a bit like a sore thumb on my table for one with only a paperback Simone de Beauvoir for company among happy families downing endless refills of fizzy drinks – I make for the buffet, where I find myself in unfamiliar territory. One might assume Chinese food to be fairly similar the world over, but of course, it isn't.

What I take to be dim sum of some kind on the first station are actually profiteroles and sugared biscuits, and, having bypassed the pizza and garlic bread, somehow I end up with a spoonful of rice pudding on the same plate as wonton and sushi and most disconcertingly bite into what feels like a small bone in something I took to be tempura aubergine. For all this I'm pleased to finally get the opportunity to try great American favourites like orange chicken (very sweet), coconut shrimp (ditto) and crab Rangoon (very deep-fried), though my favourite thing is broccoli and fried rice doused in large amounts of Tapatio salsa picante, a Californian product created by an immigrant from Guadalajara, which sits in huge bottles at the end of each station. It's an unusual experience, but not an unpleasant one . . . unlike the moment when I get into bed, catch sight of the blackened soles of my freshly washed feet and resolve to write a strongly worded letter of complaint to management the next morning.

As said management only provides a sheet, rather than any kind of blanket, I wake up freezing at 5.30am, leave my angry note on one of the desks, along with a filthy tissue I've wiped along the floor for emphasis, and depart, raging. On the plus side, the sun is just coming up over the plastic-wrapped fields, and traffic is gratifyingly light, which means I have the Point Mugu Naval Air Station, with its cheery display of decorative missiles,* to myself. I hit the ocean and my bad mood melts like American cheese on a hot burger – the tarmac is freshly laid, warmth just creeping over the cliffs, the water still and impossibly blue, and I'm in cycling paradise. Crossing the Los Angeles County Line at 8.18am, I find myself in Selling Sunset territory: huge glass boxes perch on the cliff, bypassing views of the public road in favour of the big blue beyond. Finally, Malibu, a name so aspirational it spawned both a Barbie and a regrettable rum-based liqueur.

Had I known I'd still be pedalling through in search of breakfast an hour later, I would have been rather less jubilant: well-heeled sources have since informed me that if you know a local like Pamela Anderson or Bob Dylan then Malibu is just delightful, but like Montecito before it, from the road the place certainly doesn't give much away. I'm briefly excited by the prospect of the Paradise Cove Beach Cafe, but there's nowhere in their capacious car park to lock up Eddy – and no, the primly polo-shirted staff say when they finally deign to acknowledge my presence at the door, there's nowhere safe to stow him, nor can they offer me a seat where I can keep an eye on him, so in the end, ravenous after three hours on the road, I have to grind back up the hill, muttering furiously to myself about Californians and their bloody car fixation. By contrast, the Malibu Farm Cafe, which I reach forty-five hangry minutes later, could not be more welcoming – of course they can give me a table on the pier next to the bike, no problem; even the fact that they forget the toast with my ridiculously virtuous raw Brussels sprout, quinoa, almond, arugula and avocado open-face omelet can't dent my enthusiasm for the place.

As LA proper looms, Highway 1 becomes increasingly busy with parked cars (some with people still asleep inside) and I'm glad when

---

* One is emblazoned with the word HARM, which I think is at least honest, though it turns out to stand for High-speed Anti-Radiation Missile.

the cycle path peels off at Pacific Palisades* where I stop to take a picture for my Beach Boy-fan mum. The wide golden sand is largely empty all the way to Venice Beach, where I see my first sign for this year's presidential race in the form of a house bedecked by red, white and blue KENNEDY 2024 banners. En route I pass a man on a fat-tyre bike smoking a joint and blaring reggae, a woman towing a huge dog in sunglasses, innumerable impeccably buffed and waxed rollerbladers, and a bare-chested jogger shouting; GO! GO! GO!' to himself without a shred of self-consciousness. No doubt about it, I think, I'm definitely in LA.

Ridden: 219 miles
Climbed: 8,196 feet
Pies consumed: 2, oliaberry and strawberry rhubarb
All-American foods discovered: wedge salad, breakfast muffin,
hash browns, orange chicken, crab Rangoon, coconut shrimp,
California tacos, sprout omelet

* Tragically destroyed by fire in January 2025.

3

LA – DOWN THE DONUT HOLE

In search of the Cambodian Donut King

'Mmmm . . . donuts.'
Homer Simpson

I haven't been planning to cycle in Los Angeles – the epic traffic jam in the opening minutes of the film *La La Land* made quite the lasting impression – but surviving the last couple of days has made me cocky, and the city does appear to boast at least a patchy network of bike routes, which feel potentially easier to navigate than its public transport system . . . or so I tell myself as I set off into the belly of the beast from Santa Monica pier. Initially it's pleasant and Sunday-lunchtime quiet, which lulls me into a false sense of security: the streets are all angles and sunlight, the colours oversaturated, even the lush vegetation tightly groomed. I struggle to spot anything built before the war; if San Francisco felt strange, this place is positively alien. In a glamorous rather than a Ridley Scott way, naturally.

And then the route passes under a freeway bridge sheltering a large homeless encampment. It's a desperate scene to behold, whole lives spewed out onto the pavement, a woman apparently unconscious half in and half out of a tent, and a smell that makes me want to hold my breath but, 'Hi,' I say feebly to a man sitting staring out from an old car seat – I always think one of the small sadnesses of finding yourself at rock bottom must be people pretending not to see you. There's not even a flicker to show he's heard me.

I quicken my pace towards Santa Monica Boulevard, ducking my way through some back roads to Marty's Hamburger Stand on West Pico, an LA institution since 1958, and perch on a stool round the side, watching the cooks at work assembling orders. When a hand thrusts mine through the hatch I'm pleased to find it's a good, ordinary burger, the first of a trip several people warned me would contain nothing but. Nicely crisp on the outside, served with onion, tomato, lettuce, the inevitable processed cheese, and a view of traffic – what could be more American? I think with satisfaction, mopping grease from my gloves.

Lunch so far has cost less than my morning coffee in Malibu, so I pedal back down the street to the Apple Pan (est. 1947), which aficionado George Motz declares in his book *Hamburger America* to be 'one of the best burger experiences in America'; Clark Gable was, he says, a regular, and Jack Nicholson and Barbra Streisand are still fans, 'as are many other Hollywood stars looking for a late-night burger fix'. As it's 2.30 in the afternoon, I recognise no one in the little back garden, but I do enjoy my Hickory burger – pink and juicy – though the sauce is too sweet for my taste, and it's not enhanced by a frankly absurd amount of iceberg lettuce.* Two lunches may seem excessive, but I justify it as professional curiosity: Southern California is the birthplace of not only the international

---

* I later read in the *LA Times* that co-owner Shelli Azoff believes the secret ingredient of the signature Hickory burger is not its smoky sauce, but the countervailing cool freshness of iceberg lettuce – each leaf selected for maximum crunch. 'We don't really use the outside leaves,' she says. 'It's all the heart.'

burger behemoth McDonald's, but smaller chains like Carl Jr's, Jack-in-the-Box, Bob's Big Boy, Fatburger and In-N-Out, the cult business that created the modern drive-thru. (It's also, interestingly, where several other fast-food giants including Taco Bell and Panda Express started out, a phenomenon the *Drive-Thru Dreams* author Adam Chandler partly attributes to the weather, which, he told the website LA-ist, gives life here a certain looseness and freedom from buttoned-up convention.)

As the Apple Pan also offers apple pie, I get a slice to go (which comes with a little pot of extra apple syrup, a nice touch), and head for the metro – my room for the next few nights is twelve miles away in East Hollywood, and having been on the road since 6.30am, I'm ready to let the train take the strain, even if it means listening to other people's music at ear-splitting volume. American cities, I'm beginning to notice, are incredibly noisy places – London is hardly an oasis of calm, but the size of the roads and the average vehicle makes life here especially deafening. On the plus side, however, this means people have to speak very loudly to make themselves heard, which is great if you're nosy like me.

An hour and twenty minutes later, I find myself in the slightly bizarre room I've taken in a boarding house in East Hollywood, done up like a bordello, with velvet furniture and a lot of taxidermy. In the two nights I spend there, I don't see another human being, though I do hear two (I assume, anyway) having sex next door.

Following a much-needed shower to wash the trauma of last night's motel from my skin, if not my memory, I continue my enquiries into the distinctively American phenomenon of the hamburger with a pilgrimage to McDonald's in the city of Downey, some thirteen miles south-east of downtown LA. You may well ask why I'm bothering to take three metro trains and as many buses when there are seven branches within three miles of where I'm staying, but this isn't just any old McDonald's – it's the oldest McDonald's in existence.

So what? you might reasonably say; they're all the same. Except this one isn't – instead of the golden arches that now bestride the world, the Downey McDonald's boasts one single yellow neon-tipped arch labelled HAMBURGERS crowned by a character who looks like a cross between the Little Chef and Stewie Griffin from *Family Guy*. (I discover later his name is Speedee, and he was replaced by Ronald McDonald in 1967. Even though Speedee's doughy face is an actual hamburger, I find him considerably less terrifying than the clown who took his job.) 'McDonald's', it says in an unfamiliar typeface below: 'Your kind of place.' There's also a boast that the chain has sold 500 million burgers, a milestone it reached some forty years ago.

Opened in 1953, franchised from Dick and Maurice McDonald themselves* in the days before the infamous Ray Kroc took control of the company,† for many years this renegade outpost was exempt from the obligation to keep up with developments in the wider chain; in fact, its stubborn refusal to serve Big Macs was almost the architect of its downfall. Kroc bought the failing business in 1990, but though he brought the rest of the menu back into line, the Downey McDonald's remains a stand-out in one culinary respect: unlike every other McDonald's in the continental US, it still deep-fries its dessert pies. I get very excited about this, and decide, as I've had enough burgers for one day, to order one, plus a vanilla milkshake. (Oddly they don't offer my preferred banana flavour in the US.)

There are no touchscreeens, no order numbers to remember – just a walk-up window where I interact with an actual person, albeit very briefly, before taking my cardboard tube of pie to eat in the small museum area. The golden, blistered pastry shatters with a satis-

---

* The sons of Irish immigrants from Kerry.
† The film *The Founder* offers a good introduction to the force of nature that was Kroc.

fying crunch – God, deep-fried anything is delicious – and though the filling is the usual cinnamon-heavy gloop (6/10), nonetheless I feel I'm experiencing something very special. Later, back in the room, as I tuck into the Apple Pan slice (rich, flaky savoury pastry, could have been a little crisper, but very keen on the big chunks of apple instead of the usual slurry, 8/10), I excitedly message my friend Martha who witheringly informs me that most of the world, including the UK, still deep-fries its pies, so I could have had this same experience round the corner in London. Yet the A501 would struggle to match Downey for atmosphere after sundown, with neon Speedee glowing alluringly in the blue velvet sky.

The museum more than justifies the trip anyway – as well as the original carved wooden doors from the lofty halls of Hamburger University, Chicago, it contains a hodge-podge of intriguing exhibits including a book entitled *The Good Egg: Herb Peterson, the Egg McMuffin and the Secret Ingredients of Innovation*, the McDonald's employee training manual #001 (motto: 'Nothing succeeds like success') and a very creepy moon-faced mannequin in a tuxedo. The character of Mac Tonight was launched in 1986 to try to 'promote dinner as an eating occasion at McDonald's', I learn, and played 'Mack the Knife' on the piano in commercials (until a lawsuit by the family of musician Bobby Darin put a stop to it). More recently, and inexplicably, it's been co-opted by white supremacists, and in 2019 was declared a hate symbol by the Anti-Defamation League, though this detail isn't mentioned in the caption.

As I wait for my Uber under the strangely beautiful neon baby, unable to face another two-hour transport extravaganza, I ponder the curious power of the McDonald's brand, aware I'm experiencing an entirely fake nostalgia for a time I never knew, and a business I rarely patronise, but which was once the acme of my childish culinary ambitions. (My older brother was allowed to take me once a school holiday – later, when I was at boarding school, we were permitted to enter the local branch only between

2 and 5pm on a Sunday afternoon, just after the weekly roast lunch. So cool was it as a place to hang out that we went anyway.) On the way home my driver, Tyson, tells me that Ozempic will soon put McDonald's out of business before crashing the global economy. Five stars, very cheery.

The flip side to all this fast food, of course, is LA's reputation as the faddy eating capital of the world, birthplace of the Hollywood (grapefruit at every meal) and Beverly Hills (nothing but fruit) diets, to say nothing of the mushroom or baby-food regimes periodically linked to various slender starlets. Eager to repopulate my gut after yesterday's burgers and apple pies, I decide to pay celebrity grocery-store-cum-wellness-cult Erewhon a visit. Apparently Miley Cyrus and Jake Gyllenhaal are fans, but as neither of them have returned my calls, I arrange to meet Charlotte Simmonds from the *Guardian*'s West Coast office there instead.

While munching a very un-clean but deliciously chewy cream cheese bagel round the corner beforehand, I discover the chain's name is a nod to the inventor of the macrobiotic movement, George Ohsawa, who was, it seems, a mentor to the store's Japanese-born founders, Michio Kushi and Aveline Yokoyama. His favourite book, *Erewhon,* is a dystopian Victorian satire by British author Samuel Butler about a land where health is equated with moral value, and the sinful sick are thrown in jail, a detail I find . . . quite weird?

The store, however, a brightly lit temple to every fad going, from paleo to pistachio mylk, proves less sinister than its name might suggest. Charlotte, a local, gives me a guided tour – Instagram-happy walls of plastic pots packed with sliced fruit and vegetables and peeled citrus, neatly stacked peppers, spiralised courgettes, and aisles of mysterious supplements: 'So you think, oh, I'm in a rush, these look good, and then you pick them up,' she gestures to a pack of sugar snap peas, 'and they're like, $22.' She confesses she shops here 'more than I like to admit', but when I ask her whether there's any resentment towards things like this and Courage Bagels moving into working-class areas she says she doesn't think so – 'In LA there's enough room for everyone, I don't see the mom and pop places closing. People just love to eat out here.' (Or, perhaps, I speculate, they like to go out, whether or not they end up eating much: my friend, the award-winning food writer Nik Sharma, who I meet later for lunch, claims he's seen people split a bowl of pasta between the table, everyone limiting themselves to a single forkful. Whether this is down to Ozempic or simple calorie-counting is, of course, up for speculation.)

We order a pair of Erewhon's TikTok-famous smoothies – she goes for the viral Hailey Bieber strawberry skin glaze enhanced with collagen and sea moss and I reluctantly embrace the inevitable with crazy carnivore Dr Paul's* raw animal-based recipe featuring kefir, unspecified freeze-dried beef organs, immunomilk (colostrum – i.e. the first milk a mother produces for her baby; species of mother also unspecified) and blueberries. Both cost $19 (pre-tip) and take a while to make, so, seeing an excess of processed foods in my near future, I seize the opportunity to purchase some probiotics and almost buy a tote bag too, thinking it will come in handy off the bike . . . until I discover that the Erewhon version, apparently identical to the fifteen I have hanging by the door at home, will set me back $52 and hastily ask the cashier to put it back.

My smoothie, I notice nervously, comes with a safety sticker warning about the health risks of consuming raw meat. The top two-thirds are a reassuringly normal purple colour, but I can't help noticing an ominous brown line on top of the snowy white coconut cream. Thankfully, it turns out to be maple syrup; the offal apparently blended into discreet invisibility. 'How is it?' Charlotte asks. I consider. It has the slightly furry consistency of liver,

---

* Dr Paul Saladino, formerly known as Carnivore MD – an animal-based diet influencer.

and an . . . earthy backnote, but mostly, I admit, it tastes like slightly meaty blueberry yoghurt. Oddly she politely refuses my offer of a sample.

Over an Armenian feast* of grilled lamb and buttery pilaf in Glendale a little later, Nik, who is the first to sow a seed of doubt in my mind over the origins of the colostrum – 'You laugh, but it's LA. I tell you, there was a chef here serving ice cream made from his wife's breast milk' – also admits to a sneaky Erewhon habit. 'It's so pretty in there, all the fruit and vegetables and everything, and the pretty people . . . And they do cake and stuff by the slice, which is really handy if you're watching your weight.'

I'm not, but I'm still relieved I have some exercise planned this afternoon: a trip out to the city of La Puente, about twenty miles east of downtown, to see the famous Donut Hole – described by the LA Conservancy website as 'one of SoCal's best examples of Programmatic architecture'. Programmatic is apparently a fancy term for novelty, and a drive-thru shaped like an enormous fibreglass donut definitely qualifies as that to a girl from East Anglia. I'm even more excited than I was on the way to Downey yesterday.

Though they're not an American invention, the direction they've taken since crossing the Atlantic is so different from the relatively plain fritters served on special occasions elsewhere that I feel confident in claiming the donut as quite distinct from its charmingly named Dutch oliebollen, or oily-ball ancestors, or even the no-nonsense British jam doughnut. For all the chat about clean living, Los Angeles feels like a great place to learn more: while the US as a whole has roughly one donut shop per 30,000 people, in LA, it's one for every 7,000.

* Good Indian food is thin on the ground locally, he tells me, but the Armenian and Persian food is 'fantastic'.

COFFEE BREAK
Donuts: A User Guide

Though most cultures around the world have discovered the pleasure of deep-fried dough balls, the US does seem to have taken the idea and made it its own in a quite remarkable way. Probably popularised by Dutch immigrants to the East Coast, they gained national-treasure status thanks to the Salvation Army's use of Donut Dollies to deliver morale-boosting treats to American troops during the Great War – though whether the donuts, or the women serving them, did more for morale is up for debate.

A Russian immigrant, Adolph Levitt, invented the automated 'Wonderful Almost Human Donut Machine' shortly afterwards, and installed it in the window of his Broadway bakery, a phenomenon the *New Yorker* described as not 'exciting enough to go there specially to see . . . donuts float dreamily through a grease canal in a glass-enclosed machine, walk dreamily up a moving ramp, and tumble dreamily into an outgoing basket', while noting that, nevertheless, on the writer's visit, 'the rail outside the window was heavy with people looking. A man whose straw hat moved as he chewed and a woman in a red dress were still there looking when we came back that way after more than half an hour.'

Donuts were clearly a money spinner – Bill Rosenberg opened the first shop in what was to become the Dunkin' empire in 1950 (they dropped the Donuts part in 2019, apparently feeling type-cast), and its early success is often credited to its dedication to getting the doors open in the morning. Few other places offered breakfast in the post-war period (McDonald's didn't introduce its breakfast menu until the 1970s), which allowed donut shops to corner the pre-work market among people who consider them an appropriate breakfast . . . which is apparently an awful lot of Americans. (As a fully paid-up member of team savoury before noon, this never fails to puzzle me, just as Marmite or black pudding probably would many Americans. Such insignificant differences are what keep life interesting.)

If you, like me, find yourself flummoxed by the array of choice in an American donut shop, here's a handy guide to the most common basic varieties:

- **Yeasted/raised:** As the name suggests, raised with yeast (like a classic British doughnut). Breadier and lighter than the . . .
- **Cake:** which contains baking powder and is denser and firmer in texture.
- **Potato:** a cake donut made with potato as well as wheat flour, making it slightly less dense.
- **Cider:** which disappointingly do not contain booze (cider is not always alcoholic in the US unless prefaced by the word hard) but apple juice and spices, predominantly found in the autumn in New England.
- **Old-fashioned:** made from cake batter, in a weird angular shape that yields a crunchier finish.
- **Glazed and jelly donuts:** usually yeasted, and iced, with jam inside the latter.
- **Cruller:** a cake dough, twisted or plaited before frying, unless it's a French cruller, which is made from a rich choux pastry instead.
- **Bear claw:** an oddly shaped yeasted glazed or cinnamon-sugared donut.
- **Boston crème:** filled with vanilla custard topped with chocolate icing. Without the icing it is sometimes called a Bavarian crème.

Hoisting Eddy off the J line at El Monte, I spend a couple of minutes in the parking lot trying to align myself with Google Maps. A guy on a motorbike stops and instead of stealing my phone, tells me he has a road bike himself, should get out on it more, I'm an inspiration – and then insists on taking off his glove to shake my hand. 'Stay safe,' he calls as he roars away in a cloud of fumes.

I try my best as I negotiate the six-lane Valley Boulevard, cracked and potholed, the inside lane regularly blocked by food trucks, marvelling at how low-rise and spread out Los Angeles is, as if space was literally endless out here – I barely see a two-storey structure in the entire forty-minute journey, until I spot it: a three-storey-high chocolate ring donut rising magnificently from the concrete, flanked by a heavenly cloud of white camellias. It's a very special moment indeed.

Taking a deep breath, wanting to savour the experience, I pedal slowly through the hole into a cool, dark tunnel lined with windows. One side looks into a deserted stainless-steel commercial kitchen, the other displays trays of donuts, glazed, coated in coconut flakes and multicoloured sprinkles. Though none, of course, are labelled, I confidently point at the weirdest-looking one, craggy and deeply bronzed – after all, surely nothing in this enchanted cave can be bad.

'Apple fritter,' the man behind the window says, grabbing it with gloved hands and slotting it neatly into a paper bag. He looks more closely at me – 'You come by bike? Wow, you are strong!' – pumping his arm gratifyingly. I ask if they get many ride-through customers. 'Some, but not many. Americans, they are lazy, hahaha! We get some kids, and some people on motos, but people here they like their cars . . . and their donuts, which is good for us! But not everyone can do what you do, ha! Just you do this! You are special!'

It seems safe to assume from this stone-cold serving of Truth he doesn't consider himself American, so I ask if he's Cambodian . . . but he's already turned to the SUV growling behind me. Emigrants from the South East Asian nation have famously come to dominate the donut industry of southern California, such that Dunkin' had to pull out of its first attempt to expand there in the early 90s, and only tentatively re-entered the market a decade ago. Though they're gaining ground, there are still an unusual number of independent stores in the area, and 90 per cent of them are run by first-and second-generation Cambodian Americans.

Many words, and an entire documentary, *The Donut King*, have been devoted to explaining the extraordinary story of how this came about, focusing on one man, Ted, originally Bun Tek Ngoy, who arrived in the US with his wife and children in 1975, a refugee from the violence unleashed by the Khmer Rouge. A donut franchise opposite the gas station where he worked caught his attention, not just for its wares, which reminded him of Cambodian *noum kong*, but for its potential as a business. After joining a management trainee programme with local chain Winchells, Ngoy bought his own shop within the year. By 1980, he had twenty, and his empire continued to grow as he sponsored work visas for hundreds of Cambodians desperate to get out – the chains couldn't compete with the economics of using extended family as free labour, or the furious work ethic of new immigrants. According to Ngoy himself, back then 'Dunkin' had to make at least $50,000 a month to survive . . . Cambodian donut shop; make $10,000 they can survive.'

As Nicola Twilley notes on her Gastropod podcast, this is no David and Goliath tale: 'Dunkin' has come to California, but the Cambodian independents have stayed, and now there's just more donuts to go around.' And like David dancing around the big beast, a small operation can afford to be nimbler and more reactive than a multinational juggernaut – DKs in Santa Monica was opened by a Cambodian couple in 1981, but it's the next generation, in the form of social-media savvy Mayly Tao, who can claim responsibility for shaking up the menu with things like Los Angeles's first ube-flavoured donut and the West Coast's first cronuts.

Though the Taos sold up to fellow Cambodians in 2021, when I pay DKs a visit a few days later I can't get all the flavours in one wide-angle shot. They're even helpfully labelled so I can tell ube purple yam donut crumb from homemade salted caramel bacon.

CAMBODIAN-STYLE UBE DONUTS

I'd have been delighted if any of the donut shops I visited had these on offer next to the maple bacon buttermilk crullers: deliciously bouncy and elastic inside (think Japanese mochi), with a crunchy golden crust, they're gluten free and only minimally sweet, until you add the vivid purple yam icing. I've made them slightly smaller and fatter than is traditional, like mini ring donuts of the kind that used to be sold hot from a van in the marketplace in my childhood, and replaced the traditional palm sugar glaze with a vivid purple version in tribute to Mayly Tao, who introduced ube donuts to the West Coast, but if you don't fancy either, a simple dredge of icing sugar will also be delicious on the warm donuts. The ube powder is easily sourced online. Note that like any deep-fried food, these are best eaten soon after cooking.

Makes 10
230g/2 cups + 3 tbsp glutinous rice flour
45g/¼ cup rice flour
½ tsp fine salt
3 tbsp melted palm sugar or crumbled soft brown sugar
270ml/1⅛ cups coconut milk

For the icing
150g/scant 1½ cups icing /confectioners' sugar
1 tbsp ube powder
Sesame seeds or hundreds and thousands, to sprinkle

1. Put both flours, the salt and sugar into a bowl and whisk together, then stir in just enough coconut milk to make a fairly stiff dough; you shouldn't need it all. Leave, covered with a damp tea towel, for 20 minutes for the flour to absorb the liquid.

2. Pinch off a piece of dough and roll it into a ball about the size of a golf ball. Flatten slightly, then poke a finger through the middle and work it around to turn the dough into a slender ring; too thick and they won't cook through. Store underneath a damp tea towel while you heat the oil.

3. Heat a tall pan (or a wok) a third full of neutral oil to 150°C/300°F – make sure the donuts always start at this temperature, as there's the risk of them exploding in hotter oil. For the same reason, a splatter guard is advised!

4. Add a few donuts (don't overcrowd the pan) and dislodge from the base of the pan, then leave to float to the surface. Turn over and continue to fry until rich golden (they won't go the same deep brown as wheat donuts) and cooked through, then drain on kitchen paper, making sure the oil comes back to temperature before cooking the next batch.

5. Stir together the icing sugar and ube powder and, working cautiously, add just enough water (or thinned-down coconut milk) to make a thick glaze. Dip each donut into it and sprinkle with sesame seeds. Eat warm, or allow to set.

By the time I get back to El Monte, after eating my surprisingly crisp and ridiculously sweet fritter, and then, clearly crazed by sugar, cycling brazenly through an LAPD roadblock outside a recently held-up cash depository, the trains to the city have been replaced by buses – at least, I think they have; information is thin on the ground, and the only person I can find to ask, a friendly dreadlocked stoner, is keener on taking me out for a drink. Unfortunately neither he nor the bus driver, when he finally turns up to rescue me, is any help loading Eddy onto the rack on the front ('Ain't allowed to touch no bikes,' the driver says flatly, watching me struggle), which means I barely take a breath for the next twenty minutes as I listen to the bike I've paid to fly 5,354 miles rattle his distress against the windscreen as we swoosh down the freeway at 65mph.

Ridden: 14 miles
Climbed: 59 feet
Pies consumed: 2 (Apple Pan apple pie, McDonald's deep-fried apple pie)
All-American foods discovered: hamburger, deep-fried apple pie, vanilla milkshake, cream cheese bagel,* colostrum smoothie, donut

---

* Keep your hair on: we will go into the history of the bagel once we get to New York.

4

LA – IN WHICH GWYNETH MAKES ME A SALAD

In search of clean food

'When it comes to Beverly Hills, you can have regrets but no apologies.'
Lisa Vanderpump, *The Real Housewives of Beverly Hills*

Los Angeles covers an area of 469 square miles – twice the size of the similarly glamorous Isle of Man – which might explain why it feels like several different cities rolled into one, as of course technically it is. Having tackled hamburgers and donuts, neither of which are apparently of much interest to my health-conscious hosts for the next few nights in Beverly Hills, I'm now keen to taste some Mexican food in a city where this is the largest ethnic group. My hosts Dan and Ruth have promised to take me out to one of their favourite spots this evening, but on my way to their place, I'm detouring via the oldest part of the city, the eighteenth-century Pueblo, built by the Spanish, probably on the site of an indigenous Tongva village, for some historical context.

Just a block from the eight-lane US-101, everything feels on a more human scale in the Pueblo's central square, with a band playing, a few seniors dancing under colourful bunting, and huddles of hoodied teenagers sitting scowling over quizzes from its many museums. It's a shock to be among old buildings, and I realise I've hardly seen anything pre-twentieth century since I left San Francisco. I bound into the Los Angeles Plaza de Cultura y Artes, a Latinx* community hub and museum, with rather more enthusiasm than the kids outside might deem cool, though once inside I'm quickly subdued by my ignorance with regard to Indigenous and Hispanic history.†

It's a sobering, if enlightening, visit, which finishes in the Plaza's cookery school, named for local activist Gloria Molina, and centred around a large, colourfully tiled comale, or griddle, used for cooking tortillas, toasting spices and searing meat. Ximena Martin, director of programmes, shows me around, explaining that food has always been a big part of the Plaza's work because 'as immigrants a lot of us didn't get the opportunity to learn from our grandmothers, so when we have elders coming in to teach, we see a lot of younger people coming who want to learn from them'.

They run cookery classes, talk and taste sessions and demonstrations from chefs and home cooks alike, trying to move beyond the preconception that Mexican food, 'one of the finest cuisines in the world', should be cheap and cheerful. 'We try to educate the public – on why a plate of tacos should cost $15 in a high-end restaurant where they grind and nixtamalise‡ their own corn,' she tells me. 'We want to fight back against the stereotypes of

---

* The non-gendered form of Latino/a.
† In common with many overseas visitors, I suspect, I hadn't realised the city was part of New Spain, and then, following independence, Mexico until 1849 – a history that certainly puts online complaints about people not speaking English into context.
‡ A process discovered by the Aztec and Maya civilisations of Mesoamerica, which involves soaking corn with an alkaline substance to soften it, making it easier to grind into dough, while also increasing its protein availability.

Mexican food in this country.' I can't help but remember a story I'd read in the *Guardian* just before leaving, about a $22 beef burrito in San Francisco, and the outrage it sparked when, as business owner Ricardo Lopez pointed out, people 'don't have an issue' with Italian restaurants charging the same for pasta al pomodoro.

Wishing I'd asked Ximena for some recommendations about where to find the good stuff here, I set off instead in the direction of Beverly Hills. I've seen very few cyclists in Los Angeles so far, but Westlake and Pico Union, which I pass through on my way, produce a few bikes weaving in and out of traffic – perhaps not coincidentally, both areas feel like they might be down on their luck. Indeed, I have to swerve to avoid people wandering zombie-like into the road near MacArthur Park, yet, as in San Francisco's Tenderloin, no one takes a bit of notice of me. A bicycle, I'm beginning to suspect, is shorthand for poor round here.

Not long afterwards, the roads turn residential; Hancock Park with its big houses and leafy verges feels like riding through a movie set . . . if you don't look too closely. Spotting a man passed out in a wheelchair in the hot sun opposite Trader Joe's, I wonder as I ride on by if I should have done something. Or, to be absolutely truthful, I wonder that up until the point where I find myself marooned in the middle of oncoming traffic from West Hollywood being honked and sworn at, a somewhat distracting experience, which I do not share with Dan and Ruth – kind friends of my friend Gemma's parents – when I arrive, rather pink, at their beautiful white-columned house just off Wilshire Boulevard about twenty minutes later.

Though I've never met them before, it immediately feels like staying with the parents of friends – if my friends had parents with fully-furnished pool houses the size of my flat to offer, rather than spare rooms crammed with sewing machines and dusty exercise bikes. After showing me around, and instructing me how to use the laundry (which, after this morning's ride, I don't take personally), they invite me to come in for a glass with them before we go out to eat, by which time, I discover, they've already emailed Gemma and her parents in the UK to say I've arrived safely.

Though Dan tells me he's a transplant from the East Coast, Ruth is an Angeleno; both in medicine, and on their second marriages, they moved to Beverly Hills independently to be close to the hospital where they both worked – but tonight they're taking me downtown, to El Cholo, 'a real old LA place', where my hostess has fond memories of 'drinking pitchers of margaritas before ball games as a kid' (kid, I assume, here means a young woman, rather than as an actual child, but hey, no judgement either way). A warren of cosy low-beamed rooms, the restaurant reminds me of a British pub, only with portraits of celebrity guests like Jack Nicholson and Paul and Linda McCartney ('thanx for the great veggie food') rather than Nasty Nick from *Big Brother*.

Naturally we also get a pitcher of margaritas, and some nachos and guacamole, and I order the Sonoran-style enchiladas that have apparently been on the menu since El Cholo opened in 1923.* They come as a pile of tortillas bathed in two chile sauces, red and green, plus shredded chicken and a fried egg – having only ingested half a cookie and a satsuma all day, I eat the whole plate, plus much of Dan and Ruth's dark chocolate-coloured mole, and am only kept awake on the way home by Dan's guided tour of such attractions as the Ice Age La Brea Tar Pits, Rodeo Drive and the edge of Koreatown. They both politely scoff at Nik's championing of Armenian food as in any way representative of the city – 'maybe it's big in *Glendale*, but LA has

---

* El Cholo is also credited with being the first place in America to put burritos on the menu back in the 1930s, though tonight's menu only lists a burrito dorado introduced in 1977.

the biggest Korean population outside Seoul' . . . so much so, they say, that specially chartered buses line up to take elderly Koreans out to the tribal casinos every day of the week.

Yet another LA, I think. Perhaps, I say, this city has as many faces as residents. 'It's certainly a very different place to when I was growing up,' Ruth agrees as she waves me off to my bed in the pool house.*

After a breakfast of fruit – 'You have to try these Cara Cara oranges,' Dan insists, pushing the bowl towards me, 'aren't they incredible?' and indeed they are, unusually pinkish and sweet – and excellent homemade bread, Ruth departs for a day's babysitting with the grandkids, and Dan drives me to the Getty Museum, a white marble palace perched high on a hill above the city. As he then has to leave abruptly to take his father-in-law to an audiology appointment, and there's no public transport in the vicinity, I end up getting an Uber back to Beverly Hills with a thickly accented Ukrainian, 'No, not because of the war,' he bristles, 'I've been here forty years.'

He's furious about the student protests that have erupted into violence at UCLA – and also about affirmative action, Joe Biden, gas prices, Chinese fentanyl, 'illegals' and the general stupidity of American youth, including his own son. In short, he is generally a very angry man. 'When I got my citizenship, they told me it was a privilege to vote, now look at this country, it is going down the drain.' He tells me he doesn't like Trump, but everything was better when he was in charge.

To cleanse my aura, I decide to let Gwyneth Paltrow make me lunch, with the help of the quintessential California girl's Goop

---

* Ruth will later lose her childhood home and high school to the fires in January 2025, in the aftermath this pool house becomes a refuge for her elderly parents.

Kitchen 'concept' whose mission is 'to accelerate the clean-food movement by proving that eating clean can be delicious, satisfying, and accessible'.

COFFEE BREAK
What Gwyneth Eats in a Day

'I eat dinner early in the evening. I do a nice intermittent fast. I usually eat something about 12 . . . in the morning I'll have some things that won't spike my blood sugar . . . so I have coffee, but I really like soup for lunch, I have bone broth for lunch a lot of the days . . . and then for dinner, I try to eat, you know, according to paleo, so lots of vegetables. It's really important for me to support my detox.' As told to Dr Will Cole's *The Art of Being Well* podcast, 2023

TLDR: coffee, stock and lots of vegetables

I imagine white walls, organic linen curtains billowing in the breeze and wafty music, but when I'm dropped off at Goop Kitchen Beverly Hills, I realise there's no actual storefront: instead I have to download an app to order, and then sit on the steps of a very unspiritual-looking office building with the delivery guys and wait for my phone to ping. Bypassing the Magic Mineral Broth and the G-Potle Taco Crunch Bowl, I settle on GP's Classic-ish Cobb and a kombucha, but when I go to the service door to collect it, the woman at the door handing out bags is horrified – 'No, no, YOU go to the coffee shop inside!' Apparently an actual customer approaching the delivery drivers' entrance is akin to Lady Grantham trying to hang with Mrs Patmore: extremely bad form.

Having finally located my lunch, I take it to the nearest green space, a deserted but immaculately coiffed strip of park adjoining Santa Monica Boulevard. Credit where credit's due, Gwynnie, it looks great – ripe avocado, crumbled blue cheese, tomatoes, peppers, roasted beetroot, bacon and a fudgy boiled egg – but, I realise, there's no cutlery (or silverware, as it's known in the US despite usually being made of plastic) in the bag. I look around me, give thanks no one walks anywhere in LA, and then begin furtively eating with my hands, wiping my fingers periodically on the spiky grass. It's a new low, and as soon as Dan messages to say he can pick me up on his way home, I guiltily snap the box shut, resolving to eat the rest when I have access to a knife and fork. Is clean eating with one's hands still clean in a kind of getting-back-to-nature way? I wonder as I examine my vinaigrette-soaked fingernails. Probably it would help if I'd washed them first.

GWYNETH PALTROW-ISH CLASSIC-ISH COBB

Should any Hollywood lawyers be reading, and for the avoidance of doubt, this recipe is inspired by the Goop version, rather than claiming to be it. It's best enjoyed with a knife and fork rather than fingers, and can be made ahead up to the end of step 7 (in fact, if you're making the pickled peppers, you'll need to do this the day before). Piquillo peppers aren't easy to come by in the UK, but Spanish padrón work here too.

Serves 4
2 tbsp olive oil
2 fresh beetroot (or use ready-cooked and skip step 4)

4 eggs

4 rashers of sweet-cured bacon, preferably back bacon

200g/7 ounces cherry tomatoes

60g/about ½ cup crumbly blue cheese

2 ripe avocados

2 heads of Little Gem lettuce

½ a head of radicchio

For the dressing

4 tsp Dijon mustard

1 tsp maple syrup

60ml/¼ cup red wine vinegar

120ml/½ cup extra virgin olive oil

Salt and black pepper

For the pickled peppers (or use 4 tbsp of the bought variety)

100g/1½ cups shishito or padrón peppers

180ml/¾ cup cider or white wine vinegar

1 tsp salt

2 cloves of garlic, chunkily sliced

1. If you're making the pickled peppers, slice them into fairly thick rings; remove the large rounds of seeds at the top of each pepper but don't worry about it too much.

2. Pour the vinegar into a small pan and add the salt and 90ml/⅜ cup of water. Bring to a simmer. Meanwhile put the peppers and garlic into a clean jar or other heatproof lidded container just large enough to hold them.

3. Pour the hot vinegar on top of the peppers, then seal and leave for at least 24 hours. The peppers should be submerged in the vinegar if you're planning to keep them for any length of time, so you might need to weight them down; I use a small, clean sandwich bag full of water.

4. Put the oil into a small roasting tin and roll the washed beetroot in it. Cover with foil and bake at 180°C/160°C fan/350°F or until tender. Allow to cool, then peel and cut into wedges.

5. Put the eggs into a small pan of boiling water, turn the heat down slightly and simmer for 7 minutes, then scoop into a sink of cold water to cool.

6. Chop the bacon into strips. Heat a frying pan (you may need to add a little oil if your bacon is lean) over a medium flame, and fry the bacon until crisp and golden.

7. To make the dressing, put the mustard and syrup into a small bowl and beat in the vinegar, followed, more gradually, by the oil, until well emulsified. Season to taste.

8. To assemble the salad, peel the eggs (rap them against a hard surface to start cracking the shells) and cut each in half. Cut the tomatoes in half unless very small. Crumble the cheese. Peel the avocados and cut in half, then slice.

9. Separate the lettuce and radicchio into individual leaves and put into a large mixing bowl. Add just enough dressing to coat, tossing it together, preferably with your hands, until well covered but not pooling at the bottom of the bowl.

10. Put the salad on a serving platter or divide between four bowls. Top with beetroot wedges. Add, along with 4 tablespoons of the drained pickled peppers, the cheese, bacon, avocado, tomatoes and egg. Serve immediately.

Dan drives me home down Carmelita Avenue, where spindly king and smaller, more graceful queen palm trees alternate, like something from a film set. I'm beside myself as I snap pictures from the passenger seat: 'I suppose palm trees don't feel exotic when you live with them,' I say apologetically. 'No,' he replies, 'but what does constantly surprise me is the number of people lying down in the middle of the road to take pictures, for social media I suppose.

Unbelievable!' I silently thank my lucky stars the dog, my favourite muse, isn't here, or I'd definitely be one of those people; Beverly Hills is just as perfect as it looks in the movies, the streets lush with well-tended vegetation, the houses exuding wealth – anything pre-1990 seems to be in the process of being replaced by something bigger and better, with the exception of the Witch's House, a pointy Hansel and Gretel affair, which started life in a 1920s silent movie studio, and now sits in a corner lot with a sign outside warning it's protected by an armed response security service.

My hosts have generously offered to get me a ticket to come and listen to Víkingur Ólafsson perform the Goldberg Variations at the Walt Disney Concert Hall with them this evening, but I have a friend to locate. Having messaged me from London to say his flight is delayed because of one passenger deemed 'unfit to board', which I have to assume isn't him, and then to complain about the lengthy border security queue at LAX, my friend Matt, a famously indolent comrade from university days who somehow quietly morphed into an extremely successful member of His Majesty's Civil Service without any of us noticing, has now gone quiet. Nothing as I walk down Rodeo Drive past the Instagrammers snapping themselves outside Gucci and leaning against a bizarre, angular Tesla Truck that looks like something out of *Minecraft* – silence as I munch my way through a green chili enchilada pizza with a brick-like cauliflower crust at the California Pizza Kitchen (a business set up to capitalise on the gourmet pizza trend of the mid-1980s: the Alice Waters effect), zilch when I cautiously check my phone on the way home, remembering Dan's advice not to walk around this apparently quiet and well-defended neighbourhood after dark, and no sign of him at the house either.

By 10pm, after checking the doorstep numerous times, I'm really worried – finally he calls and says rather crossly that he hadn't wanted to use his phone out here (not for the first time, I briefly wonder if he's a spy) but he's been outside ringing the bell for forty-five minutes and no one is answering. Turns out I've given him the wrong house number. Thank God no one called the cops, I think as I watch his tall, slightly crumpled figure stride briskly down the empty sidewalk, given, Dan informs me in a manner I think is intended to be reassuring, that the Beverly Hills PD response time is 2.4 minutes. 'Sorry,' I say, giving him a hug. 'Welcome to America.'

Like it or not, Matt is hitting the ground running: I've booked us on to a five-and-a-half-hour food tour the next morning, kicking off in Chinatown and entitled 'Exploring America's culinary frontier', which also takes in the sadly shrunken Little Tokyo (yet another place that claims to have invented the fortune cookie), Olvera Street, where I eat a rolled taquito covered in tangy green avocado salsa so good I wish I'd asked for the recipe while Matt was asking for seconds, and Villas, the first business to win the city's coveted Taco Madness title two years in a row, where the handmade blue corn tortillas, crunchy with toasted cheese, boast no fewer than seven toppings – gilding the lily, even by LA standards. Thirty-one-year-old Victor Villa, who is proud of the fact you won't find a taco like his in Mexico *or* California, started out with a pop-up in his grandmother's yard in Highland Park, and is now in the *Michelin Guide*.

The *LA Times* has noted that, while 'Villa is the son of Mexican immigrants . . . [his] style epitomizes . . . the L. A. dreamer, the go-getter. His queso taco . . . is deftly engineered chaos. It's a taco built on charisma. It practically takes two hands to wield. You have no choice but to be all in.'

I'm definitely all in. I just wish America had more effective napkins.

It's Matt's first visit to the West Coast, and I'm curious to find out what he makes of it as we make our way to meet Ruth for dinner at Oste (a couple of doors down, thrillingly, from a shocking-pink dog cafe, grooming salon, accessories boutique and rescue centre owned by the Real Housewife of Beverly Hills, Lisa Vanderpump). An enthusiastic and frequent traveller/spy, he professes himself frustrated by the limitations of public transport so far, particularly from the airport, but says he's been pleasantly surprised by the range of cuisines on offer today, including the deep-fried artichoke I finally got to try. 'I thought it would be more fast food . . . though,' he clears his throat as if he's about to suggest something outrageous, 'I would quite like to try an In-and-Out at some point if we have time?'

He turns the question back around. We're leaving tomorrow for Texas, and it still seems extraordinary to me that I've travelled so far from chilly, charming San Francisco to sunny, shiny Los Angeles without leaving California, and yet barely seen any of it. In many ways it's been how I imagined, the palm trees, the ocean, the burgers and Mexican food, health stores and Chinese buffets, and yet in others, it's been surprising. I hadn't anticipated the fascinating detour into farming country, or the decorative missiles. I'd known little about Indigenous history, and nothing about the Chinese massacre, or zoning laws, or the difference between Armenian and Persian-Armenian food, or about Cambodian donut shop culture. In short, I hadn't really imagined beyond the stuff I'd seen on screen. 'It's much . . . more three-dimensional,' I say, and then, realising that sounds quite stupid, 'I think I just imagined stepping into the movies, and of course, real life has a lot more . . . layers, I suppose.'

'Like a croissant?' Matt supplies helpfully.

I consider. 'Yeah. More like a cronut.'

The next day is our last in California – after giving Matt a tour of the earthquake-proofing under the house, Dan insists on driving us to the station, a round trip of almost thirty-five miles, which, thanks to LA traffic, will probably take him at least three hours all told. He brushes off our gratitude: 'So many people have helped us around the world, all I ask is that you help someone in return.' I almost cry as I hug Ruth goodbye, and not just because I'll miss out on the Friday-night challah already on the go in the kitchen – they feel like a far-flung outpost of family, and, so far from home, I couldn't feel more grateful.

I try not to make too many jokes about Dan's dire warnings on the cycling front as we say our farewells, because, if anything, he's more worried about me in Texas, where I'm heading next: 'Elections, abortion rights . . . You're certainly seeing us at an interesting time.'

Having checked our stuff into the sleeper passenger lounge at Union Station, a vast, beautiful Mission-style building impressive enough to have hosted the socially distanced 2020 Oscars, we head out unencumbered to find Matt an In-and-Out . . . though I admit, the cult-like fast food chain was on my radar too. Started in Los Angeles County in 1948, where it now has almost seventy locations, it remained there until 1990, when it finally opened a branch in San Diego.

It's been very slowly expanding ever since, and has currently got as far east as Texas; famously the chain refuses to use frozen meat, which means they can only operate within 300 miles of their own burger-making facilities. I suspect the more compelling case, though, is that they don't have to: it remains a privately owned company, the stores they have are doing good business, and the air of exclusivity gives it a certain cachet: as CEO Lynsi Snyder, granddaughter of the founders, put it in 2018, 'You put us in every state and it takes away some of its lustre.' That said, she also claimed they'd never open east of Texas in her lifetime, and they're currently planning to move into Tennessee in 2026, so maybe they'll reach Europe in time to cater my wake.

Only the Hollywood location appears to be accessible by public transport, so we brave the hordes on the Walk of Fame and the LORD JESUS CHRIST crew outside the Chinese Theatre, turn the corner, and almost immediately hit the drive-thru line. Ha! we say smugly to each other, why don't the lazy sods just walk . . . and then we see the queue inside the restaurant.

It turns out, however, that most of those people have already ordered: everything is prepared fresh by the red-and-white-uniformed worker bees in the kitchen, which means with ticket no. 91 we have to wait almost half an hour for our food, 'hardly fast', as Matt points out, though in truth we're both so excited we don't care. When our number finally comes up, it feels like we've won the jackpot; I haven't seen Matt move so fast outside a pub in decades. 'Chips look a bit undercooked,' I say as he comes back bearing our order triumphantly aloft. He gives me a hurt look, as if he's already joined the cult.

Though I'm not into the pallid off-menu 'animal fries' sogging under the weight of thousand island dressing, American cheese and fried onions, the burgers themselves ('double doubles', which, to my relief, merely suggests two patties rather than the four I'd feared; that would be 'a four-by-four') are pleasingly juicy, albeit topped with so much salty cloying processed cheese I can't taste the beef, or anything else. 'I never thought I'd say this,' I say, unable to quite believe it myself, 'but I think there's too much cheese on this.'

Matt's mind is on other things. 'Would you mind,' he says courteously, 'if I got another one?' As this may be my only chance to get it right, I ask for a single mustard-grilled burger without cheese, which I prefer, though I still can't understand the hysteria around a burger topped with thousand island dressing. (Then again, people love Big Macs too, so perhaps I'm the weird one.)

While Matt finishes his second double double, I read online that In-and-Out only fry their chips once, rather than the usual twice, or the ideal thrice, which explains why everyone agrees they suck. Why people carry on ordering them is another puzzle to add to the In-and-Out mystique. Is the hype justified? For me, no. Would I go back for more if they opened in London? Yes, at least once, especially if they were priced as competitively as here, where at $3.69 a hamburger costs less than your average drip coffee. But I wouldn't wait half an hour, and I'd definitely skip the fries.

Heading back to the station via the Broad contemporary art museum, our last stop in California is Philippe The Original, a cafe a block from the station in an area that, according to yesterday's tour guide, was LA's Frenchtown until the 1940s when they all went home to fight.* Philippe's, which has been open since 1908 (a successor to founder Philippe Mathieu's much better-named original venture the New Poodle Dog French Restaurant), is LA's longest continuously operating eatery, and claims to have invented its very own piece of art in the form of the French Dip sandwich, a gravy-sodden affair that not every French reviewer on Tripadvisor seems happy to be associated with.

Once we reach the front of the queue, I bottle on my resolution to order a wet Beef Dip (wet bread always makes me think of duck ponds) and timidly opt for roast beef dipped just once in jus instead, plus potato salad, a kosher dill pickle and a beet-pickled egg to share. I'm tempted by the pickled pig's foot too, but Matt isn't keen, and as he has to share a room with me for the next four days, it seems only polite to heed his wishes.

---

* This rush of patriotism surprises me sufficiently that I look it up and find it's perhaps as likely that Prohibition put paid to the predominantly Basque population's winemaking enterprises a decade earlier.

After adding a beer each and slices of cherry and boysenberry pie, we find a table in the lino-floored dining room next to a couple of old men eating in companionable silence, take a good look at our trays and agree we probably should have got a sandwich to share. Despite this admission, we both finish every last bite; unlike the burgers, they're emphatically beefy, the gravy giving the French-style bread a rich, juicy fattiness that makes me wish I'd been braver on that front. And they're definitely very American; the idea of your average French person disgracing themselves with something so messy, so gluttonous, so devoid of garnish or sauce, is wonderfully absurd. Philippe must have really gone native.

My boysenberry pie is merely fine; savoury flaky pastry, a generous but slightly stiff starchy filling (7/10). 'What is a boysenberry?' Matt asks.

'A cross between a blackberry and a raspberry,' I say confidently.

'Isn't that a loganberry?'

'We should get back to the station,' I say crossly. I hate not knowing things. (The next day, as we cross the Arizona desert, he informs me that it's a cross between a blackberry, raspberry, loganberry and dewberry, and we both agree we don't care enough about dewberries to have another argument.)

I've been curious to discover who uses long-distance rail here ever since I first discovered the thrilling existence of the Sunset Limited service from Los Angeles to New Orleans – Dan, who says he hasn't ridden a train since he got his MBA from Wharton in the late 1970s, confirms my suspicion that it isn't a common mode of transport. Even the lounge attendant, with thirty-five years' service at Union Station under his belt he tells us proudly, only took his first real trip last year. 'I thought I was going to go mad on there for three days, would need to drink to get through it,' he laughs when he finds out we're newbies too, 'but turned out I enjoyed myself. There's a lot to see out there.'

The thirty-hour journey to San Antonio would take just under three by plane, tickets for which start at an astonishing $36 one way. The road-based alternatives are less competitive, however: by car it's a twenty-hour trip (the Sunset Limited has an average speed of 44mph), while the more circuitous Greyhound bus takes just over thirty hours, and doesn't cost much less.

The sleeper-class waiting room this evening is filled with a mixture of older couples and tourists like ourselves, though we're the only ones wheeling a bike down to the platform on our own two legs rather than being ferried there by golf cart. Having handed Eddy over to the dubious care of the luggage car, we're shown to our 'roomette' by Harold, the smiling car attendant who'll be with us all the way to Texas. As the name suggests, it's like a room, but cuter; just deep enough, in fact, to hold two blue leatherette seats which Harold explains he'll convert into beds as soon as we're ready. Matt chivalrously offers to take the top bunk, but given his height, that feels cruel, so I subject him to two days of my feet dangling in his face instead.

With an hour to go before the whistle, we wander through the empty dining car, buy a beer from the shop and settle in the observation lounge, whose curved floor-to-ceiling windows promise a good view of the LA suburbs. Our departure time comes and goes. We buy a whiskey, then another whiskey and watch a man dumpster-diving on the opposite platform before finally giving up and retiring to bed. Assuming we ever leave LA, the train should be well into the desert by dawn, and it's vital, we agree, to be up early so we can bag ourselves prime seats in the observation car.

Some time later, I wake to discover we're finally moving, swaying gently from side to side. Though I always sleep well on trains, I'm woken several times by the engine's mournful hoots, and, half still in dreamland, imagine herds of bison careering across the track ahead of us. Bye-bye West Coast, hello South West, I think confusedly as I rock back to sleep.

Ridden: 12 miles
Climbed: 49 feet
Pies consumed: 2 (boysenberry and cherry)
All-American foods discovered: nachos, Cobb salad, green enchilada cauliflower crust pizza, LA tacos, French dipped sandwich

5

TEX-MEX AND PROUD

In search of the real chili con carne

'You don't need to go to church to be a Christian. If you go to Taco Bell,
that doesn't make you a taco.'
Justin Bieber

I wake at 5.30 to the soft pink of the Arizona desert; flat-topped hills in the distance, cacti by the track. An empty road runs alongside us punctuated by an occasional ranch house, a farm supply store, a gas station. Matt heads straight for the observation car, I detour via the swaying shower before racing to join him, only to find we have it to ourselves but for a coach-class passenger asleep on one of the banquettes with a wolf-print fleece over their face. Apparently no one else is as excited about the view as us.

'This,' Matt says carefully, 'reminds me of the time you made me sprint to get to that seafood place in Normandy when everyone else just strolled in.'

But look, I say, gesturing at the scenery. Isn't it nice not to have missed this? You can snore when you're dead.

As sleeper-class passengers, our meals are included, and we make it until half six before agreeing it's time to cash in, leaving a scattering of possessions on our seats in case of a sudden rush of enthusiasm. Matt has an omelet with cheddar, tomatoes, red pepper, onions and ham, plus extra bacon and fried potatoes, and I get grits, fruit, yoghurt and a croissant – plus an unpromising-looking skinless chicken sausage, which I hastily transfer across the table. Apparently there are limits on the amount of meat you're allowed on one plate, even in America.

After buzzing from place to place for the last fortnight, it's very pleasant to spend an entire day just looking out of the window at the changing scenery – from dusty scrub to scrawny forests of thorny mesquite – and listening to the chatter of our fellow passengers. Shortly after passing a sign for the world's largest pistachio just off Highway 70, in Alamogordo, New Mexico, I get talking to a woman – 'from just outside Dallas, but in the summer I take my RV up to New England where it's cooler, work out of there' – who delivers truck cabs around the country for a living; 'and not many gals do that, I can tell you. I drive these roads all the time, back and forth, the ten, the twenty – but I like taking the train home, taking things a little slower, seeing out the window. You fly, you just see airports.'

She's not the only person on the train to tell me she loves the British royal family – though one fellow passenger, waiting to disembark at a late-night 'smoke stop' somewhere in western Texas, hears our accents and leans forward, cigarette already in her mouth, to confide they're all shape-shifting lizards. 'BE CAREFUL,' she hisses. Matt thanks her politely for her warning and I hear her telling someone else that she'd found one on the ceiling of her apartment eating pizza: 'And I was like, woah, did no one else see that? I tell you I went straight to bed, because I am not so naive I don't believe there ain't alien life forms out there.'

We meet others too; at lunch, we share a table with Jean from Orange County, who's on her way to stay with friends in Georgia – everyone she knows left California as soon as they stopped work, she says, no one can afford to stay: 'I'll go too, once I've sold the house.'* This, she tells us over a grilled Caesar salad (me and Jean) and a patty melt and crisps (Matt), is her first train trip too: she usually drives, but her friends, 'They said why don't you try it, and I'm enjoying it so far, it's really nice to see some new places, and fun to sleep on here too.' (That said, she's planning to fly home – 'But sure, I'd do it again.')

Later, while we're having dinner with Ann, a grant coordinator at Texas A&M on her way back from a conference in Seattle – 'When I said I wanted to go by train, they were puzzled, like – do we even fund Amtrak tickets? A lot of my colleagues think I'm crazy, but then their flights back were delayed by weather so . . .' – Jean passes and asks me to stop by her roomette after dinner; she has something for me. It turns out to be a copy of *National Geographic*, a National Parks special – 'I thought you might find this useful on your travels,' she says. She has a long way to travel still, and it doesn't even look like she's opened the glossy cover, but she's insistent I take it: 'I'd like to show you how beautiful this country can be.'

Whirling columns of dust dance across the sand, and the time zone changes. I spot a canyon full of wrecked cars, and Matt a cluster of lonely white crosses on a rocky hill. A development of half-finished

---

* This state of affairs is corroborated by an Uber driver in San Antonio, who says he left because he couldn't afford to raise a kid on the West Coast. He also tells us he drives back to Orange County a few times a year to see family, non-stop, twenty-two hours and five caffeine drinks. 'I get drive-thru, buy extra so I don't have to stop to get more,' he relates proudly. 'I didn't even know there was a train.'

houses already sports an enormous American flag, while a semi-circle of rusting vehicles surrounding a trailer in the middle of nowhere have windscreens sprayed with the repeated words 'KEEP OUT'. The dirt gets redder, ranch fencing starts to appear, and late afternoon, as we approach El Paso, the conductor announces that the border wall is now visible from the right-hand side of the train. It's more of a fence really; oxidised metal slats in empty desert, giving a blurry panorama of life on the other side. Sometimes it abruptly stops at the side of a hill, and then picks up again on the other side.

'Forty, fifty years ago,' he's back on the tannoy as the station slides into view, 'the train would stop for a few hours here, and people could go over to Mexico to visit. Unfortunately these days we no longer have the time to stop, so be warned; the next train through here is in three days. If you're hungry, the famous Miss Juanita will be outside with her burritos.'

People look up, start fumbling in bags for their wallets. Matt's already on his feet: 'the burrito lady' is clearly a star attraction, and by the time we make it down the platform (the air like a furnace, even at 5pm) there's a long queue in front of a woman covered from head to toe – mask, baseball cap, sunglasses, headscarf – doing a brisk trade from a coolbox. For $3 a piece, we get foil-wrapped, warm doughy green chili beef tortillas to eat as we watch the colourful houses of Ciudad Juarez slide by on the other side of the Rio Grande; 'Just a light afternoon snack,' I say, before our three-course dinner featuring 'Amtrak signature flat iron steak' with Californian Cabernet Sauvignon. Certainly beats an M&S sandwich and a gin in a tin on the East Coast Mainline.

The train pulls in to a muggy San Antonio a merciful hour behind schedule, just after 6am. Perhaps it's the humidity, perhaps it's just all that time on board, but it really does feel as if we've arrived in a different country. As Matt points out as we walk from the station, a novelty in itself, Texas has pavements, and actual pedestrian crossings!* As I'm wheeling a fully laden bike, I'm also pleased that dropped kerbs seem to be more of a feature too; being a wheelchair user in California must be hard work.

We're staying at the Valencia, on the pretty Riverwalk, where the lobby displays over 100 glass oranges signed by celebrity guests playing at the nearby theatres, from ZZ Top to Snoop Dog (sadly without Martha Stewart in tow), and the valets are happy to park Eddy for me – where I don't ask, I'm just desperate to get stuck into the Tex-Mex, dragging Matt to Mi Tierra where, even three minutes after it opens for the day, we're only third in.

This San Antonio institution started life as a three-table cafe in 1941 to serve early-bird farmers and workers from the nearby market, and now, in the hands of the children and grandchildren of founders Pedro and Cruz Cortez, occupies a sprawling multi-room complex that can seat 500. Even before you get to the food, Mi Tierra is quite the experience: on the way to the twinkling, tinsel-decked dining room we pass an altar stacked with photographs of deceased family members, staff and friends and more religious icons than my mum's mantelpiece, under a ceiling spinning with glittery piñata. The whole place feels like a fiesta, especially when I look at the menu. Tex-Mex was my first exposure to any variety of Latin American cuisine back in the mid-90s, and though I've branched out since, I realise I really miss it.

---

* It also has a giant old sign for the Hotel Robert E. Lee, named for the confederate general and slave owner deemed cruel even by the standards of the day, and one of the first things I notice on the skyline – though it's now apartment buildings, the owner's attempts to get permission to modify the historic landmark have so far come to naught.

COFFEE BREAK
What Is Tex-Mex?

For a long time it was fashionable to dismiss Tex-Mex as 'inauthentic', though in fact, until the 1970s, it was simply considered Mexican by those who had been in Texas longer than any border. According to the *Houston Chronicle*, Tex-Mex is a term popularised by the (late British) 'food authority Diana Kennedy', intended to insult an 'overseasoned' cuisine 'loaded with all those false spices like onion salt, garlic salt, MSG, and chili powder'. It turned out to be marketing gold: 'For the rest of the world, "Tex-Mex" had an exciting ring. It evoked images of cantinas, cowboys and the Wild West.'

Chef Johnny Hernandez is proud to call his native San Antonio 'ground zero for Tex-Mex' – he freely admits that there are many parts of the US where you can get more 'authentic' regional Mexican cooking. 'Here we're much more Tejano [descendants of those who settled in Texas before it became an American state], rather than first generation. It's quite a limited cuisine,' he admits, 'more of a style than an array of dishes.'

Imelda Sanchez Lopez, vice president at Henry's Puffy Tacos, whose family have been in Texas for over 200 years ('I don't have an abuela in Mexico, I consider myself Mexican-American, not Mexican'), explains that it reflects the ingredients available, like cheddar rather than queso fresco, and the poverty of many who cooked it, who bulked out dishes to feed their large families: 'adding potatoes, bell peppers, fideo to the ground beef, for example'. She bristles at those who look down on her culinary traditions: 'We don't want to hear it's not special, because that's the food that I grew up with, the food of my parents and grandparents.'

Baseball writer Jesse Sanchez makes the same point in Gustavo Arellano's excellent survey *Taco USA*: 'Tex-Mex is important to us because it's our bond to Mexico, even for us born in the United States. And it's just Mexican food to us. Are we less Mexican or Mexican-American because we are Tejanos? We consider ourselves all part of the "Mexican food" family and are surprised to hear when people speak of our food – or us – with disdain. The critiques sound elitist to us, and that says a lot coming from a state where we claim everything is bigger and better.'

In short, Tex-Mex food is Texan food, it's Mexican food – it's American food, pure and simple. And it's also incredibly delicious.

Five of the best Tex-Mex dishes:

- **Chili con carne:*** first mentioned in print in 1857 as 'literally red pepper and meat', this is a dish indelibly associated with San Antonio, but beloved throughout the state. Beware, classic Texas chili never contains beans or tomatoes!
- **Breakfast tacos:** said to have been invented in Austin but now found throughout the Southwest and beyond, this basically means a taco that includes scrambled egg (of the firm American variety), plus things like sausage, salsa and avocado.
- **Fajitas:** popularised, if not invented, in Houston in the 1970s, this inspired combination of marinated, grilled skirt steak and fluffy flour tortillas took Britain by storm, about two decades later.

---

* A note about spelling. In the UK we use 'chilli' for all purposes; in the USA, particularly the Southwest, 'chile' tends to refer to the peppers, as it does in Spanish, and 'chili' to the spiced meat dish.

- **Nachos:** the much-disputed origin story takes place just across the Mexican border in Piedras Negras, when a local waiter, faced with American army wives on a jolly, threw together a few items lying around in the kitchen to serve with their drinks. Whatever the truth, we're grateful.
- **Queso:** a fondness for cheese (and sour cream) is one of the hallmarks of Tex-Mex cuisine, and no party in the Lone Star State is complete without a bowl of gooey yellow cheese.

Sadly fajitas aren't available for breakfast, so I settle for chalupas, fried tortillas spread with refried beans, barbacoa and fried eggs ('Sunny-side up, please,' I say, feeling as self-consciously British as when I'd spontaneously said, 'Thank you, ma'am,' to a woman standing aside for me on the train, like I was talking to the queen) garnished with pickled red onions, coriander and queso fresco, and served with guacamole and fried potatoes. Good as it is, Matt's slow-braised pork with eggs, potatoes, beans and tortillas is even better, rich and brick red with chilli – and every time one of us takes a sip of coffee, the waitress leaps in to refill our cup. I will never get used to the concept of free refills, I say – even if the coffee is generally nothing special, getting something for nothing never gets old. Even getting up for a free refill of soda gives me a guilty thrill every single time.

As we eat, the dining room fills up with couples and family groups – many of whom are opting for the menudo, or tripe soup (one thing the rather snooty Diana Kennedy did occasionally order when she was in town), a dish that perhaps swings towards the Mex end of Tex-Mex, though not one I fancy quite so early.

After grabbing a guava pie from the bakery and admiring the huge and striking American Dream mural featuring Mi Tierra's founders along with the likes of actor Eva Longoria, revolutionary Pancho Villa and celebrity dog trainer Cesar Millan, we make for the Alamo. Matt could hardly be more excited about this prospect, so I decide not to tell him my dad remembers his visit thirty-five years ago as 'very dull'.

To be honest, I think this former Spanish mission church, now a 'shrine to Texas liberty'* considered so sacred that visitors are requested to remove their hats out of respect for the dead, may be something you have to be American to truly appreciate. That said, they've recently added a museum out back, which, to my surprise, is mostly dedicated to the Phil Collins Collection – the Chiswick-born Genesis frontman is, it transpires, an Alamo fanatic. Of more interest to me is the guava pie in my bag, which I eat outside while waiting for Matt to finish admiring Phil's musket balls: more of an empanada in shape, with a soft, short, sugary pastry and a red, sticky, distinctly tropical filling, I'm afraid it's too sweet for my taste and so scores a mere 5/10.

Driven out of the marvellously old-fashioned Museum of Texan Cultures by the frigid air-conditioning rather than the fascinating coverage of every conceivable community that has made its home in Texas, from post-war Jewish refugees (guacamole makes a great substitute for Ashkenazi chopped liver apparently) to the Comanche Indians who once dominated the Southern Great Plains, we decide it's time to taste some of these converging cultures, starting at Curry Boys BBQ, where they combine Texas smoke with South-East Asian sauces. This is not a kitchen afraid of strong flavours; the

---

* The defenders of the Alamo were not only demanding their independence, but the right to keep slaves, which became illegal in Mexico in 1829. According-ing to the account of a former Confederate soldier who guarded it during the Civil War, the mission building was subsequently used for slave auctions, though I only learn this fact later at the African-American Museum.

brisket with green curry is a sharp one-two to the tastebuds, and frankly I'm not sure I've ever eaten anything quite like it, or indeed their curry queso, which is certainly my first taste of Thai-Tex-Mex.

Wandering slowly back to the mercado through a dusty low-rise light industrial district in the heat of the afternoon, hoping for something cold and sour, I clock the live band outside the Centro de Artes, and suddenly remember it's the Cinco de Mayo, which I'd imagined would be a bigger deal here. Though a few people are dancing, more are standing around drinking large chilli-crusted pints of michelada (lager with lime juice, hot sauce and salt), including two seniors in 'JESUS SAVES' t-shirts and a man with a huge, disturbingly pallid snake wrapped around his neck. 'We're definitely in Texas,' Matt says, eyeing the snake nervously.

After a somewhat later start the next morning thanks to an evening at Re:Rooted, an urban winery producing unexpectedly good Bordeaux blends, and a 7/10 artisan berry pop tart (great flaky pastry, delicious fruity filling, all spoiled by a thick layer of sugary icing), Matt gets to tick off another Spanish mission. En route through San Antonio's sprawling suburbs (which, like LA, give the impression of endless space, none of it public) we have a worrying conversation with the Uber driver, who tells us it's always been hot here, but last year it was over 100°F for three months straight. 'Not a drop of rain, the lakes are drying up, the rivers. I know a guy who bought a lakefront house that's now a mile from the water – he can't sell it for any price!' This does not bode well for my onward travel plans; it's already 75°F and 97 per cent humidity in the first week in May, and temperatures for the week ahead, when I plan to cycle east towards New Orleans, are in the 90s.

Shoving that concern aside for now, I admire the humped, tortoise-like ovens sheltering within the 250-year-old stone walls of the Mission San José, shaded by huge Mission fig trees and the thorny honey mesquite our guide tells us is 'the secret of a good barbecue'. In the mercifully cool visitor centre is a reminder that the Coahuiltecan Indians who built this mission for the Spanish, and made up the vast majority of its residents, didn't just disappear overnight: 'We're still here', a sign on the wall politely points out. A quote from one Indigenous local shows how traditions have blended in their admission that 'the way that we ate, the way that my grandmother had her little remedies and her little herbs and stuff like that, it's very native. The way we were raised was very native . . . [but] of course we thought it was just Mexican . . . now we know that they never really lost their traditions.'

Culture vulture Matt satisfied, my mission for the day is to a place almost as sacred to local hearts: the home of San Antonio's beloved puffy, or deep-fried, tacos Henry's Puffy Tacos. Henry J. Lopez may not have been the first to deep fry masa (dough made from ground nixtamalized corn) or even to call the featherlight, almost prawn-cracker-like results, puffy tacos – he probably got both ideas from his older brother Arturo, who had a taco business in California (and may himself have been inspired by the *gordita inflada* or puffed-up fatties (!) eaten in Veracruz) – but he does seem to have been the first person to really see their potential when he opened up this spot in 1978.

His daughter Imelda invites us into the kitchen to witness the birth of a batch of puffy tacos, starting with rounds of pre-rolled masa dropped into hot oil, ten at a time. They balloon impressively. Working quickly, while they're still flexible enough to bend, the chef wraps each around the head of what looks like a garden implement but is in fact a special tool the family is currently attempting to patent, and pushes it to the back of the fryer to finish cooking – it's clear it's a skilled and labour-intensive process, which takes two to three minutes per batch, and that's without all the faff of making the masa in the first place.

As Imelda explains, bringing us a tray to try, the puffed-up dough soaks up all the flavours of whatever you put in it, 'so even though it's the same corn tortilla as you might use in a taco, it tastes different'. We get spicy chicken, carne guisada (braised beef), picadillo (spiced ground beef), guacamole, bean and cheese and spicy beef fajita versions – I think the last is my favourite, because of the contrast in textures, the char and chew of the steak and the oily, fluffy dough, slightly crisp and then soft as it yields to the bite, cradling the meat like a heavenly cloud. 'We cook the steak on the grill so it's a bit juicier,' Imelda says, pleased with my reaction. 'I don't think anyone else does that in town.'

Puffy tacos are so much a part of San Antonio's identity that Henry's sponsors the local minor-league baseball team mascot, a puffy taco that runs clumsily around the field before games, chased by screaming kids. 'A student came in recently, thanked us for getting her through her degree, and asked us if she could take her graduation pictures in here,' Imelda recalls proudly. 'And we had a guy in the military bring in a puffy taco soft toy he said had been with him when he was deployed in a bunch of different places – he always kept it close, as a piece of home.'

Decorum suggests I should claim neither of us could eat another thing after that, but actually, after a respectable break involving a very sweaty walk and a visit to the tiny but deliciously cool African American Museum,* I force Matt into ordering a 'macho-sized' cheddar cheezy burger for dinner on the basis that the day after tomorrow he's going home to eat salad, while I have another two months of this to go. I confine myself to a regular-sized tostada burger, Chris Madrid's speciality, topped with refried beans, tortilla chips, onions, melted cheddar and salsa, which is, I'm afraid to say, extremely enjoyable, much as you might wish to hear otherwise. Another example of the happy American disregard for culinary

---

* Currently fundraising for a bigger site including a lunch counter. 'We're hoping some of the people who weren't allowed to sit at them here back in the day are going to come and cut the ribbon!' the enthusiastic young hijabi guide explains.

rules and boundaries, I say, as we drink pitchers of frozen *nopales* margaritas. 'Just . . . maybe it's not the best idea to eat this stuff every day?' Matt whispers, looking around.

Loath as I am to body shame anyone, it can't be denied that a couple of the kids we see returning again and again to the soda refill machine do look like their size is hampering their mobility. Everything in moderation, I say entirely hypocritically, ordering another margarita.

Breaking Matt seems to be tradition on these trips, but this time I manage to do it with food, rather than the usual cycling. He seems perfectly perky over breakfast tacos (bacon and egg for him, potato and chorizo for me) at the Cafe Alameda, where the waitress is aghast we only want one per person, amused when we have to be searched by armed officers before going into the post office to buy stamps, and positively delighted when we meet a man who claims to be a descendant of Davy Crockett himself in the entrance to San Fernando Cathedral. Like Crockett Sr, our new friend, standing with his hand reverently on the tomb of the Texas Heroes, is from Tennessee, and though this is his first visit to San Antonio, 'I've just felt . . . such a connection here I've extended my stay.' He's proud of his ancestor, who he describes, somewhat emotionally, as 'a much-misunderstood man, a great hunter, and a warrior. Disney,' he continues angrily, 'has a lot to answer for when it comes to Mr David Crockett, yes, sir.'

It could be this morning's alarming email from Dan, warning me about open carry laws in Texas,* that finally breaks Matt, or it

---

* As of 2021 you no longer need a special licence to carry a handgun in most public places in Texas, which is not at all terrifying. An Uber driver reassures us that 'while at the beginning you saw a lot of knuckleheads out with their guns', things have calmed down a bit, 'though we had a fiesta just last week that ended in gunfire . . . luckily the police came pretty quick and terminated the guys'.

might be the 90°F heat, but he's visibly drooping. He walks into our lunch venue, Best Quality Daughter, in the shadow of a recently redeveloped Victorian brewhouse, like a condemned man. 'I hope you don't mind if I don't eat much, I'm not very hungry,' he says, requesting a large iced water. Amateur, I think, ordering for both of us regardless.

The restaurant, its name inspired by Amy Tan's novel about Chinese-American families in San Francisco *The Joy Luck Club*, is the latest from chef Jennifer Hwa Dobbertin, whose mother, like Nina's back in San Francisco, came over from Taiwan in the 70s, though she tells me, 'I don't think of myself as Chinese American, I'm American Chinese, and a lot more American than Chinese. Chinese people don't see me as Chinese.'

The menu, she explains, is a reflection of her own experience growing up in her parents' American diner, eating her mum's Chinese food at home, and spending her summers helping out at her brother's restaurant in Taiwan: authentic 'in the sense that it's my story' – which includes such flights of Texan-Chinese fancy as orange chicken-fried steak, a 'very divisive' dish, according to Dobbertin: 'Some people expect it to be like Chinese restaurant orange chicken, some people expect it to be like chicken-fried steak,* but I just love it' – and curry guisada dan dan noodles, inspired by Texan breakfast tacos. 'That heavy carbload, the protein, the richness – I grew up here eating a lot of Mexican food.'

Oddly enough, however, the best-selling dish on the menu, the cashew chicken, is a version of a dish she ate in a British pub in Bangkok – 'I always used to get it when I was hungover, and I never regretted it. I'd never take it off here, it's like, 27 per cent of all orders. It may not be, well, whatever authentic is, but it's authentically American – because it's authentic to me,' she says defiantly.

---

* A Southern speciality not dissimilar to wiener schnitzel: beef steak beaten thin, then battered and fried like chicken.

JENNIFER HWA DOBBERTIN'S BEST QUALITY DAUGHTER CHORIZO, EGG AND CHEESE DUMPLINGS WITH JALAPEÑO CREMOSA

Chorizo, egg and cheese is a classic breakfast taco combo, and what better way to celebrate that by putting it into a dumpling?

[Notes: American scrambled eggs are cooked fast with a little oil on a high heat, stirring, until fluffy and dry. Look for the thicker type of round gyoza dumpling wrappers, rather than wonton ones. This makes about 50 dumplings; to freeze the excess, space them out on a lightly greased baking tray and freeze until solid, then decant them into a freezer bag. Cook from frozen. FC]

Makes about 50
For the dumplings
7 eggs, beaten
Vegetable oil
450g/1 pound minced/ground pork
10g/2 tsp white vinegar
8g/1½ tsp salt
4g/¾ tsp chilli powder
3g/½ tsp ground cumin
4g/2 minced cloves of garlic
120g/1½ cups shredded cheddar
1 × 284g/10 ounce pack of gyoza/potsticker dumpling wrappers

For the salsa cremosa
225g/½ pound jalapeños (deseed half or as many as desired to increase or decrease the spice)
50g/2 ounces cloves of garlic [about 10]
1 white onion, cut into quarters
100g/⅓ cup + 1½ tbsp neutral oil, plus extra to toss vegetables
75g/⅓ cup lime juice [about 2½ limes]

8g/1½ tsp salt
675g/1½ pounds sour cream

1. To make the filling, lightly scramble the eggs with a little oil [see note on page 107] and chill. Mix the ground pork with the vinegar, salt, chilli powder, cumin and garlic. Combine the scrambled eggs, cheese and the pork mixture. Chill.

2. Toss the jalapeños, garlic and onions liberally in oil, then cook in a large skillet [frying pan], over a medium-high heat, until everything is soft (some char is OK). Put everything from the skillet, including any remaining liquid, into a blender with the lime juice and salt. While blending, add the oil and blend until everything is emulsified. Remove from the blender. Let cool. Add the sour cream and whisk together until even.

3. To make the dumplings: place a heaped teaspoon of pork filling just below the centre of each wrapper. Wet the edge of the wrapper with water, then fold the top half over the bottom half and pinch the border to seal. Alternatively, pleat the dumplings by making small folds starting on one edge and ending on the other, pinching firmly to seal after each fold. Place on the prepared baking sheet and continue stuffing and sealing dumplings until all the pork mixture is used.

4. Heat 1 tablespoon of vegetable oil in a large skillet over a medium heat. Add the dumplings in an even layer, sealed side up. Fry for 1 to 2 minutes, or until golden on the underside.

5. Add 80ml/⅓ cup of water to the skillet, lower the heat to medium-low, and cover with a tight-fitting lid. Let steam for 3 minutes, then adjust the lid so it is ajar, allowing steam to escape. Cook until no water remains, about 3 minutes more. (Alternatively, deep fry.)

6. Use a spatula to transfer the dumplings to a serving plate, crisp-side up. Repeat the process until all the dumplings are cooked. Serve with the cremosa.

I can't get enough of the rich, savoury noodles, or the mochi cheddar hush puppies, but I notice Matt is merely picking at the roasted Brussels sprouts as Dobbertin kindly furnishes me with several Houston and New Orleans recommendations, explaining that 'Round here it's mostly classic Chinese mom and pop restaurants. I have to go to Houston for my Asian fix, there's a huge Vietnamese and Korean community there.'

Perhaps in revenge, he signs us up for an afternoon tour of the European armour exhibition showing at the San Antonio Museum of Art. 'We're going to be looking at so many pieces of armour in the next hour, and I'm gonna have a lot of questions for y'all at the end,' the guide announces gleefully as we stand in front of a seventeenth-century Dutch breastplate ('An HOUR?' I mouth at Matt, aghast) 'but I think we can all agree this really is a stunner.' The things we do for our friends.

With the end in sight, my pal rallies for our final meal together, on the riverside terrace at chef and local restaurant magnate Johnny Hernandez's La Gloria. Though the heat is still stifling, even at 7pm, the immediate delivery of a frosty margarita and a bowl of tortilla chips, guacamole and salsa helps – no wonder Texas food culture developed as it did: I can think of nothing more perfect in this climate – and then Johnny himself barrels in, sits down, and does not stop talking for the next three hours. I've never met a man with so much energy . . . or not since we bid farewell to Dan in California.

His father, Johnny tells us, was a migrant worker from the border region who left school before his tenth birthday and, sick of the agricultural work he'd been doing since childhood, managed to scrape together enough money to establish San Antonio's first cafeteria. He grew up helping there, making things like chicken-fried steak and mashed potatoes, but also what's now called Tex-Mex food (and taking it into school to sell to his classmates) before moving to New York to train at the Culinary Institute of America – 'My dad said I don't want you cooking Mexican food; French, Italian, anything but Mexican.'

Sadly his dad died when Johnny was still training, but later, during his time at places like the Four Seasons in Santa Barbara, and the Mirage in Las Vegas, he began travelling with his mum Theresa on her missionary trips to Mexico, where he discovered that the *norteño* (northern Mexican) food he'd grown up with – a lot of meat, goat, sausage, quesadillas – was very different to the typical fare elsewhere, 'And I decided to make a conscious shift, to start exploring regional traditions rather than the international food I'd trained in.'

This restaurant came out of his travels, though for a long time, he admits, he avoided the border region – 'too violent, I'd just fly into Mexico City'. Now, he's interested in exploring the cooking of this hinterland too: 'You go to Arizona, it changes a bit, California, it changes a bit more – they're more playful, not bound by tradition there, more liberal with flavours – it's a difficult terroir, very dry – I think it's an undertold story, and I really want to tell it, because it's the one dearest to me.'

As we talk, or Johnny talks at us, a succession of dishes arrives: bubbling *queso fundido*, or molten cheese, topped with a puddle of promisingly oily Mexican chorizo and poblano peppers, a refreshingly zingy ceviche selection, and a richly smoky Oaxaqueñas *mole negro* – 'It's not easy getting these recipes, you can't just come out and ask people right away, you got to befriend them, buy a lot of tacos from them,' Johnny laughs – and then a chipotle chicken enchilada and, of course, we *have to try* San Antonio's signature dish, the chile (con carne) . . . I notice poor Matt looking more and more anxious every time the waiter approaches.

But really, you can't come here without trying it: associated with the city since its earliest days when nineteenth-century tourists flocked to street vendors known as the 'chile queens' to sample their 'exotic' fare, it is described in one 1874 account as 'various savoury compounds, swimming in fiery pepper, which biteth like a serpent'. Perhaps inevitably, locals felt these ladies (whose virtue was oft called into question) were debasing San Antonio's reputation with their flirtatious sales pitches, and though chile remains the official dish of the Lone Star State, Johnny admits it's only gone on his menu relatively recently.

Perfecting the recipe 'was a real struggle', he recalls. 'I couldn't find any of the coarsely ground meat I remember my dad using, so we have to grind our own, and honestly the dish has been taken so far beyond the original concept that bringing it back wasn't easy.' Often, he says, modern chiles are 'more of a chile sauce with a little bit of meat'. What's in front of us is much beefier, less tomatoey than your average British version*, with granola-sized chunks of beef in a glossy, piquant but relatively thin sauce. It is, I can firmly say, the best chile con carne I've ever had – even without my beloved kidney beans.

Chef Hernandez seems to view bringing Mexican food to an audience brought up on Tex-Mex as an educational vocation as much as a business opportunity – to show them that though the food they're used to may be relatively simple and cheap, born as it was out of hardship, Mexican cuisine can be highly sophisticated, rich and complex. Yet when President Obama invited him to showcase it at the White House for Cinco de Mayo celebrations in 2016, he chose to take the tacos he'd promised his father he wouldn't spend his life making: a decision he describes as 'intentional . . . because can you imagine being able to serve tacos to the president?'

---

* Though, ahem, my own perfect chilli con carne contains no tomatoes, an omission which regularly horrifies friends before they actually try it.

His phone vibrates on the table for the umpteenth time this evening – it's his mum, he says, he promised he'd stop by and see her tonight. 'But I've got a little something for you to remind you of San Antonio back in London . . .' He reaches under the table and presents me with a Día de Los Muertos altar kit, and two hand-painted tiles. It's a lovely gesture, and a weighty one for a cyclist. 'I'll take it for you,' Matt says wearily as we roll home along the riverwalk, dodging water cockroaches. 'I assume . . . you're leaving before breakfast, right?'

(He messages me the following evening to tell me he has been all-but nil by mouth since the final bite of chili: not even a British Airways gin and tonic passed his lips until he landed back in London.)

Ridden: 0 miles
Climbed: 0 feet
Pies consumed: 2 (guava, berry pop tart)
All-American foods discovered: patty melt, Caesar salad, curry queso, brisket green curry, pop tart, puffy taco, tostada burger, breakfast taco, mochi hush puppies, orange chicken-fried steak, curry guisada, dan dan noodles, chile con carne

6
TEXAS – ALL HAT AND NO CATTLE

In search of Marmite ribs

'Only a rank degenerate would drive 1,500 miles across Texas without eating a chicken-fried steak.'
Larry McMurray

It's already warm, but still dark and damp outside, and a cacophonous, almost tropical dawn chorus is under way as I join the queue of passengers at the station awaiting the 6.48am Texas Eagle service to Chicago. I'm almost at the front when a guy in an Amtrak uniform, walking past, clocks me and says, 'Hey, you checked that bike?'

Turns out, unlike in LA, I'm not allowed to hand Eddy up to the train myself – in fact, the woman behind the counter almost laughs in my face at the audacity of the idea: 'Yeah, you needed to have delivered it to us forty-five minutes beforehand, ma'am.' There's nothing for it but to weaponise my Britishness; at some point around the twelfth or thirteenth sorry she's so sick of me that she relents and sends her minion out to walk me to the luggage car – I slow-jog alongside, just to show how contrite I am, promising I WILL KNOW NEXT TIME. 'Hmph,' the minion says, taking Eddy from me and dumping him unceremoniously on his rear mech. I'm too grateful to object. Thank you, Amtrak woman with a neck tattoo, I appreciate you.*

To be fair, I've had other things to think about. My initial plan had been to join the Adventure Cycling Association's Southern Tier tour from Austin all the way to New Orleans (after skipping the distinctly unpleasant-sounding 'I-35 hell route', as *Texas Monthly* describes the road between San Antonio and the state capital). It sounds wonderful, starting in Texas Hill Country, passing through the Sam Houston national forest and then descending into the Gulf coastal plain, Cajun country and the Big Easy.

The problem is, as San Antonio winemaker Jen Beckermann observed to us apropos of growing grapes here, 'we don't have weather in Texas, we have biblical events' – and one of those events, three storms back-to-back, has caused serious flooding in the east of the state. This is not something that I anticipated, but I decide I can at least get as far as Houston in safety, and take stock from there.

In the meantime, I sit back in my coach-class seat – surprisingly roomy and comfortable by British standards, if uncomfortably chilly because the US invented air-conditioning and it's not afraid to use it – and watch San Antonio roll away, peeping into the backyards of people's lives: a well-used barbecue grill outside a stonemasonry workshop, people queueing for breakfast at a homeless shelter, a deer running through a meadow of wild flowers . . . a dead deer being picked at by crows. I look away quickly, in time to see a troop of smartly dressed small boys – blue shirts, black trousers held up by braces, straw hats – follow their identically dressed

---

* I keep hearing people say this and it takes a while for me to realise they're not offering deep appreciation for my very existence, they're simply saying thank you.

father down the staircase to the bathroom. Mennonites, I guess, with a little thrill at how foreign America is. Before the day is out it will become clear I haven't seen anything yet.

After retrieving Eddy, apparently no worse for wear, in Austin, things start off pleasantly enough – I'm relishing the sheer Texasness of it all as the route heads out of town past Smokey's Smoked Meats and 'Earth Native Wilderness Training', but though the skies are overcast, I can't help noticing the air becoming rather warm. Stopping to take a picture of a sign for High Noon Road, I glance down and notice the sweat slick on my forearms. This feels very different to cycling in California, I realise, as I spot my first snakes, skunks and armadillos, all deceased and stinking to high heaven on the tarmac. I begin holding my breath as soon as I see any object in my path, just in case.

Yet, despite the huge disparity to my eyes, I see my first bumper sticker shouting 'DON'T CALIFORNIA MY TEXAS' on the way out of the city, and the further I go, the more enthusiastically they seem to be breeding. 'TRUMP 2024: THE RETURN!' 'TRUMP 2024: I'LL BE BACK' and one I'll become quite familiar with in the weeks to come: a yellow flag with a coiled rattlesnake above the legend 'DON'T TREAD ON ME'.* So numerous are they that I'm momentarily taken aback to spy a rival 'BIDEN' flag fluttering in a farmyard before I look more closely, and realise I've missed the 'IMPEACH' bit.

The pleasant little farm roads, with their vast, neatly mown plots and immaculate churches, give way to slightly less enjoyable highways with scanty shoulders and close-passing motor traffic – I even

---

* A safe distance away from the landscaped ranch house flying it, I stop to look it up, and discover it's an anti-British revolution-era flag recently repurposed to protest against 'government overreach'.

get a couple of honks, which I choose to take as encouraging in the absence of any definite evidence to the contrary, though it could equally be surprise given that I haven't seen any other cyclists out here yet. Every breath feels like sucking on a hairdryer, and I can't even muster any enthusiasm for the taqueria trucks and barbecue joints of Cedar Creek, stopping only to grab a Mexican grapefruit soda and a mango ice lolly from a gas station before powering on. When I pass a sign on a fence asking if I'm ready to meet my God, I wonder if I might be.

By the time I reach Bastrop State Park, with its historic golf shelter, I've lost all interest in my surroundings. 'Wouldn't catch me out in this,' the chirpy girl in the air-conditioned ticket booth says, snapping open her window to extort $3 from me for passing through. I attempt a wry smile, settle for a grimace, and begin an endless sequence of short but punchy hills, some of which are so steep I swallow my pride and get off and push. The first thing I google when I stop on a fallen tree to eat my lunchtime tamale is 'heat exhaustion symptoms'.

Staggering up yet another ascent, I see a sign for a scenic over-look, and, hoping to claw back some joy, lean Eddy against a tree, watch as he callously topples to the ground, shrug helplessly and am about to head towards the view when a man jumps out of a parked car and waves his arms frantically at me, pointing at the tree. Dopily I stand and stare, until he finally finds the English words to explain: 'SNAKES, BIG SNAKES, MISS! IN TREE!' Star-tled, I jump away and look. There are indeed two fat snakes coiled around the branches above Eddy. I thank him for the warning, curse myself for my stupidity* and gingerly pick the bike up (fully expecting something to uncoil in front of my eyes at any moment,

---

* Having not even considered the fact that Texas might have dangerous snakes, despite having ridden over several dead ones, I later learn it has ten species of rattlesnake alone.

Jungle Book style), then ride very briskly off, sweating more than ever. From that moment on, I do not leave the road.

Things do not significantly improve when I'm chased by my first dog – one minute I'm puffing along thinking longingly of the frigid embrace of air-con, the local enthusiasm for which is suddenly making a lot more sense to me, and the next I'm aware of something gaining on me, snapping its teeth. The sprint I put on is worthy of Tadej Pogačar himself and the dog, clearly an amateur, quickly gives up the chase and returns home to laugh about my red face with its pals, but honestly I'm losing patience with the entire endeavour; I have a leaden headache, a lump in my throat as if I'm about to burst into tears and I haven't been to the loo since I left San Antonio, despite the 3.5 litres of water I've put away. My fingertips are, I notice with detached interest, wrinkled like prunes, yet La Grange, my destination for the night, is somehow still almost seventeen miles away.

I'm having a serious sense of humour failure when I roll in after ten hours in the saddle and find no one at reception at the Oak Motel (any plans to camp slithered out of the window at the first mention of snakes), just a coaster with a Bible verse on it and a pink Easter decoration assuring me 'You are some bunny special.' Having tracked down the proprietor enjoying a nice cool drink in the garden, I discover that, despite liberal use of suncream, my thighs are a hot pink rash, and it takes several minutes under a cold shower, and several bottles of water, before I feel human enough to go in search of a terrible dinner – a limp salad with something bright orange and gloopy that claims to be Italian dressing, plus a fettucine alfredo, which when it arrives turns out to be linguine with mushrooms and a sauce of pure oil.

Clearly my accent is foxing the Spanish-speaking waitress, but I can't be bothered to try to explain, so I miserably eat around the grease and return to the motel, where I notice a slightly unnerving sign directing me to 'LOCK AND CHAIN THE DOOR' and, checking the weather for tomorrow, discover an excessive heat warning has been posted for La Grange. Even this late in the evening, it's 86°F with a 'feels like' temperature of 101°F and a humidity rating of 83 per cent. This makes me feel better about how hard I've found the day, if not the prospect of doing it all again tomorrow.

I'm away before any of the local attractions – and La Grange has a surprising number given its size, from the Texas Heroes to the Texas Quilting and even the Polka Lovers Club of Texas Museums – open, determined to make the most of the pre-dawn cool. The air is already so heavy that my handlebars are wet with moisture, but the traffic is light and it feels easier than yesterday – more open countryside, more of a breeze over the cracked asphalt.

The cemeteries are full of Czech and German names, the highways studded with historical signs commemorating long-forgotten Methodist schools and vanished 'festplatz' dancehalls. As the morning wears on, the staring cattle by the side of the road are replaced by a display of startlingly vicious-looking dinosaurs, a Republican elephant with a Texas flag painted on its haunches and, perhaps most surprisingly to me, a series of 'antiques barns'.

I don't pause to check out the world's smallest Catholic church in Warrenton, though I am sad the St John's Lutheran Food Booth ('hot food, cold drinks, warm smiles') isn't open for business. This makes me realise I'm hungry and I stop for breakfast a few miles down the road in the self-consciously pretty city of Round Top (pop. 87). The little cafe is empty apart from a group of older men and women clustered around the large communal table, who all stop talking and stare as I walk in. I smile ingratiatingly, order a potato, egg and cheese taco (the breakfast menu is simple: taco or cake) and a pecan iced coffee, and sit down with the *Fayette County Record* ('On March 17, Animal Control Officer Justin Pietsch picked up a dog in the 100 block of Lee and took it to the pound. On March 19, Pietsch set up a skunk trap in the 200 block of Lynwood . . .') to eavesdrop. The men, clustered at one end, are talking about President Biden's 'obsession' with spending taxpayers' money on 'the Ukraine and so-called refugees while veterans go homeless', as one old chap in a red MAGA hat puts it, and the size of local building plots. The women mostly seem to be discussing hip replacements and other people's marriages.

As I go out to grab a water bottle to refill, I'm hailed by two of the guys by the door, who ask me what I'm up to. I explain, admitting I've been caught out by both the weather and the wildlife, and they fall about laughing; 'Oh yeah, we got snay-yuks all right!' one says, while another chimes in, 'You think this is hot, you should come in Ow-gust, missy!' MAGA-hat, a friendly sort, comes out to inspect my bike. 'I'd be thinking of getting me one of those,' he says smiling, 'but with one of those electric motors inside, heheh. You be safe now,' he says more seriously. 'Drivers round here, they can be crazy.' On the way out of town, such as it is, I pass a house with a sign on the gate reading: 'Beware: Dog Bites Democrats' and wonder if it's his.

My breakfast companions are very keen, as people seem to be in these parts, to know how I'm enjoying 'our rollin' hills'. In truth they'd be fun in cooler weather, never big enough to engage the small ring, but lively enough to keep me engaged, and, along with the lush, early-summer countryside on the way into Brenham, serve as a much-needed reminder of the joys of cycling. It helps that, by 11.40am, I'm done for the day and seated at LJ's BBQ with a plastic plate containing a slab of juicy, tender brisket, some collard greens and the creamiest macaroni cheese I've ever had – it's like eating a sauce made from Philadelphia. Matt the Pitmaster, chopping meat behind the counter, sees my Marmite-branded jersey and asks if I want to try his Marmite barbecue sauce.

'NO WAY?' I say, genuinely excited.

He laughs and tells me he's kidding, but he does have a buddy, 'big sausage guy', who goes over to cook barbecue in Australia, and *he* makes a mean Marmite sausage. (I decide this is not the place to get into the difference between Marmite and Vegemite, especially with a man holding a large knife.) By the time I've cleaned my plate and tossed it guiltily in the trash – like free refills, disposable flatwear is taking some getting used to – the queue stretches out the door: everyone from dusty labourers to men in blue blazers and preppy loafers, and a big bearded man in denim dungarees who spends a long time on the porch staring hard at Eddy before coming in.

As I reattach my handlebar bag, a group stops to tell me they thought I was a pizza-delivery rider. Having canvassed my opinions on the late queen and Margaret Thatcher, they're replaced by a man in an enormous truck who slows on the way out of the parking lot, rolls down his window and tells me, somewhat unexpectedly given that I've not seen a single bike since Austin, that he moved to Brenham because he loved cycling round here so much, before adding the customary admonition to 'be careful'.

I'm trying but America doesn't always make it easy: there's literally no way to access tonight's motel without a car except by walking up the interstate off ramp – when I finally make it, after trying and failing to drag a fully-laden Eddy up a steep grass bank behind Applebee's instead, the Indian man behind the desk tells me I have a red face and laughs mockingly; 'I can tell you are not used to the weather.'

On the good news front, Anne, the aunt Adele put me in touch with back in California, will not only be in New Orleans next week, where she's invited me out for lunch, but has put me in touch with her cousin Harold Osborn, who is the CEO of Tabasco – hot sauce royalty! – to arrange a trip to Avery Island, where the magic happens. With only four days to get there, and heavy rain forecast over the weekend, I accept reality and book the next train to New

Orleans from Houston,* some eighty-seven miles south-east of here, which leaves in three days' time. This all takes so long (logistics being the unglamorous aspect of travel no one ever writes about, because, as you can tell if you've made it this far through the paragraph, it's very dull) that by the time I realise I'm in the home of the Blue Bell Creamery, and could have gone to the factory to watch them making delicious ice cream, it's too late.

Unable to displace the idea of ice cream, I take a terrifying ride along Highway 290 to a gas station and food mart where I decompress with a scoop of Blue Bell's black walnut and one of butter pecan under a display of decorative crosses and a sign that says 'You can take my gun when I run out of bullets', then end the day eating a Kroger organic sweet kale chopped salad from the bag, spraying Triscuit crumbs around the room, and watching a programme called *My 600-lb Life: Where Are They Now?* Today has, without a doubt, been a lot better than yesterday, and I feel I've learnt a few things, e.g. take Texan weather seriously, and rehydration tablets are not just for hangovers.

What I haven't really taken into account in my planning is just how large Houston itself is. Though I arrive in Katy, on the outskirts, just after noon, having set off at dawn, I don't get to my hotel downtown until almost 6pm, which means most of the day is spent negotiating urban traffic.

The first chunk of the ride is profoundly rural, however: country roads, unsurfaced and slow, particularly after the recent rain has turned them to bog, and only a few farmers up and about. Even the dogs are still asleep, it seems. I pass a 'cowboy church' and through

---

* On most routes Amtrak will only allow you to load and unload bicycles at manned stations, which are few and far between – Houston is one, New Orleans the next, so there's no way to pick up the train at any point in between, or indeed closer to Avery Island, despite the station at New Iberia.

a few one-horse towns where even the horse seemed to have bolted, so I'm relieved to find Bellville open for breakfast. Given that I still haven't seen another cyclist, I particularly appreciate the kerbside mechanic station where I pump up my tyres before feasting on fluffy hot cakes and a sausage kolache, a Texan speciality with Czech roots, at Newmans Bakery, an old-fashioned beige place with a distinctly Germanic-slanted menu and Latino staff. Trump Burger down the road is still closed when I ride past afterwards, but every outside surface is plastered with pictures of the man himself giving his trademark thumbs-up and fluttering flags proudly declaring 'TRUMP 2024: THE RULES HAVE CHANGED' and 'TRUMP 2024: BECAUSE AMERICA CAN NEVER BE TOO GREAT'.

I ride on, across the swollen, muddy Brazos River, where thousands of tiny birds dive for insects and a huge femur bone lies across the hard shoulder, past large houses flying flags declaring 'FUCK BIDEN AND FUCK YOU FOR VOTING FOR HIM', and then find myself on a road so broken and busy with trucks that I break my own rules and put on the *Archers** omnibus. Just in one ear, just to make it a bit more bearable, because if there's anything to make you feel better about a grim situation, it's Tony whanging on about an overflowing slurry tank.

The edge of the city comes abruptly: Google takes me down a dirt track along the side of an estate of half-built houses and there I am, in a weird, manicured residential zone with no shops to buy a drink, and no benches on which to rest, just row after row of immaculate identikit houses. The fact that over 95 per cent of land in Texas is privately owned does not surprise me in the least – one

---

* For those unfamiliar, this everyday story of country folk is the world's longest-running radio drama, according to the BBC, but I'd describe it as a soap opera with added cows. It's famously, gloriously dull – a recent storyline concerned some missing spectacles – except when it isn't: in the last few years it's also covered coercive control, modern slavery, prison overcrowding, gay marriage and abortion. I never miss an episode, even from Texas.

of the things I'm finding I like least about cycling in America is how hard it is to find somewhere to sit quietly without spending money. Outside state parks, benches seem to be an endangered species.

I push on, stopping briefly for an apple in the parking lot of an Episcopalian church where I'm attacked by large tawny flies intent on taking chunks out of my leg, and eat a pecan pie from Newmans in the shade of a gas station. The chunky pastry tastes flat and the flour oddly scorched, but the filling, all brown sugar and vanilla and chunky nuts, is quite good (6 / 10).

Eventually the mirror-glass skyscrapers of downtown Houston hove into view, and I literally feel like I'm riding into the opening credits of *Dallas*; by the time I reach the hotel, thankful for the cool, dim corridors between the glittering towers, my mouth is open in wonder in a way it hasn't been since San Francisco. After hand-washing everything I own, and with no need to be up early to beat the heat, I sleep for ten hours straight.

In fact, as I hadn't intended to be in Houston, I don't really have anything particular to tick off, so the next morning I simply get on my bike and go exploring. It's a more cycle-friendly city than I would have guessed, with lots of riders and runners out by the bayou (!), though not a bike rack in sight near the Avalon Diner where I stop for breakfast. Their chicken-fried steak, the Texas classic, is so big that it arrives on two plates; one for the buttery beef steaks (there are two of them, beaten thin and encased in puckered, golden breadcrumbs), biscuit and cream gravy, and one for their sidekicks: two fried eggs and a portion of hash browns. I feel bad about the second plate – I certainly didn't need two eggs, and I'm not keen on 'proper' (starchy, greasy, half-raw) hash browns rather than the trashy fast-food sort – but my server tells me not to worry, people rarely finish it all, which begs the question of why they make it so big in the first place. Do people really only feel they're getting value for money if there's too much to eat? I wonder. How many of them actually eat what they take home in a box?

Uncomfortably full, and hoping to discover more about the food culture of this city I've ended up in so unexpectedly, I visit three very different markets: a neighbourhood farmers' market of early peaches and delicate lamb chops; Central Market, a jaw-droppingly large cross between Whole Foods and Fortnum & Mason, where I get lost and slightly panicky trying to find my way out from the piles of giant apples and imported cheese (the British section does not do us proud, with such horrors as Wensleydale with blueberries, champagne cheddar, and a surprising number of unnervingly red varieties I've never seen at home – sorry, Houston), and the Houston Farmers Market, which is almost entirely filled with Latin American vendors. I wander the last wondering at the bowls of freshly made mole, boxes of dried prawns, bunches of cinnamon sticks, cactus paddles and strings of dried chillies, all overlaid with the heavy perfume of ripe mango. There are cooking pots you could wash a baby in, platters of cut fruit stained red with sweet, salty chamoy chilli sauce, and everywhere families pinching and prodding and discussing food.

Though I enjoy browsing, I'm not here for anything Mexican. Tucked around the side of the hall is a place called Crawfish & Noodles, serving up the Viet-Cajun cuisine developed by the refugees who arrived on the Gulf Coast in the 1970s in search of a new life. As writer, and Houston native, Dan Q. Dao recently explained to readers of *Southern Living*, the Vietnamese-Cajun crawfish I'm hoping to try 'doesn't have any actual roots in Vietnam; it's a Southern food through and through. Like Tex-Mex or Creole cuisine, it was born on American soil through a specific set of circumstances at a particular moment in time.' New immigrants of his parents' generation, he says, found in local crawfish boils the south-eastern equivalent of 'the casual, social outdoor stalls in Vietnam where you'd go to throw back a few beers while snacking on fish, shellfish, or snails'.

Sitting at the bar, server Dave, who says he's originally from the Midwest, 'where we've got crawfish, but don't eat 'em',* promises me that, daunting as it sounds, a pound of Viet-Cajun mudbugs would very much not be absurd as an individual order: 'There's more calories in the picking than the eating, trust me.' The stainless-steel mixing bowl of fiery red crustaceans arrives along with a plastic apron and rubber gloves. I look around self-consciously – it's still early, and the only other person eating is a market worker swallowing a dozen oysters without taking a breath – and ask Dave if the gloves are *really* necessary, adding somewhat proudly that I'm happy to get my hands dirty. He shrugs, 'I would, things get saucy, and these babies can be pretty sharp . . .' He pauses, assesses me, 'Hey, have you eaten crawfish before?'

Yes, I say, not wanting to let the national side down, and it's true, I've been to a midsummer crayfish party in Finland, and fished them out of the river at a festival in the Cotswolds . . . plus I've eaten absolutely loads of those Pret sandwiches with rocket over the years. Yet I can't help noticing as I reluctantly pull on the gloves, feeling very like someone about to conduct an internal examination, that these chaps are bigger than the ones I'm used to, almost langoustine sized. After standing, arms folded, frowning at my haphazard technique, Dave swoops in with a few gentle pointers (stick your thumbnail in the hinge between head and tail, then peel off the first segment of shell so the rest comes off in one clean, satisfying sweep), which I humbly accept as I work my way through the rest of the giant bowl. They're sweet, and doused in garlicky, buttery, peppery liquor that I quickly get absolutely everywhere – I

---

* He also informs me, to my amazement, that up there they burrow underground for winter, and then pop up again in the spring – 'I grew up miles from a river, and yet, every year, there they were' – which I later check online and find to be true.

have to apologise when he removes the bowl to reveal a counter stained orange with shame. He reassures me this is nothing: 'Believe me, sometimes it looks like a murder scene in here.'

On the way back to the hotel, I ride through River Oaks, a quiet and perfectly manicured residential district full of mansions so grand I can't help taking videos as I go. After a while, a black minivan stops in front of me. I pass, and then it reappears and does it again, before driving very slowly in front of me for several blocks. I can't help wondering if someone has called security on the scruffy, sunburnt woman on a bike.

VIET-CAJUN CRAWFISH BOIL

It's probably a fool's errand to try to recreate an authentic seafood boil outside the Gulf Coast, let alone across the ocean, but if you come across some fresh crawfish (crayfish, as they're known here, are an invasive species in the UK, and are available online in season) this is a great way to enjoy them. You can also find them frozen out of season, though I'd suggest substituting large raw prawns, soft-shell crab or, if you're feeling flush, langoustines. Seafood boil seasoning is a vital ingredient, and available online (I used Zaterain's concentrated shrimp and crab boil liquid), as are recipes suggesting homemade replacements. I'd just order it: seafood is expensive, so you may as well do it justice, and you can use it on all sorts of other seafood dishes too.

Serves 2, but easily ramped up if you have a pot large enough
2 oranges
1 stick of celery, roughly chopped
2 bay leaves
2 tbsp fine salt
2 heads of garlic

2 litres/8½ cups water
1½ tbsp liquid seafood boil seasoning
2 corn on the cob, each cut into 3 pieces
2kg/4½ pounds crayfish, defrosted if necessary
100g/1 stick minus 1 tbsp butter
2 tbsp coarsely ground black pepper
2 tsp cayenne pepper

1. Finely zest the oranges into a large pan and squeeze in the juice. Add the celery, bay leaves, salt and one of the heads of garlic, cut in half across its widest point, plus the 2 litres/8½ cups of cold water and the seasoning. Bring to the boil.
2. Add the corn and simmer for 10 minutes, then add the crayfish. Continue to boil for 5 to 8 minutes, depending on size – they'll be bright red once they're cooked through. If you're using defrosted ready-cooked crayfish, they'll be heated through in 5 minutes.
3. While the crayfish are cooking, peel and crush the remaining garlic and heat the butter in a small pan. Add the crushed garlic and the peppers and fry until the garlic begins to smell cooked.
4. Drain the crayfish and corn (you can save the water for stock) and put back into the pan. Add the garlic butter and toss together. Serve immediately, with finger bowls.

I leave Eddy back in the room for the final stop of the day: Ninfa's (slogan: The Best Mexican Food in Texas Since Texas was in Mexico!), which claims to have invented fajitas. As I still have a soft, doughy spot for the 'fajita kit' sold at Waitrose in the late 90s, which was my first taste of Mexican food, I feel compelled to make the pilgrimage, though looking at the sorry tents huddled under the flyover from the comfort of my cab, I'm relieved I've decided not to attempt the short distance on foot. A man lies on the pavement wearing just one shoe, his hand around a bottle, while a couple smokes outside the bar opposite. A thick skin is beginning to feel like an asset in the face of such sadness.

Feeling extremely fortunate, my only complaint about the evening is that everything arrives too fast, despite me asking if I can finish my margarita before tackling the fajitas. 'Tacos al carbon', as they're also known, were once a popular dinner among Mexican cowboys (and, one imagines, Texan cowboys and any cattle dog who happened to be within smelling distance when they were grilling steak), but it's generally agreed that Ninfa's can take the credit for popularising them with the non-cattle-herding classes, and turning a cheap cut of meat, skirt steak, into a restaurant sensation. The tortillas are thick, soft and rich, almost paratha-like, and the steak pleasingly charred and chewy, if underseasoned, something that matters less once I load it up with pico de gallo salsa, guacamole and *queso con chile*. I'm in and out in forty-five minutes, even given a helping of flan so firm Dan could earthquake-proof his basement with it, and ready for an early night. This time tomorrow, I'll be in New Orleans, the real city that never sleeps, whatever those New Yorkers claim.

Ridden: 256 miles
Climbed: 7,513 feet
Pies consumed: 1 (pecan)
All-American foods discovered: barbecue brisket, mac and cheese, collard greens, butter pecan ice cream, hot cakes and syrup, sausage kolache, pecan pie, chicken-fried steak, Vietnamese crawfish boil, fajitas, Cambodian-Czech pho kolaches★

★ Back in Europe, kolaches are always sweet yeasted rolls, filled with things like fruit, cream cheese or poppy seeds, but in the US, the same dough is wrapped around sausages and other savoury items.

7

BIG FUN ON THE BAYOU

In search of Cajun spice

'I got hot sauce in my bag, swag.'
Beyoncé

In my first five minutes cycling in New Orleans, I discover two important facts: traffic lights down here are considered merely advisory, and I'm just as scared of streetcar rails as I am of tram tracks at home. After a nine-and-a-half-hour train ride through the swampy scenery of the Gulf of Mexico in the company of a cane corso dog rejoicing in the name Trevor Badass and his owner, a proud Creole who tells me that she likes to put a little of her favourite Southern Comfort in his food, 'because if it's good for our hearts, it's got to be good for theirs, right?' I'm more than ready for my bed. Even my immense load of laundry can wait until the morning.

I'm here for an entire week, the longest I'm to spend anywhere, which is fortunate, because New Orleans has repeatedly been voted the USA's best food city, boasting a remarkable number of culinary specialities, often credited to the fact that it was under French and Spanish rule for much of the eighteenth century until the Louisiana

Purchase of 1803 brought it into the Union, though wider diversity in a port city with strong African influence probably has as much to do with it.

It also immediately feels more laid-back than Texas, more mercurial, and yes, more liberal – at Molly's Rise and Shine where I go for breakfast (a warm, crusty buttermilk biscuit sandwich with sausage, scrambled egg and cheddar, a slick of the South's beloved Duke's mayo and tangy pickled banana peppers), a sign by the register invites people to 'pay it forward' by buying a meal 'to add to the hundred free, no-barrier, hot lunches we supply each week to our neighbours in Central City via Bethlehem Lutheran Church's Community Table'.* What a lovely idea, I think, to make it so easy for someone looking forward to a good meal to share this happy feeling with someone else with just a tap of the card.

Wandering back to the main road, admiring the Garden District's large, expensively restored mansions, with their shady porches and generously spreading trees, I reflect how firmly rooted they feel, in contrast to the shacks I saw from the train yesterday, which seemed to sit so lightly upon the watery earth. This area escaped the devastation of Hurricane Katrina relatively lightly, and even the pavements seem more solid; great slabs of stone designed for graceful promenading, rather than narrow concrete afterthoughts in a universe made for motor vehicles.

The boy behind the counter at the Southern Food and Beverage Museum, on the other side of St Charles Avenue, encourages me to *laisser les bons temps rouler* by starting my tour with an absinthe cocktail. I demur, it being only just past noon on a Monday, which proves a good move, because there's so much information stacked

---

* And goes on to explain that 'BLC is an historically Black, antiracist, pro-choice, LBGTQ celebrating radical church. . . that works to provide hot meals and ADA-accessible housing in the heart of New Orleans.'

higgledy-piggledy in this former market building that, half cut, I wouldn't stand a chance. It's an idiosyncratic warren of treasure, halfway between a museum and a jumble sale with a collection including a display of old moonshine bottles, one of the food-packed St Joseph's altars erected around the city every March to give thanks to the saint for delivering Sicily from a medieval famine, and a picture of Elizabeth Begue, a Bohemian immigrant and restaurateur who served a fifty-course breakfast for $1, including wine, at her eponymous Decatur Street establishment at the turn of the last century. (I'm amazed until I look it up and discover of course that a dollar was worth about thirty-three modern ones back then. Still, fifty courses is not to be sniffed at.)

There's also a whole section on New Orleans' beloved red beans and rice, a dish traditionally made on Mondays, when the cook was busy with laundry and didn't have time to tend to anything more temperamental. In the accompanying video, historian Jessica Harris explains the 'line of red beans' running from the Caribbean to New Orleans. As I'm to learn later, the early American rice industry also relied heavily on the knowledge of enslaved Africans* – but these days beans and rice is a solidly local dish that seems to represent 'a taste of home' for New Orleans folks of all colours and origins. Coming together for that first bowl post-Katrina, one says, felt like 'a communion in church'.

---

* Enslaved people from the Windward Coast, Senegambia and Sierra Leone fetched higher prices in the Lowcountry because of their expertise when it came to creating rice fields and growing and processing the grain. 'All them rice field been nothing but swamp. Slavery people cut canal and dig the ditch . . . All been cleared up for plant rice by slavery people,' as Gabe Lance put it in 1937.

COFFEE BREAK

The Secret to Great Red Beans

- A tablespoon of vegetable oil at the end – Shana T.
- A bay leaf, a little dried basil and a little dried rosemary – Gail S.
- Smoked ham hocks – John H.
- Make them the day before – Dana N.
- A teaspoon of bacon grease – Connie W.
- Add a small can of tomato sauce to every pound of red beans – Mona D.
- Add pickled pigs' tails and some cooking oil at the end – Teara M.
- Don't soak them, rinse and boil them hard, adding water as needed, for a thick intense gravy – Scott I.
- Use an electric pressure cooker – Ellen T.
- A sprinkle of ground cloves and a dab of tomato paste – Kathryn W.
- Mash a cup of the cooked beans, then return them to the pan – Amy M.

As told to the Camellia Bean Blog (which contains many more suggestions, should you wish to experiment).

As I lean in to get a closer look at the golden buttermilk biscuit presented to Popeyes Chicken and Biscuits founder Al Copeland by grateful suppliers, I realise it is pouring with rain outside. Absolutely pelting down and me in full tourist-mode shorts and flip-flops. With only so much time I can fritter away in their second-hand book shop given that I can't carry two volumes of the classic cookbook *Who's Your Mama, Are you Catholic and Can You Make a Roux* all the way to New York, eventually I have to make a dash for it, ending up, after a detour for a collard greens melt at Molly's sister restaurant, Turkey and the Wolf, at the Great American Alligator Museum.

A private collection in an ordinary parade of two-storey Victorian brick shops, it's rather less grand than it sounds, but also a lot more interesting given that I'd forgotten they eat the things round here. After looking at the display of vintage cookbooks and recipe cards (a sign describes the meat as 'lean and when prepared properly . . . delicious'), I ask the lady behind the desk whether these days gator is more of a tourist gimmick, but she assures me I'll find it frozen in just about any grocery store. (A similar question at Avery Island a couple of days later gets the response that it's 'more of a restaurant food – like, if you get a bunch of appetisers for the table, one of them will probably be alligator boudin or something'.) As frozen meat isn't much use to me right now, I pick up a bag of alligator jerky in the gift shop instead.

The rest of the museum is an unexpectedly engaging place – did you know that alligators can eat 20 per cent of their body mass in one sitting, 'which is roughly the same as a 180lb [82kg] person eating a 40lb [18kg] cheeseburger'? I can't help noticing as I go round that the reptiles seem to attract a certain sort of eccentric, like fifty-eight-year-old Mrs Albertine Castell, pictured in 1965 with her fifty-five-year-old alligator house pet Sam, or perhaps the proprietors themselves: 'As you roam the museum you may find yourself wondering more about the strange people that collected all this junk than the actual story of the alligator,' a board near the front says, as if reading my mind. 'It's difficult for us to pinpoint where curiosity caused interest and interest begat obsession. One minute we were picking out a trinket at a Cajun gas station and the next thing we knew we owned the largest collection of alligator salt and pepper shakers in the world . . .' For someone with a weakness for croissant-shaped objects, it's a cautionary tale.

Wandering back to the hostel, avoiding the discarded crawfish shells that litter the pavement like London chicken bones, I think how pleasant it is to be somewhere built on a more human scale, with single-lane roads and terraced housing, rather than enormous lots and huge expressways. I'm just pondering where to go for my Monday red beans and rice when Nicola Miller, a British food writer who spends several months a year in her beloved New Orleans, and who has promised to show me around at some point, texts to warn that a severe storm alert has been issued for this evening. Dashing to the nearest grocery store in the French Quarter (which does indeed stock 'gator filet proudly packed for Cajun country'), passing drinkers dancing wildly in the rain on Bourbon Street, I grab a tin of 'Creole style red beans' and a sachet of microwave rice, plus a pot of banana pudding, and splash home again, jacket over my head. As I sit and eat, watching the rain lash down on Canal Street, I can't help thinking of all the people out there in tents this evening: where do they go when the weather gets bad?

By the next morning the heat has dried the ground as if I'd dreamed the deluge, though the clouds are muggy and low as I cycle, careful to stick to the cracked back roads through colourful rows of narrow wooden shotgun shacks (so called because you could fire a gun right through the front door and out the back), to meet Adele's aunt and uncle at Domilise's Po-boys a couple of blocks from the Mississippi River. Open since 1918, Anne says it's not quite as it was since 'they had to put in all that stainless steel in the kitchen' but still, she allows, it's the kind of place 'where college kids come straight from the airport'. Like beans and rice, the po'boy is clearly a taste of home for Louisianans, just like breakfast tacos for a Texan, or . . . colostrum smoothies for a certain type of Angeleno.

There are only a handful of tables, and all they serve is sandwiches – meatball, hot smoked sausage, catfish, oyster – assembled from the paper sacks of Leidenheimer bread stacked by the door. Why these are known as po'boys is lost to the mists of time, though stories usually involve one kind person or another giving out free dinners to hungry strikers or needy kids. What's not up for debate, from the first bite of crusty, fluffy baguette filled with crisply fried oysters (the most expensive filling on the menu, at $19 – a catfish version is a mere $12.50, an American cheese one $6, but really, why would you?), is the fact that there really is very little to match the pleasure of hot, salty seafood on a soft white loaf.

I notice that despite the Creole mustard that comes as standard my companions both douse theirs liberally in hot sauce – 'You don't have to,' Rob says, pushing the bottle of Tabasco towards me, 'but you really should.' Anne, who grew up here, observes New Orleans loves a strong flavour and Rob confirms that no one in his native Maine can stand their smoky chicory coffee – and when they come to visit, Anne chips in, they can't get over the sweetness of the city's famous beignets either. 'Maine folk are so thrifty too,' she laughs. 'I once caught a girlfriend shaking off the excess sugar into a paper bag for me to keep.'

As well as great sandwiches and hot sauce, they say Louisiana boasts the best fried chicken in the country – though Anne adds a little sadly that she's still never had any to touch the stuff made by the family cook in her childhood. The woman just had the magic touch, she says, and though she still has that same pot, she now uses it for jambalaya: 'It really is a good pot,' she sighs, 'but when we want fried chicken these days, we go to Popeye's: it's just as good as mine, and it's a lot faster.'

I spend the rest of the afternoon riding along the Mississippi in the sweltering humidity, looking out for alligators and worrying about small dogs straying too close to the banks. Ticking off a few more local experiences, I get a purple king-cake-flavour sno-ball of shaved ice at Ike's, where a poodle is licking its chicken version somewhat uncertainly on the deck, catch some live jazz, all brass and swagger, in the courtyard of the Royal Frenchman, and end up at Adolfo's, a Creole Italian joint above a bar, where everything, even seafood (I can almost feel Italians swooning) comes swimming in butter, cream and cheese with a dash of spicy Cajun seasoning on top.

New Orleans is not a place for the faint-hearted, I think, dodging drunks and a barefooted man in talks with police on the walk home – the energy here is quite different to anywhere else I've been so far. It's often described as the Caribbean's most northerly city, and I can see why; time seems to move more slowly, dripping like molasses off a spoon – and though it's as noisy and full of life as any LA or Houston, the melée has a more unpredictable, even slightly anarchic quality, as if everything might erupt into merry chaos at any moment.

As it's too far to cycle, Tabasco generously send a very swish car to whizz me 140 miles back east to Avery Island the next morning. Once on the freeway, I distract myself from the driver's unnerving habit of scrolling on his phone by concentrating on what's outside the window as we head over thick swamp into Cajun country – a Subway promising alligator boudin, a yard sign advertising cracklin', a concealed handgun class taking place near St Mary and a billboard warning that fentanyl makes any party drug deadly. I see floating houses on the edge of Wax Lake and worry what happens if you come out to find an alligator sunning itself on your porch – as we approach Avery Island, I even see something which might be an alligator half submerged in a bayou. It could also be a log, but we're going too fast to tell; unlike on a bike, I can't stop to check.

It's odd to find myself in the place on the bottle: my mental image of Avery Island has much in common with a Bond villain's lair, a tightly guarded tropical oasis of chilli plants and trade secrets several miles out to sea. In reality, it rises above the marshes three miles inland, a dome of rock salt topped by live oak forests and surrounded by bayou, owned by descendants of the same family who bought it as a sugar plantation in 1818, though it wasn't until after the Civil War that things heated up in Iberia Parish.

The hot sauce made there for over 150 years is widely believed to have been the world's first commercial example; an earlier cayenne sauce marketed in Massachusetts is, culinary historians reckon, unlikely to have been hot in the modern sense, and though an Irish settler, Maunsel White, cultivated Tabasco peppers (native to the Mexican state of the same name) in Louisiana several decades before they appeared on Avery Island, there's scant evidence he ever marketed the sauce he's said to have made with them.*

Certainly people were familiar with hot sauces before Edmund McIlhenny, who married into the Avery family, began producing his in 1868 from peppers cultivated on his in-laws' estate. Both British and American nineteenth-century books abound with recipes, and contemporary accounts note West Africans making sauces with the chillies brought across the Atlantic by the Portuguese as early as the seventeenth century. The tradition re-crossed the ocean with enslaved peoples: Swedish naturalist Peter Kalm reports Philadelphians consuming bottled chilli sauce in his 1748 *Travels into North America* and it seems safe to assume these were probably the same 'negroes' he records growing okra in the previous paragraph.

So Black Americans, at the very least, were seasoning their food with chilli condiments long before Tabasco came on the market. Nevertheless, McIlhenny was the first to have the connections, and

---

* Though his family did apparently attempt to do so following his death in the Civil War.

the financial means, to make a commercial success out of the idea, which means I'm now entering hot sauce ground zero in 'America's hot sauce heartland', as Denver Nicks, author of *Hot Sauce Nation*, describes Southern Louisiana. More of the population is employed in hot sauce manufacture here than anywhere else in the country: as well as Tabasco, the state is home to Crystal, Louisiana Brand, Trappey's, Panola and innumerable smaller producers, a concentration encouraged by the chilli-friendly climate and soil and the ready availability of salt underneath the ground in places like Avery Island.

Assuming that these days Avery Island is just a tourist showcase, I spend quite a lot of my tour trying to think how best to phrase the question, 'No, but where is Tabasco REALLY made?' Finally I just come out with it, and am informed that they produce the equivalent of 750,000 of those little bottles a day right here. 'In our day shift today, we'll make more bottles than my great-great-great-grandfather Edmund McIlhenny, made in his entire life,' John Simmons tells me in the bottling plant. So, I pause, every single bottle of Tabasco I have *ever seen*, from the dried-up one at the back of my parents' cupboard to the ones on the table at the barbecue goat restaurant I ate at in Nairobi, all started life here? 'Correct,' John says. I'm dumbfounded. (Call me cynical, but I still google it on the way home; if he's not telling the truth the Big Sauce cover up goes deep.)

The peppers, however, are now largely grown abroad; they plant about ten acres of seed stock on the island every year to send to growers in seven different countries, all in Central and South America, apart from one outpost, 'the president's brother grows them for us in Zimbabwe'. Though it's no doubt cheaper, these hotter climates also yield two or three crops a year, rather than the one possible in Louisiana, while the geographic spread acts as an insurance policy against natural disaster: Anne has already mentioned the levees the family built around the factory after two hurricanes brought the water rather too close for comfort. It gives the blenders more options to play with too, given that drier regions, like southern Africa, produce hotter fruit than wetter ones like Nicaragua.

Thanks to a chance remark over taco salad in Berkeley, I'm lucky enough to be getting a much more thorough look behind the scenes than your average visitor. Lisa, my guide, starts by taking me to a greenhouse of chilli plants and picks a couple for me; the reddest is small, no longer than my thumbnail, hot and when I take a cautious bite, surprisingly sweet – in fact, the only thing it has in common with the sauce on my shelf at home is a lingering fruitiness. The transformation starts when the freshly harvested chillies are ground with salt (a preservative) on the day of picking. The resulting paste is shipped to Avery Island in 50,000lb (22,679kg) batches: 'Zimbabwe peppers can take three and a half months to reach us, Central America just a week,' warehouse manager Stefan explains.

Once it arrives on site it's pumped into barrels and hand sealed, though each barrel is fitted with a one-way valve to release the gases given off as the contents begin to break down. 'When it's hot, they tend to ferment really aggressively,' Stefan continues, 'so we don't put them in the stacks right away, because those valves can pop right off.' His raised eyebrows suggest exploding chilli paste is not something to be taken lightly.

He leads me into a vast airy warehouse stacked five-high with oak whiskey casks. In the middle sits a long line of barrels with what looks like snow on top (a surprise given I'm perspiring just standing still), though when I stretch a tentative hand out to touch it, I find instead a dry, solid crust of salt. We peer into a freshly filled barrel, which he says contains peppers from Peru: 'There's maybe thirty-five farmers' work in here.' Another one, from Colombia, is four years old, significantly less full, and the paste is a much darker red, almost brown on top.

Though I'm trying hard not to breathe too deeply lest I sneeze all over someone's future breakfast seasoning, I'm then presented with a ceremonial tasting spoon, and invited to help myself, with the caveat that the mash is ten times hotter than the sauce itself, which is diluted with vinegar. My heart begins to skitter before I've even put out my tongue to take a tentative lick. It's a slow burn but then it hits me, and my eyes sting; an almost grassy heat, keen and piquant. Delicious actually, I say before I'm overtaken by a coughing fit. 'Trust me, even if you taste this stuff every day, it gets you every single time. You never get used to it,' Stefan laughs, taking a scoop from the second barrel. The older stuff is smokier, more savoury – but yes, just as hot.

The barrels of mash are aged for at least three years in warehouses the size of football fields, stacked by country and year and festooned with a gothic lace of cobwebs. Spiders apparently help keep other insects at bay, but I shudder to think of what must scuttle out as the 2021 barrels are moved out to make room for this year's batch. It's not only the thought of spiders that's making me sweat: 'Yep, second week of May, it's like someone turned the volume up on the weather,' Lisa says with apparent satisfaction, 'regular as clockwork.'

Once it's done its time, the fermented chilli paste is disgorged into huge spinning vats where mash, typically from several different countries to ensure consistency, is churned with vinegar for about three weeks straight to homogenise it. I peer into the fiery depths of mixing sauce tank no. 43 and imagine falling in; even the air in here is hard to breathe, the hot pepper of the warehouse replaced by a sharp acidity, which Nuk, the blending manager, claims not to notice: 'I've been here that long it's just air to me,' he says cheerfully, 'sweet as outside.' The solid skin and seeds are strained out (also for sale as a dry rub in the nearby shop; nothing, it seems, goes to waste that can be turned to profit), each batch is lab tested, and then at least three years after those wee red peppers were picked, the finished sauce is finally ready for bottling.

The little bottles currently rattling along the conveyor belt, and the even smaller ones found on Air Force One (and, for many years, in US army ration packs as I know from the Seabee Museum), will be sent out to 195 countries and territories around the world – Japan, to my surprise, is, John says, 'by far and away our biggest export market, but we ship a lot to Western Europe too and Saudi Arabia.' Tabasco Original is available at the US base in Antarctica (you'll find a lot of anxious Americans asking about this on Reddit before shipping out) and on the International Space Station – the final frontier might be trying to convince the rest of the world that it belongs on pizza. 'It's the single greatest host food for Tabasco, I'm not joking,' John tells me earnestly, when I admit I've never even thought of combining the two. 'It's the fat in the cheese, it just cuts right through. You need to spread the word.'

There's no pizza for lunch, but a feast of local cooking with more of the staff: egg rolls stuffed with boudin,* deep-fried pickles, bayou crabcake with crawfish étouffée – a rich, spicy roux-thick-ened stew – a bowl of gumbo and another of red beans and rice . . . plus, of course, a carousel of six different types of Tabasco to season them all. The conversation around the table touches on the differences between the local Cajun† cooking, and the Creole tradi-tions that Amanda, who has travelled out from their offices in New Orleans, grew up with.

'Where I'm from in Lafayette,' Megan says, 'we're known for sausage and chicken gumbo . . . Okra only goes in seafood gumbo.' Lisa politely disagrees, but then points out sadly that people, particularly in restaurants, don't know how to cook okra these days. 'My grandma, she used to grow it, then she'd stew it down with onions to get rid of the slime, then put it up in cans ready to use in gumbo. A lot of folks, they just chuck it in.' A New Iberia

---

* The beloved Cajun pork, pepper and rice sausage.
† According to Molly Cleaver, editor of the *Historic New Orleans Collection Quarterly*, 'common understanding holds that Cajuns are white and Creoles are Black or mixed race; Creoles are from New Orleans, while Cajuns popu-late the rural parts of South Louisiana. In fact, the two cultures are far more related – historically, geographically, and genealogically – than most people realise.'

gumbo never contains tomatoes, she goes on, while over in New Orleans, gumbo is *red* – 'But my family don't put a whole bunch in,' Amanda cuts in, 'it's like with red beans and rice, everyone makes it their own way . . . And then you go out to a restaurant and they put some random thing like pork chops or fried chicken with it!'

They will agree that Cajun cooking is country food; 'Creole I think of as city food,' Lisa says. 'Creole is more tomatoes,' Amanda chips in. 'Even the food here is different from the food in Lafayette,' Megan muses. 'I'd say down here it's more Spanish-Cajun, while we're more French-Cajun.'

So many hyphens, so many different influences and diverse traditions, I think, in a land popularly supposed to have no real food culture. The one thing these women all have in common, however, is a tradition of hunting and fishing for food – deer, duck, catfish – and the importance of gravy and rice. Pure comfort food, the taste of home: 'Sometimes you don't even know what kind you want,' Lisa says, 'you just want gravy and rice.' There's a murmur of happy agreement from around the table; city or country, Cajun or Creole, down here they're all rice and gravy people.

EULA MAE'S SAUSAGE AND SHRIMP GUMBO

Thanks to the McIlhenny Company for the permission to use this recipe

Eula Mae Dore worked for McIlhenny Company on Avery Island for fifty-seven years, running the general store with her husband Walter, and selling lunch to workers in the pepper fields and factory. Her po'boys and sandwiches were so good she was soon asked to cater for the company and family's special events and for visiting VIPs: not bad for a girl who left school at the age of ten to take care of her family after the death of her mother, who learned her Cajun repertoire from her grandmother, never trained professionally and famously never followed a recipe.

This gumbo, which was a favourite of Walter McIlhenny, President of McIlhenny Company from 1949 to1985, is taken from Eula Mae's Cajun Kitchen *cookbook (Harvard Common Press, 2015), a collaboration with Marcelle R. Bienvenu, food columnist for* The Times-Picayune, *who worked with her to distil a lifetime of wisdom onto the page. Because it's so heavy, gumbo is usually served with rice as a main course, but Eula Mae recalled, when he had dinner parties, Mr Walter often served it to start.*

(Note that andouille here is not the French chitterlings sausage, but the Cajun version, a coarse smoked pork sausage, which is well-nigh impossible to find overseas. I used Polish kielbasa, but French saucisse de morteau would also make a fine substitute.)

Serves 8

½ tsp TABASCO® Brand Original Red Sauce
2 tbsp vegetable oil
1 pound/450g andouille (or other spicy smoked sausage), cut crosswise into ¼-inch/6mm-thick slices
2 tbsp all-purpose/plain flour
½ cup chopped yellow onions (½ onion)
½ cup seeded and chopped green bell peppers (½ green pepper)
1 clove of garlic, minced
2 cups/500ml chicken broth/stock
2 cups/160g sliced fresh okra or one (10-ounce/285g) package frozen sliced okra, thawed
½ tsp salt, or more to taste
½ tsp cayenne, or more to taste
2 bay leaves
1 pound/450g medium-size shrimp/raw prawns, peeled and deveined
¼ cup/25g chopped green/spring onions (green part only)
Hot cooked long-grain white rice

Heat 1 tablespoon of the oil in a large skillet over medium-high heat. Add the sausage and cook, stirring frequently, for 5 minutes.

Remove the sausage with a slotted spoon and set aside. Heat the remaining 1 tablespoon oil in the same skillet over medium-high heat. Stir in the flour and cook, stirring constantly, until the roux is light brown, about 2 minutes. Add the onions, bell peppers, and garlic, and cook, stirring frequently, until soft, about 5 minutes. Gradually stir in the broth and blend until smooth. Bring to a boil. Add the sausage, okra, salt, cayenne, TABASCO® Sauce, and bay leaves, cover, reduce the heat to medium-low, and simmer for 20 minutes. Stir in the shrimp and green onions and simmer until the shrimp turn pink, about 5 minutes. Remove the bay leaves and serve in soup bowls over rice.

To be honest, after a sampling of Tabasco ice cream (surprisingly good) in the Avery Island Country Store, I don't want any kind of food for at least a week but I travel back to the city in style with a box of boudin and some fried pickles, plus a miniature bottle of Tabasco for future emergencies in the frozen north, where hot sauce might be less readily available. The idea of the frozen north is actually quite pleasant now I think about it – right now I can't ever imagine being either cold, or even mildly peckish again.

Ridden: 29 miles
Climbed: 79 feet
Pies consumed: 1 (the city's beloved Hubig's hand pie in lemon flavour, damp, plain, oddly addictive soft pastry, acid-yellow gloopy filling 7/10 – New Orleans does not seem to be big pie country)
All-American foods discovered: breakfast biscuits, collard greens, alligator jerky, red beans and rice, banana pudding, po'boys, sno-balls, Italian-Creole pasta, fried pickles, boudin balls, étouffée, hot sauce ice cream

8

AN INVOLUNTARY VOODOO FUNERAL

In search of Creole cooking

'There are a lot of places I like, but I like New Orleans better.'
Bob Dylan

By lunchtime the next day, I'm back in business – and when I say lunchtime, I mean 11am when the legendary Dooky Chase's opens its doors to diners. Nicola Miller, the friend who sent the storm warning earlier in the week, is already waiting outside, chatting to a teacher accompanying a small group of smartly dressed middle-school girls, on their first visit to 'a proper restaurant', a chance, she says, for them to learn 'etiquette and deportment'. Though I'm agnostic as to the value of such things, we agree it's empowering to at least know the rules, whether or not you choose to follow them; 'This is not the environment they're raised in,' Miss Cherry says, 'and let me tell you, they're excited to be here.'

Dooky's is indeed very proper, as befits the first fine-dining restaurant in the city run by,* and largely for, Black people, a Mecca for musicians like Duke Ellington and Ray Charles (who name-checks it in a song, 'Early in the Morning'), permitted to play the city's segregated venues, but not eat in them, and which famously welcomed Civil Rights leaders including Martin Luther King and Thurgood Marshall, to hold court in their upstairs room. This was one of the few places in New Orleans where Black and white activists could convene, in open contravention of Jim Crow laws – 'It was a meeting place, and if a person needed to see someone in the Black community, they'd come here, because this was where everyone met,' its late chef Leah Chase recalled.

The daughter-in-law of the founders, Edgar 'Dooky' and Emily Chase, it was Leah and her husband, musician Edgar 'Dooky' Jr, who turned the business from a cafe to the art-filled, white-tablecloth joint it is today. And though she died in 2019, Miss Leah's standards are kept up: the bosomy ladies behind us in strapless dresses are told they'll need to cover their shoulders with something or go elsewhere: 'This is a family restaurant.'

Leah was determined to elevate traditional dishes like fried chicken and Creole gumbo z'herbes, which she felt were undervalued by diners and cooks alike. She told the Southern Foodways Alliance in 2014 that for many years, the city's white restaurants didn't even have such things on the menu, and part of the reason, she speculated, was that Black people 'did not put any value on what they had or what they did, particularly their food. They didn't.' Judging by the queue outside, and the photos

---

* Most, if not all, segregated establishments were more than happy to let Black people do the work in the kitchen – Sherman Crayton, who began cooking at Arnaud's in 1936, observed, though Creole food was claimed to be a mixture of Spanish and French influence, 'The only people who seem to know all about it are neither Spanish nor French, they're Blacks.'

of Barack Obama, Beyoncé and Jay-Z on the wall, her efforts were not in vain.

Nicola and I order a mint julep apiece (well, it's almost noon), and I let her take control of the menu: Creole gumbo, much thinner than the Cajun version of the same beloved meat and seafood stew yesterday, and a fat ice-cream scoop of potato salad (many people dip it in the gumbo, she tells me, but I can't bear to spoil the latter's silky elegance); superlative fried chicken – ridiculously crunchy, warmly spiced rather than hot – with stewed okra and mustard greens, then pecan pie and peach cobbler. The pie is interesting as well as delicious: the filling in two parts, a sweet, caramel jelly below, whole nuts on top, in a rich, salty, flaky crust (9/10).

It's sweltering when we come out blinking into the daylight, but Nicola says she has somewhere she wants to show me, so we set off on foot up Orleans Avenue and through Louis Armstrong Park, ending up outside a green-painted shed with a large wooden alligator affixed to the base offering GUMBO FILÉ. Less dramatic signs above identify it as the Calas Cafe, a 'Community Based Small Business' and centre for 'Equitable Economic Development: Tremé Neighbourhood'. A couple of small tables sit on the sidewalk.

Despite the alligator's claims, this place actually deals in calas, sweet rice fritters with their roots in West African cuisine, once a popular New Orleans street food. We put in an order with the sleepy teenager who pops up in the window when I peer in, and just as we sit down, Nicola gives a shout of joy. 'He's here! I was hoping he would be – hey! Brandon!' A handsome man in a crisp white shirt and patterned trousers, braids piled on top of his head, bounds over, arms outstretched – this, Nicola tells me as they embrace, is the cafe's owner, and local food security activist, Brandon Pellerin. He pulls up a third chair, explaining that the little golden globes in front of us, dusted heavily with powdered sugar, were at risk of extinction – 'and I couldn't let them fall through the cracks. When the elders die, their recipes die with them. Go on, try one!'

I take a bite: they're like sweetly spiced arancini, rich and soft, aromatic with nutmeg and vanilla. He says that sometimes that first taste makes people cry, 'because their mothers used to make them, their aunt used to make them, and when they passed, they didn't leave the recipe. I had one woman, she came up to me and said, "I haven't had one of these for forty years, I've been searching all over, and then I found you."' Another example of food as home, I think: a sense of belonging to a community, to New Orleans, but perhaps also a connection to an older home, sparked by something so simple, yet clearly so evocative.

His own grandmother, Brandon says, made calas, but at the time he didn't realise their significance to the Black community; the opportunity they represented for Black women in particular to make money by using their daily rice as a path to economic freedom. Tremé, he explains, is the oldest Black neighbourhood in the country, and he wanted to serve his community, 'this neighbourhood of free people of colour', by giving them calas back.

There are grand plans to open a bricks-and-mortar cafe – he shows us the plans on his phone – 'to represent the West Africans who are not represented in the city's history, who built the French Quarter. This history belongs to all Louisianans, and it's been stolen from them' – but he says bitterly, though everyone at City Hall wants to shake his hand and tell him he's doing a great job, so far no one wants to actually back that up with an investment.

In the meantime, the connections keep him going – he hails passers-by, startled-looking tourists searching for the Jazz Museum, inviting them to come and sit down. They walk on by. He sighs and tells us of the 'seventy-two-year-old woman who was here the other day, she put me in check, she ordered three portions for herself, and I tried to tell her, no, ma'am, you get three calas per portion. Ooooh but she got saucy with me then: "Don't you tell me what I want," she says, "I want one for me, and two for the two ninety-five-year-olds who used to make me calas when I was a little girl."' He chuckles fondly. 'Bridging that cultural diaspora, that's the reward for me.'

DR JESSICA B. HARRIS'S CALAS

Taken with kind permission from The Welcome Table *by Jessica B. Harris (Simon & Schuster, 1995)*
Calas are rice fritters that hark back to the Grain Coast of West Africa. The Vai people of the rice-growing regions of Sierra Leone and Liberia were represented in the Southern slave census. To them, the word for uncooked rice is kala. The word means 'a stalk of cereal' to the Bambara people of West Africa, and for the Gullah people of the South Carolina and Georgia Lowcountry, kala means rice. The fritters were one of the items hawked on the streets of New Orleans by women of colour.

[Note, this makes a lot of calas, so be prepared to cater a party. I used 7g of instant yeast in place of dried yeast. Small balls are better (I used a tablespoon measure, greased to help the batter off it) and cooked them for just over a minute on each side. Keep checking the temperature of the oil as if it gets too hot, or the balls are too big, the outside will burn before the interior cooks through. FC]

Serves 6
540ml/2¼ cups cold water
140g/¾ cup long-grain rice
10½g/1½ packages of dried yeast or 7g instant yeast
120ml/½ cup lukewarm water

4 eggs, well beaten
175g/¾ cup caster/superfine sugar
¾ tsp salt
405g/3 cups plain/all-purpose flour
Vegetable oil, for frying
Icing/confectioners' sugar, for dusting

1. Place the cold water and rice in a saucepan and bring to the boil over a high heat. Lower the heat and cook the rice for 25 to 30 minutes, or until it is soft and tender. Drain the rice, place it in a bowl, mash it with the back of a spoon, and set it aside to cool.
2. In a separate bowl, dissolve the yeast in the lukewarm water, and then add it to the cooled rice. Beat the mixture for 2 minutes to aerate it, then cover the bowl with a slightly moistened towel and set it aside in a warm place to rise for 3 to 4 hours.
3. When ready to prepare the fritters, add the eggs, sugar, salt and flour to the rice mixture. Beat it thoroughly, cover it, and set it aside for 30 minutes. Heat 10cm/4 inches of oil in a heavy pan to 190°C/375°F.
4. Drop the batter by the tablespoonful into the hot oil, frying a few at a time until golden brown. Drain on paper towels, then dust with icing/confectioners' sugar and serve hot.

I leave Nicola, promising to come and find her and her husband Ed in their favourite bar later, and go back to the hostel to pick up my stuff. For some reason the Big Easy has proven more of a draw than rural Texas, and not one but two people called Claire* are joining

---

* A popular name in the Commonwealth in the first half of the 1980s, it seems – another one, a Kiwi, is looking after my flat.

me for the weekend. The first lands tonight, and has refused to stay in a youth hostel. Annoyingly, as she's just announced she's three months pregnant, I have to let her have her way.

Luggage, and Eddy, transferred to a modest hotel in the French Quarter, I join Nicola and Ed propping up the bar at the Golden Lantern between a man eating a takeaway and reading a book, and a very tall, glamorous lady in silk gloves nursing a huge cut-glass goblet of red wine. There's a vodka-heavy bloody Mary waiting for me, festooned with so much garnish I can hardly cram the straw in – it's the most salad I've had in days and barman Greg keeps popping in another pickle when I'm not looking, and then leaning over and fondly wiping pickle juice behind Ed's ear. I can't help feeling I've arrived a bit late to the party. A hen do waltzes in, raucous and shrieking excitedly, asking when the drag show starts, and Nicola leans over and quietly tells me Greg is a master of politely managing such noisy customers out after one drink.

I suggest heading over to meet Preggo Claire – a woman who used to commission me on such hard-hitting journalistic assignments as interrogating a man who could send rabbits into a trance (yes, the headline was 'The Hopnotist'), and putting together a height chart of the royal family – before I fall off my stool. She's waiting for us at a Haitian restaurant called Fritai, and her increasingly irate messages suggest the claim we're 'just round the corner' is wearing thin.

The links between these two former French colonies run deep – many Haitians fleeing the revolution at the turn of the nineteenth century ended up here. Their influence is, it's said, everywhere, but all I know about the island's food is that they're also fond of rice and beans, so I order the sos pwa black bean plate with rice, fried plantains and double cooked goat. The portions are enormous; hearty and starchy, brought to life with zingy sauces reminiscent of undiluted Tabasco peppers. No doubt there are connections to be made there too, but I'm far too full and sleepy to explore the idea further.

Finally the Southern heat has someone to appreciate it: Claire, a lizard in human form, steps out of the hotel air-conditioning the next morning and sighs happily at the muggy air. She's also very taken with New Orleans' cat population; I keep losing her to animals drowsing on porches, or winding their way through wooden fences to greet a kindred spirit.

Otherwise we have a somewhat dispiriting day – everything I'd planned, from the Beanlandia HQ of the Red Beans Mardi Gras Krewe to the smothered turkey necks and fried green tomatoes at Cafe Reconcile, is closed when it should be open (the French legacy is strong apparently), and we end up running from the rain into the greasy embrace of Popeye's Chicken and Biscuits, a chain founded on the outskirts of New Orleans that's been on my radar since Anne mentioned it approvingly a few days ago.

The Saint Charles Avenue branch is as defiantly disorganised as I'm coming to expect from New Orleans – though the juicy exchange of gossip among those waiting around in their pyjamas and sliders more than makes up for the unhurried service – but we agree the fried chicken is very decent, with a solid, crunchy crust and juicy meat, if only passingly spicy. The Cajun rice tastes satisfyingly like something well acquainted with gizzards, while the mac and cheese's chief distinguishing quality is that it is extremely yellow: I suspect the dread hand of American cheese.

COFFEE BREAK
American Cheese

Native Americans do not seem to have consumed any dairy whatsoever prior to colonisation, so the cheeses made in the US all reflect the tastes and expertise of different immigrant groups, from cheddar style to Mexican queso fresco. Artisan cheesemaking has experienced a revival in recent years: in 2019 Oregon's Rogue River Blue became the first American cheese to be crowned champion at the World Cheese Awards . . . but of course, all most foreigners think of when they hear the words American cheese are those plasticky orange slices.

Though the first processed cheese was developed in Switzerland, the Kraft brothers, Canadian immigrants of German-Mennonite heritage, patented a process in 1916 to extend the shelf-life of the cheese they sold to Chicago merchants by melting it and stirring it into a homogenous mass (emulsifying salts, colouring and other ingredients are more recent additions). Initially marketed in tins to customers like the US Army, it took fifteen years to perfect the individual slices we know today, which finally hit the market in 1950. This ultra-processed cheese now comes in various flavours, but frankly, the flavour is less important than its ability to melt into a smooth gloop – a quality much prized by cheeseburger and grilled cheese fans. As the food writer J. Kenji Lopez Alt writes, 'No other cheese in the world can touch its meltability or goo factor, and that's really what it's there for: texture.' Which is lucky, given how it tastes.

Claire #2, a London-based Australian who never misses the chance to slag off British coffee, finally arrives fresh, if not satisfactorily caffeinated, from her work trip to Minnesota just before midnight, ready for a weekend exploring the fancier side of New Orleans dining – she's not really a Popeye's kind of person. (This is a woman so grand she refuses to take ordinary Ubers after a driver we have the next morning tells us a funny story about trying to run over pedestrians in the middle of the road.)

We kick off with Saturday brunch at Brennan's, a name that often appears in close proximity to the word iconic. Today it's full of wealthy-looking couples talking over their distinctly peaky-looking offspring; Tulane University, a local private college, is graduating this weekend, and many of the younger generation appear to have taken last night's celebrations seriously. We watch one boy focus so hard on lifting his trembling fork to his mouth that his mother scolds him for not paying attention to the conversation, and later I hear someone being ever so discreetly sick in the elegant pink and green 'ladies room'.

I'll be honest, Brennan's is not the kind of menu I would be able to look in the face with a hangover; the chief ingredient seems to be butter and I am ever so charmingly upsold fried oysters with my eggs Sardou (crispy artichokes, Parmesan creamed spinach and Choron sauce, a kind of béarnaise with tomato) – because 'everyone says they go PHENOMENALLY together'. I'm reminded of the haggis Benedict I thought I might regret after a night on the sauce in St Andrews; it should be too much on one plate, but somehow, probably because everything here feels a bit over the top, it just about gets away with it.

The main event, however, is the 'world-famous bananas Foster', a dish of dramatically flambéed fruit invented at the restaurant, and ordered by perhaps 70 per cent of tables during our visit. By the time the white-jacketed Keith Floyd-a-like on flambé duty wheels his little trolley over to set fire to some rum on our behalf, we've already heard his spiel several times, but nevertheless, it's interesting to see just how much butter and sugar goes into the pan, even if I'd personally take the caramelisation a little further – the bananas, when they arrive in an ocean of buttery syrup, still have the pasty hue of my upper arms.

After breakfast at Brennan's the only way is down, and we bump heavily back to earth with a sobering visit to the Louisiana Museum, whose entire ground floor is devoted to an exhibit on Hurricane Katrina and its ongoing legacy. US government military rations sit in glass cases – menu no.18: Cajun rice, beans, sausage – with Red Cross canned water for the five and a half weeks it took to restore supply; accompanying photos show community kitchens welcoming residents home with free meals. Later in Angelo Brocato, a gelateria and pastry shop established by Sicilian immigrants way back in 1905, I notice a little brass plaque halfway up the door, well above the handle, marking the water level in the aftermath of Katrina, just two months after the shop reopened following its centenary refit. It took a year to repair the damage.

Grand Claire is delighted to be heading to the Garden District this evening for dinner: apparently gracious mansions and wide streets are more her style than the noisy revelry of the French Quarter, which, beautiful as it is, smells faintly of regret no matter what time of day you hit it.

Our destination, the venerable Commander's Palace, has the Victorian fretwork of a British railway station, but the interior is more like the Tardis – we're led through a dizzying sequence of rooms, up hill and down dale, passed from person to person like self-conscious parcels as staff pause to greet us as we pass, until at last we end up in a vast, low-ceilinged hall at the back with full-length windows and the cavernously festive atmosphere of a Chinese banquet restaurant.

The service is an odd, and very American, mix of effusively friendly and impatient – when, after our starters, already worrying about the desserts that need to be ordered in advance, we ask to see the menu again the waiter instead reels off everything on offer in a rapid list – the menu itself would apparently 'overwhelm' us ladies. I feel like saying I'd like to see a sheet of A3 try, but I don't want him to take revenge on my sherry-heavy turtle soup; I feel bad enough about it already after seeing the turtles trying to escape the pond behind Brennan's this morning.

Once so widely beloved that, until the 1950s, even Campbell's and Heinz sold the stuff, turtle soup is often said to have fallen foul of the same trend that took offal, blood and even lamb off the mainstream American menu. Also relevant, no doubt, is the fact that local turtles were eaten almost to extinction, and their hunting season is now strictly controlled. According to local restaurant critic Tom Fitzmorris, 'for decades the Commander's Palace has used as much veal shoulder as it does turtle meat in its highly-acclaimed soup' – and though pleasant enough in a rich, Frenchified way, I'm more of a fan of the smoky, dark gumbo the Claires both get, and the solid wedge of Creole cheesecake we share afterwards. The waiter, more obliging now the time for tipping is approaching, informs us the cake's manufacture is a six-day process, because they make the Creole cream cheese, a soft, tart, old-fashioned local speciality containing buttermilk as well as cream, themselves – 'and we're one of only two places to do that'.

As we wait for our luxury cab, Grand Claire points out the restaurant security guard, as wide as he is tall, packing not one but two guns on his belt. It's easy to forget that, though New Orleans may have pavements, and decent coffee, it's still very much America.

The next morning, as she packs up before an early Monday departure for London my regal friend presents me with a pack of cooling towels she's brought with her from home after anxiously monitoring my partial breakdown in Texas from a safe distance. 'I know I *said* you weren't going to die,' she says doubtfully, 'but actually I don't trust you.'

I'm tempted to put one on for our architectural tour of the muggy Garden District (guess who suggested that one), which happens, to my delight, to be led by an actual Kentucky Colonel. Despite not being a native Louisianan, he does have good intel on Sandra Bullock's tasteful grey house, with its Hansel and Gretel woodwork (I can exclusively reveal her hedge could do with a trim), and local burial customs,* but I'm mostly interested in his own history, which he dismisses with a wave of the hand – 'Oh, the colonel thing don't really mean much of anything, just that your daddy went to the senator or whoever and petitioned them for it.' I tell him it's cool. 'Well,' he sighs sceptically, 'it is something, I guess.' (I can't help noting that he pronounces this last word *guy-yesss*, which I find very charming.)

The good Lord giveth and taketh away: having had some of the best ice cream of my life at the Creole Creamery, including a delicate magnolia blossom whose elusive flavour haunts me for weeks, the Claires gang up and make me order a 'Blue Bayou' frozen daiquiri. A foot-long pipe of neon blue slush, ending in a skull and emblazoned with the words VOODOO FUNERAL, the mere act of holding it in public gives me both nascent frostbite and hot flushes of shame, and when we go into Napoleon House for dinner, I abandon it discreetly by a bin. Ninety minutes later, after muffaletta (so much meat! In one sandwich!), jambalaya, gumbo,

---

* Bodies are placed on shelves in free-standing vaults, which act as solar-powered furnaces: after a year and a day, the vault is opened and the desiccated remains tidily stowed in drawers.

red beans and cannoli, I come out to find a circle of condensation where the plastic skull once stood. 'Shame,' Claire #1 says as we stand wondering if it's been tidied up by a garbage truck or a thirsty passer by. 'We could get you another one?'

I sidestep the offer as firmly as her suggestion that we order three rounds of beignets for breakfast the next morning – these square fritters, not so much dusted with icing sugar as buried in it, are the size of Post-it notes, come in portions of three, and I've already spotted a slender Japanese couple sitting unhappily in front of the very same mistake. They're fine, if a bit chewy, but honestly, I prefer Brandon's calas.

Having offloaded all her business-class miniatures on to me, and scooped up the extra clothes she kindly brought out with her so I wouldn't embarrass her in public – 'or not fashion wise anyway' – Queen Claire is away to the airport in a sleek black SUV and to her very important job, leaving me and old Bun-in-the Oven to make our way to the station by Shanks's Pony.

As she's selfishly refusing to cycle her miniature (non-existent, she'd claim) bump through the sweltering Mississippi Delta, we board a train to Memphis, an eight-and-a-half-hour journey during which we competitively fail to spot any alligators, competitively eat Cajun crawfish crisps, and fall out spectacularly over a particularly weak game of travel Scrabble. Looking at the board after tipping it back into the bag, I notice a somewhat dispiriting vibe: 'sore', 'laden', 'rash', 'ailment' and . . . 'doofus'.

No wonder we're both in a bad mood by the time we finally get to Memphis at half past ten and find the hotel reception deserted. After fifteen minutes, someone finally appears, wiping his hands on his trousers. 'Sorry, I was in the bathroom,' he says cheerily. Claire, I notice, is glowering rather than glowing.

'Let's eat breakfast out tomorrow,' I say in the lift.

Ridden: 0 miles
Climbed: 0 feet
Pies consumed: 1 (pecan)
All-American foods discovered: fried chicken, stewed okra and mustard greens, peach cobbler, calas, dirty rice, eggs sardou, bananas foster, turtle soup, Creole cheesecake, jambalaya, muffuletta, beignets

9

CALL THAT HOT CHICKEN?

In search of finger-lickin' Southern cookin'

'You can't go wrong with fried chicken.'
Dolly Parton*

Memphis, or at least the area by the railway station, feels half abandoned this bright May Tuesday morning, the wide roads, lined with single-storey Victorian shopfronts, as empty as anything from a Hollywood western. I half expect some tumbleweed to blow down the middle as we cross from the hotel to the Arcade Restaurant. Opened in 1919 by Greek immigrants, it claims to have been a favourite haunt of the city's most famous son, and backs this up with a dedicated Elvis booth, which is, of course, already occupied, despite the rest of the place being pretty much deserted.

---

* The country legend reckons good batter was the secret of her long and happy marriage; she puts extra pepper in hers.

However hard we stare out the couple hogging the best seats in the house, they fail to move – and, unlike us, they're not even eating the sacred fried peanut butter and banana sandwich, which comes with truly excellent fries, salty enough to bring on a coronary and as crisp as the King's famous quiff, so they're clearly not true fans. If I'm honest, though I like his music, neither am I: I'm more interested in stories like Elvis flying his private jet two hours to Denver, Colorado to eat $49.95* fool's gold sandwiches, whole loaves of margarine-rubbed French bread stuffed with peanut butter, fried bacon and blueberry jam, in an aircraft hanger in the middle of the night, washed down with champagne and Perrier, than I am in his lesser-known B-sides.

We'll be travelling in slightly less style in a minivan, motor transport being the only way of getting from Memphis to Nashville as Claire refuses to countenance jumping on the back of my bike, and this being the smallest vehicle on offer at the car rental place. Though my interest in Tennessee is largely chicken-shaped with a side of barbecue, I yield to her request to visit Graceland en route, despite the fact that tickets are now $82 per person, considerably more than I remember them being when I first came here two decades ago.

You get more bang for your many bucks these days, to be fair; the visitor complex is new, as is the little minibus that ferries us across the main road to the house (for a tip), but the lush green shagpile of the jungle room is just as I remember it. I'd forgotten the kitchen though. With its TGI Fridays-style Tiffany lightshade, 70s dark wood cabinets, massive microwave and avocado accents, it's reminiscent of kitchens of my childhood, which is, I suppose, unsurprising given Britain is always at least ten years behind.

---

* $270 in today's money.

COFFEE BREAK

The King's Kitchen Cupboards

Graceland had a cook on duty twenty-four hours a day in case Elvis or his family or entourage felt hungry. Meals, according to the signboard, were 'simple southern cooking . . . Steaks, pork chops, meatloaf or fried chicken. And, of course, lots of cheeseburgers. Elvis loved homemade banana pudding [so] that was always available.'

I find the following list of items Elvis insisted on keeping in stock in a book entitled *Fit for a King: The Elvis Presley Cookbook*, in Nashville Public Library:

Fresh, lean, unfrozen ground meat
One case regular Pepsi
One case orange drinks
Rolls (hot rolls – Brown 'n' Serve)
Cans of biscuits (at least six)
Hamburger buns
Pickles
Potatoes and onions
Assorted fresh fruit
Cans of sauerkraut
Wieners
At least three bottles of milk, including half & half
Thin, lean bacon
Mustard
Peanut butter

Fresh, hand-squeezed cold orange juice
Banana pudding (to be made each night)
Ingredients for meat loaf and sauce
Brownies
Ice cream – vanilla and chocolate
Shredded coconut
Fudge cookies
Gum (Spearmint, Doublemint, Juicy Fruit – three of each)

The eight dining options at Graceland, including Vernon's Smoke-house and the Shake, Rattle & Go coffee shop, are not, let us say, universally fêted on review sites, so on the way out of town, we make a stop at Cozy Corner BBQ. Sandwiched between the Friend-ship Church of the Nazarene and the Island Community Church, the rust-flecked sign looks like it's been deliberately aged to add character but I suspect has just been there since the place opened in 1977. Now run by the founder's grandson, Bobby Bradley Jr, Cozy's sells everything from whole Cornish game hens to bologna sand-wiches, but its speciality is spare ribs. 'If somebody walks in the door and they see an "out of ribs" sign their composure completely changes, the look on their face changes, they get sad, it's not a fun thing to see,' Bradley told Eater in 2023. His grandmother, Desiree Robinson, came out of retirement to take the helm after her husband's death in 2001 – and in 2020 became the first Black woman to be inducted into the Barbecue Hall of Fame at the age of eighty-three. She's still only 'semi-retired'.

Memphis is known for its barbecue pork, served either dry (rubbed with a seasoning mix) or wet (brushed with sauce after-wards). At the Cozy, their famous ribs are trimmed, sprinkled with a 'very secret' dry rub, marinated overnight, and then browned on both sides in unusual two-tier 'pits' before being moved up to racks to gently smoke until service; sauce is available, but optional. We request a slab for two with hot sauce, plus sides of coleslaw, clove-spiked baked beans, corn on the cob and, because neither of us can work out how you'd smoke pasta without it falling through the grill, a pot of barbecue spaghetti. The order also comes with four slices of plain white bread, though we're more focused on the tender, juicy meat, which slips from the bone so easily we're soon confronted by the evidence of our gluttony: a pile of pearly clean ribs.

The sides, however, remain more or less intact, as they're all overwhelmingly sweet, particularly the gummy spaghetti tossed with barbecue sauce, which, with the best will in the world, I can't recommend. The desserts, though, are worth leaving room for: particularly the gently nutmeg-scented sweet potato pie (9/10), which, with its sturdy, plain crust, still manages to be less sweet than the baked beans.

I can't help but notice, as we attempt to wipe sticky sauce from our hands, arms and faces with hopelessly flimsy napkins before resorting to the far more effective untouched bread, that the two men at the table behind us, who have been apparently conducting a business meeting over barbecue, now have their heads bowed in prayer: 'Oh, Jesus, save us!' the older one begins, hands clasped to the heavens. Although a banner over the wood-laminate lined dining room thanks God for the Cozy Corner's longevity, it still feels a very intimate thing to witness.

Less holy: Claire's Americana playlist, which she breaks out on the very boring freeway to Nashville – why talk when you can sing along to the Backstreet Boys?

We haven't been in Music City five minutes before a bachelorette party spills into the road in front of us – Broadway is like the Black-pool Illuminations with sunshine, a shrieking, swaying mass moving from gift shop to honky-tonk bar, Boot Barn to Jimmy

Buffet's Margaritaville. Pushing through the shrieking, hollering crowds and into a quieter district of office buildings and churches, we stumble upon the city's former Woolworth store, the site of the historic sit-in that helped kick-start desegregation in the city.

The bravery of the students is hard to imagine: a fortnight into the protest, a white mob 'threw [them] from their seats, punched, kicked and spat upon them. Nashville police only arrested the student protesters,' a plaque on the pavement informs us. Yet on 6 May 1960, almost four months after the first students took their seats at Woolworth's, Nashville, without fanfare, became the first major city in the South to allow whites and Blacks to sit together in public places.

Wanting to find out more, we end up in the Civil Rights Room of the nearby public library, where an exhibit explains that many lunch counters closed, rather than desegregate, and those that did remained dangerous places for African-Americans. Some white restaurateurs, however, simply carried on as before: the president of Morrison's Cafeterias, for example, refused a personal entreaty from the governor of Tennessee to desegregate his Nashville locations as late as 1964, vowing he would never serve Blacks (or rather, his Black waiters wouldn't). It wasn't until Lyndon B. Johnson passed the Civil Rights Act later that year that such actions became illegal.

Both of us are momentarily silenced by just how recent this madness feels: the same year the Beatles formed, that Kennedy was elected president, that Nigella Lawson was born – hardly ancient history by any measure.

On a lighter note, the library also holds an extensive collection of local-interest cookbooks by the likes of Reese Witherspoon (whose grandmother Dorothea apparently made 'the best fried chicken'), Tammy Wynette (whose sister-in-law's sauerkraut surprise cake recipe does indeed sound surprising) and the Junior League of Nashville, which furnishes me with several pages of biscuit tips.

I'm most interested, however, in information about the dish that has brought us here: hot fried chicken, which has arguably become Nashville's second-biggest attraction, after its musical heritage. Though fried chicken recipes abound, nothing immediately pops up for the hot sort – Mary Eliza's fried chicken, in a Soul Food compilation put together by the African American Heritage Society of Franklin and Williamson County, contains a mere quarter teaspoon of 'red pepper'; the fried chicken in Mrs Henrietta Dull's 1928 publication, *Southern Cooking*, only the ordinary black variety.

This perhaps is not surprising, given hot chicken is primarily a restaurant dish, associated with one restaurant in particular: Prince's. Its origin story is painted on the wall of the branch we visit afterwards: 'Even in the height of the Great Depression, [founder] Thornton Prince knew how to have a good time. He enjoyed the nightlife and had a well-earned reputation as being quite the ladies' man. Of course, one person who was not too thrilled with that reputation was his steady girl. While we don't know if Prince came home one night with a faint hint of perfume or a smudge of lipstick on his collar, we do know that after another one of Prince's nights out, his scorned lover wanted revenge. And using Prince's love of fried chicken as bait, she concocted the perfect recipe.

'Instead of a lecture the next morning, Prince awoke to the sizzlin' smell of fried chicken. The trap set, Prince's jilted lover served up a plate of homemade fried chicken. Without noticing the devilish amount of peppers and spices she had sprinkled on the chicken, Prince dug in. Much to her dismay, Prince didn't fall over weeping in pain. Nope, he asked for seconds, and, at that moment, the legend was born.' As is so often the way of things, the steady girl, if she ever existed, has faded from history, leaving her cheating man to reap the rewards of her genius – he and his brothers opened their first restaurant shortly afterwards, and never looked back.

For many years this twist on a universal Southern favourite remained a largely Black obsession: historian and Nashville native

Rachel Louise Martin writes in the *Bitter Southerner* that she'd never even heard of it until she moved back home as an adult: 'and everyone was eating hot chicken, a food I didn't know'. She recalls asking Denise, an older African-American woman in her church, about it: '"Of course you didn't eat hot chicken," she said, shaking her head at me. "Hot chicken's what we ate in the neighbourhood."'

Records suggest that Nashville was, and by many accounts still is, a very segregated city, so, though Prince's attracted a select group of white customers in the know (including many musicians playing at the Grand Ole Opry), perhaps it's little surprise that Martin, who is white, didn't come across them growing up. In 1996, in what the *New Yorker* describes as 'his last official act as a lawmaker', city mayor Bill Purcell, who was in on the secret, named Prince's the best restaurant in Tennessee. Though he was smitten by their chicken, he was also, he told the magazine, moved by their unusually diverse clientele: 'This particular food is one that, literally from the start, has brought people together who otherwise would not be in the same place' – hot chicken, he realised, could be Nashville's only indigenous dish.

Naturally, a business that's been going great guns for nigh on eighty years is always going to attract imitators but it wasn't until Purcell, who could be described as a Prince's superfan, decided to launch a hot chicken festival in 2007 that the dish went viral. Suddenly rivals were everywhere, from Nashville to New England – even KFC launched a hot(ish) take. Yet Prince's remains the undisputed original, still run by Miss Andre, Thornton's great-niece, who took the business over in 1980, and told Martin, 'My customers, they try all these different places that are popping up . . . They come right back here. Might take 'em a little while, but they come back to the real thing. They tell me all the time, "You still got it." 'Course that makes me feel good. Have mercy.'

It seems only sensible to cut out the middlemen and head straight to Prince's, where we order Hot Chicken Tenders and

XXX-Hot Whole Wings, because we mean business. Stories circu-late of staff refusing to serve anyone the latter on their first visit, but we obviously look like we deserve to be taught a lesson, because this evening they don't even raise an eyebrow. As we wait in line, a man rushes up to the counter begging for water: 'The extra hot,' he gasps, 'it's so spicy I am sweating THROUGH MY NOSE.' His friends are doubled over with mirth, but behind our British bravado – practically weaned on vindaloo, etc. – we both start to feel a little apprehensive.

The chicken pieces arrive on slices of white bread already stained brick-red with grease. I tentatively pick up a wing – I'm tempted to say a prayer – and gingerly take a tiny bite. The coating is so sturdy it takes me a few seconds to get any purchase and then, as I do, I feel it, an incendiary heat that keeps building. 'It's hot,' I tell Claire. 'Oh, it's really quite hot . . . I mean, it's probably not going to kill you but . . .' My eyes fill with tears and I reach for a paper napkin to wipe my nose. 'It tastes like they've just dumped a load of raw chilli powder in there and called it a sauce.'

Having chomped our way through the wings, eyes streaming, we decide that once you've subjected your tastebuds to a certain amount of abuse, they simply leave you to it. Though I can very much still feel the burn, after a few bites I become acclimatised to the low hum on my tongue, making the hot tenders feel rather underwhelming in comparison. That said, we both spend a long time scrubbing our hands, Lady Macbeth style, afterwards – 'Make sure you get under those fingernails before you go anywhere near the loo,' Claire says firmly. Such a mum.

COFFEE BREAK

Fried Chicken USA

People were frying chicken in both Europe and Sub-Saharan Africa long before the USA was even a twinkle in a coloniser's eye, though this was usually just one step in a longer process involving braises and sauces – it wasn't until European and African traditions came together in the New World that fried chicken was allowed to stand alone in all its crisp magnificence.

But if fried chicken was brought to America by both European and African cooks, it is certainly the latter who perfected the process we know today, though more often for the benefit of their white masters and mistresses than for their own families.

For a long time, frying was primarily used as a means of preservation, and the results tended to be eaten cold, often on the road. Until the advent of the railway dining car, enterprising Black women would meet trains around the South with baskets of fried chicken to sell, using their culinary expertise to provide themselves and their families with 'relative autonomy, social power, and economic freedom' as Psyche A. Williams-Forson puts it in her book *Building Houses Out of Chicken Legs*.

Almost a century later, during the Great Migration, Black families on the move north packed their own fried chicken in shoeboxes for the journey, knowing they would not find service at segregated restaurants in the South. Expensive and labour-intensive to produce, fried chicken was sacred, otherwise reserved for Sunday dinner: the civil rights leader Ralph Abernathy once described 'the Gospel bird' as 'the best of all meals to serve'.

It was a white man, Harland Sanders, who turned fried chicken into fast food by employing a pressure cooker to reduce the frying time. Combined with tumbling poultry prices, fried chicken, for many, has become just another meal – even Prince's has switched to deep-fat fryers rather than the original shallow pans – but for aficionados, the best chicken is still skillet-fried, a slower, more labour-intensive process, which yields a thicker, better-seasoned crust. As Miss Andre herself puts it: 'When it's slow-fried, the flavours get down in there . . . There's nothing like a cast-iron skillet. I use that at home.'

We end up in Robert's Western World on the main strip, where the man in overalls making $6 'recession special' fried bologna sandwiches behind the bar (served with potato chips, moon pie (not a real pie, to my disappointment, but a biscuit) and a can of PBR) proves more entertaining than either the lacklustre band or the watery beer selection. When a drunk next to me dissolves into tears as he shows me a video of his daughter taking her first steps, we decide it's time to call it a night on Nashville. The fact neither of us is kept awake by heartburn is either testament to the skill of Prince's, or the robust nature of our digestive systems.

After a depressing visit to the nearby Belle Meade plantation, once famed 'for its traditional hospitality and wonderful Southern food' prepared by enslaved residents, we spend the afternoon listlessly wandering the strip in the rain, eating donuts and trying on cowboy boots. As we're admiring the alligator in a Stetson that graces the counter at Big Time Boots our phones both vibrate with a message from Grand Claire back in London announcing that Prime Minister Rishi Sunak has called a much-anticipated general election for 4 July, when, if the next six weeks go to plan, I should be in New York eating hot dogs and watching fireworks. Clearly he's trying to disenfranchise me because I bought the same trainers as him. I immediately go online and apply for a proxy vote: sorry, Rishi, you don't get rid of me that easily.

Claire is nonplussed when I wake her up from a nap to tell her we're heading to a family-style restaurant. 'What does that mean?' she says suspiciously as I chivvy her along, anxious not to end up queuing in the wet. 'It means you get to talk to someone that isn't me,' I reply, and oddly enough, she immediately cheers up.

In fact, both the seating and the service at Monell's in Germantown is communal – and though Annette and Rob from Florida seem slightly taken aback by our arrival, my incessant demands for them to pass me some dish or other soon melt the ice. Just as we've helped ourselves to the broccoli and cucumber salads, cornbread and biscuits already on the table – and are debating whether the brown sugar peach preserves are starters or dessert – a waitress bustles over with more food: fried chicken, stuffing, baked chicken, cream gravy, cranberry sauce, breaded pork chops, baked apple, corn pudding, macaroni cheese, green beans and mashed potato . . . 'You want more ice tea, sugar?'

It's like pulling up a chair *at* the buffet and, without the control mechanism of distance, I end up with a plate where macaroni and cranberry sit together in unholy alliance. Claire meanwhile is trying to dissuade our dining companions from renting a car in London to visit 'that place with the real cute castle, Windsor? And maybe Dover and Bath, oh, and Yorkshire like in *All Creatures Great and Small*' in two days. 'Our roads,' she says firmly, 'are not like your roads.'

Launching into the banana pudding (which really is, the servers promise, the final course), Annette professes herself very worried about me travelling solo, to the extent her husband scolds her for scaring me. As she gets up to leave, she says very seriously, 'Well, I wish you the very best of luck, really I do.' Trying to lighten the mood, I say, as I thank her, well, I just hope you don't end up reading about me in the paper! 'Oh no,' she replies sorrowfully, 'it's not normal people like *you* that we hear about, honey, just the axe murderers.'

'Blimey,' Claire says when they've gone.

As we pay I ask our waitress what on earth they do with all the leftovers: they could feed another four people again with what's still on our table alone. Oh, she says, we give a lot away, 'and my kids, they like the chicken legs and baked apples. My boy,' she laughs guiltily, 'he goes to school and shouts he had fried chicken for breakfast – I have to tell him sssssssshhhh, you AXED for that, don't you be making me look bad!'

Stuffed to the gills, neither of us feels ready for bed, and Claire mentions a place in East Nashville where, she claims, a friend pulled a cowboy at a line-dancing evening, which we both agree sounds promising. Indeed, the parking lot at Rees is almost full when we arrive – it's open-mic night, and we listen to six or seven singer-songwriters, mostly people who say they've recently arrived in the city, hoping to make it big, a couple really good. Occasionally a wandering dog appears in the hope we've ordered pizza. If only I could have had a real beer and a lift home (this may be the first time I've ever driven to a bar, and it's not an experience I'm keen to repeat), it would have been the perfect Nashville send-off.

We're on the road early the next morning; the car needs to be returned in Cincinnati this evening, before Claire catches a flight home from there tomorrow morning. The city is a mere 250 miles away, nothing in American terms – unless you're determined to travel there via Corbin, Kentucky, the small town where Colonel

Harland Sanders opened his first restaurant back in 1940, a diversion that adds another 140 miles along winding state highways.

An hour into the journey, we stop for breakfast at the Rose Garden in Silver Point, Tennessee – big rigs parked outside, the Ten Commandments hand-painted on a slate in the porch, and a sign by the door warning 'This is not a fast food restaurant, we cook each plate to order: PLEASE BE PATIENT'. Behind the counter, and the TV showing the Zoopolis 500 Turtle Race from Indianapolis Zoo, I notice another: 'IT AIN'T FOOD IF IT AIN'T FRIED'. The menu promises 'home style cookin' from the heart', and a whiteboard lists the options for today's 'meat and three': smoked sausage with green pepper and onions, beef stew or chicken and rice casserole with mashed potatoes, pinto beans, fried okra, cabbage, scalloped potatoes, green beans, corn or slaw.

Our waitress is very taken with our accents ('I watch a detective show that's set in England!'), asking us to repeat our orders (biscuits, gravy, country ham and eggs for me, biscuits, bacon and eggs for Claire) several times. When she comes back with our coffee and iced water she asks, 'Say, you girls ever tried chocolate gravy?'

No, ma'am, we say in unison.

'Well, you gotta try it, I'll bring you a bowl.'

So, along with our eggs, country ham, grits and biscuits, plus the obligatory sausage gravy (very good, this one – rich and smoky), she proudly sets down a bowl of what looks very much like the chocolate custard I was served in primary school.

'Are you thinking what I'm thinking?' I ask Claire when the waitress has refilled our coffees and bustled away.

'What, where's the chocolate sponge?'

We're still chuckling when she pops up again. 'Well, whaddya think of that?'

It's hard to explain about school dinners, and how it tastes like a richer version of a beloved childhood pudding rather than something I'd necessarily want for breakfast with bacon, so I merely say it was surprising, and ask about the sausage gravy, which really was outstanding.

She smiles broadly, and tells us that the Rose Garden usually runs out of gravy by 11am, so popular is it – 'but it's simple, you put some bacon grease in the pan, let it get nice and hot, then you stir in flour and brown it well,' she pauses for emphasis, 'then add the milk, and then the sausage – just ordinary sausage, nothing fancy, and that's it, honey.'

Going up to pay, we're ambushed by the pie selection arranged tantalisingly by the till. A page ripped from an order pad taped to the chiller lists our options: 'ALL THE PIES WE HAVE – chocolate meringue, coconut meringue, fudge, peanut butter fudge, caramel fudge, pecan, apple, cherry, chess, lemon ice box, pumpkin.' Sugary custardy chess, a Southern favourite that has nothing to do with rooks or bishops, feels like a must, as I've never tried it, Claire votes for cherry, and then votes again for pecan for the baby. (To be fair, it's not like we don't have room in the car, though sadly our stomach space is more limited.)

BISCUITS AND CHOCOLATE GRAVY

A tribute to the lovely ladies of the Rose Garden Restaurant, Silver Point, TN. If chocolate gravy sounds a little too much for you first thing, the biscuits are also great with butter and jam, or eggs and bacon – or indeed chocolate spread. Note that UK brands of buttermilk are often thickened with milk powder for no discernible reason: look for versions like M&S's Northern Irish one, which are just milk and cultures, or use 220ml/a scant cup of milk with 1 tablespoon of white or white wine vinegar or lemon juice.

Makes 6
For the biscuits
300g/2¼ cups plain/all-purpose flour

2 tsp baking powder
½ tsp bicarbonate of soda/baking soda
½ tsp fine salt
1 stick/115g butter, frozen
230ml/scant 1 cup buttermilk (see note on page 174)

For the chocolate gravy
95g/½ cup caster/superfine sugar
25g/¼ cup cocoa powder
2 tbsp plain/all-purpose flour
¼ tsp salt
480ml/2 cups milk
2 tbsp butter

1. Heat the oven to 220°C/200°C fan/425°F and lightly grease a 23cm/9 inch ovenproof frying pan or cake or tart tin. Put the flour into a mixing bowl with the baking powder, bicarbonate of soda and salt and whisk together.

2. Coarsely grate in the butter, then stir to distribute evenly. Stir in just enough buttermilk to make a soft but not too unworkably wet dough; usually I find I don't need quite all the liquid.

3. Tip onto a very lightly floured work surface and roll into a rectangle about 2½cm/1 inch thick with the short sides facing you. Fold the bottom third up to the middle, and then fold the top third down over it, then turn 90 degrees and roll out again to 2½cm/1 inch thick and repeat this three times more (so 8 folds in total).

4. Roll out again to 2½cm/1 inch thick, then cut out 6cm/2½ inch rounds. Put the biscuits on the tray or pan, bearing in mind they will spread. Bake for about 18 minutes, until golden on top.

5. Meanwhile, for the gravy, put the sugar, cocoa powder, flour and salt into a medium pan and whisk in a little of the milk to

make a smooth paste, before beating in the rest. Heat over a medium flame, stirring constantly, until thick enough to coat the back of a spoon. Stir in the butter.

6. Once the biscuits are ready, wrap them in a clean tea towel and serve with the chocolate gravy and extra butter. These are best eaten fresh, but can be revived for a day or so by a brief spell in a hot oven.

Pies safely strapped in next to Eddy, I put the Colonel Sanders Museum into the satnav and off we go, through the pretty hills of middle Tennessee, across the Cumberland River, past several Trump signs and via a red-bearded Amish man in a buggy, who tips his hat at us after I give way to him at a junction. 'Ooh,' says Claire, 'I wonder if he's married.'

'Number one, yes, almost certainly,' I say, 'he was at least twenty. Number two, he was about twenty. Number three, you're old enough to be his mother.' She bristles. 'Number four, you have a husband at home.'

'Fair,' she says.

Traffic proves worse, and Corbin larger than I'd expected, and, to my surprise, the museum is a four-storey colonnaded mansion that looks like it may have been modelled on the White House, or perhaps even vice versa. Though we can't see any trace of the 1940s cafe I've been promising, Claire takes a picture of me next to a large bronze bust of the man himself looking more like Ho Chi Minh than ever. Inside, it appears to be an office building, so I'm relieved when the receptionist directs us to a small room off the hall.

As soon as we push open the door, a man in a double-breasted white suit, with a cane in one hand and a KFC bucket in the other, turns to address us. 'My name is Colonel Harland Sanders,' he says in a nasal voice, 'and this museum is all about my life.' We're both absolutely terrified. 'Is it real?' Claire asks. I honestly don't know, I whisper. It's definitely creepy whatever it is. I'm fairly sure, as he starts up again, that it's a model, but I can't help keeping a nervous eye on him as we hastily move away.

Though small, the museum has several points of interest, the first being that Sanders (like our guide in New Orleans, the title was entirely honorary) was married for nearly forty years to a woman who remains nameless, and is only briefly touched upon, in contrast to his second wife, Claudia, who clearly had a hand in the creation of this museum, and thus gets a lot of air time. Looking this up, we discover a claim from his biographer Josh Ozersky that the pair split up because 'Josephine bore him three children . . . but seems to have been little interested in lovemaking after that – an especially unfortunate circumstance given Sanders' passionate and hot-blooded nature.' 'What is it about fried chicken and womanisers?' Claire says, giving the animatronic Sanders a wide berth as she passes.

The second, even better than the collection of Sanders-related reminiscences sent out to franchisees after his death entitled *It Wasn't All Gravy,* or the badge from his 1951 Kentucky Senate bid (VOTE FOR COLONEL SANDERS), is the ring-bound collection of letters in which KFC's pressure cooker suppliers bully the artist Norman Rockwell, that iconic illustrator of twentieth-century America, into finding time in his schedule to paint their golden goose. 'He, like yourself, is one of the pleasant and memorable experiences our country has enjoyed in the last several decades. Therefore it would be our pleasure to have the impression of our Colonel by one of the best in the field of art.' 'Out of the question,' Rockwell replies, before being worn down by their smiling persistence and unsolicited cheques. The whole file proves quite the lesson in Southern charm: the steel magnolia, the iron fist in the velvet glove.

While I'm admiring the resulting avuncular portrait, a message arrives from my dad, who has been tracking my location. 'Wondering what you are going to eat in Louisville?'

What's he talking about? I think. I'm nowhere near Louisville, the silly old codger. And yet . . . a seed of doubt blooms within me, as perhaps bloomed within Rockwell under the weight of all those letters. I decide to check where the nearest KFC is, given there's still no evidence of one on site. Sure enough, we're not at the Harland Sanders Cafe and Museum in Corbin at all, we're 150 miles northwest at the KFC corporate headquarters, in, yes, Louisville. I start to laugh, tickled by the absurd power of technology to divorce you from your environment; on a bike, there's no way I wouldn't have noticed every sign; in a car I just relied on auto-complete, then blithely followed the instructions that followed.

On the plus side, as I tell Claire, we now have some chance of returning the rental car on time so all is not lost – plus would they have let anything as impressive as a golden pressure cooker out of the mansion? I think not.

Rushed as we are, I'm determined to find some KFC to commemorate our visit. Gridlocked in the city's rush-hour traffic, by the time we finally get to the nearest restaurant, a drive-thru feels like the wisest as well as the most American option. To be honest, I'm not entirely sure I've ever had a drive-thru before, and I've certainly never been the one in charge of the ordering process. It's also at least a decade since I've eaten anything from KFC, so we're still debating what to get when we pull up to a pole that I assume contains a microphone – I'd naively expected a window, with a real person. 'WELCOMETOKFCCANITAKEYOUROR-DER,' the pole demands.

'Hi! Um, may I have a four-piece box with buffalo ranch sauce please, and coleslaw?'

' . . . And?'

'Oh, and . . . tea, can I get an iced tea with the box?'

'It comes with THREE SIDES, ma'am.'

'Oh, does it?' I panic. 'Um . . .'

'Mash,' Claire hisses at me, 'get the mash.'

'Mashed potatoes, please, and um, green beans?'

We pull forward to an actual window. 'That'll be $44.99,' the woman says.

I gape; I thought fast food was supposed to be cheap!

'Um . . . OK?'

She hands me two large brown paper bags as I tap my card, wondering what on earth has gone wrong. We find the nearest parking space and I unload the warm cargo on my lap: a vast bucket of chicken, a box of six biscuits and two combustibly hot helpings of mash and beans, plus gravy in a separate pot, slaw and sauces.

'What have you done?' Claire says, horrified, as I try to shove the gravy into a cup holder – for all I've read about American cars being designed to eat in, the Chrysler is not making it easy for me to arrange this lot.

'I don't know!' I wail. 'I said FOUR! You heard me! It must be my accent!'

COFFEE BREAK

Meals in Wheels

Drive-ins, a concept that debuted in Texas in the early 1920s, when a business named Pig Stands Inc. advertised 'Curb Service', really hit their stride in the post-war period, with the expansion of car ownership and the road network. From there it was a race to distribute food at maximum speed, with the minimum of human interaction: In-N-Out is thought to have opened the first drive-thru, dispensing for the need for at-car service, in 1948, complete with intercom ordering system, but they didn't become really popular until several decades later: McDonald's only got on board with the concept, which now accounts for a staggering 70 per cent of its US business, in 1975.

As cars became mobile dining rooms, their designs adapted accordingly: by the 1960s, glove compartment doors opened flat, to hold drinks. Cupholders appeared in the 1980s: by 2007 a PwC survey found they'd leapfrogged over fuel efficiency as a priority for the American car buyer, which might explain why the 2019 Subaru Ascent was furnished with nineteen drink spots for the convenience of its seven occupants.

The mash and beans give off the boiled scent of institutional food. The chicken smells like the last train out of London Victoria on a Saturday night. Grease runs down my arm as I bite in. We eat an unenthusiastic piece and a half each, dropping the bones in the bucket, and wonder why on earth anyone would want to eat in their car if they had the choice. No bin is evident in the parking lot, and no hungry-looking people in need of some dubious charity either, so we end up driving all the way to Newport, Kentucky with eight pieces of chicken, some mash and green beans in the van, windows open to try to minimise the smell.

Ridden: 0 miles
Climbed: 0 feet
Pies consumed: 2 (pecan, sweet potato)
All-American foods discovered: peanut butter and banana sandwich, barbecue ribs, barbecue spaghetti, hot chicken, peach preserves, corn pudding, cream gravy, country ham, chocolate gravy

10

BURGERBURGH, OHIO

In search of the original hamburger

> *'I had a dream last night that a hamburger was eating me.'*
> Jerry Seinfeld

Strictly speaking, Newport is still in Kentucky, where the South begins, but in reality, to the visitor at least, Southern Newport and Midwestern Cincinnati feel very much like one city with a river in the middle. Newport, as we drag our luggage from the car hire office to the hotel, looks different to Louisiana or Tennessee: brick houses, narrower streets, and even a single discreet 'BIDEN HARRIS' poster peeping shyly from a window. In a few short blocks, Washington Street boasts, among other businesses, three diners, two bakeries, two girly bars, a gym, a gunsmith and a knitting shop. People are out walking, and somehow it all feels more compact and urban . . . more familiar, high-street ammo merchants aside.

The dish I'm on the hunt for is less so – Cincinnati chili is definitely not chili as Jonny Hernandez serves it back in San Antonio, or even school dinner chilli con carne. At Dixie Chili, our choice of parlour, it comes as a three-way (with spaghetti, cheese and crackers), four-way (+ beans or onion), five-way (+ beans *and* onion) or six-way, billed as 'for the true connoisseur', a phrase that puts me in mind of the menu at the Wimborne Tandoori, but which here denotes chili, spaghetti, beans, onions, fresh chopped garlic, shredded cheese and crackers.

This last arrives in shallow dishes overflowing with sauce and topped with an orange curly wig of cheese. Something brown and noodley lurks underneath, which tastes nothing like any other chili either of us have ever tried. Thick with cloves and cinnamon, a profile that betrays its Balkan origins, it's said to be the work of Tom and John Kiradjieff, who arrived from northern Greece in 1921 and went into business as hot dog sellers. The chili was one of their original toppings; the diversification into, or rather onto, spaghetti came later, as did the blizzard of extras.

As with hot chicken, success spawns imitators: like almost every other chili joint, the Dixie we're sitting in has Greek roots, established by Nicholas Sarakatsannis across the river in Newport (to avoid competition with the Kiradjieffs in Cincinnati) in 1928, though the interior styling is pure 1980s. Oddly enough, the flavour is too, because for all the spices, it tastes overwhelmingly of mince, and reminds me of nothing more than school dinner spag bol with added crackers. So far from home, I actually find this quite comforting – this Macedonian-Texas-Mexican mash-up bears little resemblance to anything I've eaten in Greece or Texas, but it definitely tastes of Cincinnati, OH. I mean, Newport, KY.

On the way back to the hotel, we pop into the Höfbrauhaus for a beer. Cincinnati is proud of its German heritage, and this vast hall, with its long tables and bench seating, is the cavernous proof – though, as one German reviewer puts it, 'It is a Hofbräuhaus as one imagines it abroad. Bad German singers and mediocre food. The beer, on the other hand, is quite good. I drank several lagers, then the food was good again.'

As I have an early start, and Claire isn't keen on a session on the 0 per cent on offer, we head back to the hotel for something we can both enjoy: our Rose Garden pie haul. Encased in rich, distinctly salty pastry, they're universally sugary, vanilla-scented and, in the case of the chess, which reminds me of a Kentish gypsy tart, buttery as hell: 8/10, with a mark knocked off because sadly neither of us can finish a whole slice of any of 'em. Southerners sure have a sweet tooth.

I always feel nervous getting back on the bike after a few days off – or in this case, ten, as Eddy has had a well-earned rest since my trip to Avery Island – but I'm also excited to have no other plan today than to ride. Hugging a bleary-eyed Claire goodbye (a hug that turns emotional when I realise she's the last familiar face I'll be seeing until I get to Boston in three weeks' time, Rishi's snap election having deprived me of my Chicago-bound companion, whose husband is a prospective parliamentary candidate), I head into the damp dawn, across the Ohio River, and find myself in the foggy Midwest.

My route on this grey May morning hugs the river out of Cincinnati, then joins the old railway line I'll be following all the way to Columbus, breaking the journey after 105 miles, in London (pop. 10,442), which offers free camping for those biking the Ohio to Erie trail, of whom there are a startling number given how few cyclists I've seen on the actual roads thus far. Most, with toddlers in tow, or chatting three abreast, look like locals out for short rides, rather than overnight tourers, but I'm still anxious to make good time, lest the cyclists' campsite I've earmarked for this evening fills up for the Memorial Day weekend.

The crowds are concentrated around the towns; between them I enjoy the peace and quiet of a segregated cycle path, the smooth tarmac ribbon running through woods, under great concrete intersections (after three days of driving, I've rarely felt more grateful to be on a bike) and over endless fallen mulberries, so many they stain my legs with their purplish juice. After a bit, however, I long to see more than just trees, which, let's be honest, basically look the same wherever you are in the world.

I pause after a couple of hours in the saddle, finally warm enough to take off my jacket, for a 'lean n green smoothie', which comes emblazoned with the faintly annoying message 'BELIEVE IN YOURSELF!' My plan is to stop for lunch in Xenia, seventy miles in and two-thirds of the way to London, until I meet Paolo, who comes powering up beside me on a sleek road bike with the opener, 'Hey, what's your story?' This proves to be the only question he asks for the next ninety minutes, during which our conversation, such as it is, ranges from his dentist to his uncle who deserted Mussolini's forces and hid out in the Calabrian wilderness for the duration of the war. The distance to Xenia, a hub on the trail, is painted onto the tarmac at regular intervals, though not quite regular enough for my liking.

To make things worse, my left cleat has begun sticking, which means twice when he abruptly shouts for me to stop at a junction (he's very safety conscious, Paolo), I topple onto the tarmac. This has never happened to me before in all the years I've ridden clipped into the pedals, and has long been one of my deepest fears – but oddly, crashing to the ground with a bike on top of me doesn't hurt as much as I'd always imagined. I suspect this only makes poor Paolo more anxious about the strange British woman he's rescued, because when we finally reach Xenia, he advises me not to stop there, he knows a great pizza place – 'and I know pizza, I'm Italian!' – in the dry town of Cedarville,* not even ten miles along

---

* Thanks to the presence of a private Baptist university whose unequivocal opposition to drinking is laid out in its student handbook. As well as not imbibing themselves, students are instructed 'not to attend bars or clubs where alcohol is the primary feature', nor are they permitted to attend

the road! He doesn't have to be home quite yet, he'll show me the way. I'm grateful of course, but when he finally drops me off with many admonitions to stay safe, I sit and demolish the doughy round in blessed silence under a sign saying, 'Attitude is everything. Pick a good one.'

I push on, the landscape turning to open farmland. A deer dashes across the path, and I stop, thrilled, as a couple of groundhogs scurry into the undergrowth – even as I whip out my phone I can't help thinking of some tourists I once saw excitedly photographing squirrels in Russell Square. Red barns, grain silos and Trump flags take the place of mulberry trees and scarlet cardinals, and I cycle open-mouthed to suddenly find myself in the Midwest . . . before remembering I'm supposed to be in a hurry. When I finally pull in to London, however, I have trouble finding any sign of the campsite at the spot marked on the map. I poke around, and eventually decide it must be the wooded area by the bicycle sculptures where there are some odd raised beds enclosed by planks. With no one around to ask, I pitch the tent in the centre of one of them, just in case they're flood defences. This process takes me at least half an hour, while Midwestern mosquitos, unable to believe their luck, make free with my exposed flesh. At some point, a man arrives and begins deftly suspending a hammock between two trees, politely pretending not to hear me swearing. I give up, leave my shelter for the night leaning at a precarious angle, and demand, perhaps slightly aggressively in retrospect, to know where he got his burrito.

As well as Taco Bell, London boasts a Subway, McDonald's, KFC, Long John Silver's, four pizza places and a supermarket that sells me chopped vegetables, spinach and artichoke dip, and a bag of pretzels the size of a pillowcase. Triumphant, I return to my

---

parties 'where alcohol is being used in a manner that violates University standards . . . violations of these guidelines may result in dismissal'.

lonely tent to find it now surrounded by other, noticeably more upright examples.

An elderly local man is holding court with some authority by the picnic tables, and I ask him about the bathroom situation – 'Oh, you didn't already tell the police you're here?' he says. Only they, apparently, can give me the access code to use the loo: 'And they need to know you're here, you know, in case your folks need to get hold of you.' I explain in such an eventuality they'll probably try my mobile phone first, but that I can't seem to make outgoing calls.* He agrees this does present a problem, and we sit in silence until one of my fellow campers, having been told in no uncertain terms he's not allowed to share the code with me, offers to lend me his phone instead. The police do not seem particularly interested by my presence; presumably even in London, Ohio they have more pressing matters to deal with on a Friday night.

Satisfied I'm now square with the feds, the older man asks me where I'm from, and tells me he used to know a Brit, married a GI, came over, 'seemed as American as can be, and then her sister came out to visit, and whaddaya know, no one could understand the pair of them together. Can you do that?' he demands.

I'm not sure what he means – 'Do what?'

'You know, switch?' I clearly look blank. 'Talk in proper English too? Like this?' he prompts, speaking as if to someone with an imperfect grasp of the language.

The man with the phone clears his throat and ventures that really they could both be considered proper English, and my questioner gets flustered, says something about ACCENTS and then that his wife will be wondering where he's got to, and leaves me to my pretzels. Nevertheless, I'm very grateful to him, and to everyone involved in the London Primitive Campsite; what a

---

* Oddly enough, once I get to the north-east, it just sorts itself out, like my handset knows it's nearly home.

lovely thing to offer travellers passing through your city, a free spot and (tightly controlled) access to the Madison County Senior Center outside bathroom.

I sleep well under the pine trees; my new air mattress is comfortable, and but for the cops making their rounds every few hours, London, OH is quiet. I wake at 5am, try to strike camp as quietly as possible, and get on the road, enjoying the sun rising over the towering grain silos, and a sign outside St Paul African Methodist Episcopal: 'DONT WAIT TIL THE UNDERTAKER BRING U TO CHURCH JOIN US SUN 11AM.'

As yesterday's repurposed railway line continues all the way into Columbus, I decide to grab breakfast while it's on offer: a short stack of pancakes, two cups of coffee and a lot of chat about mowing at the M&M Diner, where the clientele is 85 per cent men in baseball caps, and the waitresses take zero nonsense. It's only when I check in to my hotel a couple of hours and twenty-seven miles later that I realise I failed to pick up my credit card after signing the check – life without chip and pin is taking a while to get used to. Having established, thanks to the hotel phone, that they have it, I'm now going to have to retrace my steps at some point over the weekend to retrieve the thing. (Fortunately I also have a debit card with me, plus Apple Pay is more common in urban areas; one of the biggest changes since my last visit to the States, when it still felt very much a cash-based economy.)

My plan while in Columbus is: eat burgers. Though the capital of Ohio is better known as the home of Ohio State, the university football team (fervour for which borders on the religious, even among folks with quite a lot of that kind of thing in their lives already) and, to a lesser extent, the university itself, it also happens to be the birthplace of Wendy's and headquarters of White Castle.

You may know the latter from the early-90s stoner flick *Harold and Kumar Go to White Castle*, but I'd argue it deserves more recognition as the business that created fast food as we know it today. Founded back when to eat out was to put yourself at the mercy of millions of individual businesses of wildly varying quality, it was White Castle that realised the value of standardisation and efficiency decades before McDonald's or KFC appeared on the scene. A 1932 advert proudly boasted that 'When you sit in a White Castle remember that you are one of several thousands; you are sitting on the same kind of stool; you are being served on the same kind of counter; the coffee you drink is made in accordance with a certain formula; the hamburger you eat is prepared in exactly the same way over a gas flame of the same intensity; the cups you drink from are identical with thousands of cups that thousands of other people are using at the same moment; the same standard of cleanliness protects your food.' What we now see, or claim to see, as fast food's weakness, its predictability, homogeneity and lack of regional or seasonal distinctiveness, was once its biggest USP.

Not only that, but, according to 'journalist, author, junk-food bard' Adam Chandler, 'White Castle's greatest contribution remains the rise and redemption of the hamburger, which forever changed the country and the world.' In his book *Drive-Thru Dreams* he argues that before the Great War, the US was a series of communities with very little shared experience that might qualify as 'American'. Only in the Roaring Twenties did the population begin to consume the same things from coast to coast in the form of movies, radio shows, Model T cars and, most important of all from my perspective, hamburgers.

Though Anderson and Ingram, White Castle's founders, were by no means the first people to put them on the menu, before them, Chandler claims, 'the hamburger in all of its scattered iterations was just a weird, peonic meat sandwich, without ideal, definition or exemplar, living in a dusty and disconnected network of fiefdoms. And you can't have a kingdom without a castle.'

COFFEE BREAK

A Brief History of Hamburgers

Though proto-hamburgers certainly existed before the United States did, there's little serious argument that the hamburger as we know it is anything but an all-American creation. It probably has its roots in the minced 'Hamburg steaks' popular in nineteenth-century America: a cheap way to consume the beef coming out of the Great Plains in staggering quantities. As the Hamburg steak was coarsely chopped and often served with gravy, we can be sure it was not designed to be picked up and eaten by hand like the modern hamburger, whose form proved much better suited to the fast-paced American way of life. Like the burrito, which is much easier to eat at the wheel than the messier taco, or the hot dog, a streamlined version of the wurst sold with hunks of bread in nineteenth-century German-American beer gardens, it's an old-world food perfectly adapted to this new life of speed and convenience.

While many claimed to have been the first to come up with the idea of squashing the round into a more practical patty (the prototype for the ultra-thin, crisp circle of ground meat now marketed as a smashburger) and serving it as a sandwich, the most credible candidate seems to be Walt Anderson, one of the co-founders of the Midwestern White Castle chain. Perfection can always be improved upon, however. The US abounds with regional burger styles, including:

Connecticut steamed cheeseburger
Midwestern loosemeat sandwiches (as the name suggests,
    crumbly, rather than tightly packed)
Juicy Lucy – with melted cheese inside. Apparently originating
    in Minnesota, the idea has caught on nationwide
Mississippi slug burger – no slugs involved, but a Depression-era
    creation where the meat is padded out with breadcrumbs
    or flour
Missouri goober burger – served with peanut butter sauce
New Mexico green-chile cheeseburger
Oklahoma fried-onion burger – with onions smashed into
    the patty
Tennessee deep-fried burger – self-explanatory
Wisconsin butter burger, topped with generous amounts of the
    good stuff

This visit, therefore, is something of a pilgrimage; I've managed to score an interview at White Castle HQ, the place where both the hamburger as we know it, and fast food in general, began. In fact, so important a role does White Castle play in the American culinary story that this was the first email I sent when I decided to write this book, way before I booked any flights. I was pretty sure I was going to begin in California and end in New York, or perhaps vice versa, but whichever way I went, it was going to be via Columbus, Ohio.

Local food tour guide Bethia Woolf has been firing other suggestions at me for weeks – she's taking the research very seriously, which is good; someone has to. As I get out of the shower – my hotel, the Graduate, is styled in the manner of an 80s college frat house, with a Shake Shack in the lobby giving the whole place the agreeable scent of beef fat – a message comes through from her: 'I hope you're hungry!'

Fortunately the 6.30am pancakes feel a long time ago, because we do not stop eating for the next six hours, starting in the wealthy suburb of Worthington, whose farmers' market, she tells me, was named best in the US by the 2024 *USA Today* Readers' Choice Awards. Bethia seems to know almost all the stallholders, but we're not here for the man hawking $199 bison skulls along with steaks and oxtail, or even the bearded Amish fellows doing a roaring trade in strawberries. Instead, we join the queue at Joya's, where chef and owner Avishar Barua, born and raised in Ohio to Bangladeshi immigrant parents, showcases the influences that have shaped his cooking, from kathi rolls and fried rice to good old smashburgers.

Bon Appetit magazine describes his food as 'both Bengali-American and unmistakably Midwestern', and it's this burger which feels like it locates him firmly in big beef country. 'If you're running a restaurant in Columbus,' he tells me as he plonks one down in front of me, along with a kathi roll, a chicken samosa and a bowl of spicy 'hash puppies' that remind me a lot of aloo tikki, 'and you put a burger on the menu, it will immediately be your number-one seller.'

'It's Midwestern comfort food,' Bethia agrees. 'In Columbus you have speciality burger restaurants, yes, but pretty much everywhere has a burger on the menu – steak houses, fine dining restaurants, they'll all do one because people expect it.'

Barua says he grew up with McDonald's, so 'I'm not a fancy chef, but I do like to have control over all parts of the process.' Hence they grind the meat themselves ('90 per cent chuck, 5 per cent smoked bacon, 5 per cent bone marrow'), smash it flat and cook it with onions ('inspired by White Castle') before going in with the Pepper Jack cheese, hot pickles, burger sauce, shredded iceberg and hatch chilli sauce, all sandwiched between two garlic-buttered potato buns 'inspired by Indian pav'. Without the chillies, he recalls, they all felt the burger was missing something: 'and we're a Bengali-American restaurant so we added spices. It's kind of an homage to a New Mexican green-chile cheeseburger.'

The results are incredibly good, but so full of sauce and relish and shrettuce that I can barely taste that carefully calibrated meat blend. This, I think later, once Bethia and I have shared smashburgers at Preston's (served with pastrami and bacon), RayRays Reload (made with lamb, topped with pepper jelly and Pepper Jack) and local chain Swenson's, where the Galley Boy comes with barbecue AND tartar sauce, is the whole problem with the genre. Squash a burger as flat as a pancake and, yes, it cooks quickly, and develops some lovely crisp edges as a bonus, but with less meat in each mouthful, it's all too easily overwhelmed by toppings, and boy, do these places love their toppings. I think of the BBQ-sauce-drenched Hickory burger in Los Angeles, and the Tostada burger in San Antonio: for a country so enamoured by meat, America seems oddly shy of tasting the stuff.

Though I find their burgers sloppy and unnervingly sweet, I do enjoy the Swenson's Drive-In 'curbside dining' experience, where a young man comes running over to take our order when we pull up with our lights on, and returns with a tray holding our food, which he clips to the outside of the driver's-side window. I ask him why the burger comes speared with a stuffed olive, like a martini. It's clearly not the first time he's had the question because, though Ethan is all of twenty-two ('I've been eating Swenson's my whole life, my high school football field was, like, a hundred yards from one so we all used to go and hang out there after school'), he confidently assures me it's 'just the way we've always done it, since we opened in 1934. I guess people back then thought it made them fancy?'

(Before we leave, Bethia also gets me to try a bologna sandwich, after I make her laugh by pronouncing it like the Italian city. Turns out this rubbery, blubbery pink luncheon meat is actually 'baloney', and not quite as bad as it looks, while also potentially falling into the category of something you have to grow up with to truly appreciate.)

My disenchantment with smashburgers is confirmed when we stop in at the Ringside, the oldest bar in town, a dimly lit basement spot popular with politicos from the nearby state capitol. Here the burgers, named after boxers (it was once owned by a former pro wrestler and boxing promoter) and prepared behind the bar, mean business: the Jack Dempsey, which we share, is a simple, chunky ½lb (227g) patty with cheese, lettuce, pickles, mustard, tomato and mayonnaise. I'd happily lose a few toppings, but it's still my favourite of the day: uncompromisingly, unapologetically beefy.

As we get up to leave, the man sitting alone on the table behind us takes delivery of a 1½lb (680g) Buster Douglas. He picks it up, realises he can't quite get his jaw around it (or perhaps doesn't care to with an audience goggling at him – because of course I sit right back down to enjoy the spectacle) and admits defeat, removing one of the patties from the bun before tucking in. Disappointed, we leave him to come to terms with his failure in peace.

Before dropping me off at the hotel with the generous, and typically Midwestern, offer to drive me back out to M&M's Diner for my credit card the next morning, Bethia recommends I check out the famous veggie burger at North Star for dinner. It's a testament to my professionalism that I obediently heave myself out again for my sixth burger of the day. Made with beetroot, from the look of it, with black beans and rice, it's welcome in that, soft and sweet, it tastes nothing like a beefburger.

BANGLABURGER

This kebab/burger hybrid is inspired by chef Avishar Barua of Joya's in Worthington, and his passions for sweeter, sloppier burgers (which Bethia would attribute to his childhood visits to McDonald's) and his Bangladeshi

*heritage. The rolls are really worth the effort, but the burgers are also deli-
cious served as little patties with salad, flatbreads and sauces.*

Makes 6
For the rolls (or use 6 soft rolls)
*1 medium floury/starchy potato or 100g/packed ½ cup cold
    mashed potato*
255g/1½ cups + 2 tbsp strong white flour
1¼ tsp instant yeast
½ tsp fine salt
1 tsp black onion seeds
40g/scant 3 tbsp softened butter, diced
1 egg, beaten
2 tbsp melted butter (optional)

For the burgers
100g/1 thick slice of stale bread
650g/1 pound 6 ounces minced lamb
1 tsp ground cumin
1 tsp ground coriander
¼ tsp ground turmeric
½ tsp salt
1 green finger chilli, trimmed and finely chopped
½ an onion, grated
1 clove of garlic, crushed
1 tsp finely grated ginger
Juice of 1 lemon
6 slices of cheddar or halloumi (optional)

For the chutney
20g/1 cup fresh coriander/cilantro leaves
20g/1 cup fresh mint leaves (stripped from stems of a larger bunch)
1½ tsp sugar

¼ tsp salt
5–10g (½–1) finger chilli, seeded and chopped
Juice of 1 lime (about 25ml/1⅔ tbsp)
25ml/1⅔ tbsp water

For the maple chaat yoghurt
½ tsp cumin seeds
240ml/1 cup thick whole milk yoghurt
2 tbsp maple syrup
¼ tsp fine salt

1. Peel the potato, then put it into a small saucepan and just cover with water. Bring to the boil, then simmer until tender. Drain the cooking water into a heatproof jug for the next step and return the potato to the hot pan. Mash until smooth, allowing it to steam dry in the residual heat, then set aside to cool before turning it into dough.
2. Put the flour, yeast, salt and onion seeds into a mixing bowl or the bowl of a stand mixer and whisk together. Add 100g/packed ½ cup cooled mash, the softened butter, the egg and 85ml/⅓ cup of the potato cooking water (or the same of lukewarm water, if not available) and mix together into a soft, sticky dough. Knead by hand or with a dough hook until smooth and elastic (it will still be very sticky, but try not to add too much flour to the surface), then cover and leave to rise until doubled in size (about 90 minutes depending on room temperature).
3. Tip onto the work surface and punch down, then divide into 6 balls of roughly 80g/3oz each. Roll each beneath your hand until smooth and round. Put into a medium, greased, high-sided baking tin. Cover and leave until well risen.
4. Meanwhile, soak the stale bread in cold water until soft and fragile, then squeeze out all the excess water, squish into a paste and put in a bowl. Add the lamb and all the other burger

ingredients besides the cheese and mix well (I use my hands), then divide into 12 balls about 75g/3oz each. Chill.

5. Heat the oven to 180°C/160°C fan/350°F and bake the rolls for 30 minutes, until golden brown, then brush with melted butter and leave to cool.

6. Meanwhile, whizz together the ingredients for the green chutney and taste, adjusting the seasoning if necessary.

7. For the yoghurt, toast the cumin seeds in a dry pan until fragrant. Set aside to cool slightly while you stir together the remaining ingredients, then roughly crush and stir in, and adjust the seasoning to taste.

8. Once you're ready to serve, halve and butter the buns and ready the two condiments, plus any shredded lettuce or cabbage, sliced tomato, etc. you wish to add, and heat a stainless-steel or cast-iron frying pan over a high heat for 2 minutes.

9. Put a couple of patties into the hot pan and squash flat with a solid spatula until as wide as or wider than the bun. Cook until well browned, then flip and repeat (add a slice of cheese to one at this point if using). If cooking them all at once, keep them warm under foil while you repeat with the rest.

10. Put any salad items on the bottom of the bun, and add one patty. Top with a spoonful of yoghurt, followed by the second patty with the cheese, then the chutney, then add the top of the bun. Serve immediately.

Perhaps worried I might have fainted with hunger in the night, Bethia arrives at the hotel bright and early to take me on a tour of some non-burger-related Columbus hotspots – in the two days we're together we sample Somali, German, Lebanese, French, Mexican, Southern, Bengali and Polish food, falooda kulfi and Cape Cod oysters, sauerkraut balls (a popular local drinking snack) and Palestinian pastries. I admit that, having swallowed the

Midwestern stereotypes, I hadn't expected such cultural diversity in a provincial city or to see such enthusiasm for all these foods among the wider population, an open-mindedness Bethia attributes to the city's colleges, corporate headquarters and its refugee resettlement programme.

Columbus is also, she tells me, the fastest-growing metropolitan area in the United States; many of the chefs and business owners we meet are returnees, or transplants from more expensive areas on the coast, attracted by the relatively low cost of living in the city. 'Funny as it sounds,' she says as we stroll around the pretty red-brick German Village neighbourhood, settled in the early nineteenth century by people fleeing unrest in Central Europe, 'Columbus was the end of the road for Europeans at that point – basically as far west as you could easily go.' The city's newer communities, kicking back in dusty work clothes at the Hispanic food truck lot we visit for ceviche and carnitas, chewing the fat at the Somali coffee shops that dot its suburbs, are just the latest in a long line of people who've ended up in Columbus looking for a better life.

This diversity is less evident in the suburban branch of Wendy's we stop at after picking up my credit card from the nice people at M&M's Diner back in London. Bethia's husband Andy recalls that growing up in rural Ohio, Wendy's was always seen as slightly more of a family restaurant than its fast-food rivals, something borne out by the smartly dressed after-church crowd here, the men in shirts, braces and pressed khakis, the women draped in modest florals.

The Son of Baconator, which I order mostly because the name makes me laugh is, to my relief, more savoury than many of the other burgers I've tried, although I still can't taste much in the way of beef. As we each tuck into a quarter,* Bethia outlines her burger thesis: that those who grew up with McDonald's Big Macs,

---

* Meanwhile Zoe, Andy and Bethia's young daughter, proves to me that, yes, people really do dip their fries in their milkshakes over here.

like Avishar, are conditioned to demand a sweeter, saucier burger experience as an adult, while anyone who preferred Burger King craves something chunkier and beefier. (Having grown up with frozen supermarket patties, it's remarkable I still like them in any form.)

On the way back to Columbus, Andy explains the Waffle House index to me, the unofficial measure used by FEMA to evaluate the severity of a natural disaster. The chain, which is open 24/7 every day of the year, states its goal is 'always to be the last to close, first to open', which means the status of the local Waffle House is a pretty good guide to how hard an area has been hit: red means branches are closed completely, yellow that they're open but serving a limited menu (which may indicate power or water short-ages), and green means the Waffle Houses are operating as normal, and basic services in the area are likely to be unaffected.* This to me seems somehow symbolic of the role such chains play in national life – in scattered communities, they're far more than just fast-food joints.

The next day is Memorial Day, a federal holiday dedicated to those who've died in the United States military, which Bethia explains is usually marked by a family barbecue like the one they're going to at Andy's parents' place in rural Ohio. Her friend Tania, a cycling fan keen to discuss predictions for the forthcoming Tour de France, kindly arrives on her bike instead, promising to escort me to the German Village for cream puffs.

Moving far enough away from Schmidts' piped oompah music to hear each other's thoughts on Vingegaard's form and Cav's

---

* Had I known I was operating at the very limit of the Waffle House's geographic reach, I would have insisted on stopping in – Ohio represents the chain's northern frontier.

chances, I also pluck up the courage to ask if she might have time to keep me company while I try yet another burger. Not just any burger either; the burger that bodybuilders who come to town for the annual Arnold Schwarzenegger Sports Festival compete to finish, the kind of burger that requires moral support – the mighty Thurmanator.

Even the description on the Thurman Cafe menu – bottom bun, mayo, lettuce, tomato, pickle, banana peppers, 12oz (68g) burger, bacon, cheddar, another 12oz (68g) burger, sautéed onions and mushrooms, ham, mozzarella and American cheese, top bun. Served with fries and a pickle spear – is hard to swallow so I'm relieved when Tania says she'll hold my hand; 'though maybe not literally – you'll probably need both to eat. I'll be interested to know what you make of it,' she adds, which feels ominous.

We order, perched on a high table – I look around anxiously, eager to find someone else stupid enough to be taking on the challenge, but everyone else seems to be eating normal food. Or normal food for Columbus anyway – 'Oh, God,' Tania says, as a large plate goes past.

The barman smirks. 'That ain't even the one you ordered!'

'It isn't?' she says, aghast.

'Oh, no,' he says happily, 'with yours we got to get a special knife to come and cut it.'

He's not lying; the behemoth, which must stand about a foot tall on the plate, arrives at our table supported by the kind of dowel you might use to anchor a three-tiered wedding cake. An attendant, who has been closely following the monster's progress across the restaurant, appears at my side wielding a carving knife and deftly cleaves it in twain. I am presented with a steaming cross-section of meat: two grey-brown burgers (medium well is the only option here) and a full couple of inches of pink ham along with the cheese, mushrooms, lettuce, peppers and whatnot. The bacon, one presumes, lurks somewhere in between the two patties.

It can only be tackled with a knife and fork, which begs the philosophical question: is it even a burger if you can't pick it up? The famously germ-phobic Big Mac fan Donald Trump would say yes; I'm not so sure. My other problem with the Thurmanator is the burger itself, which, despite being as chunky as, or perhaps even chunkier, than I could wish, tastes mainly of salt and grease, like a lump of overcooked meat in an institutional cottage pie. I'm ashamed to say we barely make it through a tenth of it. 'I hope you've got trailers on those bikes,' the table behind quips as we sneak quietly out, leaving the remains of our shame on the table.

Before we part, I ask Tania what I should do if I encounter a tornado while riding – Andy reports that it's been a lively year for twisters so far, and has advised me to download a decent weather app instead of relying, like a cheapskate, on the BBC from London. She confesses she's not quite sure, apart from seeking shelter: a ditch would be the best bet, she guesses, and 'though you might not think it, I'm pretty sure you should avoid bridges'.

Later I look it up, and find she's spot on: the Adventure Cycling Association advises riders to seek 'the lowest spot around (a ditch, for instance), cover your head with your arms, and be sure and stay away from cars and trees if possible', while the National Weather Service states that 'stopping under a bridge to take shelter from a tornado is a very dangerous idea'. Ditch it is then, I think. Relieved to have that sorted, I invest in an app that shows me actual satellite maps and promises to alert me to incoming trouble, because even though everyone claims that it's hard to miss a storm on the horizon here, I'm willing to bet I'll be looking the other way at the time, probably at some goats.

Running out of time, I tick off two non-burger-shaped Columbus culinary icons before dinner: a Columbus-style pizza, with a base like a cracker and copious banana peppers, pepperoni, and little unidentified leathery items that may or may not be meat-based, and a strawberry buttermilk cone from Jeni's Ice Cream, a national chain, which has collaborated with everyone from Dolly Parton (strawberry pretzel pie) to Ted Lasso ('biscuits with the boss' flavour), that started life right here in Columbus.

I then somehow manage a modest salad at the Little West Tavern with Leah and Michelle from the local tourist board who kindly helped me out with my itinerary, and horrify me with tales of dodging alligators on Florida cycle paths (thank God my route won't be taking me down there), make ominous noises about recent 'weird weather', and insist I try the apple hand pies with Michelle's beloved Graeter's ice cream (other fans include President Biden and Oprah Winfrey, who once declared it 'absolutely the best ice cream I've ever tasted'). The pie has soft, buttery pastry and a finely diced, nicely tart filling, and though perhaps a little heavy on the cinnamon for my taste (8/10), it is certainly better than the McDonald's version. (The ice cream is of course good too, but then I love all ice cream, apart from the chicken-stock-caramel-swirl-with-crispy-chicken-skin version I tried in San Antonio, and still can't bring myself to write about.)

Finally the big day dawns: my meeting with Jamie Richardson, White Castle's VP of marketing (and, it turns out, the husband of its founder's great-granddaughter). En route to the Castle, Bethia whisks me quickly into the Krema Nut Company, est. 1898, and one of the oldest peanut butter producers still in operation in the country. Owner Brian Giunta, whose parents bought the business when he was in high school, apologises for the slightly chaotic atmosphere; staff are rushing to fulfil orders that have backed up over the holiday weekend, and 'the dry roaster broke down last week so, if you see scratches on my hand, don't worry. It's a very simple machine because it's old, but,' he sighs, 'it's temperamental. We don't use computers, everything here is done by eye.' Jay, who is preparing to fry what Brian estimates is over $2,500 of cashews, confirms this: 'The job's all visual, it changes from batch to batch.' Peanuts, he says, are his favourite nuts to cook, because they take the longest, which makes life easier.

COFFEE BREAK
Peanut Butter: A Brief History

Growing up in Britain in the 80s and 90s, peanut butter was seen as a very North American product – and about as sophisticated as Nutella. The adults I knew ate marmalade, jam or, in the case of my dad, salty, anchovy-based Gentleman's Relish. In fact, there's a much longer history of eating ground peanuts in both South America and Africa than there is in the States where, as with hot sauce, it was eventually popularised by a wealthy white man, in this case John Harvey Kellogg of cereal fame, who endorsed nut butters as a healthy vegan dairy substitute at his sanatorium in the 1890s.

Brian explains that originally peanut butter was made from raw nuts, ground into a paste for invalids and the dentally challenged. 'Honestly, raw peanut paste does not taste good, but it does keep better than the stuff made with cooked nuts.' Once the roads improved, however, people could begin to roast the nuts first to bring out their flavour, and a national love affair was born.* By the first decade of the twentieth century, it was being made in virtually every city in America of any size, though these days the industry is concentrated in the hands of big brands like Jif and Skippy. According to Andrew F. Smith's *Oxford Encyclopae-dia of Food and Drink in America*, 'Few other products in American culinary history have achieved such influence in so many ways in such a short period of time. In the early years of the twenty-first century, peanut butter was ensconced in 85 percent of the kitch-ens of America.' How much of that peanut butter goes into that uniquely American childhood favourite, the PB&J sandwich, remains unknown.

NB: I bought the best peanut butter of my life from a road-side stand near the Chesapeake Bay.

Brian shows us the difference between the runner peanuts from North Carolina most producers use, and the smaller, sweeter Spanish peanuts he buys from Texas and Oklahoma; 'they're so much brighter, so much more flavour', and explains how they go about making 2,000lb (907kg) of the stuff a day from the big burlap sacks of nuts that sit stacked on trolleys near the door.

'First we tip them into this roasting elevator here and they spin round and round at 300°F [149°C] for about twenty minutes before we cool 'em down. Now, I know in the UK they'd just go ahead and turn those roasted nuts into butter, but here in the States, we'd choke on that stuff!' As someone who consumes quite a lot of Brit-ish-made peanut butter, I feel a bit judged for not noticing, or even caring, that our producers apparently grind the nuts skin on, while

---

* Though the USA didn't invent it; credit for that should probably go to the Incas. The peanut itself came to modern North America via West Africa, where it's also made into roasted peanut paste.

in the USA they're blanched first to remove it. At Krema, they also take the heart out (Brian shows me a little protuberance on one side of a split nut, rather like a germ on a clove of garlic) 'because it has a bitter taste. Bigger companies that add salt and sugar don't bother, but we like to call our nuts the fil*let* of peanuts,' he says proudly. 'Then we grind, package, and it's good to go.'

Before we depart, he goes behind the lunch counter, where they serve up peanut butter sandwiches to local workers, to make us both a hot and spicy peanut butter shake. Sadly Krema do not ship overseas, but if you whizz vanilla ice cream with rather less milk, a couple of spoonfuls of good-quality peanut butter, a pinch of black and cayenne peppers, and a little salt and sugar to taste, you might get close to the oddly addictive combination of sweet, cool, creamy dairy and savoury, fiery hot peanuts. If you live locally, please just go and enjoy the sensation for yourself.

White Castle's modern headquarters look disappointingly like an airport hotel, with nary a crenellation in sight, though they do boast a giant slide in reception, a 'tip of the hat to our frozen food division, where the patties slide down the production line'. Like Krema, it's a family-owned business (CEO Lisa Ingram is the great-granddaughter of founder Billy, and eight of the twenty-five current members of the fifth generation will be doing internships with the business this summer), but I doubt this family gets its hands dirty repairing machinery.

Just as Bethia is taking a sneaky picture of me on the White Castle throne,* an honour usually reserved for 'Cravers' (White Castle superfans), Jamie appears. He's a compact, bearded ball of energy in his mid-fifties, with merry eyes and a habit of prefacing

---

* Carved with Latin mottos translated as 'I crave, therefore I am' and 'Hot steamy buns'.

everything he says with the word 'candidly', which of course gives the thrilling impression I'm being let into corporate secrets when in fact he's just explaining that Billy was a realtor in Wichita, Kansas, who got into the burger business when he began helping fry cook and fellow Wichita Rotarian Walt Anderson find sites for his burgeoning restaurant chain.

Though Ingram is the one who created the fast-food business as we know it today, the culinary innovations introduced by White Castle were all Anderson's. He's widely recognised as probably the first person to flatten the meatballs and cook them on a red-hot grill, as well as replacing the standard white bread with a specially designed and much more practical bun, both developments that speeded up the production process and made the results quicker and easier to eat. Ronald L. McDonald admitted in his book *The Complete Hamburger* that, with the bun in particular, Anderson 'did something no one else had ever done' – one small step for man, one giant leap for mankind. (Where, I wonder, following him up the stairs, does the line lie between hamburger and sandwich – is one simply a subset of the other?)

As I'm pondering this classic Aristotelian dilemma Jamie is candidly confiding that 'ground beef did not have the best reputation at the time' – in part thanks to *The Jungle*, Upton Sinclair's sensationalist exposé of the Chicago meatpacking industry, published in 1905. Ingram recognised the potential of Anderson's business to change the narrative. Before White Castle, he wrote in 1926, the word hamburger immediately conjured thoughts of 'the circus, or carnival, or the country fairs, or even of the dirty, dingy, ill-lighted hole-in-the-wall, down in the lower districts of the city. The day of dirty, greasy hamburgers is past . . . For a new system has arisen, the "White Castle System".' Under Ingram's micro-management, White Castles were to be shining beacons of cleanliness, spotless stainless steel and spotless, white-clad workers. A poster on display in the canteen shows the twenty-five criteria early White

Castle employees had to fulfil before presenting themselves to customers, including 'correct[ing] bad breath' and body odour.

'Billy believed that every family, whatever their income, deserved to have a hot and tasty dinner, at a time when going out to a restaurant was a really middle-class thing to do,' Jamie says, proudly showing us a replica of the very spatula Ingram designed for squashing Anderson's patties, which, like the puffy taco shaper, looks more like a garden implement than a cooking tool. This technique both helped speed up service, and allowed them to keep the prices low by spreading small amounts of meat thinly enough to fill a sandwich. The bun, meanwhile, turned the hamburger into a portable item, opening the doors, literally, to take-away, and drive-ins and eventually thrus: 'I don't think it's a stretch to say we invented carry out,' Jamie says with studied casualness.

The White Castle System of standardisation across branches was easily replicated too, both in new locations and, before long, by other chains. In 1961, White Castle became the first business to sell a billion hamburgers, a milestone not reached by McDonald's until three years later, but Billy's steadfast refusal to franchise, which he felt would cheapen the brand and weaken his control over every aspect of the operation, is, according to Josh Ozersky's book *The Hamburger*, the reason 'why White Castle, despite its thirty-year head start, is a stable and solvent but relatively tiny chain today'.

Jamie admits that 'we could have grown faster if we'd franchised, but it would have been a dilution. A family-owned business doesn't have to answer to a Wall Street analyst or whatever either, and you can move more slowly* if no one's pressuring you . . . I've got enormous respect for McDonald's and what they do,' he goes on

---

* Change certainly came slowly to Billy; though White Castle branched out into fries during the war, when meat was scarce, you couldn't get a cheeseburger there until 1962.

carefully, 'but they're all independently operated. It's just a different play, candidly.'

As with In-N-Out on the West Coast, staying small has given White Castle a kind of cultish appeal: 'In the age of everything being instantly available and homogenous there's an ache for something different, a pilgrimage almost – on paper our lack of locations feels like a hindrance,' Jamie muses, 'but in reality it probably adds to the experience.'

Indeed, the paper packaging comes printed with the stories of those whose devotion to the brand has seen them inducted into its Cravers Hall of Fame. When we sit down to lunch, the boxes we're given celebrate Michelle Purcell of Mount Pulaski, IL, who redecorated her entire kitchen to resemble a White Castle restaurant – 'She even confessed during her induction that she had stolen one of our White Castle logoed garbage cans to complete her kitchen decor package. We didn't press charges but requested that next time she ask' – and Scott Kempf of Novato, CA, who celebrated his sixtieth birthday by travelling over 16,000 miles to visit over 160 branches, 'including the most southern, eastern and northern locations, with stops in fifteen states. And, get this, he did it all in twenty-one days. It's true – not all superheroes wear capes!'

Such is the affection with which it's held that each Valentine's Day, White Castles turn into Love Castles, taking reservations for table service, and allotting each manager a budget for decoration. 'We get so many great moments,' Jamie says happily. 'A lot of proposals, a lot of weddings, people show up in limousines, dressed to the nines – people even bring their own cellos to serenade their dates. We had 30,000 reservations last year!' Alice Cooper, Adam Richman and the City of Whiting Indiana are all members of the Hall of Fame, and Eminem, he reveals, after swearing us to secrecy, has mentioned them in his new single, 'So all being well I should be hand-delivering White Castle for fifty to a recording studio tomorrow.'

I ask Jamie, as I tuck into my very first White Castle slider (the size of a Trolli gummy burger, with a fluffy white bun, pungent with the smell of the rehydrated onions they toast them on top of, and a disconcertingly finely ground, fairly neutral patty), whether he thinks there's a reason two iconic American burger chains, White Castle and Wendy's, are both based in Columbus. As ever, he's not lost for words: 'There's a real pride here in getting to know people on a traditional level, and I think our hamburger culture speaks to that too. Like the Midwest, the hamburger is unassuming, humble, and profoundly good.'

Amen to that.

Ridden: 228 miles
Climbed: 1,601 feet
Pies consumed: 3 (apple hand pie, cherry, chess)
All-American foods discovered: Cincinnati chili, smashburgers,
bologna, vegan burgers, Columbus-style pizza, sauerkraut
balls, peanut butter, sliders

11

TWISTER COUNTRY

In search of 7,000-year-old popcorn

*'Popcorn . . . is the basis of a number of dishes which are highly in favour. It
is very commonly popped and eaten and is considered a great dainty, as well
as a treat for visitors. It was formerly popped by throwing it on the hot coals
in an open fire-place, stirring it quickly, then pulling it out as it popped.'*
F. W. Waugh, *Iroquois Foods and Food Preparation*, 1916

Having signed a disclaimer and squealed down the White
Castle slide like an unusually noisy frozen patty, it's time to
head out of the city, and into the heart of the Midwest. Bethia
packs me off with a long list of suggestions, the first of which is a
bike shop, Paradise Garage, where they try to sort out the problem
with my pedals (inconclusive) and mention that the Alaskan cyclist
Lael Wilcox rode through town last night on the second day of her
attempt on the round-the-world record:* 259 miles from Indianapolis to Newark, OH in 14 hours 33 minutes. I feel very small as I get

---

* Which she smashes in 108 days, 12 hours, 12 minutes, taking the previous
record from the Scottish cyclist Jenny Graham's already impressive 124-day,
10-hour, 50-minute circumnavigation in 2018 – I can't recommend Jenny's
book about the experience, *Coffee First, Then the World*, strongly enough.

back on the bike and pedal the modest twenty-seven to Delaware, where I'm spending the night.

If I were going at that speed, however, I'd miss the details – the proud signs in front yards celebrating their high-school graduates (teenage me would have died of shame, admittedly) and the roadside banners promoting 'natural family month'. It cannot be denied that the American willingness to share their views with passers-by does make life more interesting for the traveller; I could ride for days in the UK without finding out a single thing about the beliefs of the communities I'm moving through; here they're hard to avoid.

The man at the reception of the Pacer Inn and Suites is similarly free with his opinions, telling me cheerfully that they've had 'a TON of tornadoes so far this year!' Delaware proves a small, quiet town of the kind I haven't seen since Texas, and I have an enjoyable wander and a plate of falafel at Opa's, a Greek restaurant with an impressive bourbon selection amassed by the owner, a friendly Albanian whiskey buff. (Slightly disconcertingly, I'm seated at the bar next to the 'FALLEN SOLIDER [sic] TABLE', laid with a single red rose, a white cloth, a blue ribbon, a slice of lemon and various other items to 'honor our fallen comrades'. It's only as I get up to leave that I realise with horror I've had my bag on the 'chair [that] is empty, the seat that remains unclaimed for they are no longer here', for which I can only sincerely apologise.)

Karma is swift. The next day starts fine, with an enormous spongy cinnamon roll at the Hamburger Inn, which Nancy my waitress informs me, with great specificity, is the oldest-remaining-diner-in-its-original-location-in-Ohio. 'I grew up here, it was part of my childhood, my dad used to bring me and my sister here after Sunday school and we'd split a cinnamon roll and a hot chocolate . . . so it's very weird to be on the other side of the counter,' she sighs before asking me about British television: *Downton Abbey* and *Midsomer Murders* and the like. (Good television and hilariously bad food now seem to be the only things we're known for in the US, which is a special relationship of a kind, I suppose.)

On the way to Waldo, where I try salty, porky, sinisterly smooth braunschweiger ('I like it, but then I like anything,' the barman tells me) on rye for lunch, I spot a new political yard sign: 'Jesus Christ for President 2024' (campaign slogan, 'Only Jesus can save this nation'). As it's beginning to drizzle, I tarry a while at the G&R Tavern, ordering a slab of banana cream pie from the chiller, which must be 8cm tall, and arrives welded to the plate. The pastry is good, once I find it under the mound of whipped cream and luminous sugary custard with a strong hint of isoamyl acetate* (7/10), but I'm so clearly overfaced that they place a take-out box silently by my side. Sadly this blows off my panniers in the storm that breaks as I'm riding between Waldo and the next town, Marion, almost as if the pie, at least, had checked the weather app, and didn't like what it saw.

Marion, as no doubt you're aware, is the Popcorn Capital of the World (admittedly a title also claimed by five other Midwestern cities), and home to the world's largest popcorn festival, which has been running annually since 1981 and has, in the past, put on such acts as Gloria Estefan and Huey Lewis and the News. The Popcorn Museum I'm here to see doesn't open for another ninety minutes, so I amuse myself by paying a damp visit to the striking Grecian revival Warren G. Harding memorial ('the last of the elaborate presidential tombs'), before seeking bedraggled shelter in the Warren G. Harding Presidential Library and Museum.

Horrified by my confession of ignorance when it comes to the twenty-ninth President of the United States, they go out of their way to try to enlighten me, insisting on me bringing Eddy in away from the hoodlums of this tranquil-looking city, and gifting me a

---

* This is the chemical compound used to mimic banana flavour, though as it's only one of the many present in the actual fruit, it's not terribly convincing. Interestingly, it's also one of the main flavourings in British pear drop sweets, which also taste a little bit like nail varnish remover.

bottle of water to rehydrate as I watch the introductory film, on my own, shivering. A towel might have been more useful given today's weather, but this kindness obliges me to spend longer in the place than is strictly ideal from a timekeeping perspective: I now know a lot about Harding, including that he had affairs, loved dogs,* and was once presented with an enormous papier-mâché model of a potato by the grateful residents of Idaho Falls, Idaho. This last item, I decide, is worth the price of admission on its own, even if those generous Idahoans spelled compliments wrong.

Having discharged my debt, I head for my original goal, the Wyandot Popcorn Museum, housed in the Marion Historical Society, which also features such novelties as a display of antique telephones and a Victorian beard-trimming chart. Its crowning glory, however, is a circus tent full of antique popcorn machines amassed by the late George K. Brown, scion of the Marion-based Wyandot Popcorn Company. I'm lucky enough to, quite by chance, find myself on a private guided tour with a volunteer who joined Wyandot in 1982 and immediately found herself co-opted into helping George with his collection of antique machines. 'Forty-two years later I'm still involved,' she sighs, not entirely enthusiastically, as she takes me round the brightly painted Victorian wagons and elegant 1950s self-service machines – 'I've only missed one popcorn festival that whole time.'

I make appropriately appreciative noises over the 1927 Holcomb & Hoke Popcorn Popper ('note the paddle-style butter applicator') and the 1935 Brown-Duval Moisture Tester, but I'm mostly interested in the history of popcorn itself, as it strikes me it must be one of the very few Native American prepared foods,

---

* His airedale Laddie Boy wore an engraved silver tag, which read 'I AM PRESIDENT HARDING'S DOG LADDIE / WHOSE DOG ARE YOU?' Unfortunately Laddie's friend Oh Boy, a white bulldog, 'did not respond adequately to training to be allowed in the White House'.

along with things like maple syrup and jerky, to remain part of the modern, mainstream US diet. According to historian Andrew F. Smith, pre-Columbian Americans domesticated maize as early as 5,000 BCE. These primitive varieties were small-kernelled and hard-shelled; difficult to chew, but easy to pop open with a little heat: ears of such corn thought to be 5,600 years old have been found in caves in New Mexico.

Europeans were intrigued by this novel foodstuff, with early French explorers noting that the Iroquois popped corn by putting it into a pottery jar with hot sand, and then used it to make popcorn soup. Records suggest, however, that it did not make it east of the Mississippi until the nineteenth century, when it became a popular street food, sold at fairs, circuses, election rallies and other such entertainments. Its adoption by movie theatres, and then bars, gave popcorn a whole new audience – and, unlike sugary snacks, it wasn't rationed during World War Two, which turned its consumption into a patriotic act. Today, the US continues to be the largest ready-to-eat popcorn market in the world, consuming 14 billion quarts annually.

COFFEE BREAK

Native American Culinary Culture

'The Iroquois and the Cherokee called corn, bean, and squash the three sisters because they nurture each other like family when planted together.'

Christina Gish Hill, 'Pre-Colonial Foodways'

Indigenous American plants like corn, white and sweet potatoes, cassava and tomatoes are among the world's most widely cultivated crops – what would Indian food be without chillies, or Italian without tomatoes? Other native ingredients include chia, quinoa, wild rice, peanuts, Jerusalem artichokes, pumpkins and squash like courgettes, avocados, Brazils, pecan and cashew nuts, many varieties of bean, guava, cranberries, black cherry, pineapple, papaya, and of course chocolate, maple syrup, vanilla and allspice.

Early European settlers relied heavily on their Indian neighbours for food (indeed, they were in awe of the abundance of their harvests) but showed little apparent interest in the cuisines of the over 500 tribes living in the area now known as the USA, which have had to fight hard to keep these traditions alive. Thousands starved to death on the Trail of Tears, in which President Andrew Jackson forced more than 125,000 people from the Cherokee, Chickasaw, Choctaw and Seminole Nations to walk to their new 'homelands' in Oklahoma. The US government also funded a buffalo cull, reducing a pre-1800 population of over 60 million to a few hundred beasts in just a century. As White Mountain Apache chef Nephi Craig has said, 'You want to attack a people and wipe them out? Attack their food.'

Pushed off their ancestral lands by colonial expansionism, many tribes lost their local knowledge as well as their hunting grounds, leaving them reliant on government handouts of foods hitherto completely alien to them like lard, sugar, tinned meat and fish, powdered milk and white flour. Modern reservations frequently qualify as food deserts, with little access to fresh food and unsurprising consequences: the Office of Minority Health reported in 2018 that 81 per cent of Native American adults were either overweight or obese. There are green shoots, however, in the form of a growing movement to replant traditional crops on tribal lands and make them available to the community. Oglala

Lakota chef Sean Sherman's 'decolonised' indigenous restaurant Owamni, in Minnesota, serves dishes like smoked bison chimichurri, and corn cookies with sweet corn pudding, and rejects colonial ingredients like wheat, cane sugar and dairy. In 2022, it was named best new restaurant in the United States by the James Beard Foundation.

GREAT LAKES WILD RICE SALAD

This is inspired by the version served at the Mitsitam Cafe, in Washington, DC, which celebrates the annual wild rice harvest of the Native tribes around the Great Lakes. Zizania palustris is not actually a rice, but a grass that grows in the shallows after the spring ice melt. Ojibwe men and boys traditionally harvested the crop from canoes, knocking the heads off the plants into the bottom of the boat, then, once back on land, dancing on their haul to remove the outer husks. Women would then complete the winnowing using a birch bark basket. The Ojibwe of Minnesota still do the harvesting by canoe, but tend to use modern mills to process the seeds.

Wild rice is pricey in the UK, but filling and nutritious, and this recipe is easily customisable; in the autumn replace the courgette with cubes of roasted squash or sweet potato, or other vegetables of your choice. Nutty, vivid green pumpkin seed oil is a favourite in Austria, and can easily be found online. Good on its own, this is really lovely with poached or roasted trout or salmon.

Serves 4
200g/1 cup wild rice
500ml/2 cups chicken or vegetable stock or water
1 courgette/zucchini

12 *cherry tomatoes, halved*
2 *tbsp dried cranberries*
2 *tbsp pumpkin seeds or pine nuts, lightly toasted*

For the dressing
4 *tbsp cider vinegar*
1 *tbsp maple syrup*
2 *tbsp neutral oil*
1 *tbsp pumpkin seed oil*
½ *tsp chipotle chilli flakes (optional)*

1. Put the wild rice into a medium pan with the stock or water, then cover and bring to the boil. Turn down to a simmer and leave until tender, which should take 50 to 60 minutes. Drain and spread out on a serving plate to cool.
2. Whisk together the dressing ingredients, season, taste and adjust as necessary, then toss with the rice.
3. Use a y-shaped peeler to slice the courgette into long ribbons. Lightly salt and then arrange in a circle in the middle of the rice or strew on top as desired. Add the tomatoes, cranberries and seeds and serve.

I leave clutching a box of freshly popped corn, half of which I tuck into my panniers for later, and set off north along the Sandusky Plains Prairie Trail – prairie! I can almost see the covered wagons and smell the campfires – studiously ignoring the ominously dark clouds gathering to the north. Heading for the town of Findlay, some sixty miles away, I pass a coonhunting club, a 'We the People Are Pissed Off' flag and an increasing number of signs urging me to pray to end abortion, and then, perhaps noting my failure to immediately comply, the heavens open. It's not so much rain as a wall of water: I put my lights on at four in the afternoon, but can barely see a thing, despite periodically wiping away excess liquid from my eye sockets. This being the Midwest, there is nowhere to shelter – not a bus stop, not even a spreading tree, just open fields as far as the eye can see, so when I roll into Kenton and see the Pfeiffer Station General Store (last train departed: 1981), I stop with a squeal of brakes, whacking my head on one of the hanging baskets in my hurry to get under cover. The women behind the counter regard me unenthusiastically as I drip over their shelves of jarred peaches and elderberry jelly. Good as these things sound, they're hardly the kind of thing I can eat here, so I order a slice of dried-up pizza, a coffee and some black raspberry ice cream, at which point they warm to my 'cute accent', and a small boy comes out from a back room to gawp.

Feeling self-conscious, I squelch outside to wait out the storm on the porch, and am thrilled when the unexpected clop of hooves heralds the arrival of an Amish buggy, which halts to exchange words with a similar hearse-like vehicle approaching from the other direction, both men wearing straw hats and extravagant beards and holding large black umbrellas over themselves and their huddled children. They depart as another man, also hirsute, but presumably not Amish, pulls up in a truck and dashes into the store. On the way out, he asks where I'm heading, sucks his teeth at the answer and wishes me luck with both the weather and 'the crazy drivers'.

Despite these repeated warnings, my biggest problem is closer to home; somehow, for all the miles I've put away in northern Europe, I've never learnt the important lesson that you should never ride in damp shorts, and eight hours in the rain today has left me in such agony that I spend as much time out of the saddle as I can, pumping along for a few pedal strokes and then coasting, bottom in the air, for as long as possible on dead flat, empty roads through dead flat, empty fields, the monotony broken by the occasional grain silo or barn. By the time I limp into Findlay about 8.30pm, all I'm interested in is lying down on my front, which I do, covered in nappy rash cream, eating raw vegetables from Kroger and trying hard to forget this morning's braunschweiger.

Having covered the affected area of my posterior with the largest dressing I can find, I set off with a grim face the next morning, leaving the cleaners a $5 apology for the oily medicinal mess all over the sheets. The sun is out and oddly things feel almost OK until I stop for a waffle and some local maple syrup in Leipsic and discover, after a brief and panicky moment staring uncomprehendingly at the blue gummy stuff on the inside of my shorts, that I've melted the cushioning of the plaster, the rest of which is now apparently welded to my broken skin. There's little I can do but push on, casting beseeching looks at the Blessed Virgins who kneel, hands clasped, in every other front yard.

I'm definitely in big sky country now, riding the romantic likes of 'ROAD X' and 'ROAD 13', past towns called macho things like Defiance, a place that sounds like it might provide a good square lunch. Dustin, tending bar at the handsome tin-ceilinged Kissner's ('the oldest tavern in Ohio still owned by one family'), struggles to understand my accent, particularly when I ask him what salad dressings they have. 'All of 'em,' he says, perplexed. 'You just name it.' After the disaster with the orange Italian dressing back in Texas, I play it safe with ranch; the shock of discovering the patty melt, which I'd vaguely assumed from Matt's Amtrak experience to be something like a cheeseburger toastie, is actually fried (a fried burger in a fried sandwich! Who comes up with these things, Elvis?) is quite enough for one day. I finish with a slice of cherry pie, which is molten from the microwave, rendering the pastry soft and spongy, and the cherry filling gloopy with starch (6/10), but as I have about twenty-five miles still to cycle today, I manage to put quite a dent in it nonetheless.

By the time I reach Bryan Ohio ('the lollipop capital of the world') I'm only too pleased to get off and give my wounds a rest.

Bethia was insistent I visit the home of such nostalgic all-American treats as Dum Dums lollies and Circus Peanuts, where even the water tower is adorned with brightly wrapped lollipops. Haribo-style gummy candy seems to be taking over here just as quickly as it is at home, and I've struggled to find much in the way of my preferred cycling fuel, boiled sweets, in most stores: at the Spangler Candy Visitor Center, I hit payday.

As I'm pondering a display of antique medicated menthol and horehound cough tablets, my phone vibrates in my pocket. At the same moment I hear a squeak from the woman who's just sold me my ticket. 'Excuse me,' she says in a low voice, looking around slightly furtively, 'but do you follow American politics at all?'

I say I know a little, which seems the safest answer; enough to show interest, not enough for anyone to worry about sharing their opinions.

'Well then, Donald Trump has just been found guilty on ALL CHARGES.' Her face looks fit to split open with joy. I ask her what this might mean, and she admits she's not quite sure . . . 'But I sure am delighted!'

She's still smiling as I leave with a fistful of Dum Dums lollies.

That same evening, as I tote my washing back from the machine in an outhouse of the Bryan Inn (5.4/10 on booking. com, but also, only $48, and with washing facilities, if no working television, plus a free cockroach lying with its feet up in the bath), I get talking to a couple grilling steaks and shrimp in the back of a truck outside my room. They initially want to settle an argument about my accent – 'She said Australia, I said nah' – before informing me that they're from Arkansas but, the man says proudly, have been 'all over the world' with his job maintaining water towers. 'You mean all over the country, honey,' his partner, drinking a beer on a plastic chair next to their open door, corrects him gently. 'Well,' he shoots back, 'we've been up near the border with Canada, and down to Mexico once – that was real nice. I've seen water towers in the shape of teapots, corn cobs, all kinds.' (Oddly, they're unaware of the Dum Dums lollipop tower, but he says it sure does sound neat.)

I tell them we don't really have many water towers in the UK, or at least not that I've noticed anyway, but they're more interested in our healthcare and maternity provision – life has not been easy for them, it seems – and tell me they'll both be voting for Donald Trump, the only person who's ever done anything for people like them, she says, in November, before moving on to Princess Diana (not as dead as I'd assumed, apparently).

Just as I'm wondering where the conversation will go next, the woman asks me urgently if I tried chocolate gravy while I was in the South. She flushes with pleasure when I ask for her recipe. 'Well now, you whisk together flour, cocoa and milk, heat it up, then I add a little butter at the end, just before I put it on the biscuits. You try fried green tomatoes too?' I say yes, I had them in a biscuit sandwich. She looks shocked, more shocked than about the whole maternity pay thing: 'Oh, no, honey, in a biscuit don't count, you just have them as is, or maybe with fried eggplant, or o-kra.'

I realise it's getting dark, and I still haven't located somewhere selling sturdier surgical dressings, let alone fresh fruit and vegetables, so I make my excuses and get on my bike. 'You here tomorrow?' she asks somewhat plaintively as I switch on my lights. 'You just come and knock, I'm in all day, we can hang out!'

It strikes me that, with only one truck between them, she's effectively trapped here until her partner comes home from work, and I feel sad about it . . . but not sad enough not to leave Bryan at first light after eating a $2.99* supermarket grapefruit with my bare

---

* Currently 50p/62c in my local supermarket despite coming from a lot further away. The price of food in the States is a shock to me, even with the rampant inflation at home.

hands in the parking lot, washed down with a cup of scalding but free motel coffee.

This morning brings excitement as I cross the state line from Ohio to Indiana: another new state for me, and my tenth of the trip so far. The moment which I anticipate for miles, constantly checking my position on the map to ensure I haven't missed it, does not prove momentous (the only indication is a sign marking the spot where Ohio school buses turn around rather than risk their tyres touching enemy territory) but it puts a smile on my face, even if the flat fields look the same on both sides of the border.

I might not have anticipated tornadoes, or extreme heat, but when I planned the trip I was concerned about the mental toll cycling through the Midwest might take. I imagined riding for hours along featureless field boundaries without so much as a fence to admire, yet in fact the landscape here is rarely so empty; there's always a farm or a ranch house to look at, a flag or a church sign to provide clues about the community I'm passing through. At one point there's actually rather too much excitement, as I suddenly find myself pursued by two large black dogs down a loose track – they're fast and remarkably persistent. Mostly dogs thus far have just chased me to the limits of their property, but these two are in it for the long haul. In the end I shout, OH, WILL YOU JUST FUCK OFF at them, and they melt away like magic, shocked, perhaps, by my very unMidwestern vulgarity. I wait until I'm back on the main road to stop and calm myself with a sugary Dum Dums. My legs, I notice in a detached kind of a way, are shaking like jelly.

Terror aside, I've been dreaming of an omelet for most of the twenty-five miles since setting off from Bryan; a big, chunky American omelet, firm as a chammy leather and swollen with fillings, so that's exactly what I order at Roger's Harvest House in Hamilton, a low-ceilinged room full of denim-clad farmers wearing hats advertising feed stores and agricultural chemical companies ('It's sure good to have something in the ground at last') and ladies lunching at 11am. As ever, the waitress is hovering impatiently while I'm still distracted by the menu ads for Bob's Auto Repair and the Party Store ('complete the evening at home with candlelight, soft music and our beverages') – flustered, I pick a Farmer's Omelet, which comes with ham, cheese, onion and peppers.

'What cheese d'you want?' she demands. I sigh, jaded by endless choice. Given the vast majority of cheese here tastes the same, can't they just decide the best one for omelets and stick with it?

'Oh, errr . . . Pepper Jack?'

'Mmm-hm, toast or biscuits?'

'Biscuits, please.'

She departs without a smile, and soon brings back an omelet that, while perfectly yellow and smooth, just gives me the inexplicable ick. Scattered with random tiny pieces of shell, and plump with vast amounts of pink ham, a few soggy, oddly plasticky-tasting pepper squares, and a layer of the gloopy processed cheese I'm beginning to hate, I can't finish it. I take brief solace in the biscuits while reading advice on saddle sores online, and then, willing to try anything at this point, go outside and pull a second pair of bib shorts on over the top of the first, an act that feels vaguely indecent, despite the fact I'm putting clothes on rather than taking them off. Halfway through this indelicate operation, just as I'm hoiking them up, a large car pulls into the space in front of me, and the occupants scurry past, eyes politely averted, leaving me in such a hurry to get out of town that it takes a good ten minutes for me to realise I've put the extra shorts on back to front. This time I don't care; well aware of the slim probability of finding anywhere else to lean a laden bike in the next forty miles, I shove him against a handy telegraph pole and shamelessly swap them round on the side of the highway.

I pass through the pleasant town of Pleasant Lake, which has a rather eerie crumbling railway depot in the middle, and hit my first gravel roads since Texas. These ones are busier, the cars throwing up great clouds of white dust I have to hold my breath through, little pebbles pinging off Eddy's paintwork, but I soon realise, as I'm passed at a terrific clip by a young boy in a small buggy, why they're here; I'm now in Amish country proper. It's not long before buggies and funereal-looking carriages are everywhere, driven, I'm pleased to see, by both men and women – and I'm thrilled when one red-headed young woman raises her hand to me in greeting as we pass. Though our lives could hardly be more different (and ridiculous as it may sound), it feels like a moment of communion between two people moving at a slower pace in a world of trucks and RVs, and I begin greeting everyone I pass, just as I would a fellow cyclist.

There are a few of them here too, and it gladdens my heart to see two young girls tearing out of a farm gate on bikes as their unnervingly young-looking brother practises the horse-drawn equivalent of handbrake turns in the front yard. I decide it's easily the most interesting place I've ridden so far: instead of the neat, empty yards I've become accustomed to, the gardens are a hive of activity; women bent double among rows of lettuces or pegging out soberly coloured garments on the washing lines (another thing I haven't seen in a while), children playing among the chickens, and a great many elaborate, multi-storey bird houses. Though some fields appear to have been neatly scythed, I'm startled to see a woman using a ride-on mower in one, and, more than once, men using heavy horses to pull modern farm equipment. When a car roars into view I feel positively violent at the noisy, choking intrusion.

I stop at the Chain o'Lakes country store hoping for some good old-fashioned baking, but quickly realise, as I slink in slightly ashamed by my Lycra,* that they cater for sizeable families, not lone women. The chillers are full of enormous bags of ham and tubs of sour cream (a notice asks for large church orders to be made at least a week in advance), the aisles full of Christian colouring books, sacks of crisps and dusty candles – in the end I have to be shown a small fridge full of birch beer by a sweet but silent girl standing shyly behind the till.

'We didn't have pie for breakfast like one of our neighbours did, he thought he had to have pie three times a day . . . That was his hobby, I guess you could call it.'

Grace Heinzman, 84, Hamilton County, quoted in *Feeding Our Families: Memories of Hoosier Homemakers*, 1983

The Amish are descendants of Swiss and French Anabaptists who split off from the main movement in the late seventeenth century and first arrived in the States in the mid-1700s, though the population grew slowly until the mid-twentieth century, when it began to really take off: in 1971, there were 50,000 Amish in North America, now the number is thought to be over 400,000.

---

* 'Oh, they don't mind what *you* wear,' Andy had reassured me back in Columbus, but still, it feels wrong until I see a girl in hot pants and a bikini top outside supervising a young Amish boy loading a gas canister into the back of her truck without either batting an eyelid.

Diets, like many other things, vary greatly between communities, but the traditional Amish menu seems best described as plain: high in carbohydrates, meat and dairy, supplemented with home-grown and canned vegetables, and low in highly processed foods, though I'm surprised to see, looking at cookbooks, more reliance on industrial ingredients like shortening and even boxed cake mix than I'd expected. Indeed, as there are no specific religious dietary restrictions (though alcohol consumption is low), fast-food restaurants and supermarkets in heavily settled areas often provide buggy parking for their Amish customers. The prevailing view seems to be that life with a big family and little modern technology is hard enough without shunning time-saving innovations like Big Macs.

There's a focus on communal eating – 'There's always food,' as Elaine Jones, an Amish chef at the Carriage House in Topeka, IN, observes in a local recipe collection, 'if you're coming over or you have friends stop in on a Sunday afternoon, you serve something. We have food after a church service – that's a standard thing. We basically have the same things every time, and I think that's important. It takes stress off the lady preparing it because she knows what she's going to fix. She doesn't have to top anyone else. Takes away the peer pressure.' These things might include bread and cheese, homemade peanut butter, noodles, egg salad, ham and homemade pickles and jellies. Equally, when church members travel to help with a communal barn raising, the women prepare the food while their menfolk build the barn, and they all sit down to eat together – roast meat and vegetables, pies, pickles and the like.

One thing they are still known for, given their communities are often found in wheat-growing regions where flour is cheap, is their baking, and you'll often see pies, cookies and breads for sale by the road in Amish settlements.

The children certainly seem industrious; I pass a barefoot little girl expertly herding cows in for milking, and two boys trying to do the same, rather more ineptly but with great mirth, a few miles on. There are duck farms and basket makers, custom carriage workshops and cheese producers, and the countryside is beautiful; rolling and green suddenly – I feel quite warm towards the Amish way of life as I roll into Goshen, until I remember just how much time they have to spend in church.*

I end up spending two nights in Goshen, a city named after the land given to the Hebrews by the Pharaohs in the time of Joseph, and now known as an 'extremely prominent recreational vehicle and accessories manufacturing center'. The forecast is for heavy and persistent rain, and I sense my saddle sores could do with a rest, so I extend my stay in the Best Western, and enjoy a Midwestern minibreak, eating pretzels with Amish peanut butter, ogling ads for a hillbilly hot dog evening at the Cornerstone Christian Fellowship and generally getting the feel of a place where a shop offering 'relentlessly patriotic apparel' sits next to a bookstore that proudly proclaims: 'we sell banned books'.

On Saturday morning, I hit the farmers' market: the baker has already sold out and packed up by 9.30am, but I buy some strawberries from a young Amish boy from Middleburg and some salad leaves from a lady who throws in a bunch of garlic scapes for free. Outside, I'm disconcerted to notice the label on the kefir I've just opened for breakfast features a large Saint Bernard lying proudly between two trophies. Looking more closely, I realise it's called 'Champion's Choice', and comes with feeding guidelines rather

---

* And that I'd be expected to be married and looking after my grandchildren by now, and that I'd have to do all the washing and cleaning by hand, and also, worst of all, that they don't tend to keep dogs as pets but as livestock, etc., etc., etc. Good baking can only take you so far.

than serving suggestions for humans. Taking a cautious swig, I go online to discover testimonials from satisfied customers claiming that regular doses will make my 'hair-coat . . . just AMAZING' and leave me noticeably 'less smelly'. Both these things feel like they'd be an improvement, but after drinking half the bottle, I decide to go in and check with the vendor if I'm about to die. He laughs, winks and tells me he has a glass himself every morning, but as it would cost him an extra $50k to certify his kefir for human consumption, he only markets it for animals. (The same goes, he points out, for the raw butter and milk on sale at a few of the Amish stalls.)

Mighty relieved, and excited for the coming benefits for my hair-coat, I head to the library, where I spend a happy few hours immersed in Amish and Mennonite cookbooks, breaking only for lunch at the very retro South Side soda shop, which has an original 1940s soda fountain and a 1950s-style, chrome-trimmed dining car out back. When my root beer float arrives, an enormous ball of ice cream balanced on its rim, I regret telling the waitress, who appears to check if I want dessert just as I'm taking my first bite of salmon salad, that I'd like a slice of pie . . . but it's too late, she's already back, reeling off the options from a vast tray of the things. 'Cherry, red raspberry, chocolate, pecan, chocolate pecan, rhubarb, fudge nut brownie, strawberry . . .' There must be nine or ten – plus, she says as I'm trying to decide, they have more cream varieties in the chiller if I'd care to go and look. After inspecting them all, still chewing on my salad, I go for shoo-fly, which she explains doubtfully is 'kind of Amish . . . I guess?' When I try it later, I appreciate her difficulty in describing it, as it's like nothing I've eaten before: there's a sweet streusel-like doughy layer on top, and a kind of brown-sugar jellied substance underneath, all encased in a slightly salty pastry. It's not unpleasant, if perhaps inadvisable fare for diabetics, but I really wish I'd gone for some lovely tart rhubarb (7/10); I can't help thinking of my plant at

home, in an old tub by the back door, with no one there to pick it
and turn it into fool.

The clouds lift the next morning, and I don't have far to go;
Gráinne, an Irish friend settled in South Bend with her American
husband, has invited me to spend the night, so I make a leisurely
pace, surprised at the suddenly winding roads and thickly wooded
countryside – I even see, and chat to, another cyclist, the first I've
seen since Columbus (out on a day ride, he says, overtaking me
apologetically on his racy carbon frame). It's all going swimmingly
until a t-junction where an elderly man in a large car turns on to the
wrong side of the road, stopping just in time within an inch of my
front wheel before reversing slowly and then driving past without a
flicker of eye contact, let alone apology, leaving me wondering
whether the disabled sticker on his windscreen could perhaps indicate a visual impairment. Finally, it seems, the crazy drivers have
caught up with me.

The landscape seems to flatten out as I approach the city, so I'm
amazed when what appears to be a heather-clad, sugar-loaf-shaped
hill with what might even be a few grazing sheep near the top
appears on the horizon. I can't believe my eyes; suddenly I'm
looking at a little piece of home! I'm so pleased I even stop to take a
picture. It's only as I draw closer I realise I'm hallucinating and it's
an enormous spoil heap, the purplish heather black plastic, the
dappled sunlight on close-cropped grass just different shades of
soil, the sheep rubbish of some kind, and feel oddly bereft, and a
very long way from home.

A night with Gráinne and her family, husband Pete and three
small boys, Killian, Ruarí and Tomás, makes me feel a bit better.
The older ones have insisted on hanging a tricolour from the porch
so I can find the house – 'We only have it out for St Patrick's,'
Gráinne says quickly – and it's lovely to sit chatting on the swing

chair with a cup of tea (tea! The first cup of hot stuff I've had since leaving home) as a rotating cast of neighbourhood small boys flit in and out in search of drawing paper, plasters and snacks. She's worried what I might want to eat, suggesting several local restaurants that do delivery, but I am being nothing less than wholly truthful when I say their intended family supper of breaded chicken, roasted new potatoes and salad sounds absolutely perfect to me.

Gráinne sends me off on a bucolic route north along the river the next morning, where I almost immediately spot a beaver* floating downstream on its back, nibbling on vegetation as it goes, spinning slowly round for all the world like it's on a rubber ring in a lazy river with a piña colada in its paw. After passing a banner reading 'I'd love a mean tweet and $1.79 gas right now', I cross the Michigan state line; one step closer to its eponymous lake, where I plan to spend the night.

Battling a headwind, I cycle through a scattered settlement of lonely, austere Victorian houses and sheds with peeling paint, all very American Gothic in tone, and past a Christian summer camp site where the canoe over the gate bearing the words 'WELCOME TO CAMP' contrasts oddly with the trio of large crucifixes in the next field. By the time I get to Buffalo City and sit down to a 'working person's special' (a Velveeta† cheeseburger, crinkle-cut fries and a chocolate malt) at Redamak's, I feel bone tired and realise the constant wind is deceiving; out of it, the sun this early-June afternoon is extremely strong.

---

* Online wildlife experts are quick to inform me it's actually a muskrat, which sounds even more exotic to my ears.
† Another 'pasteurised prepared cheese product' to add to my list of regrets.

The sight of Lake Michigan through the trees proves an instant tonic: it's almost like being back on the Pacific Coast Highway, I can't get over how blue the water is, how white the sand and how expensive-looking the houses. I'm gladly anticipating a lazy afternoon on the beach once I've put up my tent at the 'primitive campsite' that's the only one I could find with space this evening. OK, so an isolated clearing in the forest a ten-minute walk from the road wouldn't have been my first choice as a lone woman with no working phone, but such is life, I tell myself, pushing Eddy up a muddy path: there are no more nutters in America than anywhere else, they just make more movies about them.

Having erected my tiny shelter (faster this time, but with frequent breaks to reapply chemicals that have no discernible off-putting effect on the flies I keep finding snacking on my flesh) and set up the solar panel in the hope of charging my devices, I put on my swimming costume and excitedly grab a towel, a book and some suncream.

Pushing Eddy back down towards the shore, I notice, to my disapproval, a lot of litter strewn on the ground – but before I can let out a single tsk I'm swarmed by a cloud of vengeful black flies, a little smaller than a horsefly, but making up for this deficiency with sheer numbers. One minute the air is clear, the next they're all over me, biting hard enough for me to shriek in panic. I drop Eddy and run, but they pursue me, so then I run back, irresolute, try to push him down the dune to the beach, realise the absurdity of this plan and retreat, sobbing now (though more with revulsion than pain), lock him up hastily and sprint clumsily down to the water, throwing off clothes as I go. Still they're clinging on; I race into the lake, feel the relief of the cool fresh water . . . come up for air and the bastards dive-bomb my scalp. The only peace I have is when completely submerged, which is not really a long-term solution, so I grab my possessions and make my way back up the dune, still accompanied by my phalanx of hungry hangers-on. More join the party as I jerkily throw all my stuff in my pannier and ride away in my swimming costume – noticing blood running from my ankle, I begin to wail and pedal faster. Fortunately, though there were people on the beach, apparently unbothered by the flies, I see no one as I leave the camp, still snivelling in self-pity.

I don't stop until I'm well away from the coast, when I put a few more clothes on, and google the nearest place selling regionally appropriate bug spray, which is how I end up in a Walmart Supercenter thirty minutes away, limbs an angry red colour and still dotted with smears of blood, combing the aisles while listening to a woman saying down the phone, 'Sure, he can take his name off the birth certificate, but he'll need to go to the courthouse, and it'll cost him $200.' I buy a can of OFF! DEEP WOODS, which promises me long-lasting protection against zika, dengue or West Nile virus (though in truth I'd just like not to be bitten) and retire to the nearest McDonald's to smother myself in the stuff in peace over a blue raspberry McFlurry.

Back at the campsite, clad in leggings, a fleece and two pairs of socks despite the lingering heat, I'm entranced to see fireflies – my first ever! – blinking in the bushes, though the mosquitos in this beautiful hell hole still drive me into bed by 8.30pm. Unfortunately my wildlife encounters are not over for the day: as I lie awake trying not to scratch, I hear some scuffling in the dry leaves, the rustling of plastic bags and then the sound of one being torn open – and realise, cursing my idiocy, I've made the rookie error of leaving the leftovers up on the table.

Fumbling around for my phone I waste precious battery googling 'are there bears in Indiana', and discover that yes, indeed, they're not unheard of. Even racoons, as my rational brain tells me this animal probably, surely is, can apparently make short work of a flysheet with their claws . . . or so some guy on Reddit claims.

After scanning an academic study on effective deterrents, I play a Spotify soundtrack of dogs barking each time I'm woken up, which is a lot: as well as the raccoons, something is munching vegetation nearby, probably a deer, and later I hear something (else?) shuffling around close to my head emitting a soft, low squeaking noise, which I have to hope is a groundhog.

Unsurprisingly, I wake early and make short work of breaking camp, gathering up as much of the racoon's cast-offs as I can find (not a fan of the old ranch dressing apparently) to stuff in the first bin I come across. Still fully covered from the neck downwards, I head down to the shore, where a single mournful slider and several abandoned cans of bug spray give some context to the litter I'd observed the day before, grab the sunglasses I dropped in my own distress, and leave with just a few hopeful flies clinging to me, praying fervently never to see the place again.

The bike path runs through the swampy grasslands that run parallel to the shore, but it's muddy and flooded in places, and nice as it is to see deer, wild turkeys and even a slow-moving turtle, I quickly decide that, after the night I've had, I'd prefer to take my chances on the highway. It's only after two hours on the road that I finally feel brave enough to peel off some layers in the loo while waiting for my breakfast porridge. The countryside is nice, but right now, Chicago feels safer.

Ridden: 439 miles
Climbed: 6,391 feet
Pies consumed: 3 (banana cream, cherry, shoo-fly)
All-American foods discovered: popcorn, braunschweiger,
shoo-fly pie, Velveeta

12

THAT'S AMORE

In search of the deepest of pizzas

'We're mostly macrobiotic, but sometimes I take the family out for a pizza.'
John Lennon

Riding between the glassy lake and the skyscrapers into Chicago's famous skyline is truly the most thrilling entrance to a city I can imagine – after the low-rise landscape of the past few days, everything here suddenly seems big and shiny and exciting. My youth hostel in the Loop, the downtown area apparently devoid of any decent places to eat, is appropriately cavernous too, which means there's no one to hear me scream when I get into the shower and discover a tick sucking happily on my thigh. Fortunately this is one hazardous beastie I do feel well equipped to deal with, but having deployed the dog's tick remover to flush it down the drain,* I feel in sore need of a drink. Flo & Santos, a Polish-American sports bar, pizza and pierogi joint (that classic

---

* Something I later regret; always take a photograph of the tick against a light-coloured background (and the spot where you were bitten so you can keep an eye on the area) and then drown it in alcohol or freeze it for several days before disposing of it. Turns out they survive just fine in water.

combo), provide me with a large cold gose wheat beer, which feels sour and salty enough to count as a rehydration aid, and a tavern-style pizza, Chicago's lesser-known but arguably most popular local style of pie.

Everyone I ask in the few days I spend in the city tells me they eat deep-dish pizza maybe once or twice a year, usually when out-of-towners come to visit. This much thinner variety is designed with everyday practicality in mind; crisp enough to pick up with one hand while the other holds a drink, it's topped right to the edge so it can be cut into bite-sized squares for easy consumption. Options on offer tonight include Chicago's beloved Italian beef, and buffalo chicken and blue cheese, but I go for the Polish, with kiełbasa, sauerkraut and smoked bacon. It's actually not so different to the Columbus-style pizza, if perhaps a little less like a cracker, and is indeed dangerously easy to eat whether you're drinking or turning the pages of a horribly fascinating account of the damage humans have wreaked on the Great Lakes – which hold a fifth of the world's surface fresh water. Reading it,* I realise why I haven't yet seen a freshwater fish on the menu, anywhere.

The first person to let me into the secret that native Chicagoans rarely eat deep-dish is Bill, the guide on the excellent free walking tour my hostel puts on a few times a week. I learn much else of interest, including that the city is built on the land of the Miami, Illinois, Ottawa and Potawatomi people, and the name is thought to be a corruption of the Miami-Illinois word shikaakwa, meaning place of the stink onions, referring to the ramsons that once grew wild on the banks of the Chicago River – though naturally I spend most of the tour trying to steer him back towards my favourite subject.

* Dan Egan's *The Death and Life of the Great Lakes.*

Finally I break him. 'Yeah, people in Chicago love to argue about pizza – we have people calling themselves pizza historians here, that's how seriously we take it. People say deep-dish isn't authentic,' he shrugs, 'but, hey, I like it. Go to Giordano's, get the stuffed spinach; that's where me and my family go to celebrate. We wouldn't eat it every day though, a slice is a meal.' (I mentally dismiss this last observation as hyperbole – who can stop at just one slice of pizza?)

One of the other significant things about Chicago is its history as the centre of the world's meatpacking industry; less of a tourist attraction these days than the pizza, but at the stockyards' peak in 1900, they attracted half a million bloodthirsty sightseers annually. Some of the packers even offered guided tours, advising skipping certain stops if 'weak of stomach'. Though it's hard to imagine it made for a fun day out, I ponder whether this willingness to face up to the reality of slaughter is perhaps preferable to our modern squeamishness given Americans continue to be among the largest consumers of meat in the world,* something I can well believe given how difficult it is to avoid on menus.†

As the yards closed in 1971, victims of decentralisation and the decline of rail transport, there's not much left to see in the area, but I head down there anyway, on the bus to give my saddle sores a chance to heal.

Having skipped lunch, my first stop is Paco's Tacos, which occupies a space at the back of La Internacional Supermercado on Ashland and W. 46th Street. I order carne asada (skirt steak), el pastor (marinated pork) and rajas con queso (poblano pepper with cheese) tacos, and squeeze in between two families at the counter.

---

* In 2021 the USA consumed 149kg per person according to the Food and Agriculture Organisation of the United Nations, second only to Portugal at 154kg.
† Though statistics on vegetarianism seem broadly similar between the USA and UK, there are noticeably fewer meat-free options on menus and shelves in the US, where gym-bro protein obsession has gone mainstream.

Chicago is widely claimed to have some of the best regional Mexican, as opposed to Mexican-American, food in the country, and the production line in the kitchen here is a pleasure to watch as I nurse my sugary horchata: one man dancing around the grill, turning over tortillas and filling tacos, another briskly dressing the baskets for service, and a smiling burgundy-haired woman solely employed bundling coriander and lime slices into bags for the constant stream of takeaway orders. The tacos are so generously filled the tortillas are double stacked, street style – they're all so good I want more, but as usual, the napkins are worse than useless (America, what do you have against absorbent paper napkins?), and I'm aware a queue is building as I smear grease around my face, so I hop off my stool in search of some old-school Chicago beef.

A Packing Town museum is marked on the map, but it doesn't seem to be where it's supposed to be, and no one I ask has even heard of it.* In the end, I ring a random bell on an old red-brick factory that occupies the same spot and ask if I'm in the right place – 'Sure,' a cheerful voice answers, 'come on up!'

Taylor meets me in the atrium and takes me up an echoey tiled staircase that reminds me strongly of school, explaining what goes on at the Plant, as the building is now known. Though it does indeed house a small museum, it's primarily a research and production facility for what she describes as a 'collaborative community' of food-related businesses, brought together for their mutual benefit and to build a more sustainable 'local, circular economy'. To be honest I don't quite grasp everything she tells me but there's clearly a lot of interesting stuff going on: an urban farm (when she takes me up on the roof I can see someone

---

* Later I find a thread describing the three-decade-long active gang war between various rival factions in Back of the Yards, advising that you should always look like you know what you're doing. Bumbling around on foot is apparently not advised, but clearly I look so out of place that naively I never feel in the least unsafe, whatever the reality.

tending some very bushy greens next to the anaerobic digester, which, funding allowing, will one day provide food-waste processing to the wider community), a beekeeping-by-bike collective, an American artisan cheese supplier, a coffee roaster and an algae science business where, Taylor says, they're currently working on developing the first lab-grown shrimp.

The number of tenants engaged in plant-based meat alternatives is striking given the building began life in 1925 as a packing house for meat processors Buehler Brothers,* a business started by immigrants from Stuttgart in 1867 with a particular expertise in smoked and roasted meats. The Buehlers chose this location because of its proximity to the Union Stockyards, the more than square mile of slaughterhouses and meat-processing plants that earned the city the title Hog Butcher to the World. The speed and efficiency of the mechanised 'disassembly' lines at the Armour plant, once the largest factory on the planet, inspired Henry Ford: in 1890 a skilled butcher and his assistant took eight to ten hours to slaughter a cow and prepare the beef for consumption, a process reduced here to thirty-four minutes with the aid of up to 200 different skilled and unskilled workers.

Conditions for this largely immigrant workforce, initially Irish and Central European, then Eastern European, and latterly African-American and Hispanic, sound beyond grim, and the Yards were hotbeds of early union activism. Taylor recommends I read *The Jungle*, intended as an exposé of human exploitation, but which, depressingly, caused a public outcry about food safety instead, capitalised on by the likes of White Castle – 'It's intense, but it gives you a good idea of what went on in a place like this. I was like,' she pauses, 'oh.'

---

* It became Peer Foods in 1944, presumably in response to anti-German sentiment.

From the bus window, I glimpse an old limestone stock yard gate, the only remnant of what was once here, replaced by acres and acres of industrial park.

Dinner this evening picks up the same thread: my friend, the very talented pastry chef Nicola Lamb, has put me in touch with Tim Mazurek, food enthusiast and author of the blog Lottie + Doof, who has very kindly agreed to show me round his favourite local hot dog joint, hot dogs being perhaps the best known* product of Chicago's meat-based heritage. Indeed, death is all around us as we stroll around leafy Oak Park first; after weeks of anxious anticipation, prompted by thoughts of Biblical plagues of locusts, I've finally hit the cicadapocalypse zone. It seems cicadas spend most of their life underground as nymphs, living on the sap of tree roots, only popping up every few years in winged form to mate, lay eggs and then die – and I'm lucky enough to be here to witness the emergence of both brood XIX and XIII, coinciding for the first time since 1803.

As soon as Tim, his partner Bryan and I turn away from the main drag in search of the Frank Lloyd Wright homes the area is famous for (which Tim informs me 'leak like crazy'), the noise of the insects becomes, if not deafening, then certainly omnipresent. I realise with mounting horror that the base of every tree is surrounded by piles of dull papery corpses, while their live brethren rest on the trunks, red eyes glowing somewhat demonically. Suddenly it dawns on me that the weird hissing noise I stopped to record in a wood near Hobart yesterday, taking it to be some sort of ominous fighter jet, was actually the mating song of millions of cicadas. 'We've seen a few having sex,' Tim says, 'butt to butt' – they only have one position apparently, Bryan interjects – 'so hopefully you'll see some too, you know, for the full experience.'

---

* Yeah, yeah, but had you heard of Italian beef before you watched *The Bear*?

They're determined to show me all the sights, so we hop in the car to River Grove, and park outside an unreconstructed 1960s tiki bar (set up somewhat improbably by a couple tired of the funeral business), where we're served by a boy with the whitest, shiniest smile I've ever seen. He blushes deeply as he struggles to light Bryan's Painkiller – I, of course, always on the hunt for a blue drink, go for the Blue Hawaii, which is the colour of a Hockney swimming pool, just the way I like it. Sitting in this softly lit, woven-grass cocoon, with its heavy wood carvings and animal-print banquettes, I feel very much like I'm in one of those episodes of *Mad Men* where Roger and Don go to California and life turns technicolour – or perhaps the Aztec Zone of the Crystal Maze.

The couple debate whether to bother driving to dinner just down the road – 'We could walk?' Tim suggests, before Bryan points out that without the car, we'd lose our table, because Gene & Jude's Hot Dogs doesn't offer such frills and furbelows. Indeed, the owners proudly boast it's been serving up 'no seats no ketchup no pretense no nonsense' from this brightly lit, angular stand since 1950. What the place (which looks like something from an Ed Ruscha photograph) does have in abundance is Chicago-style dogs: all-beef sausages in a poppy-seed bun with chopped onion, a sweet pickle relish and pickled serrano 'sport peppers' plus a generous squirt of mustard.

True 'dragged through the garden' examples also include tomato, a pickle spear and a little celery salt, but this, a Depression Dog, comes with something much better on top: French fries. And not just any French fries: potatoey, almost British-chippie-like French fries made in house, before your eyes: when we go in, one of the dozen or so Latino guys behind the counter is feeding potatoes into a hand-pulled chipping machine while the others take and prepare orders. 'Whoever takes your order, he's your guy,' Bryan says, 'so you need to keep your eye on him.' Oh, and don't even think about asking for ketchup, they both warn: it's not traditional in Chicago, 'but here they go one step further; ask for ketchup and they tell you there's a McDonald's down the street, which is kind of a sick burn.'

The whole slightly chaotic experience is more like trying to get served at a pub on a Friday night than the usual soulless interaction with a fast-food computer terminal, but once we've managed to claim our order from 'our guy', we head back to the car, deliberately parked where we can lay the bounty out on the bonnet and recline against the crash barriers behind. This evocatively American set-up still doesn't prevent me spilling mustard all over my trousers as we watch a kids' soccer team spilling out of a bus to get dinner, a group of men checking out each other's kit cars, and some youths on motorbikes pulling wheelies on the road outside. ('Is this a bit like a tailgate?' I ask eagerly. 'I've always wanted to go to a tailgate.' Tim says he's never been to a tailgate.)

We also split a tamale, because my host confesses that even as a native Chicagoan, he's never tried this particular mass-produced local speciality either. The warm paper packet decorated with a vaguely Mexican-looking beauty holds a yellow cylinder of corn mush filled with a ruddy substance we take to be ground meat, but with a spicing that tastes faintly South Asian to my palate. It may be very little like a Mexican tamale (sources suggests it's actually a spin on the Delta tamale brought to Chicago during the Great Migration) but I find it quite tasty, as ultra-processed foods regrettably so often are.

Tim is very concerned, on the way back to the station, to hear where else I'm eating during my stay in his city, and visibly perturbed by my plan to take a food tour of classic Chicago dishes – 'I'm just worried where they're going to take you,' he says, peppering me with several alternative recommendations, and an invitation to an event he's doing as part of the James Beard Awards here on Sunday.

What lovely people, I think, riding the train back, and resolving to be more open and welcoming myself in future, a state of mind that lasts until I wake up the next morning to find the communal bathroom full of teenage Girl Scouts trowelling on make-up.

Keen not to let him down, I take two of Tim's suggestions on board the very next day, hitting up a Serbian restaurant in honour of the city's large Balkan and Eastern European population (enjoyably fatty chunks of smoked pork and a rich red pepper paste followed by a disappointing apple pie/strudel-type affair, which tastes like citric acid (4/10), and then their favourite date-night spot, Lula in Logan Park, for dinner. Casually elegant, it's more Tartine than Commander's Palace, embracing, this evening, a family celebrating a birthday party, a stylish pair of colleagues with angular haircuts discussing the media landscape, and a lone woman drinking a glass of natural wine and eating the best Caesar salad of her life (me). Reimagined with pickled celery and dill, fennel pollen and nutritional yeast, it's unapologetically untraditional, but believe me, as a Caesar salad devotee, it works.

(Though it's not an American classic as yet, I must give an honourable mention to dessert too: a salty-sweet pecorino cake with sour cherry, olive oil ice cream, pistachios and candied Castelvetrano olives. I wasn't sure how I'd feel about candied olives, but they remind me of Scandinavian salty licorice; so intense you can feel your teeth singing; simultaneously too much and just enough.)

LULA CAFE CAESAR SALAD

Taken with kind permission from **The Lula Cafe Cookbook: Collected Recipes and Stories by Jason Hammel** *(Phaidon Press, 2023)*
We've all had Caesar salads in our lives that spoke of dystopian collapse – brown, shredded romaine, crown-cracking croutons, Parmesan dry as plaster – so I thought I'd point out a couple factors in our version. First of all, the lettuces are tender, juicy, local Little Gem romaine, mixed with

escarole for a bitter note. Next, the celery, which in my opinion is the most underappreciated vegetable of all time. We lightly pickle ours for a sweet, tangy crunch. Our croutons are made from sourdough and toasted in olive oil, just long enough to make them crunchy on the outside and chewy inside. We source our salt-packed anchovies with care. We freshly grate the cheese and crack the pepper. And then we add a little house-made fennel pollen salt, some dill, and a flash of zested orange.

NB: Full disclosure here, I took the idea of cooking celery and blending it for this dressing from Jeremiah Stone and Fabián von Hauske Valtierra, the chefs of Wildair in New York City, who do such madness as grilling and juicing green cabbage for a salad dressing. That blew my mind.

[Note: blend oil here refers to a 50:50 mixture of extra virgin olive oil and neutral vegetable oil.]

Serves 4
Caesar dressing
80g/3 oz celery, diced
100g/⅓ cup + 1 tablespoon blend oil (see note)
1 egg + 2 egg yolks
15g/½oz grated Parmesan
1 tbsp roasted garlic purée (see below)
2 tsp red wine vinegar
1 tsp Dijon mustard
¾ tsp minced anchovy
½ tsp nutritional yeast
½ tsp minced garlic
¼ tsp salt
¼ tsp black pepper
1 tbsp olive oil

Marinated celery
2 tbsp white balsamic vinegar
1 tsp sugar

2 tbsp blend oil
⅛ tsp salt
100g/1 cup/3½oz thinly sliced celery

Fennel pollen salt
½ tsp fennel pollen
2 tsp Maldon sea salt
½ tsp coarsely ground celery seed

To serve
2 heads of Little Gem lettuce, cleaned and leaves separated
1 head of escarole, cleaned and torn into irregular pieces
120g/4 cups/4oz sourdough croutons (see below)
70g/2¾ oz Parmesan, shaved, plus extra to garnish
1 tsp lemon juice
8g/½ cup/¼ oz dill sprigs, stems removed
Grated zest of ¼ orange
Salt and black pepper

1. Make the Caesar dressing: place a small saucepan over a low heat. Add the celery and oil and cook until the celery is soft and translucent. Remove from the heat. Once cool, transfer the cooked celery to a blender, along with the egg, yolks, Parmesan, roasted garlic, red wine vinegar, mustard, anchovy, nutritional yeast, minced garlic, salt and pepper. Purée until smooth. With the machine running, add the olive oil in a thin stream and continue blending until thoroughly emulsified.
2. Make the marinated celery: in a mixing bowl, whisk together the vinegar, sugar, oil and salt. Toss with the celery and set aside.
3. Make the fennel pollen salt: combine all the ingredients in a bowl and set aside.
4. To serve: in a mixing bowl, toss the Little Gem and escarole with the dressing, marinated celery, croutons, shaved Parmesan,

and lemon juice. Taste for seasoning, but leave underseasoned as you're about to dust with fennel pollen salt. Divide among 4 plates and garnish with dill, more shaved Parmesan, a little orange zest, and a sprinkle of fennel pollen salt and black pepper.

For the roasted garlic purée

3 heads of garlic, top sliced to expose the cloves
550g/18fl oz/2½ cups vegetable oil, plus extra as needed

1. Preheat the oven to 150°C/130°C fan/300°F. In a small baking dish or loaf pan (tin), add the garlic and the oil. If the oil doesn't cover the garlic all the way, add more to submerge it.
2. Cover the dish with foil and cook the garlic until golden, tender and lightly roasted, about 1 hour. Leave to cool, then store the garlic in the oil. When ready to use, squeeze the roasted garlic purée out of the cloves.

For the sourdough croutons

60g/¼ cup/2fl oz/olive oil
½ sourdough boule (120g/4oz), crust removed and not particularly fresh, torn into chunks
Salt

1. Heat the oil in a large sauté pan until fragrant, then add the chunks of bread and a little salt. You'll need 2 hands and some skill to 'toss' the bread over the heat frequently until a golden crust forms on all sides of the croutons. If you find this hard, lower the flame and use tongs to turn the bread as it toasts on every side. The benefit to tossing it in the pan is that you can easily adjust the distance of the pan's bottom to the heat, which increases your control over the toast.
2. Sometimes bread can brown unpredictably and rapidly, hence the caution here. You want something toasty on the outside and still soft in the centre. An additional splash of olive oil may be

needed for particularly spongy or dried-out sourdough. Do not walk away from this or answer the phone or anything else. When golden brown, immediately cool in a single layer on a tray or rack. This is like toasting marshmallows over a fire.

I start the next day with a black coffee* and a trip up the 110-storey Willis Tower, where I amuse myself watching people squeal as they step gingerly out onto the reinforced glass balconies, until it's my turn and I panic like the dog on a cattle grid. It's merely an amuse-bouche to get myself in the tourist mood, however, for today is the day of the Iconic Chicago Foods Tour.

Our group convenes at Lou Malnati's – which, even Tim admits, is 'not the worst place' for deep-dish pizza – a motley crew of visitors from all over the States and Canada, plus one long-suffering local whose demeanour suggests she's already had enough deep-dish to last her a lifetime. Our guide, Casey, an actor from 'ranch central' Dodge City, KA tells us that the deep-dish was created by one Ric Riccardo, a Chicago restaurateur who fell in love with Neapolitan pizza while serving in Italy during the war. His business partner, Ike Sewell, 'being a Texan, said, well, I bet we can make it a little bit bigger', and so, it's said, the mighty deep-dish was born. (This account is disputed by historians, who reckon actual chefs might have had something to do with it, but the truth is, there's no hard evidence either way.)

I ask Casey whether it's true no one from Chicago really eats deep-dish pizza. 'Well, yes and no,' he says maddeningly. 'I'd say Chicago was just a pizza town in general; we have tavern-style, Neapolitan, Roman, deep-dish, stuffed . . .'

---

* Thanks to Cecilia back in San Francisco for the Starbucks gift card, which she chose because she imagined it would be more useful to me than something more artisan – in fact, this is almost the first branch of Starbucks I've seen.

American Pizza

The website Serious Eats lists no fewer than thirty styles of American pizza, before you even get into individual topping combinations like my secret weakness the Hawaiian, which was actually created in Canada. Here's a lunchtime buffet:

California pizza: thin crust, with fancy toppings like goat's cheese, zucchini flowers or truffles. California is also the place to point the finger of blame for chicken pizza.

DC jumbo slices: absolutely huge slices of pizza, available only in cheese or pepperoni flavours. Treat with caution: reports suggest a single slice can top 1,000kcal.

Detroit pizza: thick, rich, almost foccacia-like rectangular crust topped with cheese, then tomato sauce, right to the edge, so the cheese caramelises on the pan.

Grandma pizza: thin crust, baked in a rectangular pan, as if in your grandma's oven if your grandmother was from Turin,* not Dublin, topped with simple cheese and tomato.

Midwestern (tavern/Columbus-style): thin, very crisp, topped to the edge and cut into bite-sized rectangles.

New England Greek-style pizza: thin, oily crust, proved in the tin, rather than stretched to order. Feta and olives are available, but by no means mandatory here.

New Haven apizza: crisp, charred, chewy and ideally topped with clams and garlic, hold the tomato.

---

* Yes, I know Turin is not a traditional hotbed of pizza making.

New York slice: medium-thick crust, slightly chewy, and sold by the slice, which means it should be robust enough to hold its own weight rather than sagging under the weight of toppings.

Rhode Island strips: also known as party pizza, with a thick rectangular crust, thick tomato sauce and no cheese.

St Louis style: unyeasted, crunchy, cracker-like dough, processed cheese and sweet tomato sauce.

Trenton/New Jersey tomato pie: thin crust, cheese topped with sweet tomato sauce.

'I mean, a deep-dish is a lot of food,' the lone Chicagoan pipes up, 'and to be honest, when visitors come they always want to have it' – she rolls her eyes – 'so, yeah, that's enough for me.' Her friends look like this is the first they've heard that she didn't want to tag along today – but my eyes are on the two enormous pans that are heading in our direction. Each pie, for I see now why they're known as such here, must be at least 5cm (2 in) tall, maybe 30cm (12 in) or more across, and, to my surprise, is topped with a blistered roof of thick tomato sauce scattered atop a layer of molten cheese like cocoa powder on a tiramisù. This reversal of the natural order, I'm informed, is to stop the crust going soggy, as whole tomatoes are used, and also, perhaps, nowadays, to help with that Instagramma-ble 'pull' of hot, stringy cheese. In truth I find both elements a little bland; my favourite bit is the crust, which, Casey informs us, is made with butter, which explains why it tastes more like a rich pastry. Suddenly I understand that the deep-dish is a cheese pie masquerading as a pizza, and from this moment on, I'm a die-hard fan of the concept, if not this particular execution.

I'm already pondering how I could make it better as we move on to Al's Beef, a thin-sliced roast beef sandwich in the same chewy

'French'-style bread (i.e. not actual French bread that turns into a rusk after an hour and a half) also used for New Orleans po'boys. Like the LA French Dip it's drenched in gravy, but the Italian Beef – as fans of televisual stress fest *The Bear* will know – comes with a secret weapon in the form of giardiniera, an oily chilli and vegetable relish. Portillo's hot dogs follow ('Classic late-night food,' our local friend sighs, looking happier, though with their chilly, soggy tomatoes, they aren't a patch on last night's version to my mind), then Obama's favourite popcorn (cheese and caramel, a revolting-sounding combination I find puzzlingly moreish), and we finish in the sweet embrace of a brownie, though not the original brownie. The original brownie, or so it's claimed, made its debut at the Palmer House Hotel downtown in 1893, though as with the deep-dish pizza, there doesn't seem to be evidence to support this. Nevertheless, they still sell vaguely chocolatey little squares with apricot jam and walnuts for $8 in the foyer coffee shop, should you want to remind yourself that not everything was better in the old days (lovely-looking hotel when I pop in afterwards to try one though, much nicer than the youth hostel, I must say).

Feeling like today has been altogether too touristy, I jump on a train south to Bryn Mawr, a district that doesn't seem to get a lot of tourists if the double takes I get walking down E. 71st Street towards Mama Africa's Marketplace are anything to go by. A perfumed treasure trove of chunky Cameroonian beads and gorgeously colourful Yoruba cloth, the walls are hung with masks and art, and the fridge is full of the freshly baked bean pies I've come for. The friendly man behind the counter, splendidly outfitted in cream robes, tells me I've just missed Imani, the lady that makes them – 'and you came at the right time; when she delivers them, they don't last long!' He advises me to get the cream-cheese-topped one, 'that's the most popular', and eat it cold, so I do, on the train home.

The bean pie has been intriguing me ever since I saw a passing mention of it in a book about African-American cuisine. Created, it's said, by Lana Shabazz, cook to the Nation of Islam's Elijah Muhammad, as a dessert suitable for the low-sugar, largely vegetarian and minimally processed diet he prescribed to his followers (a rejection of the soul food he believed was poisoning the Black population), food historian Dann Woeller has termed it 'the ONLY true American Muslim food, created in this country'. Intended as a replacement for sweet potato pie, sweet potatoes, according to Elijah, being 'good for hogs but not for you', it was once sold to raise funds for the Nation – Chicago alone used to have three such bakeries on the South Side. These days, it's tougher to track down, so I'm happy I've made the trek,* especially as it's surprisingly tasty: sweet and custardy, with delicate spicing and the distinct but not unpleasant earthiness of beans. It also may have the simplest ingredients list of any pie I've eaten so far: navy beans, eggs, milk, butter, cane juice sugar, wheat flour, unbleached flour, cinnamon, nutmeg, spices and cream cheese. It's a definite 8/10.

For my final pie of the day, I walk the two miles to Nancy's in the West Loop, which claims to sell the stuffed pizzas mentioned by Casey, and am delighted to discover they take thirty minutes to bake, which gives me a stay of execution with a beer and a book. 'You know it serves, like, two to three people, right?' the guy behind the bar warns before putting it through. Oh, yes, I say, don't worry, I know. And, OK, I probably couldn't have finished the lot even had I been hungry, but by God I give it a good go – stuffed, it seems, refers to the fact that these have a homeopathically thin top crust, an apparent homage to the Italian Easter pie, though try as I might

---

* Later, reading up on them, I discover that the Nation of Islam is classed as an extremist hate group for its anti-semitic, homophobic, racist rhetoric by the Southern Poverty Law Center, 'and mainstream Islamic groups reject the group and do not consider its members to be Muslims'. Few foods seem to come without some difficult history here.

I can't detect one above the garlicky riot of cheese, spinach, giardiniera peppers and tomato I'm presented with tonight.

I decide to walk home as well, which is probably not recommended late at night, especially given that I have to cross the entry and exit ramps to the I-90, and cross the road to avoid a fight, but does, as I'd hoped, mean I can actually go to sleep when I finally hit my bunk.

In what's quickly becoming the world's least healthy dietary regime, I put away two pizzas the next day too – let no one say I'm not dedicated to my craft, should gluttony be a craft – one at Tim's favourite, Pequods, which I feel I owe him after embarrassing him with the food tour, and one at the Chicago Pizza Oven and Grinder Company, recommended to me by someone on a train. The former turns out to be a dark neighbourhood bar (neon beer signs, sport on the TV) in the residential area of Lincoln Park,* and already half full of hungry pizza fans as I lock my bike up outside at 11.30am.

One of the good things about this place is that they do an individually sized pizza, and not just in the 'any pizza is a personal pizza if you try hard enough' sense; it's 7in (17.5cm) across (and only about half as tall). The other great thing is that they deliberately char the top, so the sides develop a little ruff of toasted cheese like a lizard's frill, which makes it hard to stop eating, though reluctantly I do, because I'm not sure if my travel insurance covers self-inflicted coronaries. (I then spoil this good work by having a five-layer 'rainbow cone' ice cream down by the lake because it's a local tradition – proof that Instagrammable food existed well before the platform itself, for why else would you ever pair orange sherbet with strawberry and chocolate ice cream.)

---

* Nothing to do with the similarly named band, fellow millennials – that's after the park of the same name in Santa Monica.

Finally, after a blessedly food-free afternoon in the Art Institute, I head over to the Chicago Pizza Oven and Grinder Company where I have been unable to score a reservation. It's a popular spot, apparently, and I have to queue even to put my name on the list. 'Current wait is looking like an hour and a half,' says the girl. Such is my determination to tick off every pizza style going that I merely say sure, even though I have a policy of never queuing for more than fifteen minutes for any food. It's also cash only, I discover when I order a pint of Guinness at the bar on the basis that it'll take me at least half an hour to drink it. When the barman hands me the bottle, without even offering a glass, I realise my error. Had I known what was to come I might have ordered a vodka chaser, for, open-minded as I'm trying to be on this trip, it turns out the pizza pot pie is not for me.

The menu tells me the pot pie conceit was dreamt up by the owner in his Chicago law office, 'an individual serving, "made from scratch"' – those inverted commas are concerning from a legal man – 'with triple-raised Sicilian bread-type dough, a homemade sauce consisting of olive oil, fresh garlic, onions, green peppers, whole plum tomatoes and a special blend of cheeses; sausage made from prime Boston butts; and doorknob-size, whole, fresh mushrooms'. Leaving aside why anyone would want a whole mushroom in their pizza, or the wisdom of trusting a lawyer to design a pizza, the pale, flabby saucer that arrives reminds me of nothing more than a filled Yorkshire pudding in a crap pub: it's too weak even to contain the filling, listing drunkenly to one side of the plate. Their salad, however, served with a sour cream garlic dressing, is good, but not two-hour-wait good. I have absolutely no idea why it's so hyped, but the fact it's opposite the site of the famous St Valentine's Day Massacre, masterminded by local boy Al Capone, probably doesn't hurt its business with tourists.

On the way home, I make my reckoning. Of the deep-dish pizzas I've tried, my favourite crust is Lou Malnati's buttery version, my favourite filling Nancy's garlicky one, and the best cooking came from Pequod's, because who doesn't love charred cheese? Though I haven't managed to tick off a pizza puff, the deep-fried late-night favourite served up by hot-dog stands and convenience stores, I feel I've done the city proud, even if Tim might justly feel I've not seen the best it has to offer. After all, no one comes to London and just eats fish and chips . . . or at least, no one sane.*

Turns out I'm not done with pizza, though I don't know this when I arrive at Middle Brow in Logan Square the next morning to see Tim interview pastry chef Natasha Pickowicz about her book *More Than Cake*, clutching a slice of blueberry pie from nearby Bang Bang Pie (superlative flaky crust, fruity filling with zero jammy gloop, just bursting balls of juice, 8.5/10 as I find the streusel topping a little sweet for my taste). Afterwards we all share a sour-dough pizza that's neither tavern nor deep-dish, but chewy and charred and topped with pickles and potato chips and chopped dill, a combination which feels extremely Chicago somehow, playful and vaguely Polish.

I should stop there, but with a few hours to kill before my train east to DC, I embark on a reckless rush of gluttony, hitting 'Chicago's Horniest Farmers Market', which sells everything from Romanian pastries to healing crystals (can one farm a crystal? I wonder), Miko's Italian Ice and finally Jibaritos y Mas for the iconic Chicago Puerto Rican sandwich.

The jibarito (whose name means hillbilly in Puerto Rican slang) was created by Jajuya-born Juan C. Figuerosa in 1996, inspired by a recipe for a plantain sandwich he'd spotted in a newspaper from

---

* In truth, London is not the best place to get fish and chips, but if you're visiting and want to try some good ones, I'd recommend hopping on the train down to Knight's Fish Bar in West Norwood, where Gary still fries in beef dripping in front of a photograph of the late queen. Cash only, mind.

home. Instead of bread, it utilises fried green plantains, squashed flat and filled with layers of steak, mayonnaise, lettuce, tomato, onion, garlic and American cheese, though I go for their vegetarian version with avocado instead.

I'll just have a bite, I think – I'm not terribly fond of plantains in general, or indeed mayonnaise or American cheese, and I've already eaten enough today to keep me going until I arrive in the capital tomorrow afternoon.

That one bite is fatal: the only thing that stops me devouring the whole thing is the fact that every time I pick it up, bits spill out onto my trousers. It's a work of genius: the combination of hot, crisp plantains and cool, soft avocado and tomato, plus the powerful garlic sauce on top proves irresistible – fortunately, given I'll be smelling of it for the next twenty-four hours, like it or not. Perhaps, I think hopefully, as I pedal towards the station, it will at least buy me some space on the train.

Ridden: 41 miles
Climbed: 469 feet
Pies consumed: 3 (apple strudel, bean, blueberry streusel)
All-American foods discovered: tavern-style pizza, deep-pan pizza, Chicago dog, hot tamale, Italian beef, brownie, bean pie, stuffed pizza, pizza pot pie, jibarito

13

I HAD A HALF-SMOKE BUT I DIDN'T INHALE

In search of Presidential restaurants

> '*I do not like broccoli, and I haven't liked it since I was a little kid and my mother made me eat it. And I'm President of the United States, and I'm not going to eat any more broccoli!*'
> George H. W. Bush

Although the 6.40pm Capitol Limited departure for DC is quiet, the conductor, apparently taking against me on sight, seats me next to a woman who wishes to talk. For eighteen hours. Initially I'm delighted, until I've heard her brilliant ideas to solve the problems of 'African poverty' (the kola nut), fish stocks (netting across the ocean) and Somali pirates (actually I won't share her solution to the Middle East conflict here, but suffice it to say the UN doesn't need to follow up) on repeat. Tony Blair keeps being mentioned, but in what capacity I can't quite tell as her confidences are delivered in an urgent whisper, and occasionally, she'll just laugh silently to herself for a while instead.

As luck would have it this service has no observation car to escape to (China's fault, she says darkly when the attendant delivers the bad news) so when she gets up to go to the loo about 9.30pm I seize my opportunity to wriggle into my sleeping bag, put my eye mask on, ear plugs in and turn my face firmly to the wall. To her credit, she doesn't wake me up, but about eleven hours later I have to admit defeat and use the bathroom myself. This of course blows my cover, so, though I politely tell her I really am trying to finish my book (even the gruesome horrors of *The Jungle* being preferable to this), every so often she'll tap me on the shoulder and, when I take one of my earphones out, hiss something like: 'Is Boris Johnson still in politics?' 'Have you ever been to Wick?' and 'Midsomer seems a nice place to live apart from all the murders. Affordable.' Raw garlic is nothing to her, apparently.

The landscape offers some covert distraction in the form of the Allegheny Mountains, the pretty historic town of Harpers Ferry ('people like it, I don't know why') and the wide river valleys of Pennsylvania and West Virginia, but I'm still glad when we part company in DC, her for a connecting service to Baltimore, me to a hostel in Adams Morgan.

I've come to DC for two reasons: first, because I hope its world-class museums will shed some light on various aspects of the national food culture, and second as a jumping-off point to visit Monticello, home of Thomas Jefferson, sometimes described as America's founding foodie, in neighbouring Virginia. While I'm here, however, I'm also determined to pick over the crumbs left by more recent leaders of the free world.

I start with the current occupant of the White House – though he'd probably kill for similar coverage right now, President Biden attracted an extraordinary amount of criticism in 2023 when he and Jill were seen ordering the same entree, a fennel sausage rigatoni (which is, I note, described by a Washingtonian review as 'the perfect dish if you're having a bad day'), at the Red Hen in

Bloomingdale. 'Who does that?' screamed the *Washington Post*. I can see why neither of them fancied being the one who had to pass the plate over; it's incredibly rich, and very good, as it ought to be for $26, and having also put away a glass of Jill's preferred Barbera (her husband, like our own Rishi Sunak, is teetotal), I walk back to Adams Morgan happy.

Oddly, though DC public transport provision seems to be good, it proves of absolutely no use to me during my stay – no wonder there are so many helicopters in sight as I cycle down the Mall the next morning towards the National Museum of the American Indian. A sign on the wall inside this beautiful curved building surrounded by native planting and running water reminds visitors that 'once upon a time Indians were the Americans. Soon after Europeans arrived, they called the New World America. And they called the original inhabitants Americans. Not American Indians. Not Native Americans. Just Americans.'

Like the LA Plaza, the museum delivers a lot of hard truths. But there's much beauty on display here too, including, along with the art, a strikingly lovely collection of ladles representing the communal aspect of Native dining traditions, where all ate from the same pot.

In common with many of the Smithsonian Museums, the NMAI has a busy restaurant, the Mitsitam Native Foods Cafe, that's worth a visit in its own right. I have a fry bread taco (a contentious dish among those fighting to restore old foodways, given this flat donut-like object is the less than healthy product of government flour and lard handouts) filled with bison chili, and then pay a quick visit to the White House Museum, which is, by contrast, almost empty.

I admire the delicate Lyndon B. Johnson eagle-themed state china place settings from Queen Elizabeth's 1976 dinner with President Ford (New England lobster, saddle of veal, peach ice cream bombe with raspberries) and pictures of the very ordinary-looking family kitchen Jacqui Kennedy added to the second floor. I discover that three or four good-sized squirrels were required for Andrew Garfield's favourite soup, that Ronald Reagan had a special cup on Air Force One to prevent his jelly beans (a habit he'd swapped his pipe for on Nancy's insistence) spilling in turbulent weather and that Pat Nixon caused consternation on her first night in the mansion with a request for cottage cheese,* something staff then had to drive around DC searching for, but oddly enough, there's only one mention of the Trumps, with a picture of Melania looking fetching in emerald green.

Louise, a college friend I haven't seen in twenty years who I meet for a drink afterwards, suggests this may be because the couple simply didn't do much to, or indeed in, the White House during their tenure: 'Not many state dinners went on, and those that did tended to be at Mar-e-Lago.' A former White House Correspondent for the *Washington Post*, she tells me she was at Ben's Chili Bowl when Obama famously paid with a 20-dollar note and refused to take the change. 'There was a big debate in the press pool about whether he'd said, "nah, we straight" or, "no, we're straight",' she recalls, chuckling. She encourages me to get a luminous-green grasshopper hard shake along with my huge slab of fridge-cold chocolate cream pie with ganache so rich I have to push it away (7/10, soggy pastry and altogether too much of a good thing topping wise), and we talk about the future. The analogy of the frog in the boiling pot features.

On a brighter note, she's keen to know where I'm planning to eat, telling me that DC has historically been considered a terrible town for food (later I read an interview with Secretary of State Antony Blinken where he claims that, 'Back in the day, you could count the restaurants on one hand'). That briefly changed under the Obamas – 'We were cool for a while, but then it faded,' she

---

* Her husband meanwhile often had it for breakfast, topped with ketchup.

sighs, but she says the city ought to at least offer some decent pies –
'We're kind of Southern here, if not quite' – and suggests I try a
place called Henry's Soul Cafe: 'Get the sweet potato.'

He may not have done much entertaining at the White House,
but Trump doesn't seem to have eaten out much either; the only
restaurant I can confirm he visited during his term was the BLT
Prime steakhouse in his own hotel where his standard order was
apparently prawn cocktail and twenty-eight-day dry-aged New
York strip steak and fries. Though I'd prefer mine served rare, and
with mustard rather than ketchup, I could have worked with that,
but as the restaurant is no more, that avenue is closed to me.
Instead I book into the Bombay Club, an Indian restaurant near the
White House favoured by the Clintons, and also patronised by
President George W. Bush, John Kerry and Nelson Mandela. The
Michelin Guide notes it 'still functions as a club for politicians and
Beltway insiders. Polished and sophisticated with just a hint of
spice, Bombay Club's environs are a nostalgic nod to the clubs of
the British Raj.'

Leaving aside the question of whether anyone alive is nostalgic for
the Raj, as someone outside the politico club I do not feel terribly
welcome there. The thali is decent, but the service frostier than the
kulfi – I get the impression that as a woman dining without a secret
service detail I'm an inconvenience, and they largely ignore me until,
confused by a foreign credit card, they usher me over to the machine
to enter my pin and then leap in horror as I press to confirm the
amount, clearly anxious about their tip. 'NO, NO! WE WILL BRING
IT TO YOU.' On the way out I pass a photo of Bill in a colourful
90s tie shaking the hand of the owner, Ashok Bajaj. Presumably he
didn't have to wait fifteen minutes for his gin and tonic.

I have to be up bright and early the next day to make it to Monticello; predictably, the website only gives directions by car, but I

manage to work out I can just about get there and back in a day on the train if I take Eddy with me too. But the 8.15am is thirty-eight minutes late into Charlottesville, which means, given the time on my ticket, I have to ride hell for leather through the town, and then sweat through muggy woods all the way up to the entrance – as the name suggests, Jefferson built his dream house on top of a hill.

The temperature mid-morning is already 79°F, humidity 85 per cent, but there's no time for a drink; I'm bundled onto a minibus and into my group, who look understandably confused when I observe that the house's architecture reminds me of that of Welwyn Garden City, the Hertfordshire new town that was once the UK home of Shredded Wheat. The views are quite different, however, across acres of forest to the rotunda of the University of Virginia, widely considered the most beautiful campus in America. Even this pleasure was segregated: Jefferson's slaves looked on to a ten-foot fence instead, separating them from the magnificent vegetable garden they tended.

Our guide, Grace, a young woman from Alabama with a fine sense of drama, invites us, as we stand in the library, to recite the first sentences of the Declaration of Independence together. Unfortunately I'm standing at the front, which means I can only look down in embarrassment as everyone else begins more or less confidently, 'We hold these truths to be self-evident, that all men are created equal . . .' Worried I'm about to be hounded from this sacred ground for insufficient enthusiasm, I keep quiet when, after reading his self-penned epitaph, Grace invites us to consider how we are building on his legacy of freedom, but it all rings a bit hollow, particularly after my next tour, which focuses on the experience* of the 400 or so enslaved people Jefferson held at Monticello during his lifetime.

---

* For more on this, I recommend Clint Smith's *How the Word Is Passed: A Reckoning with the History of Slavery Across America.*

Our group is all white, except for one Black couple, who remain silent but for the moment when an Australian asks if it can really be true that the middle-aged Jefferson made the enslaved teenager Sally Hemings his mistress – 'Because wasn't there quite a big age gap?' 'MmHMMM,' I hear the woman respond quietly, rolling her eyes at her husband.

We walk the length of Mulberry Row, where the enslaved people were housed, as our guide Ashley explains that they had to fit their own farming around hard physical work on the estate, going out fishing early in the morning, and tending small gardens late into the night to supplement their scanty rations of a peck of cornmeal, four salt herrings and a half pound of pickled beef or pork per person per week.

As an example she tells us the story of the Herns, Isabel and David, who had twelve children. Isabel, Ashley says, grew potatoes, strawberries and other small crops, which she could make a little money from selling to the house if Jefferson was away and the vegetable garden wasn't in cultivation. Their daughter Edith proved a skilled cook, and Jefferson took her to DC to work in the kitchen at the age of fifteen, and kept her there more or less permanently, even as he travelled back and forth between his two residences. Finally he brought her back to her family at Monticello in 1809, installing her as head cook; visitors described her food as 'always choice'. After the president's death in 1826, Edith and nine of her ten children were sold as part of the Jefferson estate. Free relatives managed to purchase her, and her two youngest children, on behalf of her husband, Joseph Fossett, who his master had set free in his will. The couple moved to Cincinnati in the late 1830s, and eventually also managed to scrape together the money to free their son Peter (who later became a successful caterer along with his brother William). Edith died in 1854.

COFFEE BREAK
French Connection

Jefferson's preferred style of food has been described as 'half French, half Virginia' – after spending five years in Paris as a representative of the Confederation Congress, he came home with a taste for French food and wine. He took with him, when he went in 1784, the enslaved nineteen-year-old James Hemings (who was also, as it happened, the half-brother of Jefferson's late wife Martha Wayles Jefferson), and put him to work learning the delicacies of French cuisine, apprenticing in restaurant and aristocratic kitchens. Jefferson paid him well during their stay, no doubt because he was technically free on French soil and could potentially have absconded with his newly acquired skills.

Back at Monticello, Jefferson had a new kitchen installed with a state-of-the-art stew stove, which allowed for the more precise control of cooking temperatures vital for recipes such as custards and emulsified butter-based sauces. His love of European dishes like macaroni cheese, pommes de terre frites and ice cream helped popularise them with the American public – though he did not invent, or even introduce them, as is often claimed. Such were the prodigious quantities of butter employed by the kitchen at Monticello that the dairy could not keep up, and slaves were sent each winter to bring hundreds of pounds from his Poplar Forest estate ninety miles to the south-west, and then to Charlottesville to buy more on the commercial market.

Though he never succeeded in growing wine grapes on the estate, Jefferson was noted as the foremost American wine buff of his day, advising Presidents Washington, Madison and Monroe on the matter. He stocked his cellar with Italian and French table wines, rather than the fortified wines popular in Britain during the period, and had a dumb waiter installed from the wine cellar to the dining room.

Four years after his return from Paris, Hemings asked Jefferson for his freedom. Jefferson agreed, on the condition that Hemings trained his replacements first – one of which was his younger brother Peter, who worked with Edith Hern Fossett. Tragically James died, apparently by suicide, in Philadelphia just five years later.

The thousand-yard vegetable garden below Mulberry Row, first planted in 1770, was carved from the side of the mountain by slave labour.* Divided into fruit, root and leaf squares, with orchards, vines and berries slightly downhill and delicate crops like figs and peas planted against the north-west wall (which should have provided Jefferson with a great advantage in the annual neighbourhood contest to produce the first peas of the season), it's a truly lovely spot to pause and reflect, a privilege no doubt not afforded to those who built it. Even remaining within the culinary sphere, rather than touching on his complicated views on slavery as a whole, Jefferson, undoubtedly one of America's greatest thinkers, seems a mass of contradictions it's difficult to reconcile; a man who prized the abilities of his cooks, and took the trouble to train them properly for his benefit, yet who seems ultimately to have seen them as little more than kitchen implements.

---

* The historian Michael W. Twitty has written, 'slavery begins with food': sugar, yes, but also cacao, coffee, rice, peanuts, corn and the many other crops produced, and still produced, with involuntary labour.

JAMES HEMINGS' SNOW EGGS VIA AFRICA

The snow egg recipe that James Hemings leaves behind is a fairly straightforward rendition of a French classic, flavoured with delicate flower waters, presumably something he picked up during his time in Paris. Remarkable as it would have been at the time, given the precise heat control required for things like meringues and custard, no one needs another recipe for iles flottantes. So I've reimagined it with bold West African flavours; tangy pink hibiscus flowers, fiery ginger and peppery calabash nutmeg, though you could substitute a good grating of standard nutmeg if you prefer. Note that if the water is too hot, the meringues will cook too fast and then collapse; make sure it doesn't boil!

Serves 4
480ml/2 cups whipping/heavy cream
½ tsp ground ginger
2 cloves, lightly crushed
1 calabash nutmeg, crushed into pieces
4 eggs
120g/¾ cup caster/superfine sugar
Hibiscus powder, to serve

1. Put the cream into a medium pan and gradually whisk in the ginger. Add the cloves and nutmeg, bring to a gentle simmer and maintain for about 5 minutes, then take off the heat and leave to infuse for 20 to 30 minutes.
2. Meanwhile, separate the eggs, putting the whites into a large clean glass or metal bowl and the yolks into a smaller heatproof bowl with 40g/scant 4 tablespoons of the sugar. Whisk together the yolks and sugar to dissolve the sugar.
3. Heat the cream back up to just below the boil, then beat a little of it into the yolk and sugar before pouring the whole

    lot back into the pan. Turn the heat down and cook, stirring continuously, until thickened; it should coat the back of a wooden spoon such that you can draw a distinct line through it.

4. Pass the mixture through a sieve into a bowl, then set this in a sink of cold water to cool down more quickly.

5. Once ready to serve, beat the egg whites until thick and frothy, then beat in the remaining 80g/ ½ cup of sugar until the meringue is glossy and firm enough to be held upside down.

6. Fill a wide pan half-full of water and bring to a very gentle simmer. Using a large spoon dipped in cold water, plunge heaped tablespoons of the meringue mixture into the simmering water and poach for 90 seconds, then carefully turn and repeat. Lift out with a slotted spoon, shaking off any excess water, and drain on kitchen paper.

7. Divide the custard between shallow bowls and top with the meringues. Finish with a jaunty sprinkle of hibiscus powder.

Too late for lunch at the cafe, I buy a large box of Virginia peanuts (examining them with newly critical eyes thanks to my education back at the Krema Nut Company of Columbus) and head back down the hill with an appetite for Jefferson's beloved macaroni cheese and ice cream. Many of the diners in Charlottesville have already closed for the day (6am–2pm seems fairly standard here) and the Virginian, just across the road from the UVA campus, though very much open for business, for reasons best known to itself only serves mac and cheese from 5pm.

    Grumpily revising the schedule, I huff six miles back out of town for a pre-dinner ice cream (or perhaps late lunch?) from Kohr Brothers, an offshoot of a New Jersey seaside institution, which claims to have invented soft-serve just after the Great War. Which of the Kohr brothers made the breakthrough depends on which branch of the business you're talking to, but the Kohr in question added egg yolks* to the milk- and sugar-based ice creams popular in the States at the time, ran it through a new-fangled continuous flow machine, and called his new creation frozen custard.

Ice cream

The US didn't invent ice cream, it arrived fully formed from Europe (with roots as far afield as China), but it can take most of the credit for ice cream culture as we know it – from saucy sundaes to the modern cone, they all took shape in America. Perhaps most importantly, it was an American, Nancy Johnson of Philadelphia, who patented the first mechanical ice-cream-making device in 1843, and another, Jacob Fussell of Baltimore, who began to manufacture it on a large commercial scale not long afterwards, removing the dessert from the realm of artisan producers and high-end kitchens. On his death, the *New York Times* reported that he'd 'made a fortune in ice cream', ushering in the golden age of the drugstore soda fountain, which was soon said to outnumber saloons in many places.

Indeed, Prohibition only encouraged the American taste for sundaes, sodas and floats – brewers like Anheuser-Busch switched to ice cream, cafes and hotels converted their bars to soda fountains, and by the time the Eighteenth Amendment was repealed in 1933, there was one in nearly every town. The popularising of the cone, whose origins are hotly disputed, at the 1904 St Louis

---

* Jefferson's own recipe calls for two bottles of good cream and six egg yolks, but sadly he was a century too early for the soft-serve machine.

World's Fair, the invention of soft-serve by the Kohr brothers of Brooklyn just after the Great War, and the introduction of pre-packaged frozen treats like the Eskimo Pie in the 1920s only added more opportunities for Americans to enjoy the stuff. (Novelist John Dos Passos pondered, in a review of e e cummings' *The Enormous Room*, why his fellow countrymen seemed so resistant to innovation in art when they were so willing to embrace 'the experiment of surrounding ice-cream with a layer of chocolate'.)

Roadside ice cream stands popped up as car ownership took off, followed by chains like Dairy Queen, founded in 1938, and Howard Johnson's – which started life as a soda fountain. It was Johnson who saw the potential in choice; his restaurants famously offered twenty-eight flavours, and offered a free cone to anyone who could prove they'd tried them all. ('I spent my whole life developing scores of flavours,' he famously complained, 'and yet most people still say, "I'll take vanilla."')

Yet HoJos paved the way for 'luxury' brands like Baskin-Robbins, Häagen-Dazs (Polish-born, Bronx-raised founder Reuben Mattus explained that 'the only country which saved the Jews during World War II was Denmark, so I put together a totally fictitious Danish name and had it registered . . . Häagen-Dazs doesn't mean anything. [But] it would attract attention, especially with the umlaut') and Vermont's hippy-ish Ben & Jerry's, still famous for its chunky, funky flavours, though now owned by Unilever. The average American eats 20lb (9kg) of ice cream a year according to the International Dairy Foods Association, with 73 per cent eating it at least once a week. The top three flavours remain vanilla, chocolate and strawberry. Sorry, Howard.

The teenagers behind the counter are sweetly amazed I've come all this way to try it – 'You're from LONDON, ENGLAND? What are you doing in our town?' 'Does it rain all the time there?' – and earnestly tell me they hope I enjoy my stay in their country. I certainly enjoy my frozen custard; swirled into an impressive point, like a shaving-foam beard, it's nevertheless surprisingly dense and rich, and not in the least like the ephemeral vegetable-oil pleasure of a Mr Whippy. By the time I've cycled back to Charlottesville in the Southern summer heat, devoured the mac and cheese (also very rich) and a cold beer (very fast), and got back on the train, I feel more than a little queasy.

The landscape, which I have more chance to appreciate now I'm not worrying about missing my tour, is very pretty, however: an odd mix of English pastoral and sub-tropical, thick ropes of vine hanging from huge oaks. At one point I think I glimpse an improbably Saxon-looking church spire through the trees and feel quite homesick – until I realise it is, of course, a grain silo.

It's mid-June, seven weeks into my trip, four to go, and my last day in the kind-of-South, as Louise described it. Temperatures have climbed even higher, not helped by the many tour buses idling on the Mall, pumping out fumes and hot air. To try to cool myself down I ride along the Potomac, head craned for a breeze, listening to the skim of blades on the river below the infamous bulk of the Watergate complex. Abe Lincoln (largely indifferent to food, apparently enjoyed apples) is shrouded in scaffolding as I glide the length of the reflecting pool and arrive at the National Museum of American History in time to be the first person of the day to admire Julia Child's draining rack. I always love nosing at other people's kitchens (the great woman donated hers, custom built to accommodate her 6ft 2in frame, to the Smithsonian in 2001) and find myself particularly covetous of her pegboard of hanging tools and well-used butcher's block, even as I remind myself my workspace in London is about the same size as Julia's kitchen table.

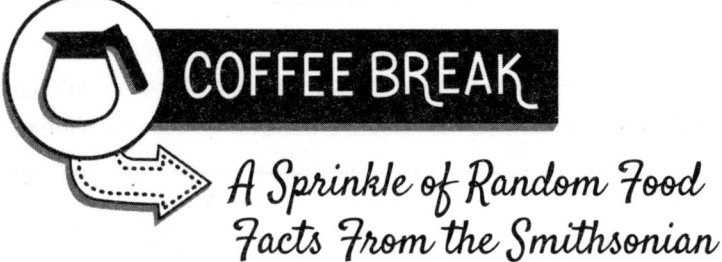

COFFEE BREAK

A Sprinkle of Random Food Facts From the Smithsonian

House-party favourite Ernst & Julio Gallo, once marketed by the actor Peter Ustinov as 'possibly one of the finest wines you, or I, will ever taste', was set up with the express aim of becoming 'the Campbell Soup company of the wine industry'.

In 1970 the United Farm Workers called for a nationwide boycott of all lettuce growers in the Salinas Valley, to protest against the pay and living conditions of the workers. Presidential opposition explains the wonderfully cutting badge on display reading 'NIXON EATS LETTUCE' – five years later, California passed the Agricultural Labor Relations Act.

At-home pizza consumption nearly tripled between 1985 and 2017.

In the late 1980s, Californian vegetable processors came up with a novel way to salvage imperfect carrots, by using industrial peelers to pare them down and market them as 'baby carrots' (this shakes me to the core, as I have consumed many bags of these oddly smooth vegetables in the last few weeks without ever stopping to consider how they could be quite so uniform).

In 2017, 31.1 per cent of American women and 23.7 per cent of men were on a diet (a startling 56.4 per cent of women and 73.7 per cent of men were considered overweight and obese that same year).

Such is the popularity of my next stop, the magnificent National Museum of African American History and Culture, that I decide to start at the cafe before tackling what Louise has warned me is a vast and absorbing collection. It's a wise strategy; heading out after juicy fried chicken (no fried fish on offer today, to my disappointment), collard greens and excellent cornbread (almost more like a corncake, sweet and buttery, with a crisp bronzed top), I have to battle my way past a hungry queue that already stretches way out into the lobby at 11.50am.

I work my way up the building chronologically from the grim lowest basement, finishing with celebratory stories, including, in the culinary sphere, such icons as Laura 'Dolly' Johnson, head White House cook to Presidents Harrison and Cleveland and a successful caterer and restaurateur in her own right, Leah Chase in New Orleans and the award-winning Swedish-Ethiopian-American chef and noted Arsenal fan Marcus Samuelsson in New York.

Still deep in thought, I nearly get run over on the sidewalk outside by a young boy on an electric scooter wearing a t-shirt reading 'Don't Tread on Me' and then a red-faced woman in hot pursuit, whose sweating back proclaims, 'Around Here We Take Care of Our Own'. When I google this slightly sinister-sounding slogan, I discover it's a reference to a controversial country song about small-town justice, with a video banned by some networks for allegedly glorifying gun violence and perpetuating racist stereotypes. Lovely.

Wearily, I ride up to Henry's Soul Cafe, and find it's operating as a takeaway, so I get a piece of sweet potato pie to go, and find a patch of shade. It has a fantastic consistency: not too rich, not too starchy, almost like a thick purée, but the pastry is forgettable and it's so incredibly sweet I have to throw half of it away when I get back to the hostel to pack (7/10).

My final destination in DC is the aforementioned Ben's Chili Bowl, which, as well as the Obamas featured in the mural outside (Bill Cosby was discreetly painted out after his fall from grace), has welcomed everyone from Duke Ellington and Ella Fitzgerald to Martin Luther King Jr and, perhaps inevitably, Bono. It's a classic fast-food joint; red, white and wipe clean, with a big sign along the back wall declaring it 'HOME OF THE ORIGINAL CHILI HALF-SMOKE', a coarsely minced, mildly spiced sausage that's one of the few distinctively DC foods the nation's capital can call its own.

Opened by Ben and Virginia Ali in 1958, when U Street was a largely Black neighbourhood, the Bowl stayed open during the riots following the assassination of Dr King – Stokely Carmichael, head of the Student Nonviolent Coordinating Committee, used it as a base for activists, Dr King himself came in for chili cheeseburgers. When the area hit its nadir, they began closing the doors early, as customers refused to come out after dark. Now, gentrification has apparently brought a new crowd – as a framed article from the *Washington Post* puts it, 'while the area has changed the clientele remains diverse', which it certainly is this evening; extended families, tourists like me, teenagers in the back room cheering the TV, lone guys tapping away at emails at the counter. I sit up there too, under the bright lights, watch the staff sidestepping past each other as they turn dogs and toast buns, pondering the fact that none of the devoutly Muslim Ali family has ever even tried a half-beef, half-pork half-smoke. Smoky and juicy, with just a hint of heat, I can confirm, despite my suspicions regarding topping meat with meat, they're delicious; the chili more of a savoury gravy than anything else, without much in the way of heat – quite different from either San Antonio or Cincinnati chili, very different from the chunky bison chili at the National Museum of the American Indian, but not bad in its own quiet way.

As I leave, I notice that Bill Cosby's still up on the wall inside. The Alis are clearly a loyal bunch.

Ridden: 54 miles
Climbed: 2,500 feet
Pies consumed: 2 (chocolate creme, sweet potato)
All-American foods discovered: fry bread tacos, bison chili, chocolate cream pie, grasshopper shake, soft-serve, cornbread, sweet potato pie, chili dog

14

THE CHOWDERHOUNDS

In search of shellfish

'Wicked pissah'
Mark Wahlberg

Creeping out of bed at 3.30am as silently as a clumsy person on the top bunk of a metal-frame bed can, I pack in the corridor, retrieve Eddy from the loo and slip out into the humid night. It's a thrill to glimpse the ghostly white dome of the Capitol glowing on the horizon, though the only other cyclist I see out, primly clad in a helmet and hi-vis, shouts 'POP TART' at me as we pass at a junction. I puzzle over this for ages before realising I've misheard – he called me a fucktard: a random act of rudeness so bizarre it makes me laugh all the way to Boston. Clearly the South has had enough of me, bless its heart.

After a brief nap as the train rumbles through DC suburbs, I find myself rapt by the view from the window, changing from swampy Southern marshes to the urban landscapes of Baltimore, Philadelphia (where I sorely regret not being able to get off for a cheesesteak and a hoagie – sadly Amtrak tickets don't work like that) and the unmistakable skyline of New York. I watch the sun rising over the sleepy Gunpowder River and later, high in the sky, glittering off the choppier waters of New England, fringed by white clapboard houses and fishing boats, though by the time I get to Boston, the early-afternoon sky is ominously pewter.

I only just make it to shelter in time – instead of joining the queue for a fried fish sandwich at the Barking Crab, as planned, I end up in the health cafe chain Sweetgreen, watching the rain pour down on poor old Eddy stuck outside. With aspirations to be the McDonald's of the millennial generation, Sweetgreen proudly posts its 'core values' around authentic food (don't get me started) and sustainability on its walls, so I'm genuinely taken aback to discover that, of the ten salads on offer, all but two contain chicken or beef. I go for a hummus crunch, which is nice enough, though I'm caught off guard by the number of options the impatient woman who assembles it for me offers in rapid-fire, heavily accented English – you want kale? You want pita? Dressing? How much? – and sit down feeling, as so often, slightly like the simple country cousin in this situation.

Finally, after chasing the last chickpea around the cardboard container for a bit, I have to admit defeat and brave the rain to find the room I've booked for the next three nights. Two longer than I intended to spend in Boston given I'm on a mission now to push north, almost as far as the Canadian border, to Maine and the start of the Atlantic Cycle Route – but as it transpires public transport doesn't reach that far at weekends, I'm stuck here until Monday. And while I'm sure Boston is great, I'm already impatient to get back on the road, especially with a friend arriving to actually ride alongside me for a few days.

Caroline, a faithful companion on many previous trips – whose mad notion to cycle from Saint Malo to Marseilles inspired my book *One More Croissant for the Road* – is the only person brave enough to have volunteered for a cycling leg on this one. In fact, cycling is what she's here for, but life can't all be bucolic roads and leafy campsites, as I remind her when she complains mildly that she didn't come all this way to spend her precious holiday drinking beer in a rickety bunk in a room so small we have to take it in turns to get out of bed.

Though she claims to only be interested in the wild north, I notice she keeps stopping on the way to the pub to take pictures of things like the sun going down behind Dunkin', and gesturing to quite ordinary buildings and saying things like, 'This is mad. It's all like something out of a film.' In short, she reminds me of myself, two months ago, and if I'm honest, still on occasion. I suspect it's difficult for Americans to understand the shock of finding yourself in a landscape you've only seen on screen for most of your life – yellow school buses, red fire hydrants, steam rising from manhole covers, counter service at the diner, all conspire to make every day feel like you've stepped onto a new movie set.

When we finally arrive at said pub, which is supposed to do excellent burgers, it's packed to the gills with people in green – apparently the Boston Celtics are playing, though who and at which particular sport I don't discover until later.* Unable to even see the bar, let alone a free table, we end up at an almost empty Polish restaurant round the corner where they serve cold lager, crisp potato cakes with goulash and sour cream, stuffed cabbage and pickle soup, all in hearty Eastern European quantities. Having over-indulged (as I've never been to Poland I can't guess if these quantities have been scaled up for the local market, or are typically generous), I wake up in the night sweating and terrified I'm going to fall from the death bunk onto Caroline's tidy pile of French toiletries, imagining her peeling off her silk eye mask to berate my corpse for squashing her bougie face wash.

Wanting to ease my friend in gently on her first morning, I select a breakfast spot that offers croissants and espresso rather

---

* The Dallas Mavericks NBA team.

than hash browns and drip coffee. In an attempt to distract her from the paper cups, I gesture at the Saturday-morning athleisure on show and observe that, like the French, American women seem to favour a fairly conservative colour palette. Glancing at the sleek black Lycra and tastefully neutral sweatshirts (no clashing London neon here), Caroline says with some finality: 'In France, no one would go out dressed like this outside the gym. Never.' That said, she does enjoy her roasted peaches and yoghurt, so apparently Boston isn't all bad.

As it would be ridiculous to fly a bike over for five days on the road, and rental options are inexplicably pricey, she's borrowing one from an old friend in Cambridge, Massachusetts – though I have my private doubts about the city bike's suitability, she wobbles off on it fine, if on the wrong side of the road, and I'm relieved that we quickly settle into our old rhythm; me navigating with more enthusiasm than accuracy, Caroline behind concentrating more on the scenery than safety.

After the traumatic taxidermy of the Harvard Museum of Natural History, we take in a couple of New England classics in the form of a lobster roll and a bowl of clam chowder on the other side of Harvard Yard. The roll, arguably the most truly American of all the country's many iconic sandwiches,* is surprisingly generously filled, and tastes like it's been fried in salted butter, but the chowder is creamily bland, as if the star ingredient has been dropped in at the last minute. Despite this, the meal is more successful than our evening visit to an Irish pub foolishly selected without the advice of former Boston resident Gráinne – of which I will only say that it was nice to have some proper, solid bread and butter for a change – or the hot, cross day that follows, which reaches its nadir in the cafe of the Boston Tea Party experience. Over paper cups of bad tea, to the sound of tourists sticking

* Did we agree a hamburger is not a sandwich?

it to the Brits by tossing plastic bales into the harbour, I promise my grumpy little frog she is going to LOVE Maine. We just have to get there first.

This endeavour takes most of the next day, with a lunch stop between buses in Bangor, where the ticket office is full of Mennonites. When we finally get off the bus in Bar Harbor, a pretty, touristy town on Mount Desert Island, some ninety-eight miles from the Canadian border, I realise with dismay that to get to our campsite we're going to have to ride back along eight miles of the busy road we've just driven down. Caroline, chatting to the driver, discovers the shuttle is actually a request service, and, quite reasonably, suggests waiting to catch the return leg instead.

Suddenly doubting myself after so long on my own, worried she's regretting coming, that the daily distances I've planned will be too great, the roads awful, that her bike will be uncomfortable and that she'll hate it all, I counter that maybe we should just get going, given that we're here to cycle. It comes out more sharply than I intend, and Caroline looks hurt, accusing me of claiming she's lazy when actually, she says crossly, she just thought it might be a good idea to get to the campsite sooner rather than later.

She gets up and begins strapping on her panniers, telling me over her shoulder I've made her feel like shit. This, of course, makes me feel terrible too, and we have a deeply passive-aggressive row in front of a woman also waiting for the next bus and trying desperately to pretend she's not there. It ends with Caroline getting on her bike and pedalling off, forcing me to follow her, still insisting cravenly she's right, we should get the bus. I'm tense with shame and regret all the way to the campsite; we rarely argue, and I'm uncomfortably aware that I've taken my own anxiety out on her because I don't want to worry her with the truth: that in my optimism, I may have bitten off more than even we can chew.

On the plus side, the scenery here, with its thick pine forests and flat, pebbly beaches, is stunning, and though our camping pitch is gravel (I wake in the night with hundreds of sharp little rocks digging into my flesh, a literal bed of mortification), we luck out at the little cafe across the road, a farm-to-table place where the deck looks out onto the vegetable garden, and I spot a couple of deer behind the twinkly fairy lights strung out by the fire pit. Encouraged by the local beer, I abase myself one final time* before she tells me to shut up, she has something new to worry about.

'Mate, tell me the truth, are there bears round here?'

I confess I don't know, but think privately it seems fairly likely, given how far north we are. Back at the campsite, having polished off some local mussels and a wood-fired pizza with homegrown kale – in its simplicity some of my favourite food so far – we call into the office to ask nervously about local wildlife, and whether they might happen to sell bear spray. The woman behind the desk laughs a lot and says we're more likely to see a chipmunk, but nevertheless, I quietly stash my food in a crevice above the bathroom block before returning to the tents; if my Virginia peanuts are going to get stolen, I don't want to be woken up to hear it this time.

Seeing proud former Scout Caroline gamely coaxing a spark into some foraged pine cones and sticks, the man in the pitch next door, who's been tossing an American football around with his young son, kindly offers us the remains of their firewood – 'we've toasted all the marshmallows we can eat, be my guests' – so we end the night sitting round a blazing inferno while she reads to me from a completely ridiculous Neanderthal romance called *Tales of the Cave Bear*. All seems well with the world again, I think, as I try to get comfortable on my gravel mattress . . . just as long as I don't tell her how far we have to cycle tomorrow.

---

* I say that, I'm still apologising for it to this day.

Unfortunately my fears on the traffic front prove well founded; there's only one road on and off Mount Desert Island, lined with ads for camping with wolves, whoopie pies and lumberjack shows – 'Forget diamonds!' one sign claims, 'lobster is a girl's best friend' – and in peak tourist season, it's pretty busy, though not with bikes; apparently we're the only ones foolish enough to take it on.

Though I thought I was immune to trucks at this point, we're both exhausted by the continuous noise when we flop into Ellsworth for breakfast ninety minutes later; crab Benedict for me (crab being, in my opinion, nicer than lobster as well as cheaper), a salmon bagel for Caroline, plus several cups of coffee and a slice of blueberry pie for later.*

To make matters worse, it's hot, already in the mid-seventies, and Caroline's panniers, secured to the bike by a well-used portable rack too wide for this particular seatpost, keep bouncing off onto the rolling hard shoulder, while her handlebar bag exhibits an unhelpful tendency to disgorge its contents onto the tarmac whenever she gets up any speed, which rather takes the wind out of her sails. When I spot an enticing sign for the National Salmon Hatchery and suggest turning off the main road, with its endless views of evergreens and not much else, she's enthusiastic – 'Finally, some quiet,' she sighs happily, breathing deeply as I, scenting a niche museum in the vicinity, speed up.

Oddly enough, though there are plenty of people cavorting with dogs down by the lake, the visitor centre, with its displays of antique fishing lures and depressing tales of pollution and overfishing, is deserted. Concerns, I learn (Caroline is on her phone), were raised

---

* Handsome browned crust studded with crunchy granulated sugar, and a generously fruity, if somewhat loose and starchy, filling (7.5/10).

over salmon stocks in Maine as early as the 1860s, and this particular hatchery has been trying to boost the numbers since 1871. From 1912 until 1954, the first fish caught each year in the Penobscot River (named for the native tribe that once relied on, and honoured, the salmon) was sent to the president – the original recipient, the magnificently fat* William Taft, ate his poached with a cream sauce.

Poor old Eisenhower forty years later only received one such fishy tribute before the river was judged so polluted that the sport was outlawed for a decade. No wild Atlantic salmon has been reported in a commercial catch since 1986, and the Gulf of Maine population was declared an endangered species at the turn of the millennium. Since then states across New England have poured millions of dollars into conservation work, and, the *New Yorker* reports, if progress remains steady, the US Fish and Wildlife Service might take it off the endangered list in about eighty years or so. Most Atlantic salmon on US menus (where it's by far the most popular fish) now comes from farms as far afield as Norway and Chile. That said, my favourite exhibit is a newspaper clipping from 1941 headlined 'Dennysville Male Anglers Unhappy', which records the recent prowess of several local women at catching salmon, 'while the men were 100 per cent unsuccessful' and feeling 'mighty mean about it'.

Outside, we pose with a handsome sculpture of the 'king of fish', before returning, reluctantly, to the roar of the Acadia Highway and our route south. Lunch, at Crosby's Drive-In in Bucksport, a low-slung seventy-year-old local institution with walk-up windows staffed entirely by giggly teenage girls, is a chewy fried clam roll with tartare sauce – clams are huge here, I notice, the size of skinny chicken nuggets. While I wait for our order to be called, Caroline disappears into the dark of Snowman's Grocery Pizza

---

* Though Taft is America's heaviest president by some margin, it is not true that he had to be buried in a piano box.

Subs Video opposite, a cream shack with a large handwritten sign advertising fresh fiddlehead ferns stuck up next to more permanent adverts for worms and crawlers, notices about hunting licences, and a flyer for a children's competition to win a junior rifle. She's unable to find anything to better secure her pannier, but returns to report they have a beautiful selection of skinning knives if I'm interested.

We cross the Penobscot River by Fort Knox (a place I'd always vaguely assumed was somewhere in the middle of a desert, full of gold, but which turns out to be a massive grey stone building on the water, surrounded by dense forest), and decide to sack off the official route in favour of a somewhat longer (nineteen miles versus twelve and a half along the coast) but quieter road through the forest, with some lovely heathland, almost Alpine meadow views from the top of its many, many hills.

This is the first, but sadly not the only, time we regret deviating from the Atlantic Coast Bicycle Route; by the time we finally rejoin it, reaching the holy grail of the Stone Fox Farm Creamery at 5.46pm, fourteen minutes before closing time, I can barely do any more than croak my order for scoops of wild blueberry and grape nut* through parched lips while my companion lies prostrate on a bench outside, having confessed she doesn't 'care for ice cream. I've never told you before because I know how much you bang on about it, but I just don't like it,' she whispers, eyes already closed. I have to say, I'm shocked and disappointed – you think you know someone! – . . . but also quite pleased she doesn't want to share.

Our motel for the evening is charmingly located in the middle of some all-night roadworks, which sit between us and the ocean. As soon as the sun begins to dip in the sky we lose our enthusiasm for trying to worm our way through them in search of a chilly swim – instead, we spend the evening sitting on the porch outside our

---

* Nothing to do with grapes or nuts, this is a classic American breakfast cereal.

room, drinking beer, eating salad from the Edwards Brothers supermarket in Searsport and speculating excitedly about the black-and-white Certified New York State Escort Vehicle parked out front. I'm convinced we're bunked up next to a dangerous escaped felon on their way back to the Big Apple for trial, but after Caroline has passed out from exhaustion halfway through an episode of extreme survival show *Alone*, I discover it's actually a safety vehicle for a wide load – a disappointment that feels in keeping with the day as a whole.

With the good luck characteristic of all our expeditions (in the past Caroline and I have had heatstroke in the Highlands and been almost drowned by rain in the South of France), we've arrived in Maine at the start of a heatwave. Temperatures, I see looking at my weather app, are predicted to be well above average for the time of year, but I can't bear to wake the peaceful sleeper next to me, who clearly needs a rest from both me and her bike. Consequently, we don't end up leaving Searsport until after 10am. As we pull away, a fellow guest sitting coolly in the shade watching the roadworks calls out to us to 'take it easy and drink plenty of water, girls!'

Today is Juneteenth National Independence Day, a federal holiday commemorating the end of slavery in the United States, so I'm aware that things might be shut – but in fact, up here in rural Maine the most we hear about it is a man grumbling to his wife that the bank is closed for 'some sort of made-up holiday'. Otherwise it seems to be business as usual.

Not wanting to take any chances, however, we stop at the first cafe we see. Just as Caroline is slathering mustard on her Scotch egg (an unlikely find so far from home) a man appears from the kitchen, points at my Marmite top, and says jovially, in a broad northern English accent, 'Oh, you've got to be British, wearing that!' Russell, who owns the place with his Romanian wife, tells us they've been here for over thirty years, can snowmobile right the way across the Canadian border from their land and winter in Florida, before roaring off in a Mercedes convertible, so I suspect he may not share our complaints about the relentless traffic.

Having crossed Belfast Bay to the music of halyards clinking on pleasure boat masts, we stop again an hour later for brunch – a pretty port with a working boatyard, Belfast delivers more farm-to-table cooking at Chase's Daily, where we order beet salads with walnuts and blue cheese and hearty wedges of frittata. While I sit morosely worrying about our progress, Caroline, happily oblivious to my concerns, gets chatting to a young blond man on his laptop who says he lives in a converted bus in the woods with his German (American) wife and their two small boys. 'We've been all over the country but Maine, Maine is something else, man.' His wife would like to move to Europe, he says, 'But I couldn't put up with all the rules you got over there.' (When probed about the nature of these rules he hastily changes the subject, so we assume it has something to do with guns, though he seems a gentle, friendly sort.)

Like Russell he insists that, though it's not on our intended route, we shouldn't miss Bayville, a cluster of cheerful painted cabins and swanky-looking beachfront vacation houses scattered along a narrow wooded road, lawn chairs looking across the water to the islands rising from the heat haze in the distance. When the little local road tumbles to sea level, Caroline can bear it no longer, and insists on running in, fully clothed, shrieking with pleasure. Mindful of my experience with the saddle sores (which seem, thank goodness, to have healed well), I merely paddle enviously. Just south of Ducktrap we pass a Windsor Chairmakers workshop and having mercifully stopped dripping, she spends a happy half-hour chatting to the crafts-men about Shaker furniture while I make a fuss of the resident dog. Sinking back into the comfort of an elegant tiger-maple rocker, I see we're only twelve miles from the campsite, and relax; if she's happy, I'm happy.

Once we reach the beach at Camden, I'm so confident nothing is going to go wrong that I accompany her screaming into the ocean, where we splash away the day's sweat, joyous as labradors. The water, warm on top, is quickly icy once we get out beyond the seaweed – but still not quite as cold as San Francisco. Mind you, the air temperature on this mid-June afternoon is about 20°F (11°C) higher than it was on the Pacific Coast in late April.

No good ever comes of tempting fate: when we get back to the bikes we discover a flat tyre on Caroline's steed; try as we might to look capable in front of a stream of curious locals, neither of us can find the source of the puncture. In the end, mindful of early closing times in this part of the world, she replaces the inner tube instead, and we pedal off, spirits only slightly dented, to dine on Maine potato pizza, piled high with roasted local spuds, spinach, mozzarella and sour cream (how comforting it is to be in a place that seems to value potatoes as much as I do), at a spot on the outskirts of town with a couple of guys playing guitar on hay bales outside. When we get to the campsite, a little way down the road, it's dark and the reception is already closed for the night, but our pitch details hang from the noticeboard – we're deep in the woods, past the ghostly ranks of huge white motorhomes and trailers that line the gravel paths, satellite dishes out, flags fluttering from tow bars. The moon is already hanging low over the satiny water when we discover the tyre has gone flat again, so the day – not a bad one all told – ends with my pal sitting outside the lavatory block in a swimming costume and a headtorch, having another go in front of an attentive audience of mosquitos while I hang around ineffectually offering to help.

Today, I say firmly when I hear the noise of a zip next to my head at six the next morning, we *really* have to get a move on. Record-breaking temperatures are predicted, and I've scored us a free bed courtesy of the Warmshowers app* sixty miles away with a man who's promised to make us yet more pizza.

Nevertheless, already hungry after our early dinner, we decide to stop at a promising-looking bakery in nearby Rockland to grab a quick – 'quick!' we agree – pastry and a coffee. Finding them still closed, we detour to their cafe round the corner where, side-stepping the fresh Maine lobster menu (lobster scramble, lobster tacos, clawfather sandwich), I opt for the efficient-sounding granola, yoghurt and blueberries, while Caroline wins big with a steaming, spicy bowl of the huevos rancheros I immediately wish I'd ordered too. I'm consumed with envy, and jittery about time, and then we finally go back to our bikes and discover Caroline's attention-seeking tyre is in no hurry to leave either. Clearly it requires professional attention before we hit the sparsely populated coastline.

Somewhat miraculously the town (pop. 6,936) boasts two bike shops, only one of which is currently closed. In the other, Maine Sport Outfitters, where furry lobsters compete with bivouacs and bug spray for attention, Austin doesn't take long to find the microscopic piece of metal embedded in the tyre wall, while chatting about local cycle routes ('You can't miss Owl Point, seriously'), making sure we're aware of the severe heat warning in place for the area today, and generally proving that wherever you go, bike people are very often the best people.

Pathetically grateful, we obediently head to Owl Point along quiet, tree-lined roads. I leave Caroline flossing her teeth on a bench by the general store ('home of the seven-napkin burger!') and ride a swift loop, via Lobster Lane, with its decorative array of colourful floats, to the neat white lighthouse, where the sea sparkles in the sun like frost on freshly fallen snow, and a sudden breeze makes it feel, for a brief delicious moment, like pedalling through a walk-in freezer. If Santa Barbara was peak California, this is the New England I dreamed of.

---

* Couchsurfing for cyclists rather than anything dodgy.

Unfortunately, I do not heed this strong hint from the universe to stick close to the cool of the coast, and instead decide to deviate from the official route in search of quieter roads in the backwoods with less in the way of climbing, which is, needless to say, an error. A serious one this time; the temperature is 96°F with a feels-like 102°F, and I can barely see for sweat dripping in my eyes. We make regular stops, ostensibly to check in on each other, but also, in my case anyway, to try to force more air into my lungs – Caroline assures me she's fine, she just needs to take it slow. Oh, I'm fine too, I tell her, unconvincingly. Yet at Thomastown, where we pause for ginger beers and a sweet, spongy whoopie pie (5/10), I barely have enough moisture in my mouth to swallow, people in the grocery store stare at us open-mouthed, and a genial man light on teeth leans out of a truck window to tell us we're 'crazy ladies'. The woman behind the counter at Beth's Farm Stand, where we buy blueberry sodas and lie in the shade in silence, swaddled in Grand Claire's cooling towels, is more brutal in her assessment: 'You're idiots.' She's right; a customer stopping just to stare at us claims it's ten degrees cooler by the water, helpfully adding, 'I'd head down there if I were you.'

By the time we make it to Jefferson for a root beer float and a lemonade, we're so desperate we debate asking one of the owners of the many pick-up trucks parked outside for a lift . . . after all, we reason hoarsely, Americans are so kind surely one would agree to help, but then, hallelujah! A sudden breeze blows up. It's already 4.30pm, and with an inexplicable three hours ten minutes still left to cycle, we grit our teeth and decide that at least the gathering clouds will offer some relief from the sun. 'Honestly, mate, even rain would be better than heat,' Caroline says. 'I'd actually welcome it.'

A few minutes later, out in front on the road in the middle of nowhere, I see a huge black animal, which, as I grow closer, resolves itself into a dog, staring silently from the bushes – and then, as our eyes meet, the heavens open, like someone's pulled a plughole in heaven, and we realise that of course rain here isn't just refreshing drizzle, or a short, sharp shower. No, ma'am, American rain means business.

It's not long before the deluge is sluicing down the hills in muddy torrents, and despite my hastily dug-out lights, I can barely see further than the yellow line in front of me – the rivulets of sweat earlier had nothing on this. My rim brakes, only adequate at the best of times, become near useless, and in the end we wobble to a halt on a small bridge, which offers no shelter but does at least have a set of crash barriers we can lean the bikes up against. Crouched under trees as thunder cracks directly overhead, we discuss the best course of action regarding the lightning periodically splitting the sky in angry forks. Caroline reckons we should get away from the trees, I'm worried about being the tallest thing on the tarmac – and also, I realise as I stare miserably down at my bare, muddy legs, which look very soft and vulnerable against the carpet of soggy pine needles, uncomfortably aware we're now sitting ducks for any lurking ticks. At least bears will surely be staying indoors if they know what's good for them, I say weakly, trying for a mirthless laugh.

The occasional car roars past in a cloud of spray, the hollow we've been eyeing as a prospective hunkering-down spot is now a small pond, and with no way to check the forecast or the map in such conditions, we eventually decide to pedal slowly and cautiously on in search of civilisation. In my head I think, well, rubberised tyres must surely be earthing, but I can't tell Caroline this cheering fact, because I can barely see her up ahead, just the reflection of a blinking red light in the running water.

It takes almost half an hour to find shelter, in the form of the United Baptist Church of South Jefferson, which has an overhanging roof just about wide enough to keep our heads dry if we flatten ourselves against the wooden walls, and allows me to at least partially dry my fingers enough to operate my phone. It is, I note incredulously, still at least two and a half hours from Bath and our Warmshowers host and it's now 6.30 in the evening. I do a secretive little search for accommodation, turning away slightly, not wanting to offer false hope, and discover that, although we've passed nothing since the ice cream shop, there's a bed and breakfast less than three miles away, and it has a room. Admittedly three miles in the wrong direction, but loath as I am to give up on the offer of a free bed and homemade pizza, I'm yet more loath to cycle another thirty miles in this weather, so I casually mention it to Caroline as something that could maybe, potentially, be an option to consider? The way she instantly clasps her hands in front of my face in prayer suggests she's given it thorough consideration, so I hastily book it, send Joe my fulsome apologies, imploring him to eat a pizza for us too, and, ignoring the light show up above, head back along the road to a place where this can become just another funny story to add to our long list of holiday disasters.

The landscape here is so empty that, approaching a dilapidated trailer with a sign outside informing passers-by that 'JESUS SAYS I AM THE WAY THE TRUTH AND THE LIGHT' – I think, well, if this is where we're staying, so be it, because the Clary Lake Bed and Breakfast surely was sent by God. That said, I am relieved when our home for the night turns out to be a handsome old farmhouse into which Linda and Rick welcome us without either a scriptural verse or a batted eyelid, given that we're dripping horribly all over their wooden floors.

It gradually comes out that they've only just got back from a trip to Kansas and Colorado themselves, and were still sitting in their driveway trying to muster the will to brave the rain when our booking came through, sending them into a tailspin. Rick is running about with fans frantically trying to release some of the heat that's been gathering in the upstairs rooms in their absence while Linda kindly offers to wash and dry our clothes, and by the time we've both had baths a pile of warm, dry laundry is waiting on the chair outside the room.

We agree a time for breakfast – muffins are promised! – and, not wanting to impose on the couple's kindness any further, I assure her we've already eaten. We lie on the narrow bed cramming in New Orleans alligator jerky and Virginia peanuts, which I'm accused of having deliberately concealed up to this point ('YOU HAD PEANUTS THIS WHOLE TIME? BEARS LOVE PEANUTS!' my companion shrieks angrily, though it's hard to take her seriously clad only in a t-shirt covered in kittens), while I mug up, somewhat belatedly, on lightning strikes. The National Weather Service advises that 'the safest location during a thunderstorm is inside a large enclosed structure with plumbing and electrical wiring. These include shopping centers, schools, office buildings, and private residences.' In the absence of such luxuries, 'an enclosed metal vehicle such as an automobile, van, or school bus makes a decent alternative'. No mention is made of alternative alternatives if you don't have a car available.*

'Did you know,' I say conversationally, 'that in the United States, lightning routinely kills more people each year than tornadoes or hurricanes?' But Caroline, having finished the bear-baiting peanuts, is already fast asleep.

MAINE BLUEBERRY LEMON MUFFINS

With grateful thanks to Linda Gallion of Clary Lake Bed and Breakfast, Jefferson, ME.
Everyone gets to experience this Maine recipe, which came to me from a neighbour and long-time Maine resident, during their visit. I hope

---

* The UK Met Office advises: 'If outside avoid water and find a low-lying open place that is a safe distance from trees, poles or metal objects . . . Squat close to the ground, with hands on knees and with the head tucked between them. Try to touch as little of the ground with your body as possible, do not lie down on the ground.'

you enjoy making them yourselves. They are the best with fresh Maine blueberries.

[I have made these with full-fat yoghurt with success, and also add a pinch of salt – there's no need to defrost the blueberries if using frozen. Use a dessertspoon to portion – I leave them in for a little longer, until well browned. FC]

Makes 15

2 eggs
120ml/½ cup canola or other neutral oil
170g/1 cup sugar
250g/1 cup non-fat yoghurt
325g/2 cups plain/all-purpose flour
1 tsp baking powder
½ tsp bicarbonate of soda/baking soda
1 tsp grated lemon peel
120g/1 cup fresh or frozen Maine blueberries

1. Heat the oven to 200°C/180°C fan/375°F. In a large bowl, beat together the eggs, oil and sugar. Stir in the yoghurt.
2. Add the dry ingredients just until blended; fold in the blueberries. Spoon into a greased muffin pan. Bake 18 to 25 minutes until slightly golden on top.

Ridden: 170 miles
Climbed: 9,898 feet
Pies consumed: 2 (Boston creme, blueberry, whoopie)
All-American foods discovered: clam chowder, lobster rolls,
crab Benedict, clam strip rolls, grape nut ice cream, granola

15
FUN TIMES WITH FUNGI

In search of free food

'They didn't simply allow me to escape reality for a while, they let me redefine reality.'
Prince Harry

I wake to the clop of hooves on the road outside, and jump out of bed as a black buggy disappears from sight. 'AMISH!' I shout to Caroline excitedly, keen she should see this fascinatingly American phenomenon for herself. 'Come and look!' Rick told us last night about these relatively recent arrivals to the area from the South, and explained how, though they've quickly established several successful businesses, they've also made driving at night a scary experience for rural motorists such as himself – their buggies, he said, have no real lights or even reflective triangles, they don't use seatbelts or car seats, and sadly (at this point he threw up his hands in despair), there have already been several fatal accidents.

I get back from the bathroom to find all in uproar; Caroline's passport is, like almost everything else we possess, still damp – but unlike my Irish version, which, though wrinkly, has all the important stuff on a stiff plastic insert, the République Française photo page is printed on ordinary paper. As she waves it in front of my face, almost hyperventilating with panic, I realise that the ink has run, lending her ghoulish green face the alarming appearance of an evil cartoon character. Initially, I think this is quite funny, until I go online, where the doomsters and gloomsters lurk, and realise it's very possible she could actually have trouble getting back into the country looking like the Mask.

After discreetly researching whether you have to pay for your own repatriation flights, I urge her to ring the nearest consulate as soon as possible to solicit advice. In the meantime, there's Linda's splendid breakfast spread, which I at least enjoy: fruit salad, fruit yoghurt in little glass sundae jars topped with a pert raspberry, boiled eggs, bread, butter and jam. The much-anticipated platter of blueberry muffins arrives warm from the oven as I'm pouring half and half into my coffee. They're both slightly crisp and deliciously fluffy, not too sweet, and full of last year's fruit, picked right here, and she insists we pack some to go in a paper bag, a gift I accept very gratefully indeed.

At 9am, sodden shoes jammed on to dry feet, and bikes loaded up, Caroline rings the embassy in Boston and, despite her gloomy prognostications about how helpful her fellow countrymen will be in such situations, has an animated conversation in rapid-fire French. 'OK,' she says, hanging up. 'He was actually lovely – he's going to show the vice consul the passport, but he says I need to get to Boston this afternoon to collect an emergency letter because they're closed over the weekend, and obviously I'm flying on Sunday, and I do really need to be back at work on Monday because I have a big meeting in Paris on Wednesday so . . .' While she's talking I'm googling, and discovering we're about three and a half hours' ride from the nearest railway station in Brunswick, and Brunswick itself is three and a half hours by train from Boston. The consulate, meanwhile, closes at 5pm. Rick, heading out to his woodworking barn to teach a furniture course, stops to say goodbye, and Caroline asks, with studied casualness, if he might know anyone she can pay for a lift to the station; the nearest taxi service seems to be a thirty-minute drive away in the wrong direction. 'Oh, sure, I can take you,' he says cheerfully without missing a beat. 'People have always been so kind to us – you know, someone did something similar for me fifty years ago, and I never forgot it.'

Given the aforementioned class, it turns out he actually means poor Linda will drive us, but if she's upset at having her day ruined by a two-hour drive to Brunswick and back, she doesn't show it, and before long we three, and both bikes, are crammed into their car and on our merry way. The drive, across the wide, lazy Kennebec River and through Gardiner, has some lovely moments, and our chauffeur agrees that, however much she travels, the US still amazes her with its variety and beauty. Rick, she says, has always been a keen cyclist, and for a while they went everywhere by bike, didn't even have a car, in fact. That such people exist here gladdens my heart, and we thank her so fulsomely – an angel sent from above, I may have said – she's embarrassed: 'You know, just pass this on, help someone when you're in a position to.' That's two people I've promised that to so far on this trip, I think guiltily as we wave her off, giggly with relief.

With our final leg to Portland off the cards for Caroline, we enjoy a leisurely coffee, a poke around the bookshop (which also sells such bumper stickers as 'EVERY TIME YOU SAY WOKE GOD MAKES ANOTHER DRAG QUEEN' – I'm struck by how often bookstores here seem to be hotbeds of liberal politics, a phenomenon I've never particularly noticed at home), and another creamy bland chowder while we wait for the train – but Caroline's head is already at the consulate in Boston and we're both relieved when she's safely on board. As we say our goodbyes, she confides that yesterday, at the peak of the heatwave, she'd worried she was going to faint. I'm furious with her – 'I told you to say if you felt bad. You have a HEART CONDITION!' – but as she quite reasonably observes, what could either of us have done about it, really?

I watch her go, madly blowing kisses from the window, and feel both sorry to lose her infuriating, hilarious company . . . and mildly grateful I'll only have to worry about myself for the next two weeks – from now on it's just me all the way to New York. As I tried, ineptly, to explain after the Bus Station Incident, as a self-employed, single, childfree person, feeling responsible for someone else's happiness is quite a stressful business. This is especially true when that person is a beloved friend who has paid through the nose and used up precious holiday allowance to come and join you on a trip where you're reluctantly but necessarily in charge. As the dog would confirm, I'm not really management material.

I ride south to Portland, where I'll now be spending the night alone, missing those bloody panniers wobbling around in front of me, but content in the knowledge that if the day takes a turn for the miserable (and it is already very humid, the clouds so thick and low it's like cycling underneath a feather duvet), I'll be the only one suffering.

I'm surprised to find that cycling in Maine's biggest city shakes me up a bit – all those days in the forest have made a softy out of me and, misreading cycle lane signs, I very narrowly escape being hit by a speeding car as I cross the I-295 on my way into town. I'm still in shock when I get to the centre, and find it abuzz with Friday-night fun – people sharing platters of oysters, a wedding party tumbling raucously from a bar. Suddenly I long for company: Caroline would have enjoyed the energy; alone, I feel hemmed in by roads and buildings. I slink around in the drizzle, looking in the windows of seaweed shops and jauntily nautical weed stores like Captain's Cannabis, before taking a seat at

Becky's Diner on the waterfront, far enough away from the action to be blessedly calm.

Though it's just the kind of place I would have chosen for myself, Becky's is the family business of a friend-of-a-friend, Aaron, who tells me that the eponymous Becky is 'kind of a hero in our family. She had five kids as a single mother and started selling breakfast to lobstermen off the dock at like, 4, 5am every day, built the entire business from scratch. Everyone in the extended family has worked there as a rite of passage.' It certainly has a family vibe this evening; perched at the counter, I get chatting to a Texan girl a few seats away who has to come up to Portland 'pretty often' for medical appointments, and always makes time to eat at Becky's – 'You don't find many places that do fresh blueberry pancakes,' she explains with relish, making short work of a short stack, 'particularly not in Texas.' The waitresses are friendly too, singing together as they refill the sauce bottles and wipe down the counter around a couple of teenagers feeding each other chips. I eat my watermelon salad and hot breaded clam cakes with tartare sauce, half listening to the murmuring chat about boats. By the loos, a cluster of children goggle silently at the tank of lumbering lobsters awaiting their fate.

Becky's aside, I find Portland as a whole too big and busy for my mood right now. I'm keen to skip town, yet the next morning I wake to heavy rain, and end up sitting gloomily in the Holy Donut, picking at a potato old-fashioned ring (gratifyingly stodgy, if not noticeably potatoey) and watching the cars splash past along the harbour. Eventually deciding conditions are probably not going to improve however hard I stare, I head out reluctantly into the downpour.

It rains, I would estimate, for 70 per cent of the day, and is chilly enough for me to add another layer beneath my waterproof but once I'm out of the city I feel much better; Caroline would have loved this stretch, I think, as the coast reveals itself to be, by turns,

Cornish, with beaches strewn with wet black slate and pretty wild flowers, and East Anglian, as the soggy gravel path runs dead flat through whispering reed beds and muddy rivulets, before settling into a Blackpool-esque stretch of motels and gift shops. The water is grey and angry, and the only people on the beach today are clutching surfboards. I stop to eat a pastry I picked up at the ZU 'micro boulangerie' on the way out of town, and am set upon by mosquitos and a perfectly groomed power walker who tells me, discreetly sotto voce, that I have mud 'up my ass', as if my entire personage wasn't utterly caked in filth – I could hardly be happier.

My dad, still dot watching, messages to ask me if I'll be lunching at the Bush family compound in Kennebunkport. Hastily I google this, and discover I will indeed be passing by, though in the end I get no closer than the roadside 'Anchor to Windward' George H. W. Bush Memorial (4.7 star rating on Google). There's a Texas flag flying outside the grey stone house on the distant promontory, but I can't for the life of me see how you get in. Shame, I would have liked a taste of Laura Bush's famous cowboy cookies* if they'd had some in the tin, but as it is, I settle for another cup of chowder and a salad at a restaurant round the corner handy for both the Kennebunkport River Club, Maine's 'premier private club', and a shop selling nautical antiques. Despite the unpromisingly tony surroundings, the chowder, eaten at a picnic bench to spare the moneyed diners inside the sight of my grimy limbs, proves the best yet, with big generous chunks of potato and briny clam, while the blueberry pie I follow it up with is unusual, with a golden, sturdy, almost hot-water-like crust, and a stiff, tangy filling as if it's been set with apples, rather than the usual mealy cornflour (7.5 / 10).

---

* This oat, coconut and roasted pecan recipe beat Tipper Gore's gingersnaps in the *Family Circle* First Lady Bake Off in 2000. Sadly *Family Circle* went out of business in 2019, so we will never know what Melania Trump would have put up against Jill Biden . . . or indeed Doug Emhoff.

I slightly fall out of love with the place, however, when the friendly woman behind the counter tells another customer wondering where to put their empty drink cans, 'Oh, just in the bin, sugar, we don't recycle here.' Given my lunch alone has created quite the pile – one cup and lid, two boxes, for salad and blueberry pie, a can of lemonade, a plastic cup of water, two dressing pots and two packs of disposable cutlery – I can only imagine what their waste collection must be like.

The traffic is heavy as I follow Route 1 through Wells and Ogunquit, and the driving seems to be becoming worse – one woman, her SUV pulled out across the bike lane, stares blankly at me as I gesture at her to please reverse a little to allow me past, forcing me into the speeding flow of cars to detour around her. 'Oh, yeah, people are mad round here,' a guy on an electric bike confirms when we're stopped together at a set of lights. Even the two-wheeled traffic increases – I have to race past a couple towing their luggage behind them at one point, anxious not to get stuck behind them on a hill. I say hello as I pass, and they look similarly amazed, but from now on I see at least one or two cyclists a day, which is nice, though unlike in the Midwest, no one seems much inclined to chat.

The architecture changes too, begins to look more stereotypically New England: Queen Anne houses with severe gables softened by gingerbread woodwork, proudly upright white weatherboard churches, their plainness only partially relieved by lines of tall narrow windows. My motel in Kittery, where I'm staying because it's considerably cheaper than Portsmouth across the water, is pure 1970s, however. Finding a heater tucked away in a cupboard, I take a chance on burning the place down by leaving it on full blast in the tiny bathroom, wet clothes draped on every surface, while I go out for a bowl of clam pasta.

The rain has quieted to a mere all-encompassing dampness as I ride across the Piscataqua River and into a new state (my sixteenth of the trip!) the next morning. After almost a week in the vasts of Maine, I'm finally entering New Hampshire, and I stop at a German cafe for a celebratory cortado (not very German admittedly, but after so much watery drip coffee* I'm just happy to be drinking something strong) and a cider donut (which sadly doesn't contain any actual alcohol to warm my cockles) before continuing south. The morning is soft and misty, the green water of the Sagamore Creek as smooth as glass, and despite the drizzle, it's a pleasant route through marshes and lakes full of flowering lilies, the occasional restaurant, always strung with ropes of colourful buoys, offering steamers, fried clams and lobster dinners.

The gaudy resort of Hampton looks depressed in the weather, with just a few holidaymakers wandering around disconsolately, perhaps waiting for Big Steve's Italian Sausage to open its doors. Even the giant lemon-shaped lemonade stand is shuttered against the drizzle. At the cafe where I get a wild blueberry smoothie bowl with fruit and granola, I notice almost everyone else is tucking into greasy-looking hot breakfast sandwiches, and regret my po-faced, if aptly Puritanical, choice.

Some way down the road, inland now, I pass a poster advertising the fifth annual Fourth of July Declaration of Independence recitation event in North Andover Common and, trying and failing to imagine such festivities, think I couldn't possibly feel more foreign. That's before I stop at a deli in wealthy Andover for a sandwich. The many options listed above the counter all have names I don't recognise – American, Sicilian, Capicola, Italian – without further explanation, and there are eight choices of bread, and four of mustard before you even get down to the business of the fillings

---

* My Californian friend Sarah is of the opinion that this taste for large, weak coffees is down to the Scandinavian influence.

themselves. Beginning to empathise with people who struggled with the concept of choice following the collapse of the Soviet Union, I ask what's in the Sicilian and, understanding very little of the response – I'm sure they spoke more slowly in *The Sopranos* – but too embarrassed to request a repeat performance, I nod confidently and say yes please. Having eaten it, I'm still little the wiser, but it's made to order,* seems to involve a lot of different types of cured meat, one of which may even have been Tony's favourite gabagool, but no bologna, and it tastes good. Which is, I suppose, all I really needed to know.

It's funny how themes recur in a country that can otherwise feel too big to have much in common: back in Maine, some 2,350 miles from Mexico, I spotted a political poster for the Republican congressional primary promising that the candidate would 'secure the border'; here a gubernatorial candidate runs with: 'Don't Mass up NH', just like those people back in Wyldwood were anxious to ensure no one California-ed their Texas.

I, however, only realise I've crossed the state line when the Massachusetts plates start outnumbering the New Hampshire ones, though as I pass through the leafy commuter towns of Billerica, Chelmsford, Tewkesbury and Bedford, the terrain seems increasingly English, just with even fewer public conveniences. As it's Sunday, not much is open in general; I stop at a run-down garage and buy a horrible sugary bottled Starbucks latte as a preamble to asking to use the loo. 'Oh, no, honey, it's out of order,' the woman behind the desk says brightly, before telling me she went to Britain in 1981 with the Girl Scouts – 'all rain and cathedrals'.

There are no handy bus shelters to hide behind either – just spindly pines and woods that turn out to be private gardens, neither of which feel ideal for my purpose. Once again I'm struck by the

---

* The American taste for customisation seems to be keeping the sad pre-packed sandwich trend at bay for now – and long may this continue.

small, unexpected ways travel is hard without a car here; everything seems to be private property, there are few public lavatories outside retail outlets, and in small towns, these cafes tend to be small businesses that keep commendably civilised, if personally inconvenient, hours. Plus, given the price of everything, it's getting expensive to keep buying soft drinks I don't want just to have a wee. I start feeling quite cross about how everything in this country is treated as a commercial opportunity – even water fountains seem to be few and far between these days – and then thankfully I spot a portaloo near a kids' baseball field and forget all about my revolutionary fervour.

Perhaps, I muse as I wheel more cheerfully into historic Concord, it was something in the air around the site of the first battle of the War of Independence, which allows the town to declare itself the birthplace of the nation. Oddly enough, as well as a thrusting priapic memorial labelled Faithful Unto Death, where some men are standing to attention talking gruffly about freedom, the town is home to a shop called Best of British, which sells tea cosies, tubs of Bisto and, rather boldly, a gluggle jug painted with the Irish tricolour.

The Colonial Inn where I'm staying the night even smells authentic – fried food and beery carpets – and I feel very at home in the dark, low-ceilinged bar, and quite jolly as I finish off a pint, some unexpectedly good fish and chips (made with the unprepossessingly named scrod), and a bowl of Indian pudding,* which tastes like a gingerbread-spiced Weetabix. (Historians, I discover, googling it as I wait, are divided as to whether it has any relation to Native American cornmeal mushes sweetened with maple syrup, or is simply the stodgy spawn of British boiled puddings, but either way I'm a fan.)

---

* Harvard's Hasty Pudding Club, est. 1795, serves a pot of hasty, or Indian, pudding at every meeting, and counts no fewer than five US presidents among its membership.

Struggling to digest this hearty meal, I embark on an ambitious after-dinner walk up to the Old Manse, former home of Ralph Waldo Emerson and Nathaniel Hawthorne, a dark, dripping route that takes me past the site of the battleground (and, to my surprise, a familiar fluttering poppy and a Union Jack on the grave of a British soldier 'of the 4th the King's Own Regiment of Foot fatally wounded at North Bridge'). Hearing what sounds like raspy breathing from the trees I quicken my pace, then, thoroughly spooked, turn back, eager to return to the lights of the town. Later, in bed, I realise it was probably just frogs.

Two good things happen the next day. The first is that I see my first cairn terrier, just outside Bedford, after a quick visit to Thoreau's famous Walden Pond (bikes prohibited; the great essayist was a keen walker who thought nothing of a ten-mile hike through the snow to pay his respects to a tree). More excited by the dog, I perform a hasty u-turn. The owner is taken aback by my enthusiasm – 'Oh, there's quite a few of them round here' – but fifteen-year-old Garney ('slowing down a bit, but still likes his walks') comes snuffling over to say hello, which leaves me grinning from ear to ear. The second is that I meet Diana, not a cairn, but yet another friend of my friend the Norwegian-American food writer Signe Johansen, who has generously offered to put me up at her home in Newton, ten miles outside Boston.

To be honest, when Signe said Diana was a forager, I'd assumed that meant the woman liked to go out at the weekend and look for mushrooms. In fact, it turns out, she's a professional who discovered her passion for wild food while working as a sound engineer and designer in Los Angeles, of all unlikely places, and now runs a business supplying restaurants and leading Edible Excursions tours back in her native New England. Monday not being a peak day for either of those activities, however, when I arrive at her wood-shingled bungalow I'm greeted by Mitzy the dog (a two-terrier morning!); Diana is inside watching a Gordon Ramsay show about foraging in Cuba with the curtains drawn.

As she opens her kitchen cupboards to make tea – no bags here, just jars and Tupperware containers of mysterious ingredients – filling a pan with water and adding a chunk of something called chaga, some rose petals, a few spruce tips, she tells me how she taught herself her trade from books and the combined wisdom of Boston's Mycology Club, the world's oldest continuously operating association for amateur fungi enthusiasts, which apparently counts Harvard professors among its membership.

'What's . . . what's chaga?' I ask somewhat nervously, looking at the dark brown mass looming below the floating carpet of needles and petals in the pot. She explains it's a parasitic fungus, mostly found on birch trees, which is thought to have various immune-boosting, anti-inflammatory properties and has been used for centuries by Native cultures, though she also stresses that as yet there have been no human trials. Trying not to be put off by the word parasitic, I take a sip; it tastes oddly savoury, not unpleasantly so, but unusual enough to keep me on my toes as Diana shows me her vast collection of jams and jellies, syrups and salts, occasionally opening one to give me a taste of magnolia and rose soda, or lobster mushroom seasoning salt. The experience is like being in the kitchen with Willy Wonka, a whole larder of truly American ingredients I have almost no knowledge of, and as a cook, albeit one currently on sabbatical, I find it utterly thrilling.

My host casually throws together a lunch of 'yard salad' using leaves and herbs picked from the garden, cheese and cured meat, plus blushing rainier cherries and pickled chicken of the woods mushrooms, sea beans and an elderflower and lilac jelly 'that's really good with the cheese', while Mitzy leaps about on the lawn nibbling delicately. 'She just loves wood sorrel,' Diana says fondly. 'It's in our salad too actually.'

Afterwards I take Eddy over to the nearest bike shop, Landry's, for new brake pads; somewhere along the way, and probably in Linda's car, they've been knocked out of kilter and one has clearly been rubbing itself bald. When I get back, I find Diana pouring vodka infused with young beech leaves, juniper berries, shagbark hickory bark and magnolia flower into a large jar along with some black locust flower syrup – 'This is for you, for the road,' she says in a tone that brooks no polite resistance. 'We're going out to find dinner.'

As we don't have time to head too far afield, we drive to her allotment (me still awkwardly clutching my drink) where we gather purslane, sorrel and other leaves (and I inadvertently pull up one of her beets thinking the leaves look tasty), inspect the progress of the tomatoes and corn – 'should be knee high by the Fourth of July,' she says with satisfaction – and filch a few ripe redcurrants from a neighbouring plot; just a couple, just to test them. (Unlike many states, which have lifted early-twentieth-century prohibitions* on the fruit's import and cultivation in recent years, blackcurrants are still banned here thanks to their role in spreading white pine blister rust, white pine apparently being a species of particular importance to Massachusetts.)

The allotments are an interesting snapshot of the area's immigrant make-up – the currants belong to Russians, who also cultivate gooseberries, beetroot and vast waving seas of dill, while the chillies and napa cabbage suggest the influence of Asian-American palates. We find eerie ghost pipe mushrooms wiggling through the soil and wild blueberry bushes in the nearby woods, and Diana tells me that, in North America at least, if a berry is blue, and has a 'crown' on the bottom, it's safe to eat: 'huckleberries, hackberries, bilberries, low and high bush blueberries, etcetera'. The same, she says, goes for what she calls coned fruits, like raspberries,

---

* Explaining why purple candy and soda in the US will almost always be grape rather than blackcurrant flavoured.

blackberries and so on: 'Doesn't matter what colour they are, any berry in the shape of a cone is edible!' Which is a relief to know, should I get stranded in any forests on the way down to New York.

She excitedly shows me some wild hop shoots curling over a fence, and I say, all blasé as we pick them for salad, oh, yeah, we get these a lot at home. Later, preparing dinner, she calls me in from the garden where I've been flirting with Mitzy to tell me that I've added some deadly nightshade to our salad. Shamefaced, I blame the car cocktail.

Saved from myself, we sit out in the fading light eating sumac-rubbed pork loin with black walnut molasses, white beans, sautéed hop shoots, wild ramp sauerkraut and blessedly non-toxic salad, and talk about politics, and food, and the untapped potential of magic mushrooms when it comes to connecting with the world around us, and then she makes me watch a surprisingly fascinating, if quite trippy, film called *Fantastic Fungi*. Mitzy, who's clearly seen it before, retreats to her bed, and not long afterwards, I go too, dozing off happy and well fed under framed photographs of dogs.

DIANA BURNELL'S SUMAC-DUSTED PORK LOIN WITH BEEFSTEAK MUSHROOM GRAVY

With thanks to Diana of Edible Excursions Wild Food and Foraging Tours
This is the dinner Diana cooked for me when I stayed with her and her lovely little dog in Newton, MA. As a forager she has wild mushrooms on tap in season, but if you're not so lucky you can use dried porcini or similar as indicated below.

Serves 4
For the pork
450g/1 pound pork loin fillet
1½ tsp sea salt

Ground black pepper

1 tbsp sumac powder (you can also use 1½ tbsp of za'atar as a
    substitute)

1 tsp ground cumin

Olive oil, to cook

For the beefsteak mushroom gravy

450g/1 pound beefsteak mushrooms (porcini or maitake/hen of
    the woods will also work) [if using 45g/1½ ounces dried
    mushrooms, soak in boiling water for 30 minutes before use]

90g/6½ tbsp butter

Pan drippings from the pork loin

1 clove of garlic, finely chopped

1 leek or shallot, trimmed and finely chopped

½ tsp ground black pepper

½ tsp flaky salt

4 tbsp plain/all-purpose flour or gluten-free alternative

480ml/2 cups beef or bone broth/stock

1 tsp Worcestershire sauce

A few sprigs of fresh marjoram or thyme, or a pinch of dried
    marjoram or thyme

*Optional – for a creamy mushroom gravy, add 60ml/¼ cup of
    heavy cream [whipping or double cream] at the end

1. Pat the pork dry with a paper towel. Heat the oven to
   200°C/180°C fan/375°F. Sprinkle all over with the salt and
   some ground black pepper. Combine the sumac and cumin (or
   use about 1½ tablespoons of za'atar), then massage the
   seasoning mix evenly onto the loin.

2. Oil the base of a baking pan just large enough to hold the
   pork, put it inside and drizzle a bit of olive oil across the top.
   Cover the pan loosely with a piece of aluminium foil with a
   few holes in it.

3. Bake the pork for 18 minutes, then remove the foil and flip the loin. Cook for an additional 5 to 7 minutes. Remove from the oven and let the loin rest, covered, while you make the gravy. Save any of the juices left in the baking dish for this next step.

4. Finely chop the mushrooms. Transfer to a sauté pan, turn the heat to medium-low and sweat the mushrooms for 4 to 5 minutes, until they begin releasing their juices; this is where much of their deep umami flavour lies (add a little of the soaking liquid if using dried mushrooms).

5. Add half the butter, any pork pan drippings and the garlic and turn the heat up to medium. Cook for 1 minute, then add the chopped leeks or shallots. Season with the pepper and half the salt and cook for 5 to 8 minutes, until the white parts of the leek are translucent.

6. Add the remaining butter and melt. Pour in the flour and stir constantly for about 3 minutes. Once browned, add the broth, Worcestershire sauce, and marjoram or thyme. Whisk constantly until the gravy begins to thicken.

7. Cover and simmer on low, stirring occasionally for 5 to 7 minutes. Once the gravy reaches a consistency to your liking, take it off the heat. Taste and add more salt if necessary.

8. Serve the gravy over the thinly sliced pork loin for a truly heavenly fall [autumn!] meal. Pair with roasted potatoes, grilled cabbage wedges or mashed cannellini beans.

I'm touched, the next morning, to find myself greeted by freshly toasted English muffins – thought I'd make you feel at home, Diana says with a grin – and homemade mulberry jam (finally, I say, someone who does something with all the fruit I've been cycling over for weeks!), and sorry to leave both her and Mitzy, who is gratifyingly pleased to see me come into the kitchen in a way Wilf rarely is. Though we've never met before, the last eighteen hours have felt like spending time with friends, and I'm in a buoyant mood as I continue south, the sun already blazing hot at eight in the morning.

Reaching Providence, Rhode Island (number seventeen: states mount up quickly round here) by lunchtime, and enticed by the gas station signs offering homemade chourico, the smoked Portuguese cousin of both Spanish and Mexican chorizos, I stop at a pastelaria in Fox Point for a messy but satisfying chourico and hot pepper roll, a pastel de nata and a bean cake that, being almost entirely made of sugar, makes me quite nostalgic for the austerity of the Nation of Islam bean pie.

The cycle path follows a former railway line east for a while, past an old textile mill on the Pawtuxet River and a food bank, people queueing in battered cars and shiny pick-ups alike, before depositing me onto the wide shoulder of RI Route Three. Concentrating only on eating up the miles and making it to my primitive camp-site, just across the state line in Connecticut, before dark, I suddenly realise with a sinking heart, as I pass the Middle of Nowhere diner, already closed for the day, that I've inadvertently bypassed the only supermarket or source of food within an hour and half of my desti-nation, and no longer have either emergency peanuts or alligator jerky to tide me over. Grimly I turn around and pedal back along the hard shoulder, the wrong way, which seems safer than having to cross four lanes of traffic twice in fifteen minutes, to discover the supermarket is down, and then up, a long hill, and, of course, on the other side of yet another four-lane highway.

Severely overheated, I wander around indecisively, coming away with two tomatoes, an avocado, a cucumber, goat's cheese, salted Cape Cod crisps, a peach and 2 litres of water, plus some chocolate milk for immediate consumption on the ground outside the store, as more respectable shoppers give me a warily wide berth. Having managed to balance the rest on top of my now permanently gaping panniers, the afternoon goes downhill figuratively, if not literally, when Google encourages me down not one but two 'roads' that turn out to be rough, boulder-strewn forest tracks alternately flooded with deep sand or muddy water and peopled only by the eerie dead of the Douglass cemetery (last burial 1910). The surface is so bad I end up pushing Eddy much of the way, trying not to let myself get freaked out by gunshots echoing in the trees (hunters, surely), or the fast-encroaching night.

By the time I finally reach the campground in the Pachaug State Forest after narrowly escaping death under the wheels of a speeding pick-up passing far too close on a near-empty road, my feet sodden with mud, and having taken almost three hours to cover barely thirteen miles, I'm furious. My mood does not improve when the rangers swing by the little clearing I've been assigned within three minutes of my arrival, as I'm battling to put my tent up in the last rays of light, to furnish me with several pieces of paper and vehicle parking permits, despite my assurances I need neither. Fortunately, they leave just in time for me to dash into the swimming pond (against regulations at this hour, but I'm past caring), allowing the cool green water to wash off some of the day's grime, eat my salad in the company of a large beetle and several smaller but less welcome mosquitos, think enviously how much better avocados are in the States, and toss the paper permits in the recycling before it's too dark to see.

In bed by 9.15pm, weighing up the need to rehydrate with the distance I am from the rustic loo, I listen to the people next to me discussing Yankees form at a volume more suited to a Brooklyn bar, and then, when I finally drop off, am woken up by something very close to the tent, rustling. When I wake for good at 4.45am to a chamber choir of birdsong, I discover that 1) racoons like peaches too, which is breakfast gone, and that 2) however early the hour, and remote the place, a man will always manage to walk past while you're having a wild wee. Still, at least there are no bloodsucking flies, and for this small mercy I remain extremely grateful.

After yesterday's hot, boring slog along hard shoulders strewn with detritus (if there's a good reason why New Englanders throw empty miniature bottles out of car windows at a much higher rate than people in, say, Ohio or Texas, I'd like to hear it), this morning's roads are smaller and pleasantly rural. I pass some charming goats relaxing by a barn, and Griswold, sunflower capital of New England, and stop in Norwich, which claims to be the rose of Connecticut. It feels a bit wilted today, but there's a warm welcome at the Old Tymes restaurant on the way out of town – from the staff at least. As I'm attempting to excavate the processed cheese from the creamy cloak of gravy that smothers my ultimate biscuit sandwich (as featured on the Food Network, the menu says proudly), a couple come in, very slowly – the man, who is large enough to have trouble walking, has a particular table in mind where he can be comfortable. Once he's been helped into his seat, and decided on a backwoods breakfast with hash browns and a muffin – 'buttered, with extra bacon' – he begins sniffing loudly. I look up, and he quickly looks away.

'Does something smell kind of off to you in here?' he demands. His wife says, distractedly, she has a cold, so can't tell.

'It's kind of musty,' he complains, 'I smelled it as soon as I walked in.' I decide, hot with shame, it's time to get back on the road in my gently steaming trainers and sweaty kit – I can't get away fast enough when one of the waitresses, coming out to water her hanging baskets, engages me in friendly conversation about my trip. Nervously pulling up at the Hadlyme Country Market a couple of hours later, hoping to be in and out before anyone smells me, I spot a sign for a 'historic ferry'. Looking at the map it strikes me that this could cut a handy few miles from today's journey by negating the need to travel upstream to a bridge, only to have to come back down on my way to New Haven. I ask the lady behind the counter if it's running. 'Oh, sure, it's three dollars,' she says, 'right, Blake?' The young guy behind me in the queue assents.

'Plus, you get to jump the queue on a bike,' he says, 'they just load you right on.'

Suddenly, the day seems even brighter, the sky blue, the summer foliage vivid, the breeze from the water, with its gently swaying reeds, pleasant. Ten miles shaved off the day's total without even trying, I think smugly as I career downhill to the shore, whistling merrily to myself. Something that may or may not say 'CLOSED' under the next historic ferry sign does give me a little pause for thought but, I reason, I've checked with a shop literally on the road to the ferry; they'll know the hours off by heart. Naturally, when I get there, the ferry is closed for maintenance.

As I sweat angrily back up the hill towards something called Gillette Castle (insert King of Shaves joke here) on a road Google claims to be 'mostly flat' and I'd describe as anything but, a man in a pick-up truck winds down his window, forcing me to stop. 'Hey,' he says, 'were you wanting the ferry?' I sense an angel in disguise. 'Yes!' I say eagerly. He sucks his teeth, 'Yeah, I've just been out putting up the closed signs and when I passed you coming down I thought to myself, well, I bet she's heading for the ferry.' After a pause I'm unable to fill politely, he goes on, 'We've still got a few hours' work to do I'm afraid, but come back tomorrow, she'll be running!'

I'm about to retort that doesn't really help when he explains they get tourists from all over; I really should stay and experience the 'second oldest ferry in Connecticut', and he's so touchingly enthusiastic about it all I can't bear to admit I was only hoping to use the boat as a shortcut. Instead I thank him warmly (everything about me currently is warm), continue back up the hill and cross the bridge at East Haddam instead, before turning onto a road that turns into a track that finishes abruptly at an actual river that I have to wade through with a fully laden bike. Perhaps there was a bridge here once – I pass a sign on the way out to civilisation that warns 'Abandoned road: pass at your own risk' – but by the looks of the pile of stones in the river I'd say it's been a good century or so. A little later, my phone tries to take me down a road that exists in a map of 1878, but no longer, and fed up, I find the nearest main road and stick on it for the next twenty miles all the way into New Haven.

By now it's so hot I can feel it radiating from the tarmac, but the only place I can find to stop on Route 80 is a crash barrier on the narrow hard shoulder, so I lunch on a bag of crisps with trucks whizzing by metres from my damp trainers, and wonder what on earth Google Maps HQ in Mountainview, Cal. has against cyclists in New England. To make it worse, New Haven seems to sprawl for hours, the sun is relentless, a man in a tipper truck on the wrong side of the road tries to drive over me, and then simply hoots his horn until I concede my space, and downtown has some sadly desperate-looking beggars – though frankly, by the time I pull into the hotel, I win the prize for person you'd least like to share a small elevator with. Fortunately, I chose it for its laundry facilities: robe on, it all goes in the machine, even my shoes.

While they're spinning away, I festoon the room with damp camping gear, then, clad in clothes still warm from the dryer,* take a walk around the Yale campus, which looks like a cleaner, CGI version of a British university, peopled by earnest, shiny-haired joggers who don't look like they've ever heard the fateful word, Jägerbomb. While it's all very charming, no neo-Gothic architecture could hope to compete with the beauty I have in my hand half an hour later in Louis' Lunch, recognised, it proudly claims, by the Library of Congress as 'the Birthplace of the Hamburger Sandwich' way back in 1895.

For once, the eternal question of whether a burger counts as a sandwich is redundant, because here the meat is served between

---

* Though I've never had a tumble dryer at home, I can't deny there's a point to them after all.

two slices of white bread, toasted to provide structural integrity in the face of the copious juices that spill from the 1½in- (4cm-) thick medium-rare patty, and topped with tomatoes and onion, but nothing more (unless you want processed cheese, which I do not). As at Gene & Jude's, ketchup is strictly forbidden; indeed the Lassen family, now in its fourth generation in the business, believe that their burger is good enough not to need any condimental help whatsoever.

Josh Ozersky disputes that this counts as a hamburger – 'If you say it can be on toast, you're essentially redefining the hamburger out of existence. The hamburger as the world knows it means a sandwich of ground beef on a bun' – but whether or not Danish immigrant Louis Lassen can take credit for the hamburger over second-generation Swedish-American Walter Anderson in Kansas, who masterminded the bun, it's one of the best minced-beef and bread products I've had; chunky and emphatically beefy, though I'd still prefer Anderson's bun to the toast, which has disinte-grated under the sheer volume of liquid exuding from Lassen's filling by the time I get to the second half (a failure that repre-sents a serious disadvantage in the all-important ease-of-eating-on-the-go stakes).

The table at which I sit munching happily away is heavily scarred with the carvings of generations of student patrons, but this evening the only other customers are two guys jabbing greasy fingers at a laptop, who I decide are surely maths geniuses on the verge of a major breakthrough, and a man labouring over a cross-word who calls out every so often for help. The guy at the counter might not know the name of the second-highest peak in North America (Canada's Mount Logan, as you ask), but he is able to tell me how they cook the burgers, showing me the curious vertical cast-iron contraptions where each patty, held firm in a cage, is grilled on both sides simultaneously for about six minutes. Flames are visible through the door as he clunks it shut. 'A hundred and twenty-four years old,' he tells me, 'and the toasters aren't too far off. You're eating history.'

After inexplicably assuring the crossword man that the acronymous band behind the song 'Xanadu' is ABBA, I beat a hasty retreat. The day that started so unpromisingly has finally come good, and I'm full and clean and sleepy enough to think it was almost all worth it, despite the brambly claw marks across my legs from my unplanned forays through the forest.

Before I shut my eyes, I have decisions to make; though I know I need to be in New York in four days' time, I haven't yet worked out how to get there. Looking at the map, I'm drawn to the idea of coming in from the east, via Long Island and the fancy Hamptons, rather than continuing around the Connecticut coast and approaching from the north as the Adventure Cycling Association suggests.

The problem is that everyone else prefers Long Island too, and the campsites, which get mixed reviews of the 'if you like to sleep DO NOT camp here' variety, all seem to have one-week minimum stays and require the purchase of a $33 non-resident key before booking. At the other end of the scale, even the most run-down-looking hotels at the east end of the island start at $450 per night, it being a summer Friday, and me being Last-Minute Larry. Having gone through every option on every booking site I can think of, I have to concede, yawning widely, that I've brought this on myself: Saturday is my birthday, and had I thought ahead, I could have treated myself to an advance deal. As it is, I'm probably going to end up sleeping in a bus shelter, should they even have such declassé things in the Hamptons.

I go to bed cross, and wake up in the middle of the night thinking that if I want to see New York money at play, then I'm not going to do it from an overpriced 'down-to-earth' motel with brown paisley sheets and no hairdryer, so I book in to a place wildly out of my budget on Shelter Island, which looks like a Polo Ralph Lauren advert come to life, and go back to sleep feeling considerably poorer but a lot happier. Surely, after all those cockroach-infested motels and primitive campsites, I've earned it.

Before I head over to embrace my new life on credit, I have one last rendezvous in New England: a date to eat New Haven's best-known culinary speciality in the company of chef and food writer Brian Levy. We meet at Modern Apizza on State Street. 'The first thing you have to know about pizza here,' he says as I slide into the booth opposite him, a queue already forming in the doorway just before noon, 'is . . . Did you notice how it's spelled?' I nod: a-pizza. 'Well, it's actually pronounced a-beetz. Something to do with Sicilian dialect.' Though Brian studied architecture at Yale, he confesses he didn't eat much of the local style of pizza when he was here, 'But I believe clams are the usual thing, though I don't really care for them on pizza myself. We can get them though?'

My first instinct is to say, oh, no, we'll get something else, but American assertiveness is clearly rubbing off on me so we end up ordering a medium 16in (41cm) (!) pie, darkly blistered, almost burnt around the edge, chewy and robust, topped with mozzarella, garlic, oregano and briny little clams, and served with chunks of lemon to squeeze on top. We get through about two-thirds of it, which I think isn't bad going, and he takes the rest to go, though whether it's a great idea to transport clams three hours in a heat-wave is, as he observes, tbc. I tell him as he packs it up that I'm inclined to agree that clams, like chicken, have no place on a pizza and he cocks his head and says, 'You know what, I've changed my mind, I don't mind a bit of chewiness.'

Brian is curious to know, as we chat over a coffee, if I tried deep-dish pizza while I was in Chicago. I admit, slightly sheepishly, I've developed quite a taste for it. He shudders, tells me he had a Midwestern friend in grad school whose mother sent him frozen ones from home, 'And honestly, they were pretty gross.'

Yet another person I have to convert to the joys of the cheese pie, I think, as I pedal off to the station en route to New London, and the ferry to my final state: New York.

Ridden: 379 miles
Climbed: 15,321 feet
Pies consumed: 1 (blueberry)
All-American foods discovered: hot clam cakes, potato donuts, cider donuts, scrod, sweet potato fries, Indian pudding, burger sandwich, New Haven apizza

16

IN WHICH I MEET THE BIG DUCK

In search of how the 1 per cent eats

> *'The Hamptons is more than a place. It's a natural world of endless blue
> skies, the ocean, green fields, and white fences, rusticity and elegance with
> a quality of light that drew artists here decades ago. It has been home, my
> refuge, and always an inspiration.'*
> Ralph Lauren

Having not bothered to check train times, I'm blessed with a
two-hour wait at New Haven station, reading hopefully
about Long Island farmstead blueberry pies in Brian's beautiful
book* (which he kindly presented me with after I assured him I
would be delighted to pedal it the 120 miles to New York), while
eking out a single luridly coloured ice lolly. Incredibly, despite this
delay, and the number of moving parts in this travel plan (viz. a
train, two boats, a bus and a bike ride), it all works out and I arrive

---

* *Good & Sweet: A New Way to Bake with Naturally Sweet Ingredients*, which
comes highly recommended, particularly the aforementioned blueberry pie.

at the ferry ticket counter just in time for the 6pm service to Orient
Point. Hearing my accent, they inform me cheerily that my boat,
the MV *Cape Henlopen*, served in D-Day, 'Neat, huh?'

If I'm honest, I might have preferred a newer model, but at
least it has a bar. I realise, as I sit with my pint and a copy of *New
York Magazine* (coverline, 'Are Republican Women Okay?')
everyone around me sounds like Tony Soprano. A knot of men
discussing property values are putting away a lot of booze for
people with car keys on the table, and I hear one say, 'Oh, I don't
lease the land from him, it's like a handshake thing, ya know?'
Towards the end of the eighty-minute voyage, a woman holding
a large glass of wine approaches and begins loudly berating one
of their teenage sons for his US Marines t-shirt: 'You don't
deserve the shirt, take it off, turn it inside out, you gotta earn
the shirt!' The boy squirms uncomfortably as the men around
him laugh.

Having made it onto the North Fork of Long Island, and my
final state (I feel quite emotional as I take a picture of Eddy under
the Welcome to New York sign), I find myself the only person on
the shuttle across to the next ferry terminal, at Greenport. The
driver is chatty, telling me the island is so beautiful she sometimes
stops the bus to take a photo of the sunset, passengers or not. I'm
disappointed to hear the rich and famous, as usual, selfishly hide
their houses behind high walls, but I perk up when she tells me
about Justin Timberlake's recent arrest for DWI in Sag Harbor.
'He's our replacement Billy Joel,'* she says delightedly. Not only am
I to beware of men in double denim, but my new friend warns me
to be careful in the long grass – 'deer, and ticks everywhere' – as we

---

* The latter having recently listed his Oyster Bay estate for $49 million
to 'spend a little more time in Florida like old Jewish guys from Long
Island do'.

rattle along the narrow roads at such speed I can't even bear to look at Eddy banging about on the windscreen.

As the second ferry, to little Shelter Island (pop. 3,253), the crab-shaped blob of land caught between the lobster claws of the North and South Forks, pulls out from the cluster of fishing boats I get a glimpse of the shoreside houses hidden from the road, now glowing in the setting sun. It deposits me in the island's only real settlement, a scatter of streets, and I make my way over to the hotel through darkening elm woods. The first thing I notice, as I approach, is a vast American flag flying outside – and I mean huge, it must be the size of a small European car. The second is the line of pristine white Adirondack chairs beneath, which give the surreal impression I'm riding into an Instagram post.

The sweet chino-ed teenager in charge of valet parking looks a bit surprised when I pull up the drive, admitting they don't get many guests arriving on two wheels, 'But hey, it's cool, I love to mountain bike.' From that point on, however, although everyone is perfectly pleasant, I get the distinct sense that I don't quite slot into the hotel mood board; no one is actually rude, but I clearly don't give off a sufficiently demanding (or, no doubt, wealthy) aura to merit putting oneself out for. (The exception is the young Irish guy at the pool bar who tells me he's looking forward to getting back to €3 pints – 'I paid $40 for a daiquiri the other day down in Montauk – $40! I mean, Jaysus fuckin' wept!' He stops abruptly, and apologises for his language. I grin and tip him generously for making me feel briefly at home.)

The media for the last fortnight has been full of speculation around the first presidential debate, and I manage, somehow, to crash a private watch party in the hotel 'nook' – clutching a Manhattan (because at least I have the grace not to help myself to their drinks and pizza), I find myself cross-legged on the floor in front of a vocal but fast-shrinking crowd. Clearly this is not going as they hoped because, long before the end, the last guest hands me the remote control, saying angrily that they're going to bed, they can't watch any more – 'Enjoy,' he shoots bitterly over his shoulder.

I wake the next morning to a barrage of messages from the UK, half demanding to know if I saw the debate, half wishing me a happy birthday. It feels like tragic tradition that I always seem to end up on my own on my big day on tour – in France abject self-pity earned me a hug from a maître d' in a Michelin-star restaurant, in the UK, an invitation to dinner at the home of Indian food writer Maunika Gowardhan, so here, after a dip in the cool, green ocean, I decide to simply drift and see what the day brings me.

Briefly, I even consider not leaving the hotel – having been on the move for ten weeks, it might be a nice treat – but it's not long before my natural nosiness, and skin-flint tendencies, see me back on the bike and off in search of a birthday breakfast that isn't a $27 bagel. The counter at the drugstore serves me up a cream cheese number with coffee for not much over $5, and for that I also get to earwig on the conversations between the locals – the cook, and many of the customers, dressed in work clothes, speak Spanish, Greg, the guy in charge, English, and chat switches between the two as someone else comes in seeking advice for where to get a table leg welded locally ('the place by Commander Cody's' in case you're also wondering).

Full and happy, I spend the morning completing a leisurely circumnavigation of the perfect little wooded island, noting the many gardeners out titivating the pristine lawns in preparation for the weekend and the novel BIDEN HARRIS yard signs, and startling the resident ospreys who wheel around me squawking to defend the nests perched on top of telegraph poles. The sun is out, and a light sea breeze makes for ideal cycling conditions, even away from the coast (though not far away; the island is only twenty-nine square miles, and a third of that is nature reserve). Commander

Cody's Fish Shoppe where lobsters jostle for supremacy in a tank labelled 'Please do not touch me, I am super duper expensive' offers lobster dinners starting at $35 and lobster rolls for $28 (plus tax), but as it's still a little early for either, I ask the guy behind the counter how much one of the big boys would be – about $40 he says, which almost feels like a bargain round here. Later, passing a little store with several workman's vans pulled up outside, I decide instead to get a picnic lunch in the form of a goat burrito, which I tuck in my jersey pocket, where I can feel it warm and heavy against my back, like a small, tightly swaddled baby. Too self-conscious to take its oozy, oily deliciousness anywhere near the hotel, I eat it perched on a rock painted with a US flag, overlooking the water. While I'm there, several cars arrive, take a picture of the rock and leave again, presumably not noticing they've also captured a woman licking goat grease off her fingers.

Determined to make the most of my considerable financial investment, I head back to resume life as a wealthy woman of taste and find someone's left an ice bucket containing a magnum of champagne above my damp and, it must be said, still slightly pongy trainers. I assume it's gone to the wrong room until I see a card with my name on it from my brother and sister-in-law. I can't stop smiling – partly because who wouldn't at surprise champagne? But also because it's lovely to feel special on your birthday, particularly when you're spending it alone. Not feeling quite up to popping the cork just yet, I skip downstairs with the bucket to ask the bar to keep it chilled for later, a request they seem to find strangely perplexing, and spend the afternoon as the only person reading by the pool in Intersport Stornoway's stoutest swimwear.

At some point, I realise if I'm not going to consume 1½ litres of sparkling wine and nothing else for dinner, I need to make a quick sortie to the village, where the only option open is the Marie Eiffel Market ('real food the French way'). Lobster rolls are priced at an astonishing $45 (to go), which, birthday or not, I can't bring myself to shell out for a takeaway sandwich. Waiting to collect my comparatively competitive $23 crabcake salad, I watch drunk boys in ripped t-shirts casually ordering several hundred dollars' worth of food, while a woman who I guess from her accent, to be Marie herself, scolds one of the girls behind the counter. When I see the size of the crabcakes, two of them, each no bigger than a Pizza Express dough ball (or a hush puppy, in American measures), served on a few limp, *wet* lettuce leaves (Marie, you've been away from home too long: *où est votre essoreuse à salade?*), I feel like doing a bit of scolding myself, but it's my birthday, and I'm British, so I meekly take the box and leave.

Resplendent in my smartest outfit (i.e. my only dress), sporting all my jewellery and make-up (earrings, necklace, mascara), I go downstairs to reclaim my champagne. This takes a while, but eventually the bar manager returns with an ice bucket. He doesn't offer to help me with it, so I bear it proudly aloft through the busy throng on the terrace, take a ceremonial picture to send to my family, and then look closely at it to see if I have goat stuck in my teeth and realise it's not the same bottle: the Reserve in my earlier picture had fancy black foil; this one is sealed with the gaudy gold of ordinary Brut! Do I *look* the kind of scruffy cyclist who drinks entry-level champagne? I think crossly, marching back across the lawn and up the steps with the whole set-up.

Resolving this no-doubt honest mistake takes another while, and yields nothing in the way of apology, but finally I get to sit under the flag in my Adirondack chair, watching the sun set over the water, breathing in the drifting, evocative scent of cigars from around the firepit, and feel happy. I feel even happier when I take the bottle back to the room and discover TLC has a *90 Day Fiancé* double bill on, so I can sit in bed, eating chocolate mousse and drinking champagne, and feeling, briefly, like the queen of the bloody world.

Remarkably, it's not until I'm on the South Ferry from the other end of the island the next morning that I start to wonder if a magnum of champagne, however fancy, might be slightly beyond my capabilities these days. Even then, the thought quickly passes as I myself pass the hotel where poor Justin had that single, fateful martini and settle back into life on the road, where, if I'm honest, I'm much more at home – my penultimate day in the saddle, and I finally feel every inch a confident American cyclist.

Once I'm out of Sag Harbor the Montauk Highway is much like any other large, busy road, albeit with more plastic surgeons than average. In Southampton I fall foul of local by-laws for attempting to ride my bike down Main Street – 'Excuse me, ma'am,' a teenager wearing a CROSSING GUARD gilet says, stepping out in front of me, 'but you have to walk that down here or take the back lots.' As I'm on a shopping street choked with Range Rovers and Teslas, I'm taken aback – 'Sorry, you're allowed to drive a car down here, but not ride a bike?' He nods apologetically, 'Because, like, there are cars behind you and stuff?'

This has, I decide, furiously pushing my heavy bike down the sidewalk, to be the most ridiculous place I have ever been, and I'm only too delighted to leave, passing, as I go, a vast queue of traffic heading in the opposite direction, as New Yorkers rich enough to escape the city for the weekend, but not rich enough to charter a helicopter, crawl east. I've been keen to visit the Hamptons ever since seeing it on some reality TV show years ago, but in reality, I don't think it's the place for me. Or perhaps, much like Malibu, it's just not the place for my budget.

That dream shattered, I turn north, away from the south coast and through the forest towards Port Jefferson, where I finally have a free Warmshowers bed lined up for my last night on the move. Just beyond a sign telling me the verges are sponsored by Surburban Exterminating, I receive the exciting news that I'm entering Flanders, Home of the Big Duck. This, when it finally appears some five miles down the road, exceeds my wildest expectations: a white cement duck about twenty feet tall and twice as long from beak to tail, just plonked by the side of the highway next to that even rarer beast, the American public lavatory.

What a fine thing this is, I think, jauntily approaching the glass door set into its breast, where a couple are loitering with no obvious intent. It seems to be locked, though I can see people in the duck's internal cavity – I turn and ask if the waterfowl perhaps operates a one-in-one-out policy, like a nightclub. 'I guess,' the woman says uncertainly. So, we wait. And wait. Finally the people inside leave, clutching shopping bags, and the couple are admitted, but its doorman motions for me to stay where I am. A carload of girls arrives, speaking, I think, Korean – before they can make the same mistake as I did, I explain the duck seems to only entertain one group at a time. 'But,' one of them says, 'what is inside? What is it?' I say I'm not sure, so there we stand, the six of us, queuing outside a giant duck for we know not what. After a few minutes the same girl, following some lively discussion among themselves, asks me, 'Is it a gift shop?' and I tell her again I have no clue, and then it's finally my turn to be inducted into its mysteries.

Having secured the door behind me, the duck's custodian returns to his seat in silence: getting information out of him is like plucking down through a pillowcase – all questions lead to the same book, *The Big Duck and Eastern Long Island's Duck Farming Industry*, for sale on the counter. A few newspaper articles on the wall, however, explain that the Big Duck, inspired by the programmatic architecture of California (alas! how long ago the Donut Hole seems!), was built in 1931 for a local farmer, who used it to sell his Pekins. A framed flyer depicting the Duck in its prime mentions freshly killed ducklings, broilers, fryers and young roasters, dressed ready for the oven: 'our speciality', nearby a tin sign urges, 'Enjoy Long Island Duckling, famous for its succulent flavor.'

What happened to all the ducks then? I ask its taciturn guardian. He grunts, 'No one round here these days wants to live next to a duck farm.' I buy a sticker, and make way for the Koreans.

Maybe it's his thick New York accent that prompts me to stop for a huge, if disappointingly dry, breaded eggplant and 'muzzarell' hero sandwich at a lovely spot on the banks of the Peonic at Riverhead, followed by a chocolate egg cream (a New York speciality that's a kind of fizzy chocolate milkshake involving neither eggs nor cream) at the Snowflake Ice Cream Shoppe opposite – like it or not, there's no avoiding the fact that the city is now breathing down my neck.

EGGPLANT HERO

This is the hero I wanted to eat in Riverhead, but on Long Island they clearly have health in mind. Sadly, however much we food writers may try to convince you otherwise, there is no substitute for frying aubergine: it soaks up oil like a sponge and that's precisely what makes it so delicious. Soft and oily, crisp and cheesy with a rich red sauce, aromatic basil and milky mozzarella, this is a special-occasion sandwich.

Makes 4
2 medium aubergines/eggplants
Salt, to sprinkle
60g/½ cup plain/all-purpose flour
50g/⅔ cup panko breadcrumbs
50g/1½ loose cups finely grated pecorino or Parmesan
2 eggs, beaten
Olive oil, to fry
4 hero or ciabatta rolls
A small bunch of basil
A ball of fresh mozzarella

For the sauce

2 tbsp olive oil
1 onion, chopped
4 cloves of garlic, chopped
¼ tsp chilli flakes
¼ tsp dried oregano
2 × 400g / 14-ounce tins of chopped tomatoes
1 tsp balsamic vinegar
A knob of butter

1. Cut the aubergines / eggplants into roughly 1cm / ½in slices and arrange on a baking sheet or chopping board lined with a clean tea towel or kitchen paper. Sprinkle lightly with salt, then turn over and sprinkle the other side with salt. Top with another clean tea towel or kitchen paper and leave for 30 to 60 minutes.

2. Meanwhile, make the sauce. Heat the oil in a medium pan over a medium-low heat and fry the onion until soft and translucent. Stir in the garlic, chilli and oregano and fry for another minute or so, then add the tomatoes. Bring to a simmer, then turn down the heat and allow to bubble gently away for about 30 minutes until thick. Stir in the vinegar and butter and season to taste.

3. Pat the aubergines dry and line the tray with fresh kitchen paper. Cover the base of a frying pan with 2 tablespoons of olive oil and heat until a drop of water sizzles when you flick it in. Fry the aubergine slices on both sides until just soft, then drain on the paper. (You'll probably need to do this in batches, adding more oil, unless you're halving the recipe or have a huge pan.)

4. Put the flour on one plate and the breadcrumbs and grated cheese on another, and beat the eggs in a small bowl. Put the oven on low. Quarter fill the pan with more oil and heat until a breadcrumb dropped in begins to brown immediately.

5. While it's heating, dip each aubergine slice in the flour, shake off the excess, dip in the egg, letting the excess drip off, then roll

in the breadcrumbs to coat. Fry until golden on both sides, and put into the oven to keep warm.

6. Halve the rolls, spread with the tomato sauce and strew with basil leaves. Add the aubergine slices and tear in the mozzarella. Eat in happy silence.

The further I get from the Hamptons, the more Long Island feels like the America I'm more used to: the usual political and patriotic signs are out in force, and in the parking lot of the Coram Diner, where I stop for a slice of cherry pie (underseasoned soft pastry, gloopy but pleasantly tart filling, 6/10), a bungalow is slung with a grimy banner, 'INTERNAL MEDICINE: NOW OPEN'. The menu, large and ring bound, offers roast Long Island duckling Hawaiian style ($21.95), the placemat adverts for local funeral homes.

My host for the evening, Nancy, has told me that when I get to Port Jefferson I should look for the red house with bicycles hanging out front, adding, 'Just ask people where Mike the Bikeman lives!' When I arrive, she's sitting drinking tea in her pretty garden, but immediately leaps up and shouts, 'TIFFANY! PINK!' gesturing at my neon pink jersey and down at her pink shoes, before telling me to dump my bike and come join her. As I wonder awkwardly how to drop in my real name without seeming rude, she fetches me a beer from the fridge in the shed, full of bikes her husband is in the process of repairing and restoring – 'You just help yourself, Tiffany, make yourself at home,' she says, and I decide the moment has passed – and we sit down briefly, before she jumps up again to give me a tour of the house and the vegetable patch – 'I think my son forgot to water the cucumbers' – show me the tandem she and Mike ride on tour, and suggest I might like to sleep in the spacious RV parked in the yard. She's a whirlwind of energy, just like Dan back in LA, Johnny in San Antonio or Bethia in Columbus – it's like enthusiasm flows from the taps in the refreshingly uncynical land of the free.

Born in Sag Harbor (her great-grandfather was a bartender at the site of Justin's downfall), Nancy has traced her ancestors back to Joseph Smith (of Mormon golden tablet fame), Stephen Hopkins, who came over on the *Mayflower*, and Princess Di. Despite, or perhaps even because of this unusual mix of genes, I warm to her immediately; indeed it would be hard not to like someone who has an enormous Father Christmas in their living room in late June, attired in a tie-dye kaftan and sunglasses for the summer because she couldn't be bothered to lug him down to the basement.

I'm her first Warmshowers guest, she says, and not long after telling me this she claps her hands to her forehead – 'Tiffany, I forgot!' – and runs inside to get me several large fluffy towels for an actual warm, even hot, shower. When I emerge, feeling far more cosseted than I did at last night's four-star hotel, Mike is back from his bike ride, and we sit and eat a homemade dinner in the soft dusk – delicious chicken and spinach burgers with giant couscous, roasted aubergine, tomato and feta with salad (Yotam Ottolenghi, I've missed you) and chat about cycle touring. Mike has crossed the country several times, and tells me he thinks the Californian coast the most beautiful ride he's ever done. Politics inevitably comes into our conversation too: Nancy gestures to the stars and stripes that line the driveway, saying that she's a patriot and proud to be, but she increasingly feels like the right have 'stolen our flag'.

I try to explain, in turn, how odd all these flags seem to me, having grown up in a country where they're rarely seen outside national beanos like the coronation,* though the more I think about it, the more it feels like an unbridgeable gulf between national identities. An ostentatious display of flags in the UK, in my experience at least, tends to be read as shorthand for the kind of

---

* Until 2008 it was against the law for public buildings to fly the national flag apart from on eighteen sanctioned days a year, which included the monarch's birthday and wedding anniversary.

views that became known, derisively, during the Brexit campaign as flag shagging. Here (though Nancy's anxiety suggests there are nuances I'm missing as a visitor) it often seems to represent nothing more than a simple love of home and community. (Obviously I do not mention the phrase flag shagging.)

After dinner, Mike takes me to Tara's, his local bar, a friendly, cash-only place with a pool table and baseball on the screens, where I try and fail to help a very drunk woman from Limerick work the jukebox. As we leave, I notice the sign outside: 'WE GOT LOBSTAA! $11'. This, I think, is a part of Long Island I could very much warm to.

COFFEE BREAK

The Price of a Lobster Roll En Route

$11 (whole lobster, but no roll) – Tara Inn, Port Jefferson, NY

$28 – Commander Cody's, Shelter Island, NY

$29 – Home Kitchen Cafe, Rockland, ME

$30 – Becky's Diner, Portland, ME and the Red House, Harvard, MA

$32 – Mabel's Lobster Claw Shack, Kennebunkport, ME

$32.99 – Rose Eden Lobster House, Bar Harbor, ME

$45 – Marie Eiffel's, Shelter Island, NY

I sleep well in the RV, with a soft breeze on my face and playing in the trees outside. Though they're still asleep when I leave, Nancy has left coffee on for me. On my thank-you note I finally pluck up the courage to tell these lovely, generous people my name isn't in fact Tiffany.

It's a funny feeling, this last day on the road proper. Having braved Los Angeles, Houston and Chicago and lived to tell the tale, I have no excuse not to at least try to ride around New York too, but there's a definite difference between just jumping on the bike to get from A to B, and touring for the pleasure of it. Much as I'm looking forward to going home and seeing the dog's silly little face, I'm going to miss this feeling, the freedom of long days in the saddle, the fleeting glimpse of other lives from my narrow perch, the familiar strangeness of America, its lovely, welcoming people and, of course, its many wonderful pies.

The streets are quiet, and the sky a little leaky as I wind my way west, climbing in humid woods and freewheeling along winding country lanes, passing the occasional market garden and through the pretty, arty village of Stony Brook. Gradually the landscape becomes increasingly suburban, the houses neater, closer together, and I realise with regret that I've probably seen the last of rural America for this trip. That said, we're still far enough out for a few final political statements, and there's a grand selection on show this morning, including one house flying no fewer than three flags stacked on top of each other: the stars and stripes, 'TRUMP WON You know it I know it' and, at the bottom, the Italian tricolour.

I detour for breakfast at the busy International House of Pancakes in Commack; I've always wanted to see what's so international about it, but the menu proves all American, from waffles to t-bone steak and eggs, and, intriguingly, a chicken fajita omelet. Remembering the farmers' omelet fiasco in Indiana, I decide to stick to what they presumably do best; three fluffy buttermilk pancakes with gratifyingly greasy crispy bacon. The sun finally comes out with not entirely welcome strength on the Jericho Turn-pike, and I soon find myself perspiring on an unlovely road running parallel to the Long Island Expressway, where gated communities called things like the Hunt Club and the Hamlet proliferate. A truck honks angrily at me to get out of its way at a set of lights; at the next a man rolls down his window and I brace myself for more of the same, but instead he just wants to know where I've been, where I'm heading – 'I used to do that,' he says wistfully, 'before.' He nods to the sleeping child behind him. 'Ride safe!'

Suddenly the Big Apple, the end, and everything all feels very real, and after getting a bit flustered negotiating the terrifying traffic around somewhere called the Manors, I stop at a 7-Eleven for a small BIG GULP of lemonade and a packet of Extra CHEESY CHEEZ-ITS, which I eat on the kerb, feeling flat and despondent. With rain forecast, I force myself to push on, and soon, almost without warning, and whether I like it or not, I'm engulfed by the city, racing down Queens Boulevard past Filipina bakeries and Turkish grills, men playing chess under the railway tracks and Peruvian restaurants, so much to look at all around me, and then I see the famous skyline and realise with relief I've made it to New York – and, against all odds, I'm somehow still alive.

Ridden: 175 miles
Climbed: 5,590 feet
Pies consumed: 1 (cherry)
All-American foods discovered: crabcakes, eggplant hero,
New York egg cream, CHEEZ-ITS

17

NO SLEEP IN BROOKLYN

In search of the Sturgeon King

*'Next time someone tells you bipartisanship is dead, show them how
Cynthia Nixon putting lox on a cinnamon raisin bagel sparked
outrage from pretty much everyone.'*
Sheldon Gilbert (@sheldongilbert), 11 September 2018

Somewhere in the last ten weeks I've got it into my head that my
journey should end at the Brooklyn Bridge, which offers not
only a pleasing symmetry with the Golden Gate in San Francisco,
but a stupendous photo opportunity – and so, despite the ominous
colour of the sky (when I can see it between buildings) I bypass my
hotel in Williamsburg and keep on riding, even as a wind gets up
and rubbish begins to dance alarmingly across the cycle lane. Struggling to work out the best spot for a victory selfie, I get caught out
when the rain finally follows. Brooklyn Bridge, I can reliably inform
you, is not waterproof; in fact the stuff cascades through it like God
turned the shower on. Welcome to New York, I think, watching a
rat scurry for cover as the cold trickles down my back.

After huddling pointlessly against one of the piers for five or so
minutes, I decide to strike out into the deluge and celebrate my

achievement with that most luridly golden of medals, the Taco Bell Nacho Cheese Doritos taco. Having been diligently searching out salad since the end of April, assuming that at some point down the line fast food would be my only option, I've suddenly realised that, having made it across the country and almost out the other side, I'm at serious risk of missing out on a cheesy nacho the size of my hand. Oddly enough I just haven't seen that many branches of the Californian chain (whose founder, Glen Bell, was inspired by visits to the McDonald brothers' first San Bernardino drive-in), on my travels . . . but nevertheless this culinary carbuncle has lodged itself in my consciousness.

Abandoning Eddy outside a 'cantina' huddled underneath the dripping tracks of the Broadway Brooklyn line, reasoning that few people are desperate enough to steal a muddy bike in the pouring rain, I spend a very happy two minutes in the company of said taco, which is filled with 'seasoned beef', lettuce and cheese, with extra red cabbage, guacamole and black beans. On its own, it weighs in at a surprisingly modest 170kcal – about the same as two apples (though my customisation adds another banana's worth).

As I eat, I read Antonia Hitchens in the *New Yorker* on my lunch: 'The Doritos Locos Taco, or D.L.T., is designed to target taste buds using "dynamic contrast" – in this case, the sensation of biting through the crispy shell to the fat-laced filling.' To add to its appeal, the combination of crunchy taco shell, minced beef and iceberg lettuce instantly transports me back to the 1990s, when taco shells came in little yellow cardboard boxes and were filled with chilli con carne bulked out with plenty of kidney beans and topped with grated cheddar, and this brief trip down memory lane is thus both comforting and extremely enjoyable . . . a childhood treat given the American treatment.

Wiping my fingers carelessly on my sodden shorts – not long before I peel them off for good! – I head back into the rain: by the time I get to the hotel, my trainers are so wet they leave puddles as

I squelch self-consciously across the lobby to check in. One long hot shower later, I'm shoving down a thick, fluffy grandma slice and a plastic cup of red wine from a box at Best Pizza round the corner, and not long after that I'm in bed, and fast asleep. I've got this far; now for the final, and arguably most difficult, challenge: choosing where to eat in the Big Apple, one of the great restaurant cities of the world.

The first day of July dawns fine and sunny – in a week I'll be home, I realise with a start, recalling how distant this moment once seemed – and after handing over a large plastic bag from the Mexican supermarket in Santa Barbara to Maria at the service laundromat round the corner (a handwritten sign behind her head reads: 'Refund policy: no refund'), I get a coffee (large, weak, fudge-brownie flavoured) and lay down the cornerstones of my eating itinerary.

First, of course, there must be bagels, preferably accompanied by some sort of pickles and smoked fish – as Becky Hughes, whose *New York Times* byline declares she does not toast her bagels, observes, there are 'few things New Yorkers like to argue about more than bagels', which surely must mean they're pretty close to the local heart. Second, I want to find out more about Italian-American food; the red-sauce joints of the Rat Pack and the Sopranos and the New York (pizza) slice. Thirdly, there will be hot dogs, not to be confused with the Chicago or even the DC variety, on the Fourth of July, and of course while I'm here I have to have at least one piece of New York cheesecake, and a black-and-white cookie. And, given the city is famous for the diversity of its cuisine, that feels like a legitimate excuse to eat everything else I come across too. But first, bagels. Or beigels, depending on your facility with Yiddish.

COFFEE BREAK

The Knotty History of the Bagel

Though bagel-adjacent breads are found everywhere from north-west China to southern Italy and the Levant, the boiled and baked wheat-flour rings (the hole in the middle helps this dense bread cook through more evenly, much like a ring donut or a bundt cake) we know today evolved as a cousin of the Germanic pretzel, and are closely related to the Polish *obwarzanek*; the word is usually agreed to come from the Yiddish *beigen*, to bend, and they travelled to the Americas with Eastern European Jews. Until the second half of the twentieth century, however, they remained largely within the community: as late as 1960, even the *New York Times* felt the need to explain to its readers that bagels were 'an unsweetened donut with rigor mortis'. Bagel manufacture at this point was a skilled trade, strictly controlled by members of the International Beigel Bakers Union, who guarded their secrets, and their rights, fiercely.

That all changed when Murray Lender, whose Polish-immigrant father and uncles ran Lender's bakery in New Haven, CT, decided to break into the burgeoning frozen food market with what marketing materials glossed as 'Jewish English muffins'. The company invested in a new automated bagel-rolling machine invented by a maths teacher from California, which could turn out 400 bagels an hour with little to no skill, compared to the 120 an experienced baker could hope for. Once they realised frozen bagels required pre-slicing . . . the NY bagel was ready to go national.

The advent of machine-made versions, it is said, sounded the death knell of the traditional chewy bagel of yore, which has been replaced with something more akin to a soft, ring-shaped roll. But it's still possible to get a great bagel – traditionalists argue over whether they're better in New York or Montreal (where they're smaller, denser, sweeter and baked in a wood-fired oven), while realists head to Los Angeles, which now has a bagel game to match either of them. Top tip: wherever you are, don't order the rainbow bagel.

The queue at Apollo Bagels in the East Village on a Monday morning in early July is considerably shorter than the Monday-morning line at Courage Bagels in LA in late April, which might say something about the relative availability of decent bagels – I'm quickly out with my aggressively charred, almost burnt sourdough rings (toasting is anathema to local bagel purists, but not me) topped with cream cheese and cool, savoury slices of tomato, sitting on a bench in the sun, forgetting the trauma of the first few minutes of Manhattan cycling. It's the first place I've been where it's not the drivers you have to look out for so much as your fellow riders; red lights barely merit a pause in pedalling, signalling is for wimps and one smartly dressed woman, clearly on her way to work, undertakes me on a blind corner, headphones on, zero shits given.

The crusty, tangy Apollo version is definitely not a traditional chewy, dense New York bagel, but it still feels appropriate fuel for a trip to the Tenement Museum to learn more about the history of both German and Jewish immigrant communities. The Lower East Side, I discover, standing in a dark basement that once housed Schneider's Lager Bier Saloon, was the first district of New York where English was not the dominant language, a fact that prompted panic among the city's Anglophone majority. Yet, our guide says, as we consider how quickly this German population dispersed and almost completely assimilated (leaving behind a few clues in places like Columbus, Ohio's German Village, or the Hofbräuhaus in Newport, Kentucky), many beloved all-American traditions, from hot dogs and beer to pretzels and mustard, have their roots in Deutschland. Indeed, 45 million Americans reported German ancestry in the most recent US census.

As I admire the model sausages on the table, the guide explains this area was once the most densely populated place on earth: once the Germans became settled enough in their new home to branch out, they were replaced by southern and eastern Europeans (many of the latter Jewish), African Americans, Puerto Ricans and other Latin Americans, and more recently, arrivals from South and East Asia. It's a pattern you can see as you walk around the area, as I do afterwards in search of lunch: the Buddhist Association of New York Guang Ji Temple sits across the road from Mendel Goldberg Fabrics (est. 1890), a Dominican diner and a shisha bar – different communities may have come and gone over the last century and a half, but all life is still here. I watch the uniformed chauffeur of a huge black SUV patiently smoke cigarette after cigarette as I perch in the window of Scarr's Pizza trying to maintain some dignity in the face of a New York slice dripping with hot honey and pepperoni grease, and so long it's served draped across two paper plates. (The girl next to me, struggling to stop cheese falling on her elegant cream dress, takes a break from discussing her new puppy to announce plaintively down the phone, 'Gramma, I really am having an issue with this pizza.')

Before picking up my laundry from Maria's tender care, I treat myself to a thorough laundering in preparation for my re-entry into normal, civilised society by riding up to Murray Hill in Queens for a scrubdown in a Korean spa, and then, more pleasurably, a huge mound of shaved multigrain-flavoured ice in an adjacent cafe.

It's like eating a mound of sweet fresh snow topped with syrupy red beans and chewy mochi, toasted almonds and ice cream, and quite simply one of the most interesting combinations of tastes and textures I've ever tried. I'm hooked – reviews suggest most people share a portion between three or four, but I only learn this after I've finished the lot. It's only ice, after all.

Clean, or cleanish after the cycle back to Williamsburg, I pick up my neatly pressed clothes and promptly spill deliciously oily beefy broth all over them at the Birria Landia taco truck parked by the freeway: $4 each, less than the price of the average coffee in this city,* with plentiful benches nearby to sit and enjoy the parade of humanity in search of tacos: pushing strollers and walking frames, holding hands and beer bottles, arriving on bikes, leaving in cabs. Worth the sacrifice, as long as I don't bump into Maria on the way home.

Continuing my exploration of Jewish New York, I head uptown the next morning to Barney Greengrass, the Sturgeon King, on the Upper West Side, a resolutely old-fashioned 'Jewish deli institution since 1908', Google notes, 'known for smoked fish & not taking credit cards'. (Though, Gary Greengrass informs me once I get to the till, they do take cards, it's just the machine isn't working right now.) Otherwise the place is a perfect time warp that doesn't seem to have changed since Irving Berlin had a weekly borscht order and Groucho Marx described the sturgeon as 'monumental'. The main room is lined with shelves packed with jars and bottles, and counters behind which wise-cracking, white-coated staff stand ready to cut you sable or whitefish, or reach into a large vat to retrieve your choice of tiny, knobbly half or fully sour pickles. A sign on the wall

---

* According to Eater NY, in May 2024, 'The average cost for a cup of coffee is somewhere around $6 to $7 after add-ins, tax, and tip.'

invites customers heading for the Hamptons to let them pack a box of smoked fish on ice; it's that kind of place.

I go next door, to the faded dining room, where a small boy in a paper crown is enjoying a birthday bagel with his grandparents, two Japanese tourists are silently sharing a plate of lox and a group of ladies is gossiping busily over latkes and apple sauce by the window. Taking a seat in the corner, where I have a good view of the action, I order a plate of scrambled eggs heavy with huge chunks of salty smoked sturgeon,* salmon and onion, an everything bagel, smaller and chewier than yesterday's, and a generous slab of the densest, richest cream cheese I've ever tasted. It's all exactly how I remember it on my last visit a decade ago, and I'm happy as a clam as I stroll back down Broadway with a black-and-white cookie tucked into my pocket, eating a crunchy half-sour pickle like a popsicle, on my way to meet friend and fellow writer Charlotte Druckman in the West Village.

PERFECT PICKLES

OK, I won't swear these will be quite as perfect as the ones displayed in an enormous jar between the lox and the pickled herring at Barney Green-grass – they've had a bit more practice – but making your own is a peculiarly satisfying project, and also allows you to judge exactly the level of fermentation that suits your taste. They start off crunchy and salty and pleasingly green, like a pickle from The Busy World of Richard Scarry, *becoming softer and sourer the longer you leave them. Knobbly little pick-ling cucumbers can be found in greengrocers and farmers' markets in summer, but the baby cucumbers increasingly sold in supermarkets make a decent, if slightly less meaty, substitute.*

---

* Anthony Bourdain, who once described it as serving the 'quintessential New York breakfast, period', preferred his just with lox.

Makes 1 large jar
75g / ¼ cup fine sea salt
12 pickling or baby cucumbers
6 cloves of garlic
2 bay leaves
1 dried red chilli
1 tsp coriander seeds
1 tsp caraway or dill seeds
1 tsp yellow mustard seeds

1. Dissolve the salt in 500ml/2 cups of hot water, then top up with the same of cold water – the exact ratio doesn't matter too much as long as it adds up to about 1 litre or 4 cups. Leave to cool completely.
2. Trim any remaining stalk from the ends of the cucumbers, as the flowering parts contain an enzyme that can make your pickles mushy. Pack into a clean jar just large enough to hold them.
3. Peel and lightly squash the garlic cloves with the back of a knife. Add to the jar along with the herbs and spices. Fill up with the cooled brine; you shouldn't need it all but keep it to top up the jar if necessary.
4. The cucumbers should be completely submerged; if they float, weight them down with a clean object; I use a new food storage bag part filled with water. Loosely cover the jar, put into a bowl or tray to catch any overflow and leave for a couple of days in a cool place.
5. After a couple of days the cucumbers should have gone a dark, dull green and the brine should have begun to cloud. Keep an eye on them, and top up the jar if necessary. After 3 to 4 days you should have half-sour pickles, after about a week they should be fully sour; how long you leave them is up to you.

6. Once you're happy with the result, seal tightly and refrigerate or keep in a very cool, dark place like a cellar where they should be good for a year.

Charlotte tells me her grandfather was friendly with the original Barney Greengrass, and her dad, who grew up visiting the store with him, knew Mo, Barney's son, and now she herself knows Gary, whose sturgeon she considers consistently the best in the city. (I confess I'm not sure I've ever had sturgeon before, so it's good to know I've gone in at the top.)

As Charlotte is, among many other things, the co-author of the Sweethearts, a newsletter 'for people who love pastries, confections, breadstuffs . . . and New York City', I've asked her to take me on a mini pie tour of her home turf, accompanied by an impossibly cute ball of snowy fluff by the name of Gena G, a joyful little furby masquerading as a Coton de Tuléar.*

Gena G seems to love everyone and everything, and trots enthusiastically in front of us as we visit Red Gate Bakery (tragically already closed for the Fourth of July holiday), Janie's Life-Changing Baked Goods (cookies made from pie crust), and Petee's Pie Co., where there are so many options on the counter – black bottom almond! Berry dream! Guava mascarpone icebox! Rhubarb streusel! – that I struggle to pick, which means, of course, that I have to try them all.

The rhubarb streusel is my favourite with its rich, flaky pastry, a filling almost perfectly balanced between tart and sweet, and a nutty, deliciously soggy streusel topping that server Crystal tells me is made with brown butter and hazelnut: the perfect marriage of

---

* If you're not up on Madagascan fauna, this is, allegedly at least, a breed of dog, though not one that bears much resemblance to the sentient Scottish doormat awaiting me in London.

textures (crisp/soft) and flavours (sour/sweet) with that little extra element in the form of the nutty streusel to set it apart from a standard recipe: a clear 9.5/10. 'I just really like the crust here,' Charlotte says, licking her fingers, 'it's salty, you know?'

I also, I say, like the way the juices soak into it so the bottom's a bit gooey.

'Yes, but you still get those crisp edges?'

'Hey, I didn't even *like* pie until I started here,' Crystal, originally from Dallas, interjects – 'I was more of a cake girl. But our owner, she's Southern, so that's why she makes good pie.'

Charlotte agrees, pouring a cup of mineral water for Gena G, adding, 'I feel like pie isn't really a New York thing, so it's easier for me to be objective about them.'

(On the way back, Gena G is so exhausted by all her socialising, we take turns in carrying her. I'd estimate this angel in a fur coat weighs about the same as one of Wilf's sturdy little terrier legs.)

Somehow, I also manage to fit in my black-and-white cookie, a New York icon said to have been created by Bavarian immigrants, on a bench in Chelsea next to a man who informs me that popcorn can cure dementia (*huge* news for Marion, OH if true). Though they look like snappy, shortbread affairs, underneath its coat of contrasting icing, the biscuit itself is more like a light cake. Indeed, apparently Italian-American versions sometimes have a layer of apricot jelly between the two, which surely makes them quite a close relative of the British Jaffa Cake, also a cake masquerading as a biscuit, or perhaps, for tax purposes, vice versa.

BLACK-AND-WHITE COOKIES

New Yorkers, please don't come after me; this version is based on the mighty Melissa Clark's recipe for the New York Times, *but the topping is entirely my responsibility. Traditionally they're coated in a vanilla and chocolate glaze, but I decided instead to pay homage to the German heritage of Glaser's Bake Shop on the Upper East Side (opened by Bavarian immigrants in 1902, run by their descendants until 2018, and said to be the originator of the black-and-white) by using poppy seeds and lemon instead . . . nothing to do with how much I hate cleaning up melted chocolate, honestly. (If you'd prefer a traditional topping, Melissa's original recipe is available online.)*

Note also that black-and-white cookies are more like spongy British Jaffa Cakes than biscuits, but much richer and twice the size; if you'd prefer smaller ones, use a tablespoon measure and reduce the cooking time.

Makes 12 large cookies
280g/2 cups plain/all-purpose flour
1 tsp baking powder
½ tsp fine salt
¼ tsp bicarbonate of soda/baking soda
80ml/⅓ cup sour cream
2 tsp vanilla extract
1 tsp finely grated lemon zest
115g/½ cup/1 stick butter, at room temperature
200g/1 cup + 2½ tbsp caster/superfine sugar
2 eggs, beaten

For the icing
300g/2 cups white icing/confectioners' sugar
A pinch of fine sea salt
4 tbsp lemon juice
45g/⅓ cup poppy seeds or hundreds and thousands, to coat

1. Heat the oven to 200°C/180°C fan/375°F. Line three baking sheets with baking parchment and arrange the oven shelves accordingly.

2. Combine the flour, baking powder, salt and bicarbonate of soda in a large bowl. Whisk together the sour cream, vanilla and lemon zest in a jug. Put the butter and sugar into the bowl of a stand mixer or a mixing bowl if using hand beaters.

3. Beat together the butter and sugar for about 5 minutes, until light and fluffy, scraping down the sides of the bowl as needed. Slowly beat in the eggs until thoroughly incorporated, then, reducing the speed of the beaters, add a third of the dry ingredients followed by a third of the wet ones, beating until you have a thick batter.

4. Dollop scant ice-cream scoops or soup spoons of batter onto the prepared baking sheets, spacing them out well as they will spread. Bake for 12 to 15 minutes, until lightly golden and springy on top, turning the baking sheets round after 6 minutes so they bake evenly. Bear in mind they shouldn't brown on top as overbaking will leave them dry. Cool.

5. Put the icing sugar into a medium bowl and add the salt. Stir in the lemon juice until you have a fairly thick but still liquid icing.

6. Once the cookies are cool, working one by one, dip the flat sides into the icing, then, holding a piece of card or similar over half the cookie to shield it, and with a plate underneath to catch the excess for reuse, sprinkle with poppy seeds and shake to distribute evenly.

7. Allow to set for an hour or so before serving. Like any cake, these are best eaten as soon as possible.

After a large, ice-cold martini, the kind of bold, no-holds barred drink America does reliably well, with British chef Jess Shadbolt outside her restaurant King, and a superb dinner at the Musket Rooms, another female-led kitchen recommended by Charlotte (where the dish the kitchen sends out from the vegan tasting menu, carrot with spring garlic, tofu and celtuce,* is so good I regret not ordering the whole seven plant-based courses; God knows I could do with them), I wake the next morning in a kind of panic – my time in New York feels like it's slipping through my fingers like so much slick red-sauced spaghetti. There's just so much to eat and so little stomach space to accommodate it, and I cycle around frantically trying to tick off just a few of the recommendations I've had: gorgeously elastic Trinidadian doubles at A&A Bake and Doubles in Bed-Stuy, where an elderly dreadlocked gentleman sits just inside the door greeting everyone with a 'good day, my brother'; one of the best pies I've had so far, a blueberry and lavender streusel at Four and Twenty Blackbirds in Park Slope with buttery, flaky pastry and soft, whole berries suspended in thickened, faintly floral juice (9/10), and a surprisingly light and moussey New York cheesecake at Eileen's in Manhattan – and that's all before my lunch date at Hamburger America with Melissa Clark of the *New York Times*.

Owner George Motz, a former filmmaker, is what might be described, in only the most loving terms, as an obsessive: as well as two books, he's produced a documentary about the American hamburger, hosted a Travel Channel show and a YouTube one, and taught a course on the subject at New York University. During the pandemic he began selling Oklahoma fried-onion burgers from the window of his Brooklyn apartment, using a wooden slide made from a kitchen cupboard to maintain social distancing, and in 2023, he opened this more public shrine to the patty, a luncheonette in the heart of Soho. The menu offers just three choices: a classic smash burger, his beloved fried-onion burger, and a rotating monthly special, which right now is a Chester, from Long Island: 'buttered grilled American cheese on white bread with a smashed patty'.

---

* They also, somehow, manage to produce a Marmite ice cream so improbably delicious that I almost question whether I need to go home after all.

'The voice of the American home cook', known to her friends as Melissa, is waiting for me by the counter, watching the grill staff tend each burger as carefully as if it were an $80 fillet steak – these are the hot seats, but if you're happy to sit out back, you can order immediately, so, as she's on deadline, and I'm greedy to get stuck in, we do: a fried-onion burger and a Chester special, to split. The Chester, rich and oily and a little over-salted for my taste, reminds me strongly of the fried patty melt back in Defiance, Ohio, while the fried onion is sweeter and beefier and, in my opinion, benefits from the absence of processed cheese.

We chat about American food, New York food – her early years growing up in Brooklyn, eating dim sum and pizza, but also with parents who spent, as she's written elsewhere, 'countless weekends fussing over Julia Child's terrines and Jacques Pépin's coq au vin, which my mother might slather on leftover challah, and my dad might spike with soy sauce . . .' She describes this not so much as a lack of respect for tradition, as 'an intense culinary curiosity, a playful exploration of the delicious', which I think sums up the American attitude to food in general. If you like something, why not try to make it even better? Even I'd concede perfection is not a zero-sum game.

Waving goodbye to Melissa, I jump back on my bike, feeling more confident now I know the drill, i.e. that no one takes any notice of the lights, and pedal off to meet my friend (and former editor) Malik, at a chai shop near his place in Soho. Several years after relocating from London, he's still thrilled by the food scene here; growing up, he says, 'I only ate Asian food, so now I get really excited by *everything!*' (He does tell me he sometimes leaves a 30 per cent tip at his local Pakistani cafe though – THIRTY PER CENT! I say aghast, you've been away from London too long – so maybe he also misses home a little.)

I end this social whirl of a day with dinner at my friends Ed and Jackie Schneider's apartment in Midtown. Ed is a retired food and drink writer for the likes of the *New York Times* and *Washington Post*, while his British wife, Jackie, spent her career at the United Nations round the corner from their apartment. Ed's invitation warned me that they eat very modestly these days after a lifetime of sybaritic indulgence. Modest is great, I say truthfully, as he pours me one of his house negronis and proffers a platter of Vermont cheese and cured meat ('The cheese when I arrived in the States,' Jackie shudders at the memory. 'It was in a bad place. Much better now, thank goodness') before we move to the dining room for arroz with fennel and broad beans paired with a marvellously garlicky aioli and a chardonnay from Finger Lakes, 'because I thought it would be fun for you to try some local wine, no clue what it will be like'.

They're curious to hear my impressions of their country and, like Melissa, surprised in particular by my observation that the small-town America I've seen over the past couple of months has been a largely chain-free zone – that culinary life away from the freeways is dominated by mom-and-pop joints, with very few of the coffee and casual-dining chains that dominate the British provincial market. I confess that sometimes, when I'm travelling, I crave the anonymity of such places, where I can sit and use their Wi-Fi for an hour for the price of a coffee, and yet, I tell them, still struggling to believe it myself, such soulless pit stops were few and far between. All we see of the US abroad is big business, but my view from its small towns was very different.

Perhaps, we agree, the sheer size of the US means that, if you want to get anywhere, you're likely to fly and then take the freeway, so your experience will largely be of the fast-food giants and strip malls that proliferate there, on the edges of towns. This can leave you with the depressing impression that many American communities don't really have a centre when in fact they usually do – you just have to take the long way round to get there.

When I get back to the hotel, the burger presses I so admired in Jackie's kitchen jangling in my bag ('Honestly, I have more, I only use them for toast, take them'), ESPN2 is showing highlights of last year's Fourth of July Nathan's Famous Hot Dog Eating Competition at Coney Island. I lie on my bed, full as a drum and watching the action, unable to quite believe I've made it this far – and the biggest event, the jewel in the crown of American gastronomy, is just twelve short hours away.

Ridden: 38 miles
Climbed: 1,063 feet
Pies consumed: 6 (guava mascarpone icebox, black bottom almond, rhubarb streusel, pecan pie cookie, apple pie cookie)
All-American foods discovered: bagel, New York slice, scrambled eggs with smoked sturgeon and salmon and onion, half-sour pickles, black-and-white cookies, Chester burger, Oklahoma fried-onion burger

18

THE GURGITATORS

In search of a $10,000 prize

'You know what makes me really sick to my stomach? It's watching you stuff your face with those hot dogs. Nobody, I mean nobody puts ketchup on a hot dog.'
Dirty Harry

'A sport for our degraded times' according to the *Guardian*,* competitive eating is often held up as the grotesque poster child for bloated late-stage capitalism – sadly history suggests we've always been like this. Though it's best to refrain from any speculation on the subject of loaves and fishes, I will call as evidence London poet John Taylor's 1630 pamphlet on the so-called Great Eater of Kent, Nicholas Wood.

Apparently designed to drum up public interest in the lucrative freakshow of his prodigious appetite, Taylor likens his subject to the notoriously gluttonous Roman Emperor Aulus Vitellius, 'who at one supper was served with two thousand sorts of fishes, and seven thousand fowles', and boasts of Wood's ability to put away a

---

* Ahem, my employer.

whole sixteen-shilling sheep, raw, at one meal, though '(pardon me) I thinke hee left the skin, the wooll, the hornes, and the bones'. Other notable achievements include eighteen yards of black pudding (London measure), 'three-score pound of cherries', and even 'a quarter of fat Lambe, and three-score Eggs' – which is ten up on Cool Hand Luke, even without the sheep.

Perhaps a new country, rich in natural resources and with a greater appetite for novelty than decorum, was always going to be especially susceptible to the lure of public over-consumption – again and again on my travels I've discovered dishes with old-world roots transformed almost beyond recognition by the sheer abundance of their new environment. Pizzas loaded with meat and cheese rather than a scraping of tomato and oil; fat California rolls dwarfing slender maki; sticky, sweet, deep-fried orange chicken instead of skinny braised feet, and plump burritos spilling six or seven fillings in place of a simple traditional trio of meat, salsa and beans.

Indeed, records prove the US has long been in particular thrall to feats of gluttony; in 1793, a newspaper in York, Pennsylvania reports 'two young men of this Country, an hour after dining' undertaking to eat 'twenty-four ginger Cakes each, to be provided to them gratis provided they accomplished it'. The lust for gustatory competition quickly became so much a part of a certain element of the American national character that it even travelled abroad with them: Jason Fagone's excellent book on the subject, *Insatiable*, informs me that 'US troops have battled with food on navy battleships and inside Trident submarines; they have staged eating contests while stationed in Paris in 1918 (pie), Italy in 1945 (pie), Vietnam in 1968 (eggs), and Beirut in 1984 (dog biscuits)'.

By the dawn of the twentieth century, pie-eating races were common at Independence Day festivities, but perhaps no Fourth of July celebration is as quintessentially, even iconically American as the Nathan's Famous Hot Dog Eating Contest, which, it's often claimed, dates back to 1916, when Polish immigrant Nathan Handwerker started selling sausages from a cart at Coney Island. In reality, as legendary PR man Mortimer Matz admitted to the *New York Times* in 2010, he and his partner Max Rosey came up with the idea in the early 1970s, when they began working on the venerable hot dog company's account. Nevertheless, having now reached its real half-century the annual spectacle is nothing less than a national institution, and one that, to me, perfectly encapsulates the larger-than-life, slightly anarchic spirit of American food culture. Almost as soon as I decided to make this trip, I knew my real journey must finish today, on the Fourth of July, right here in New York, with the apotheosis of American food – or perhaps its nadir, depending on your views on competitive eating.*

George Shea, the competition's current press guy, is also the one who recognised its viral potential when he took over promotion in the 1990s, telling *TIME* magazine, 'I thought it was funny and absurd, and I love things that are absurd. So we always treated it as a sport, called it a sport, called them athletes.' It was Shea and his brother Rich who founded the International Federation of Competitive Eating in 1997 to bring together such events around the world (blueberries in Missouri, fish balls in Bangkok); six years later, in confirmation of its only partly tongue-in-cheek status as a sport, ESPN snapped up the rights to broadcast the hot dog contest live across the nation. Only two mornings beforehand, I'd switched on the television while getting dressed to find George on Fox 5 explaining, with regret, the big story around this

---

* In the event's defence, Nathan's Famous gives 100,000 hot dogs to the Food Bank for New York City every 4 July, and the International Federation of Competitive Eating's website proclaims it to be a supporter of the charity Feeding America.

year's contest: sixteen-time champion Joey Chestnut (the record*
holder, with seventy-six dogs literally under his belt) will be a
no-show after signing a deal with vegan wiener pusher, and
Nathan's rival, Impossible Foods.

'The contest is bigger than Joey, bigger than anyone here,'
George tells viewers. 'Joey's always welcome, he's never banned,
he's the face of America on the Fourth of July.' Next to him on the
breakfast sofa sits current women's champion and record holder
(forty-eight in ten minutes) Miki Sudo of Florida, who tells the
hosts she hopes to 'hit that magical fifty before I retire', and her
partner, and fellow competitor, Nick Wehry (a mere forty-five),
who is clearly hoping Chestnut's absence will give him the chance
to move up the rankings. The couple met in the gym the morning
of the 2018 contest; three years later, after eating fifty hard-boiled
eggs in just over three minutes, Nick dropped to one knee and
proposed. As Chestnut has won sixteen of the last seventeen
contests, without him† this year, as I hear one commentator
observe, 'the mustard's gonna be extra spicy'.

---

* According to research by James Smoliga, a sports medicine specialist at
High Point University in North Carolina published in the Royal Society
journal *Biology Letters* in 2020, the 'maximum possible limit' is eighty-
four dogs in ten minutes – making humans faster eaters even than bears and
coyotes, though probably not than wolves. Clearly data can only get you so
far: in 2003 Takeru 'Tsunami' Kobayashi took on a Kodiak bear on television, and got trounced.

† Instead, Chestnut is competing with soldiers at an army base in Fort Bliss,
Texas – 'What a great way to honour our troops,' Shea adds magnani-
mously.

COFFEE BREAK

The Skinny on Hot Dogs

More than just the long boi of the hot meat sandwich world, in the first half of the last century, the hot dog was, according to historian Andrew F. Smith, 'America's chief iconic food item'. Street-food vendors saw hand-held potential in the sausages and bread served in the beer gardens set up by German and Central European immigrants, and by the 1860s these new sandwiches were fast on the way to becoming the great democratic food of the age. They became known as hot dogs in the dying years of the last century, possibly because of the German fondness for the long and slender dachshund, possibly as a nod to jokes about what exactly went into their sausages.

Unlike the original frankfurter, the modern American hot dog tends to be made from beef, rather than pork, or sometimes a mixture of the two meats, and is usually served skinless. Unlike the frankfurters I grew up with, they tend to be grilled, rather than boiled, or deep-fried so they burst open. Though the basics differ little from place to place, distinct local styles of presentation have evolved:

California: bacon-wrapped dog with grilled onions and jalapeños

Chicago: chopped raw onion, pickle spear, sport peppers, tomato slices, celery salt, yellow mustard, green relish in a poppy seed bun ('in the garden') but never, ever ketchup

Hawaii Puka dog: lemon-garlic sauce, tropical fruit relish, passion-fruit mustard, sweet bun

New Jersey Italian: deep-fried dog, mustard, peppers, onions, fried potatoes in a pizza dough roll

New York: with steamed onions, optional sauerkraut and spicy brown mustard

North Carolina: beef chilli, coleslaw, chopped onions

Philadelphia (an endangered species): beef sausage, fried fishcake (yes, fishcake), slaw or pepper hash, mustard and onions

Seattle: cream cheese, grilled onions, optional sauerkraut and jalapeños

Washington DC: half-smoke: mildly spiced half pork, half beef, smoked and topped with chilli, yellow mustard and onions

---

Unfortunately, I fail to appreciate just how many other people enjoy a bit of spice as I cruise down Ocean Parkway to the shore, relishing the holiday quiet – a few people already lighting up grills and joints in Prospect Park as (actual) dogs dash happily in and out of the pond, a scattering of elderly Hasidic men on benches beside the cycle path, faces turned to the sun like so many grey-bearded crows. Shea's colleague Allison, who has kindly furnished me with a friends-and-family pass, tells me that the women's contest starts at 11am, but she'd recommend coming around 10am, 'to be safe!' Though I'm at the waterfront by 9.30, I find myself distracted by Little Odessa in all its garlicky glory, and at 10am I'm still enjoying a flaky, egg-washed Tajik lamb samsa and a strong coffee from an Uzbek coffee shop on the main drag at Brighton Beach, a place where pallid men in sliders peer into vats of pickles, and trays of overripe melons block the pavement.

Noticing the time and hastily brushing the crumbs from my face, I ride cautiously over the loose slats of the oceanfront board-walk, where the concession stands are just waking up for a busy day of cotton candy and fried clams, past the Ferris wheel and the screaming, soaring loops of the ninety-seven-year-old Coney Island Cyclone, towards the epicentre of the action. Though the beach is as yet only dotted with people, it does strike me uneasily that things are becoming busier the closer I get to the Nathan's Famous concession at the corner of Stillwell and Surf Avenues. Locking Eddy up next to a PETA truck urging me to go vegan, I follow a man wearing a t-shirt featuring a flag-toting squirrel on a motorbike towards the scene of the action – 'Sorry,' the squirrel is saying, 'can't hear you over the sound of freedom ringing!' though in reality freedom here appears to sound more like an excruciatingly amplified oompah band.

Fighting through the thickening throng, I confirm, once the hurdles of accent and hearing have been overcome, that my name is on 'the list', allowing me to smugly waltz past all those queuing to enter the mosh pit – but once through, still leaving me pressed against the back fence, unable to see much more than a sea of stars-and-stripes Stetsons. It's extremely hot – already 81°F and climbing – and as far as I can tell, there's neither shade nor refreshment on offer, so I'm thankful for Melissa's sage advice about bringing a hat, even if the only one I have with me sports a French tricolour, which seems a bold choice in this rampantly patriotic crowd. (By the time the day is out I'm wishing I had my bike helmet too.)

As I flatten myself against the metal barriers (still half an hour to go before things kick off) I notice some people with my wristband slipping through a gap into the inner sanctum where the press and VIPs lounge on a set of bleachers. I waggle my wrist hopefully at the girl policing it, and shout a hoarse plea for clemency. She calls over a vast security guard, who confirms there is a special area for mere friends and family (not, it seems, actual VIPs) and it's already full. But, he says, looking me up and down doubtfully as I try my best to look like someone who hasn't eaten thirty-four slices of pie in the last eleven weeks, he might be able to squeeze me in.

Following his reassuring bulk like a baby elephant trotting obediently after a bull, I find myself in a second pen, no less crowded but at least closer to the action, and, more importantly, worthy of my exalted status as the proud owner of a sweaty wristband. Employing tactics honed in many years of snaking to the front of gigs, holding a half-empty bottle of lukewarm NYC tap water aloft in place of a pint – 'excuse me, excuse me, sorry, ouch, excuse me' – I manage to establish myself in a spot a few rows back from the action but on top of a boxed-in camera cable, which helpfully gives me a good couple of inches of extra height, allowing me to actually see some of what's happening on stage.

The contests themselves are a mere ten minutes each, but there's no let-up in entertainment as we wait – the oompah merchants are followed by a guy in western gear strumming a guitar, succeeded by a troupe of oiled, muscular men in tight red vests and stars-and-stripes short shorts aggressively twirling the American flag and a woman in a similarly patterned dress singing 'God Bless America'. As the first notes ring out, I notice many of the people around me remove their foam hot-dog-shaped hats and clasp them reverently over their hearts. Trying not to smile, I look down respectfully and notice I am one of the few here not sporting flag-patterned footwear.

Eventually George Shea himself, natty in a blazer and straw boater, appears, and begins his patter – 'Ladies and gentlemen, it is the Fourth of JULY, the greatest holiday in the YEAR, and we have been given the honour to be ALIVE at this time, to be AMERICANS, to be NEW YORKERS, to be in Coney ISLAND!' It doesn't feel much like an honour, trying to peer over the slightly musty dreadlocks now blocking my view (it's only later, when fans begin chanting his name, that I realise they belong to the 6ft 3in legend that is 'Crazy Legs' Conti, a man who once put away 2.71lb (1.3kg) of green beans in six minutes) and I'm relieved when the female competitors file onto the stage to Shea's legendarily epic introductions, delivered in a sing-song tone I find oddly mesmeric.

'She is the vortex at the centre of the vortex,' he announces grandly as Sudo emerges, holding last year's pink mustard belt above her head, 'the spiral that spins at the core of the American spirit, the force that drives the swirling gyre of life itself, and she rejects the false wisdom of acceptance, she is here to win, and win only, and her legacy is a vessel that will carry her name to the far shores of time. One hundred and four hard-boiled eggs, fifty-two ears of corn, sixteen and a half pints of ice cream, forty-eight Nathan's Famous hot dogs and buns, rank number three in the world, rank number one in the world for women, with nine victories here on the corner of Surf and Stillwell,' he's almost shouting now, 'I. GIVE. YOU. MIKKKKKI. SUDOOOOOOO!'

The field, assembled from qualifying heats around the country, are a surprisingly diverse bunch: as well as Sudo and her main rivals, Mayoi 'Ebimayo' Ebihara, 28, of Tokyo (116 pieces of sushi in sixteen minutes) and Michelle 'Cardboard Shell' Lesco, 40, Tucson, Arizona (5¼lb / 2.4kg of mayonnaise in three), there's the sole local resident in the competition, Julie Goldberg, 38, a political science PhD from Queens who trains with Conti, and Laurie Marie Mele, a 60-year-old personal trainer from Pennsylvania (fifteen cannolis in six minutes) who hasn't missed a contest in fourteen years.

As they take their places at the long table, already stocked with plates of hot dogs and buns (five per person, replaced once empty) and enormous cardboard cups, some holding water, some left empty for their beverage of choice, I notice the main contenders frowning down, focused on pouring their own drinks and rearranging their set-up, while the rest of the field smiles a little nervously at the crowd, apparently just happy to be here, rather than concerning themselves with the $10,000 winnings they have no realistic prospect of scooping. The men in short shorts stand behind each woman with a scorecard. Directly in front of the stage, facing away from me, are the official judges in their black-and-white-striped referee shirts. Sudo checks her hair in her phone camera and winds her stars-and-stripes bandana more securely around her bun as Shea tells the audience that when she shakes her head – 'we call it the angry pony' – that means she's 'in the zone'. She cracks him a brief, tight grin, clearly keen to get going.

After a roaring countdown they're off, in a frenzy of busy hands and furious jaws: Lesco finishes her first dog in just seven seconds. It's a neater affair than I expect – after pushing each pair of sausages into her mouth, Sudo daintily wipes it on her sleeve, 'always the lady, always so elegant', Shea observes. While Miki's movements look almost mechanical, Lesco next to her seems to will the food down by painful force, periodically squatting down and thumping her chest to make room, while tiny Ebihama on the other side dances barefoot on the spot, looking skyward, her eyes almost popping as she crams in another playdough-like mouthful of soggy bread. Lesco, who's admitted recent dental work could hinder her chances, soon falls behind, and with two minutes to go, Sudo has a twelve-dog lead over the Japanese woman – as she passes the fifty mark with ten seconds to go the audience applaud wildly, but she just keeps feeding them in, managing to flip over one more number before time is called.

The final score is 51 to Miki Sudo, 37 to Ebihara and 23 to Lesco, who looks distinctly uncomfortable. Ebihara, meanwhile, begins to cry. But as Shea says, there can be only one champion, 'in her, nature has fashioned a warrior red in tooth and claw, and her soul shines like magnesium set afire against the dark mountains of night, with fifty-one Nathan's Famous hot dogs . . .' Sudo checks her hair again, coughs into her hand; I wonder if she's going to be sick, or in competitive eating terms, suffer a reversal of fortunes (a disqualification offence), but like the pro she is, she simply smiles at the camera as he hoists her arm into the air in victory.

Looking around, she pulls both runners-up into a hug, appearing to say something comforting to the crestfallen Ebihara, who, she tells Shea, pushed her harder this year than she's ever worked before. Max, her two-year-old son with Wehry, runs on stage, and Shea thrusts the mic into his face for his thoughts on his mother's record-breaking achievement: 'I WANT ANOTHER HOT DOG,' he wails.

With ninety minutes to go before the men's contest, I start to look enviously at the gallons of cold iced lemonade being set out on stage for a minor sideshow, the annual chugging competition. Having seen quite enough of that kind of thing in my university days, I ask the woman on the gate whether I might be able to go out and get a drink of my own. 'Oh, you can go,' she says, 'but you might not make it back through that crowd,' so I make do with eking out my remaining millilitres of warm water and watch the 6ft 5in Eric 'Badlands' Booker (fifty mini cheesecakes in six minutes) set a new world record for downing a gallon of lemonade in twenty-one seconds. No one else even gets close, but the younger man next to him, a vlogger from Michigan by the name of Chris Lafon, suddenly begins to do a convincing *Exorcist* impression that sends the crowd into baying whoops of disgusted joy with every fresh emission. It's an unpleasantly visceral reminder of the grossness of what we've gathered here to witness, and a man in a neatly pressed polo shirt leads him away backstage, still miserably spewing liquid, as another staff member smirkingly films his exit.

Stage hastily mopped, there's a parade of flags by the New York National Guard, a Brazilian man singing Britney Spears, an opera singer doing Puccini, some heavily made-up teenagers with a cheer routine, a stirring rendition of the national anthem for which all the hats come off again, followed by a drum circle and two rounds from some more mature ladies shaking their pom-poms – something tells me there's a delay, but finally, just before 12.45pm when I'm so hot I'm drooping like a soft-serve in the sun, the male contestants file onto the stage.

Shea has already tipped his boater to the elephant in the room, declaring himself 'personally devastated' by Chestnut's absence: 'I love Joey Chestnut more than anyone here – I would take a bullet for Joey,' he pauses, 'and I'm very confident in saying that because the circumstances are very unlikely to happen.' He is now free to move on to those that have turned up. To my surprise, before Wehry he introduces, 'with forty-five donuts, 12lb [5.4kg] of strawberry shortcake . . . the number-one ranked eater in Great Britain with a UK record of thirty-four hot dogs and buns', a bloke from South London named Max. If I'm honest, had I had to pick the fellow Brit out of the giants at the table, I would have gone for the man taking grinning selfies while everyone else is earnestly preparing their drinks.

'LADIES AND GENTLEMEN,' Shea thunders, 'this is when our nation comes together as one . . . WE ARE ALL AMERICANS RIGHT NOW . . . ten minutes, all you can eat, count it down with me, ten, nine, eight . . .'

Thirty seconds gone, and one of the favourites, Geoffrey Esper of Oxford, Massachusetts (2017 and 2019 Hooters Wing-Eating Champion), has already put away four dogs, the Australian James Webb (338 pistachios in eight minutes), who's feeding in three dogs at a time like a hungry anaconda, is at thirty-five before the contest is halfway through, but Patrick Bertoletti, 39, of Chicago (eleven corned beef sandwiches in ten minutes) gradually pulls ahead. Not a neat eater, Pat, from what I can see, wet bread spilling continuously from his mouth in a nauseating stream, but in the end, the technique works and he triumphs with fifty-eight dogs, a personal record.

His comeback is likened to Michael Jordan's, having taken an almost ten-year break before his return in 2022 – 'Always the bridesmaid, never the bride, but today I'm getting married!' – he gloats to ESPN, explaining that he lost some weight, trained a bunch . . . and 'There was an urgency, with Joey not here, I knew I had a shot.' Stanford finishes with a very respectable thirty-two, two fewer than he managed in the qualifying event in Sussex, but ninth out of the fourteen-strong field, and only one dog behind Georgia's Gideon Oji, at 6ft 9in the tallest man ever to compete.

My urgency, meanwhile, after almost three hours penned in without shade, is to make like a tree – the queues at the hot dog counter here rival a beer tent at Glastonbury, so I decide to ride back to the city, grabbing a Nathan's Famous at a gas station in Clinton Hill instead. It has a charred flavour and a pleasant snap to it – oily and salty and covered in mustard, I enjoy it more than I anticipate after seeing so many mashed between furiously masticating jaws this morning, but though I could put away another, I think two would probably be my limit, should perhaps be anyone's limit given that even without condiments they're 300kcal a piece.

Traversing Prospect Park, busy now with parties around grills, kids playing and music blasting, I find myself cycling in the slipstream of a group gleefully discussing Biniam Girmay's recent stage victory in the Tour de France – 'an African up there on the podium, representing!' – and feel one step closer to home, and two weeks watching other people pedalling from the comfort of my sofa.

The final piece slots into the puzzle underneath the clock at Grand Central, at four o'clock on the Fourth of July, where I have an appointment with Lucinda, the same schoolfriend who insisted on a rendezvous at the Arc de Triomphe in the middle of a twelve-lane Paris roundabout, having talked her down from her initial suggestion that we should meet at the top of the Empire State

Building. Unable to find a wheelchair-friendly entrance to the station, I end up carrying a fully-laden bike down two sets of stairs, ruining countless selfies and almost losing my balance a couple of times, but it's worth it to see a familiar face, even if it is frowning down at a phone as I make my triumphant entrance.

My final thirty-six hours in the United States takes place on a quite different plane to the world of filthy motels and trucker-friendly diners – my well-connected and eminently respectable companion has booked us a room in the Harvard Club, a Midtown oasis of softly polished wood where the dress code* is posted on the hallway noticeboard and the man guarding the entrance looks at poor Eddy like something unpleasant on the sole of his shoe before haughtily directing me to wheel him round to the service entrance. Once he's safely chained to a subterranean pipe, everyone proves very nice, including the staff of the Penn Club across the road in which I find myself lost later – turns out all these Ivy League blue-blazer zones look exactly the same to peasants like me. Plus, I've never had a fancier corned beef hash than the one I'm presented with at breakfast in the grand, double-height dining hall the next morning.

HARVARD CLUB OF NEW YORK CORNED BEEF HASH

With thanks to Executive Chef David Haviland

I confess it wasn't until I got in contact with the Harvard Club to ask them for the recipe for their very superior corned beef hash that it

---

* 'Jeans in good repair' are permitted except after 5pm on weekdays in the main dining room and hall, and Bermuda shorts are acceptable on the rooftop from Memorial to Labor Day. Hats may only be worn for religious or medical reasons.

struck me I was letting myself in for corning* my own beef, as the stuff
sold under the same name in the UK tends to come in a tin from Argen-
tina. If you live somewhere it's commercially available (e.g. the USA),
then by all means skip this step unless you enjoy a project that takes up
half a shelf in your fridge for a week, but otherwise, the biggest effort
here is going to the butcher to buy the necessary brisket; otherwise it's
all pretty simple, very delicious, and leaves you extra left over for salt
beef sandwiches. Prague powder is a curing salt that helps give your
corned beef a nice pink colour, but, more importantly, slows spoilage.
Although I'm wary of nitrites in general, as cured meat hopefully
doesn't make up a large proportion of your diet it's probably better to be
safe than sorry here.

    * 'Corn' refers to the large kernels of salt used to cure the meat, rather
than anything yellow and sweet.

Serves 8
566g/20 ounces floury/russet potatoes
2 tbsp olive oil
2 medium onions, finely diced
2 green bell peppers, finely diced
450g/1 pound cooked lean corned beef *, cut into 3½cm/1 inch strips
60ml/¼ cup corned beef fat, roughly chopped

1. Heat the oven to 180°C/160°C fan/350°F. Pierce the potatoes
   with a fork and wrap them in foil, then bake until tender, about
   1 hour. Cool, peel and cut into quarters lengthwise.
2. Heat 2 tablespoons of olive oil in a sauté pan over a medium-
   high flame, then add the onions and cook until tender. Add the
   peppers, season with salt and pepper to taste and sauté until the
   onion caramelises. Remove from the heat, transfer to a large
   mixing bowl and allow to cool.
3. Using a meat grinder fitted with the large/coarse plate, pass the
   potatoes, corned beef and corned beef fat through the grinder

into a large mixing bowl, with the onions and peppers. (If you do not have a meat grinder, finely dice the potatoes and corned beef instead.) This can be done a day in advance if desired; it also can be frozen.

4. We cook our corned beef hash as individual portions in an 18cm/7 inch non-stick pan, over a medium-high heat with ½ tablespoon of oil. Add 240g/1 cup of hash, flatten to a 1.3cm/½ inch cake and cook until crisp and brown; about 4 minutes each side. Transfer to a plate and serve.

★To make your own corned beef
225g/¾ cup fine salt
50g/4 tbsp dark brown sugar
1 tsp black peppercorns
1 tsp allspice berries
1 tsp yellow mustard seeds
1 tsp coriander seeds
6 cloves
1 tsp juniper berries
1 bay leaf
11g/2 tsp Prague powder (see note on page 361)
1.5kg/3 pounds 4 ounces flat brisket, trimmed of excess fat

1. Put the salt and sugar into a large saucepan with 1.6 litres/6½ cups of water and bring to the boil. Meanwhile, toast the peppercorns, allspice, mustard and coriander seeds and cloves in a hot dry pan until fragrant, then cool slightly and roughly crush. Add to the pan along with the juniper berries and bay leaf and the curing salt. Allow to cool.

2. Trimming off any large pieces of surface fat, put the beef into a container large enough to submerge it in the brine, then pour in the cooled brine. Cover and refrigerate for a week, turning every 2 days so it brines evenly, then rinse before use.

3. Put the rinsed brisket into a large pan and cover generously with
    cold water. Bring to the boil, skim off the foam, then turn down
    the heat and simmer very gently for about 3 hours, or until
    tender all the way through.

With the whole of New York still talking about the presidential
debate, the focus at the Fourth of July party I've been invited to is
on another contest altogether – as the polling stations close, the
huge television at the British Consul's residence opposite the
United Nations is attracting far more interest than the magnificent
views or the equally magnificent Stinking Bishop on the coffee
table, left over from some high-end British diplomacy no doubt.
Consul Hannah Young, yet another friend of Signe's, and her
husband Archie, the UK's Ambassador to the UN General Assembly, give us a warm welcome, as do the other guests, who seem to
be a mix of diplomats and fellow Brits and their partners: one
recalls that when he told an American friend the election had been
called for Fourth of July they thought Rishi Sunak was trolling the
entire United States – 'I had to explain that in the UK, Independence Day is just a movie.'

Of course, as soon as Lucinda lets slip why I'm here, everyone
has questions. An Irish economist gestures at the view – the
soaring skyline of Queens, the red neon of the Pepsi Cola sign
reflected in the inky water of the East River – and asks me whether
'all this' has lived up to my expectations. It's a big question, but in
a sense it has – just as 'all this' conjures up visions of *Home Alone 2*,
and *When Harry Met Sally*, the country as a whole still feels weirdly
familiar yet strangely unreal, from the rundown Midwestern
motels straight out of *Planes, Trains and Automobiles* to the French
Quarter streets that take me right back to *Live and Let Die* (a film
that, incidentally, kicks off in the United Nations building right in
front of me).

I don't say this of course, because presumably you get used to the cop cars and the cowboy boots after a while, and anyway, I suspect this isn't really what she meant, so I reply no, in many ways it hasn't been in the least as I imagined. For a start, I haven't died so far – in fact, though I've seen a few guns, the only thing that's felt dangerous here has been Mother Nature, mostly in the form of weather and imaginary bears. The cycling has, for the most part, been easy despite all the dire prognostications, and despite the fact that life here seems to be as fast-paced and shiny as ever, forever fixated on efficiency, convenience and endless choice, I've also had a glimpse of a smaller, quieter side of America less commonly seen on screen. Community fish fries and radical bookstores, small towns where everything shuts at six, and of course, the many, many independent restaurants,* coffee shops and diners that aren't Mystic Pizza or the Krusty Krab. From big cities to farm country, it's been easier than I expected to find good, freshly prepared food – albeit not the most diverse range – and harder to find vegetables that aren't fries or iceberg lettuce (endless choice only goes so far, it seems). While it's true things are more spread out than in smaller, more densely settled countries, any traveller who says they can't find a decent meal here isn't putting in much effort – you might not be able to walk to it, and it almost certainly won't be your easiest option, but it will be there somewhere.

It's a place of enormous resources, and careless with them; I confess I still can't get over the abundance of packaging and dispos-able plates, the portions, the bottomless drinks – but I've never tasted avocados or oranges like the ones in California, or blueber-ries and clams as big and sweet as in New England. I wax lyrical about Amish strawberries, Gulf crawfish, Texan beef and Midwest-ern dairy – America really is the land of plenty, which makes its

---

* Seven out of ten of which, according to the National Restaurant Associa-tion, are single-unit operations, rather than chains.

appetite for highly processed products, from trashily delicious cheesy corn puffs to the pricey snacks marketed as health food, all the sadder, especially since the US is full of such creative cooks. It's just such a bloody fun place to eat.

I tell them (are they regretting setting me off?) about the Bangla-burger in Columbus, and the mochi hush puppies in San Antonio, the collard greens melt in New Orleans and the pickle pizza in Chicago . . . basically I've had a ball here, I wrap up hastily, sensing I need to let these people get home to their kids, and swallow hard, realising I already feel nostalgic, and I've not left yet.

And then Hannah is at my elbow, asking if anyone would like a cup of tea, and I remember there are a few things worth going home for.

Ridden: 36 miles
Climbed: 761 feet
Pies consumed: 1 (pecan, the next day)
All-American foods discovered: New York dogs, corned beef hash

EPILOGUE: BUT HOW WAS IT *REALLY?*

In search of a conclusion

'America: Not a Melting Pot, Not a Salad . . . but a Chili Bowl.'
James D. Coan

*'Over the years, I learned to choose from the best opinions . . . [I]n almost
every case, the American version was much better. It was only later that I
discovered there was a serious flaw with the American version. There were
too many choices, so it was easy to get confused and pick the wrong thing.'*
Amy Tan, *The Joy Luck Club*

Like Rishi Sunak's government, my days are numbered. I drop
Eddy at Bicycles NYC on the Upper East Side, where they
promise to box him up safely for me to collect on the way to the
airport – riding up there slowly, savouring the wide roads, quiet this
morning, stretching out the pleasure of Central Park as long as
possible, reflecting on my experience. Remembering how scared I
was, all those weeks ago, about getting on a bike here, about being
on my own – and yes, there have been moments where I've been a

bit nervous, alone in the middle of a forest, or crossing a Chicago freeway after dark, but actually, the only bad things that have happened to me have largely been thanks to my own ignorance when it came to continental climates and native fauna. America looked so familiar I fell into the trap of thinking it was just like home, when in fact, in so many ways, it's very different. Scottish midges have nothing on those flies, for a start.

Some small things I love about the USA

How hospitable people are, and how keen you enjoy their country / The mind-boggling diversity of landscapes and cultures / They bring you iced water without you having to ask! / The appetite for words – excellent public libraries, a tradition of high-quality, long-form journalism and an independently minded community of small bookstores / The easy way people chat to strangers on say, the bus, or in the queue for food / Ice cream, everywhere / The way you'll see kids playing in the street and running in and out of each other's houses / Free refills! / The quality of avocados / The variety of cheese-flavoured snacks on offer / Counter dining; great for solo travellers / Biscuits / The number of independent cafes and restaurants / Unashamed curiosity; people aren't afraid to ask questions / Frozen margaritas / Fireflies / Lake swimming (not with flies) / Empty roads / Small towns / The general cheerful positivity and lack of cynicism – outside politics anyway / Yard signs / Peanut butter.

Some small things I don't love about the USA

The out-of-control tip culture and unpredictable sales tax situation / The unnecessary use of disposable plates and cutlery in sit-down restaurants / Weak drip coffee / The car-centred architecture – a lack of sidewalks, safe crossings, even dropped kerbs / The lack of vegetarian options – or meat /fish that isn't chicken or shrimp / The way servers hurry you through your meal then deliver the bill before you're halfway through your food, saying, 'No rush!' / The sugar in almost everything, even bread / 'American' cheese / The death of headphones / Lack of public lavatories / One-dollar bills that don't fit in my wallet / Everything from hairbands to crisps only comes in huge packs / Segregated dog parks that deprived me of canine company / The paucity of benches and truly public spaces.

Some things that are just . . . different

You're expected to 'bus' (clear) your own table in many cafes / Flags / The idiosyncratic opening hours – don't assume anything will be open past 6pm outside major cities! / All the tiny private cemeteries in the middle of nowhere / The casual way people juxtapose 'Welcome to my porch' and 'NO TRESPASSING' signs / The endless mind-boggling choice when ordering food or drink / Lawn signs proudly proclaiming your child has graduated from kindergarten / Exciting but very dangerous wildlife, e.g. raccoons / So much ice in drinks, so much air-con in buildings.

My last day is, thanks to Lucinda, occupied with museums and gift shops, though I do manage to pull her into the Golden Diner for winningly springy honey butter pancakes and Culture Espresso to try their award-winning chocolate chip cookies, which, like the Levain one I shared with Melissa earlier in the week, I find too sweet for my taste.* Suddenly I regret not hunting down more cookies on my travels – so much to eat, I say sadly, so little time.

COFFEE BREAK
Chocolate Chip Cookies

The cookies, or biscuits, that came to the States with European immigrants tended to be dry and crumbly, designed to keep well and then be revived by dunking into tea, or wine, like Italian biscotti, or British Rich Tea. But with the advent of chemical raising agents, and the increasing availability of sugar, across the Atlantic they developed a distinct character of their own: moist, chewy and sweet.

The most famous American cookie of all is surely the chocolate chip version popularised, if not invented, by Ruth Wakefield, proprietor of the Toll House Inn in Whitman, Massachusetts in the 1930s. Her recipe, published in her own cookbook in 1937, caused such a spike in Nestlé semi-sweet chocolate sales locally that the company launched ready chipped chocolate, with Wakefield's instructions printed on every pack.

---

* According to the US government, the average American eats (or drinks) thirty-four teaspoons of sugars a day, seventeen of which are added to things like cookies, condiments, sodas, even bread. Certainly things do seem sweeter here, even coming from a country not averse to the stuff.

These days, the ccc is a gold-chip example of the American passion for tinkering – there are almost as many perfect recipes out there as there are bakers, from Hillary Clinton's homely oat-flecked versions to Snoop Dogg's Rolls-Royce PB – chocolate chip cookies. And yes, I did use him as an example just so I could get his book, the wonderfully titled *From Crook to Cook*, in this book somewhere.

We finish with clams casino and eggplant parm at Gene's in Greenwich Village, a dimly lit, old-school Italian beloved of locals like Sarah Jessica Parker, which is almost empty tonight. Clearly all the regulars are in the Hamptons for the holiday with their Barney Greengrass sturgeon. Over the tiramisù I start to feel rather glum, even though Lucinda has already put together a pre-flight schedule that enables us to hit three Upper East Side museums in a single morning, and, I note, leaves me in a good location for a final burger at J. G. Melon before I go back to collect Eddy.

Fortunately, my old friend is not a woman with much patience for self-pity – 'But you said last night you've had fun?' she asks briskly, as we sit at the Crimson Bar of the Harvard Club after dinner, awaiting our martinis. I run quickly through all the things I've eaten, all the people I've met – all the ordinary, kind, complex people so different to the cartoon Americans in the media – all the scenery I've . . . experienced. It seems an age ago that I was gawping upwards in chilly San Francisco, eating a tamale on a fallen tree full of rattlers in Texas, waving at the Amish in Indiana – and somehow, despite all the warnings, and my own hopeless naivety, I've survived everything from heat exhaustion to raccoon raids and endless, endless flags.

'Not fun exactly,' I say, 'but it was certainly a wild ride.'

'Did you do what you set out to do, at least?' she says (the bar is a mobile-free zone, so I have her undivided attention for once).

Hmmm . . . I say. Well, I wanted to find out whether there was any such thing as American cuisine, I suppose . . .

'And is there?'

Bloody hell, it's like being back on the school debating team with her.

'I think there is, yes,' I say, fighting the urge to tell her to just buy the book like everyone else,* because, after all, she has flown all this way to see me. 'I mean, obviously there are hamburgers and hot dogs and chocolate chip cookies and all the stereotypical things, which I don't think are any less worthy of being called cuisine than, say, coq au vin, or jollof rice, or . . . or sashimi, but there's more to it too. I feel like food culture here has an openness, a lack of rules you don't find anywhere else. OK, some of the people I met might get cross about beans in chili con carne, or ketchup on hot dogs, but in general Americans seem to be up for anything – it's almost like no twist or mash-up is off limits . . .'

I pause, take a thoughtful sip of my icy drink.

KING OF MARTINIS

Inspired by the absolutely killer martini I enjoyed with Jess Shadbolt sitting outside her restaurant King at the junction of 6th Avenue in the warmth of a July evening, to the sweet music of honking horns and blaring sirens. Just like being back home.

Per drink
½ tsp fine salt (optional)
Ice
60ml / 4 tbsp gin or vodka (or adjust ratio to suit your own tastes)

---

* Thanks!

15ml/1 tbsp chilled dry vermouth
1 strip of lemon peel or big green olive

1. Put the martini glass into the freezer along with the bottle of spirits and chill for at least half an hour. Dissolve the salt, if using, in 1 tablespoon of warm water and leave to cool.
2. Half fill a mixing glass with ice and add the gin or vodka, vermouth and a tiny dash of salt solution, if using. Stir for 30 seconds, touching the glass as little as possible to keep it cold, then strain into the chilled glass.
3. Twist the lemon peel over the top of the drink, then wipe it around the rim of the glass and drop it or the olive in. Serve immediately. Repeat at your own risk.

'Maybe because almost everyone is an immigrant,' I continue, inspired by the booze, 'they're already, even unconsciously, invested in more than one culture, so their food reflects that. It's not that they're not serious about good food, but they're not pretentious or defensive about it, they're not constantly trying to find or protect one "authentic"' – I mime air quotes – 'version of a dish. They're happy to tinker, to personalise it to suit their own tastes. They just seem . . . very open-minded in comparison to us in Europe. In fact, I'm going to try to be more American in the kitchen from now on. It might sound weird,' I say slowly, in the manner of someone experiencing a great revelation, 'but I reckon this trip has changed me.'

I think back to the Viet-Cajun crawfish and the tostada burger I enjoyed in Texas, the avocado jibarito in Chicago and that unusual barbecue spaghetti in Memphis. The white clam pizza, apologies, apizza, in New Haven, Prince's hot chicken, the sprout omelet on Malibu Pier, Linda's blueberry muffins, this morning's mochi pancakes – even the Doritos taco. All dishes that, it seems to me, for better or worse (sorry, spaghetti) could only have been created in the States – and yet I've been irked by the negativity I've encountered online since I touched down here.

'Am sorry to say . . . all the food looks khaki and dire . . . !' one person comments underneath an album that includes James Beard award-winning croissants, clam chowder, salad, blueberry pie and spaghetti vongole. 'Let all the blossoms bloom, but most of those look f'ing minging,' another opines re. the pizzas in Chicago, and I get a lot of vomity emojis: 'Maybe it's my aged tastebuds but much of the food you're trying is on the nauseous side.'

Someone labels my utterly delicious* biscuits with spicy pork sausage gravy in South Bend 'probably the least appetising dish I've ever seen' and lots of people are very sweetly worried about my heart, my cholesterol and my general health, prescribing a detox on my return to that famous hub of healthy eating, Great Britain: 'USA: LAND OF 0 VEGETABLES, but we all knew that, didn't we?'

The thing is, although more than a few places don't seem to have much fresh stuff on the menu (NB: mac and cheese is not a vegetable, America), and it can indeed be hard to find salads without meat, cheese or sugary, creamy dressings, these are also problems I found (albeit to a lesser extent) in both France and the UK, yet flicking back later I notice no one said how horrible and unhealthy all those fry-ups or cassoulets looked. In any case, restaurants aren't representative of how any population eats at home, and the fabulous produce available here gives me hope that those who do have access to it† enjoy a better, more varied

---

* Run, don't walk, to the Early Bird Eatery – the sausage gravy is incredible.

† About 39 million people – 13 per cent of the US population – live in low-income and low-access areas, more than one mile (urban) or ten miles (rural) from the nearest supermarket or large grocery store, according to the USDA's most recent food access research report, published in 2022. Within this group, researchers estimated that almost 19 million people – or 6 per cent of the nation's total population – had limited access to a supermarket. – Taken from the Annie E. Casey Foundation website.

diet (expensive though that must be*). While I wouldn't claim the homes I ate in – with Adele and family in Berkeley, Dan and Ruth in Beverly Hills, Gráinne and family in South Bend, Diana in Newton, Nancy and Mike in Port Jeff and Ed and Jackie in Manhattan – represented a cross-section of American society, certainly all the meals, from Trader Joe's breaded chicken to foraged salads, bore little relation to the popular stereotype of US cuisine.

Access is, of course, a problem, and it would be foolish to pretend the food system in the States, in common with that of many other countries, isn't in urgent need of reform for this and many other reasons – but to allow multinational chains to colour your opinion of the entire nation's diet and culinary skills is like assuming that Sweden is entirely furnished by IKEA, or that all Brits are Hollywood villains. In reality, most of us are much less charming.

American food has such a bad reputation for being junk, I say finally, draining my glass, and OK, it's definitely not *all* great – if I never see a square of processed cheese again it won't be too soon – 'but I find it exciting.'

'Still?' she asks.

Still, I say. I'd turn right round and cycle back the other way, if it weren't for that pesky little dog.

POSTSCRIPT

When I wearily push Eddy out of the doors of Heathrow on Sunday morning, accompanied by Gemma, and little Freddie, who have kindly come to drive me home, I find Sam waiting in the chilly

---

* That $2.99 grapefruit in Bryan, Ohio still stings.

dawn with my beloved – who promptly runs towards Gemma, tail wagging so hard he can barely stay grounded . . . after all, he hasn't seen her for at least ten minutes.

What am I, chopped liver? I demand, holding my arms out pointlessly. Sadly, as Sam points out, he'd almost certainly prefer me if I were.

(AS AMERICAN AS) APPLE PIE

What have I learned about pies on my travels, apart from confirming that I love them? The charms of the best examples I tried hinged on the contrast between a savoury, crisp pastry shell and a sweet filling, whether tart and fruity or rich and creamy. I also loved those that threw a third texture into the mix, like whole pecans, or crunchy streusel.

This recipe, which is, I warn you, designed for flavour rather than showstopping social media good looks, incorporates all these elements, and is an homage to some of the culinary influences that have shaped modern American cuisine: a buttery French crust golden with cornmeal, one of the most important of Native crops; the sweet potatoes that so reminded enslaved Africans of the sweet yams of home, spiced here with Mexican vanilla and chilli and South Asian cinnamon, topped with soft, buttery apples (a fruit that originated in China) and finished with crunchy native pecans. You can even serve it with Italian mascarpone spiked with lemon zest . . . or indeed with a glass of Irish or Scottish whiskey. Or both; because in America, anything goes.

Makes 1 × 23cm/9 inch pie (8 to 10 slices)
For the pastry
125g/1 cup minus 1 tbsp plain/all-purpose flour, plus extra for rolling
1 tbsp coarse cornmeal

1 tsp demerara sugar, plus extra for sprinkling
¼ tsp fine salt
100g/1 stick minus 1 tbsp very cold butter, cut into 1cm/½ inch dice

For the apple filling

About 800g/1 pound 12 ounces tart eating apples, e.g. 6 Granny
    Smith
About 80g/½ cup caster/superfine sugar
A knob of butter

For the sweet potato filling

250g/1¾ cups peeled and diced sweet potato
1 small cinnamon stick
1 nutmeg (or ¼ tsp grated nutmeg)
¼ tsp chipotle chilli flakes
1 vanilla pod, seeds scraped
50g/scant ⅓ cup caster/superfine sugar
375ml/1½ cups + 1 tbsp whole milk
85g/⅓ cup + 1 tsp double or whipping/heavy cream
2 eggs
¼ tsp fine salt

For the topping

100g/1 cup pecan halves
1 tbsp maple syrup
Pinch of salt

1. Put the flour, cornmeal, sugar and salt into a large bowl and
   whisk to combine. Add the diced butter to the flour mix and
   toss to coat. Press each piece of butter flat with your fingertips –
   don't overwork it – then stir in just enough water (about
   25ml/1½ tbsp) to bring the mix together into a smooth but not
   wet ball of dough. Wrap and chill for 20 minutes.

2. Put the dough on a floured work surface and shape it into a roughly ¾cm-/¼ inch-thick rectangle. Fold the top third of the rectangle down into the centre, then fold the bottom third up over it. Turn the pastry 90 degrees and repeat the folds. Roll out and use to line a deep pie dish about 23cm/9 inches in diameter, making sure there's enough slightly to overhang the sides all the way around. Roll that up onto the rim of the pie dish and crimp between thumb and fingertips (watch a video online if this makes no sense). Keep any offcuts wrapped and chilled. Cover completely and chill for at least 2 hours and up to 12.

3. Meanwhile, cut the apples into chunky half-moon slices (no need to peel unless you'd like to). Weigh them (you should have about 675g/1½ pounds), then add 10 per cent of the weight (about 4½ tbsp) in sugar. Toss together and leave to sit for at least 10 minutes, or until they start to release their juices, then fry, in batches if necessary, in the butter over a medium-high heat until golden and softened but still retaining their shape. Allow to cool.

4. Put the sweet potato cubes, whole spices and vanilla seeds, sugar, milk and cream into a wide pan. Bring to a simmer, then turn the heat down low and leave to bubble away, stirring frequently so it doesn't stick or curdle, for 40 to 50 minutes until the sweet potato is falling apart and the liquid is thick.

5. Remove the whole spices (cinnamon stick, vanilla pod and nutmeg if you used one) from the sweet potato and purée the mixture with a stick blender. Beat the eggs in a heatproof bowl, then whisk in a little of the purée to temper them before whisking them into the rest of the purée. Stir in the salt.

6. Heat the oven to 200°C/180°C fan/390°F. Prick the base of the pie shell in a few places with a fork, then line with baking paper and beans or other weights. Bake for 20 minutes, then remove the weights and paper and bake for another 7 minutes.

7. Take the shell out of the oven and turn the heat down to

180°C/160°C fan/350°F. Arrange the apple pieces, minus any syrupy liquid that's gathered around them, in the pie shell, then pour the sweet potato custard on top. Bake for 30 minutes, until the custard is just set but still wobbly.

8. Toss the pecans with maple syrup and a little salt to coat, then delicately arrange on top of the pie. Put back into the oven for a further 10 to 15 minutes, until the top is just firm and the pecans toasted. Allow to cool before serving.

VITAL STATISTICS

Pies eaten: 34 (one every 2 days)

Average score: 7

Top scorer: rhubarb streusel with brown butter and hazelnut streusel (Petee's Pies, New York)

Poorest pie: Boston creme pie, Boston (to be fair, if I'd done my research on what to expect, it might not have felt like such a swizz; it's not a pie, it's a cake)

Miles cycled: 2,064 miles (578 miles more than the UK, 613 miles more than France)

Total ascent: 60,679ft (3,022ft less than the UK, 15,295ft less than France thanks to the lack of Alps or Highlands en route)

Top speed: 44.9mph (0.6mph more than the UK, 14mph faster than in France; clearly I've got *slightly* better at descending)

Average speed: 10.6mph (very similar to the UK, 1mph faster than France)

Punctures: 0 (but a new set of brake pads 2 months in) – all credit to Schwalbe Marathon Plus tyres

Minutes before Wilf forgave me for going away: tbc

BIBLIOGRAPHY

The Taste of America, Colman Andrews, Phaidon Press, 2013

Taco USA: How Mexican Food Conquered America, Gustavo Arellano, Scribner, 2012

Diners, John Baeder, Harry N. Abrams Inc., 1978

The Bagel: The Surprising History of a Modest Bread, Maria Balinska, Yale University Press, 2009

Drive-Thru Dreams: A Journey Through the Heart of America's Fast Food Kingdom, Adam Chandler, Flatiron Books, 2019

Chop Suey USA: The Story of Chinese Food in America, Yong Chen, Columbia University Press, 2021

Big Flavors from Italian America: Family-Style Favorites from Coast to Coast, Cooks Country, 2020

America Day by Day, Simone de Beauvoir, Phoenix, 1998

Eula Mae's Cajun Kitchen: Cooking Through the Seasons on Avery Island, Eula Mae Doré and Marcelle R. Bienvenu, Harvard Common Press, 2002

The Death and Life of the Great Lakes, Dan Egan, W. W. Norton & Co., 2017

Fried Chicken: An American Story, John T. Edge, G. P. Putnam's Sons, 2004

The Potlikker Papers: A Food History of the Modern South, John T. Edge, Penguin Press, 2017

Made in Chicago: Stories Behind 30 Great Hometown Bites, Monica Eng and David Hammond, 3 Fields Books, 2023

Insatiable: Competitive Eating and the Big Fat American Dream, Jason Fagone, Yellow Jersey Press, 2006

American Cuisine and How It Got This Way, Paul Freedman, Liveright Publishing Corporation, 2019

Gastropod, Cynthia Graber and Nicola Twilley (podcast)

The Lula Cafe Cookbook, Jason Hammel, Phaidon Press 2023

High on the Hog: A Culinary Journey from Africa to America, Jessica B. Harris, Bloomsbury, 2012

Pizza: A Global History, Carol Helstosky, Reaktion Books, 2008

Travels into North America: Containing Its Natural History and a Circumstantial Account of Its Plantations and Agriculture in General, Vol. 1, Peter Kalm, Forgotten Books, 2020

Blue Highways: A Journey into America, William Least Heat Moon, Atlantic Monthly Press, 1982

The Fortune Cookie Chronicles: Adventures in the World of Chinese Food, Jennifer 8. Lee, Twelve, 2009

The American Way of Eating: Undercover at Walmart, Applebee's, Farm Fields and the Dinner Table, Tracie McMillan, Scribner, 2012

The United States of Adventure: A life-changing journey by bike through every state of America, Anna McNuff, (self-published), 2018

The President's Kitchen Cabinet: The story of the African Americans who have fed our first families, Adrian Miller, University of North Carolina Press, 2017

Crumbs: Cookies and Sweets from Around the World, Ben Mims, Phaidon Press, 2024

Far More Terrible for Women: Personal Accounts of Women in Slavery, ed. Patrick Minges, Blair, 2006

Coast to Coast: A Journey Across 1950s America, Jan Morris, Faber & Faber, 2010

Hamburger America, George Motz, Running Press, 2018

Hot Sauce Nation, Denver Nicks, Chicago Review Press, 2017

The Hamburger: A History, Josh Ozersky, Yale University Press, 2008

Food America: The Remarkable People and Incredible Stories Behind America's Favorite Dishes, David Page, Mango Publishing Group, 2021

A Ride Across America: A 4,000-Mile Adventure Through the Small Towns and Big Issues of the USA, Simon Parker, September Publishing, 2024

More Than Cake, Natasha Pickowicz, Artisan, 2023

Old Glory: An American Voyage, Jonathan Raban, Eland, 2018

American Tacos: A History and Guide, José R. Ralat, University of Texas Press, 2020

The Jungle, Upton Sinclair, Penguin Classics, 1985

The Good Immigrant USA: 26 Writers on America, Immigration and Home, ed. Nikesh Shukla and Chimene Suleyman, Dialogue Books, 2019

Oxford Encyclopaedia of Food and Drink in America, ed. Andrew F. Smith, Oxford University Press, 2012

Popped Culture: A Social History of Popcorn in America, Andrew F. Smith, University of South Carolina, 1999

Travels with Charley: In Search of Modern America, John Steinbeck, Penguin Classics, 2001

Louisiana Eats! The People, the Food and Their Stories, Poppy Tooker and David G. Spielman, Pelican Publishing Company, 2013

The Cooking Gene: A Journey Through African American Culinary History in the Old South, Michael W. Twitty, Amistad, 2018

National Dish: Around the World in Search of Food, History and the Meaning of Home, Anya von Bremzen, One, 2023

The Chez Panisse Menu Cookbook, Alice Waters, Random House, 1982

Iroquois Foods and Food Preparation, Government Printing Bureau, Ottawa, F. W. Waugh, 1916

Ice Cream: A History, Laura B. Weiss, Reaktion Books, 2018

Building Houses Out of Chicken Legs, Psyche A. Williams-Forson, University of North Carolina Press, 2006

You and I Eat the Same: On the Countless Ways Food and Cooking Connect Us to One Another, ed. Chris Ying, Artisan, 2018

ACKNOWLEDGEMENTS

(This is, I'm afraid, probably incomplete as I managed to pour a bottle of water over my laptop in the writing of this book and didn't manage to recover all my notes, so apologies, and thanks, to anyone who recognises their work and isn't featured.)

If it takes a village to raise a child, it takes a city to produce a book, particularly one like this, which has relied so much on the generosity and wisdom of others. Naturally it wouldn't have got off the ground in the first place without the combined efforts of my agent Sarah Ballard, ably assisted by Eli Keren and Olivia Bignold, and my publishers Katya Shipster and Melanie Tortoroli; thank you for, in the immortal words of Jon Bon Jovi, keeping the faith I could do it and come home in one piece. It would certainly look much the poorer without Sarah Hammond and her team, and the (bald-)eagle eyes of Annie Lee – and of course the work of Lexi Bickell and Kara Nielsen in forcibly shoving it before the world. As ever, thanks also to the many people at HarperCollins and W. W. Norton who I never meet, yet who work so hard to get the book out in the world, and of course to booksellers, some of my favourite people.

In the States, thank you to Johan and Benedetta Duramy, Nina Shen Rastogi, Adele, Richard, Felix, Simon and Hugo Price, Cecilia

Callas, John Law, Chris Radcliffe, Daniel and Ruth Fink, Charlotte Simmonds, Nik Sharma and Paddington, Kelly Just and Amtrak, Caroline Donaldson-Sinclair, Kirsty Dillury, Emilie Dujour, Jen Beckmann, Imelda Lopez-Sanchez, Jennifer Hwa Dobbertin, Anne and Rob Gardiner, Harold Osborn and everyone at Tabasco, Brooklyn MacKenzie, Johnny Hernandez, Jessica B. Harris, Brandon Pellerin, Bethia Woolf, Andy Dehus and Zoe, Fiona Pettitt, Leah Berger, Michelle Wilson, Avishar Barua, Tania Sherry, Gráinne McEvoy, Pete Cajka, Killian, Ruairí and Tomás, Tim Mazurek and Bryan, Natasha Pickowicz, Nicole Rucker, Keia Mastrianni, the team at Middle Brow, Jason Hammell, Emily Takoudes, Louise Radnofsky, Rick and Linda Gallion, Diana Burnell, Brian Levy, Nancy and Mike Olsen, Aaron Rosen, Hannah and Archie Young, Charlotte and Gena G. Druckman, Melissa Clark, Malik Meer, Neda Toloui-Semnani, George Shea, Allison O'Donnell, Jess Shadbolt, Ed and Jackie Schneider and Bicycles NYC.

Over here, my fixers and friends Nicola Miller and Ed, Ali, Iain, Molly, Martha and Fergus Hollingshead, Lucy Smart, Dr Alice Taylor, Emily Fedouloff and Robin Taylor-Fedouloff, Bob Granleese, Tim Lusher, Don Sloan, Signe Johansen, Jill Mead, Lorna Wing, Nicola Lamb, Tracey Smith and Phaidon, Dennis Nothdruft, Jenni Gwiazdowski and Condor Cycles, particularly Claire Beaumont and Adrian Lamb. Jenny Coad for moral support, services to travel and delivering joyful news en route in the form of Jasper. Sam Goldsmith and Gareth Williams, Claire Nelson and of course Gemma, Pam, John and my little pal Freddie Roberts for chauffeuring, portering, flat-sitting and putting up with Wilf and his furry nonsense, and as ever, my long-suffering family for all the moral support in the form of seaside writing hideouts, messages about *The Real Housewives of Beverly Hills* and birthday champagne.

And, of course, those brave souls who came out to keep me company: Matt Gould, Claire Cohen and Casper, 'don't you dare name me' Claire, Caroline 'don't call me Caroline' Craig and

Lucinda Orr. Thank you for so gamely agreeing to come out and be part of my big adventure, for putting up with my marginally less-furry nonsense and being pushed to the limit of your stomach capacity and heat endurance, for broadening my cultural horizons with medieval armour, Scrabble, YouTube influencers, German and Austrian art and . . . the Clan of the Cave Bear. Most of all, thanks for always making me laugh.

Lastly, I must express my gratitude to Wilf for never, ever letting me get above myself.

TABASCO® is a trademark and service mark of McIlhenny Company, Avery Island, Louisiana 70513 and is used with permission. TABASCO.com

CANADA

San Francisco

alinas

San Luis Obispo

Los Angeles

Tucson

El Paso

Austin

San Antonio

PACIFIC OCEAN

MEXICO